D0925095

REGARDING FRANK CAPRA

ERIC SMOODIN

Regarding Frank Capra

Audience, Celebrity, and American Film Studies, 1930–1960

DUKE UNIVERSITY PRESS   DURHAM AND LONDON 2004

© 2004 Duke University Press. All rights reserved.
Printed in the United States of America on acid-free paper. ⊚
Designed by Rebecca M. Gimenez. Typeset in Sabon by Tseng
Information Systems. Library of Congress Cataloging-in-Pub-
lication Data appear on the last printed page of this book.

This book is dedicated to the

memory of Mildred and Solly Smoodin,

and to the marvel of Sofia Malka

Contents

Acknowledgments

Of course it's tempting here to refer to the last scene of *It's a Wonderful Life*. Most of us are familiar with it. After seeing what life would have been like had he never been born, George Bailey comes to understand the nature of friendship and community when most of the population of Bedford Falls helps him out. But to acknowledge all of the people who have given me so much support while I've been working on this book, I prefer a slightly less overdetermined moment in a different Frank Capra film, *Mr. Deeds Goes to Town*. Longfellow Deeds has just inherited twenty million dollars and must leave Mandrake Falls for New York. The whole town turns out to wish him well, and Longfellow sums up the entire experience, for himself and to the city slickers who are taking him away: "Gosh, I've got a lot of friends."

So have I. Ann Martin has been a fabulous friend, colleague, and work partner. She and Bob Reynolds are always supportive and encouraging. Jon Lewis has read and given advice on significant parts of this manuscript, and he, too, has been both a great friend and a wonderful partner on another project. Inderpal Grewal and Al Jessel, and their children, Kirin and Sonal, have become like a second family. Carolyn Dinshaw and Marget Long have been around this book for years, and they've always been ready to talk about Capra and go with me to see Capra films. Other friends, like Richard Neupert, Jennifer Terry, Leyla Ezdinli, Mark Anderson, Kate Toll, Monica McCormick, Naomi Schneider, Julie Brand, Sumiko Higashi, Minoo Moallem, and Shahin Bayatmakoo, have all provided intellectual help and also very good company.

In 1997, I had the good fortune to go to the Frank Capra Centennial in the director's hometown of Bisacquino, Sicily. I would like to thank the people who organized the event and took part in it, and who also became great friends: Franco Marineo, Federika Timeto, Marcello Alajmo, Rosanna Cataldo, and Vito Zagarrio in particular, but also Vincent Schiavelli and Franco Pollo.

I've had something of an interesting career path while working on this book. I began the project in Washington, D.C., at American University. I would like to thank my colleagues in the Literature Department there, and also Michael Ragussis and Pamela Fox. From Washington I moved to Berkeley, and many of my colleagues at the university there have been wonderful to work with and to have as friends. I would especially like to thank Linda Williams, Donald Moore, Bill Hanks, Jenna Johnson-Hanks, Bill Worthen, Shannon Steen, Sharon Marcus, Deniz Göktürk, Sharon Lyons Butler, Althea Grannum-Cummings, Karl Britto, Gary Handman, Mary Ryan, Kathy Geritz, Josh Stein, Michael Rogin, Ron Choy, Jane Taylorson, Maxine Frederickson, Elizabeth Waddell, Nicklaus Largier, Karen Feldman, Richard Hutson, and Kathleen Moran. In addition, Judith Butler, Tony Kaes, Kaja Silverman, Gavriel Moses, and Carol Clover have always given help, support, and advice, and George Breslauer and Ralph Hexter provided valuable institutional support.

I broke up my time at Berkeley by working as an acquisitions editor at the University of California Press. A number of people at the press became good friends and helped immensely in my on-the-job training. I would like to thank the entire "Wednesday Group," and give special thanks to Anna Weidman, Reed Malcolm, Julie Christianson, Nola Burger, Nicole Heyward, Mari Coates, Rachel Berchten, Blake Edgar, Howard Boyer, Doris Kretschmer, Charlene Woodcock, Stephanie Fay, Sam Rosenthal, Mary Francis, and Gabriel Alvaro. As this book goes into production, I begin a new position at the University of California, Davis. My colleagues here in the Programs in American Studies and Film Studies have been welcoming, interested in my work, and extremely supportive.

I would like to thank other friends I've made while working at these various jobs: Kathryn Fuller-Seeley, Shelley Stamp, Catherine Jurca, Dana Polan, Caryl Flinn, Heather Hendershot, Gina Marchetti, Bill Germano, Patricia Zimmermann, Cathy Davidson, Karen Ishizuka, Haidee Wasson, Lee Grieveson, Barbara Klinger, Lutz Koepnick, Charles Maland, George Custen, Roger Rouse, Cathy Jones, Kathy Newman, Peter Limbrick, Amy Bomse, James Clifford, Jackie Stacey, Greg Waller, Eric Zinner, Micah Kleit, Richard Abel, Peter Goodrich, Michel Rosenfeld, Arthur Jacobson, Tom Rockmore, Joe Margolis, Christine Overall, Joe Pitt, Vicki Weiss, Elizabeth Young, Adria Blum, Carl Mora, David Baird, Surina Khan,

Paola Bacchetta, Mary Anita Loos, Cari Beauchamp, Ella Shohat, Robert Stam, Scott MacDonald, Robin Wiegman, Steve Seid, Edith Kramer, Kenneth Turan, Jeffrey Edwards, Judith Mayne, Dorothea Olkowski, Marilyn Schuster, Susan Van Dyne, and Paul Buhle, among many others.

It's been a dream working with Ken Wissoker at Duke University Press, who encouraged me years ago and who has waited for a long time for this book. Everyone at Duke has been great, and I'd especially like to thank Courtney Berger. Justin Faerber has helped immensely, and several anonymous readers made substantive suggestions for improving this project.

Friends and mentors from graduate school have been extremely helpful, in particular Janet Bergstrom, Frank Tomasulo, and Nick Browne. I owe a great debt to Richard deCordova, whose work was so exemplary and whose attitude was so wonderful. All of his friends miss him greatly.

I have had the help of many terrific student assistants. In particular I would like to thank Pearl Latteier, Melissa Riley, Catherine Zimmer, Jun Okada, Catherine Shozawa, Guo-Juin Hong, Jonah Ross, Michael Sicinski, Julie Chu, Jenna Gretsch, Kierston Johnson, Donald Vallis, Kris Peterson, Melinda Chen, Chris Roebuck, Michelle Probert, Ruth Haber, Scott Ferguson, and Minette Hillyer.

Several friends whom I've known seemingly forever remain incredibly supportive, in particular David Lash, Fred Davidson, Robert Ring, and Mark Zakarin.

I've been assisted immeasurably by a host of librarians, curators, and archivists. I want to give special thanks to Leith Johnson, cocurator of the Wesleyan Cinema Archives, which houses Frank Capra's papers. Leith provided wonderful access to the collection and expert advice on how to use it. I also want to thank Jeanine Basinger, curator and founder of the archive. The librarians at the Margaret Herrick Library in Los Angeles, especially Howard Prouty, were extremely helpful, as was everyone at the New York Public Library, particularly Laura O'Keefe, and at the Motion Picture Reading Room in the Library of Congress. Those who administer the always-endangered Freedom of Information Act responded quickly and completely to all of my requests.

My family has been helping me with this project for years, sometimes much longer than any of them might realize. My aunt, Esther Friberg, gave me the first film book I ever read. In 1971 I told her that I had watched *It Happened One Night* on television and that I had loved it, so she gave me her copy of Frank Capra's just-published autobiography, which had come from one of the many book clubs she belonged to. My sister, Roberta Smoodin, was talking with me about Capra films then and she still does now, and in between we've watched a million movies together. More recently, Dale Jarvis has become a valued friend. My mother-in-law and father-in-law, Doris and Arthur Kaplan, have lived through this and other projects with me, and they've always been wonderfully supportive. I also want to thank Mitchell and Heidi Kaplan and Henry Flax and David Norton.

Caren Kaplan has read every page of this book too many times to count, has watched every Capra film imaginable, and has continued to be my model of a scholar and a writer. She is Ellie Andrews, Babe Bennett, Clarissa Saunders, Ann Mitchell, and Mary Bailey all in one. And she makes me feel like the richest man in town.

When I was just about through with this book, my mother, Mildred Smoodin, died. She had been a one-woman Frank Capra clipping service for years, and she also came up with a terrific title, for the book or one of the chapters, that I could never quite figure out how to use: "On the Topic of Capracorn." Both she and my father, Solly Smoodin, always supported my interest in film and made it possible for me to study the movies seriously. When I watched *It Happened One Night* on television that first time it was with them, and both of them, in different ways, are very much at the center of this book.

At the very end of this project, Sofia Malka Smoodin-Kaplan came into my life and Caren's. It's hard now to imagine having come this far without her. I can't wait for all of us to watch *It Happened One Night* together.

Introduction

Audiences, Film Studies, and Frank Capra

In his autobiography Frank Capra identified the audiences for his movies as "a thousand pairs of eyes and ears." The description is both accurate, given the number of people who might attend a film screening, and also a little bit monstrous, an invocation of a hydra-headed, all-seeing, all-hearing spectator. As such, the image seems just right for a classical-era director who, like Capra, needed to respect and believe in his audiences and also, quite possibly, fear them just a little. Later in his autobiography Capra seemed less ambivalent about viewers and also absolutely certain of his connection with them. "I simply did my thing with film," he wrote, "and the people responded."[1]

Did they ever. For a variety of reasons—because of Capra's celebrity, changes in archival methods, practices of industry trade journals, and even because Capra was something of a packrat, unable to throw much out—we are left with extraordinary evidence of just how those audiences reacted to this director's movies. In fact, probably more than most filmmakers from the era, Capra attracted this kind of attention. By the early-to-mid 1930s, after a number of box office successes and concerted publicity efforts by his employer, Columbia Pictures, Capra almost certainly had become one of the two most famous directors in the country (probably only Cecil B. De-Mille was better known, with Charles Chaplin's fame coming mostly from his acting rather than his directing). Capra also was among a very select group of filmmakers (besides DeMille, Walt Disney comes to mind, and perhaps some of the heads of the studios) who could compete with major movie stars in terms of celebrity and media attention. As a result, there is a great deal of material assessing Capra's work, generated by fans, the news media, the government, and other groups and institutions.

Capra participated in more kinds of film production than perhaps any other major director from the period: studio-produced feature films, independent films, military filmmaking, and educational films, for example. In doing so he made films that were directed at very broad audiences in the domestic and international markets for feature films, as well as at relatively small audiences such as enlisted men and German prisoners of war during World War II and junior high and high school students during the 1950s and 1960s. The responses from these viewers varied for each film; sometimes Capra seemed to be channeling perfectly the desires of his viewers, and sometimes he invoked the wrath of all those pairs of eyes and ears. The response was never monolithic, and Capra's audiences should at all times be thought of in the plural.

These audiences assigned themselves to fairly self-evident identity groups, and were also often understood that way by the various experts—the sociologists, film scholars, psychologists, teachers, and others—who concerned themselves with movie viewing. That is, they were children, or men, or women, or Americans, or they fell into other, similarly monolithic, categories. But they also understood themselves to be responding to movies as members of other, less obvious, groups, and were also often classified that way by those same experts. Such classifications add great nuance to our own understanding of viewers and of the best ways of studying them. Most important, these classifications were not based on the readily apparent, seemingly unchosen categories of age or gender or race or nationality, but were instead frequently chosen for viewers by governmental and private institutions. Thus we can study Capra's audiences as groups that were designated prisoners of war, or military conscripts, or high school students following specific courses of study, or criminals. By examining these classifications and these audiences, as well as the ways they were understood during the period in which Capra's films appeared, we can understand new ways of thinking about identities and the relationships between viewers, about the constitution of viewing subjects, and about the history of the concerns with the ways that spectators have interacted with the movies they have watched.

The seventy-year accumulation of material from Capra's viewers coincides well with recent developments in film studies. Over the last ten to fifteen years the discipline has taken a renewed interest in movie audiences, in theorizing and historicizing the empirical evidence that viewers have left behind, understanding the data that tells us who these audiences were and what they watched, and determining where they saw movies.

A number of scholars have contributed to this reception studies project: Janet Staiger, for instance, has produced significant work on various aspects of the historical audience; Gregory Waller has studied audiences and exhibition practices in a single town in Kentucky; Charles Maland has examined Charles Chaplin as a cultural icon; and Jackie Stacey has examined women's memories of the actresses they watched in Great Britain in the 1940s, 1950s, and 1960s. Melvyn Stokes and Richard Maltby have edited two volumes on audience studies that consolidate much of the best new historical work, and Annette Kuhn has analyzed memory, the status of oral history, and filmgoing in the United Kingdom during the classical era.[2] More broadly, scholars have grown increasingly interested in the production of what we might call film culture, in the ways in which fans have learned about movies and experienced them; for example through fan magazines, or in the context of dish nights, bank nights, and other theater contests and giveaways, or as part of a day of shopping downtown. This type of analysis might also include the location of theaters and an examination of the ethnic, race, class, and gender backgrounds of the people who went to movies. Indeed, perhaps the most significant argument in film studies over the last decade has been the one between Robert Allen and Ben Singer in *Cinema Journal* about the audiences for Manhattan's nickelodeons, concerning where they saw films, how frequently they went to movies, and, more broadly, the proper methodology for carrying out this kind of historical reception project.[3]

The discipline's interest in these issues has also been responsible for the recovery of the significant historical texts of audience studies. In just the last few years, and in the example of just one journal, *Screen* has recovered the findings about film spectatorship of the somewhat ominously named Mass Observation unit in postwar Great Britain, and has published the first English translation of Emilie Altenloh's 1914 dissertation about filmgoers in Mannheim, Germany, *A Sociology of the Cinema: The Audience.*[4] By placing emphasis on issues of reception, film studies has returned, in a manner of speaking, to the discipline's concerns of at least seventy years ago. Film studies is almost certainly one of the least historicized of the academic disciplines, and there often seems to be an assumption that it began in earnest in the United States only in the late 1950s or early 1960s, with the importation of French (typically auteurist) theory. But, in fact, film studies had flourished long before this. Precise evidence can be difficult to come by, but the 1950s and 1960s probably mark only the movement of film studies firmly into the sphere of the humanities. Before this, at least since the late

1920s, the study of cinema had been as much a social science as anything else, and a principal object of study was the audience.

Film Studies and the Film Audience

A discussion of the tensions in early U.S. film studies might begin with two of the significant practitioners. In 1939 Margaret Farrand Thorp wrote that "there are other people who make the movies besides the artists and technicians in Hollywood," and then added that these were the "eighty-five million Americans [who] go to see a picture every week." She continued that "in whichever direction justice lies it is undoubtedly true that no art has ever been so shaped and influenced by its audience as the art of cinema." Thus Thorp, a sociologist, began *America at the Movies*, a major scholarly study published by Yale University Press. We can learn a great deal about Thorp's methodology from the very title of the book and also of her chapters: "Eighty-Five Million a Week" and "What Movie Tonight?" for example.[5] For Thorp, the proper study of cinema was the audience and the relationships between films, the film industry, and consumers. On her frontispiece she turned the audience into the stars of her book with a photograph of a theater full of viewers watching a movie.

At about the same time as Thorp's study, Robert Gessner began teaching his "History and Appreciation of the Cinema" class at New York University, which will, as I show in chapter 2, become significant to this study of Capra's audiences. Gessner examined a different facet of cinema each week with such headings on his syllabus as "The Early American Spectacle," "Legend and Fantasy in Germany," "The Moving Camera in Germany," "The Psychological Film," "Contemporary Soviet Naturalism," "The American Film of Protest," and "An American Classic" (Capra's *It Happened One Night*). As with the title of Thorp's book, the title of Gessner's class and these syllabus headings give a strong indication of Gessner's approach. Unlike Thorp's book, though, Gessner's class seemed clearly centered on the history of texts, on the nature of the films themselves, and on ways of making meaning from them by clustering them around national and generic concerns, differentiating one film from the other, and ranking them.[6] That is, Gessner stressed something like what we would now call textual analysis, the examination of a film's production of meaning similar to models from literature and art history.

There were ample precedents for the approaches of both Thorp and Gessner. Of special interest here, though, is that as soon as intellectuals

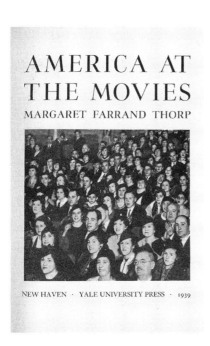

AMERICA AT
THE MOVIES
MARGARET FARRAND THORP

NEW HAVEN · YALE UNIVERSITY PRESS · 1939

The audience as main character on the title
page of Margaret Farrand Thorp's book about
viewers, movies, and the film industry.

began taking the cinema seriously, they just as often focused on issues of audience as on meaning, aesthetics, and style. As early as 1909 Jane Addams, in *The Spirit of Youth and the City Streets*, paid as much attention to theaters as she did to the films themselves. This interest was very much in keeping with the era's reformist concern over the sites of children's leisure: not only movie theaters but also parks and playgrounds.[7] About twenty years later film had fully entered the academy not only as a humanities discipline related to literature and art but also as a branch of study related to sociology, with a specific interest in audience activity. The most famous example here, of course, is Robert Lynd and Helen Merrell Lynd's study of Muncie, Indiana—the Middletown of their book's title—in which filmgoing habits and other modern consumer activities received significant attention.[8]

Shortly after the Lynds's work, issues of reception came to dominate film studies with the publication of the research sponsored by the Payne Fund, which concentrated on the effects of the cinema on children and adolescents. The very titles of some of the studies demonstrated this emphasis:

Mondays, 8.00 to 9.45 p.m.
Fifteen sessions, from September 27 to January 10.
Fee for fifteen sessions: $10.00
Single admissions: $1.00, to be secured in advance at 20 Washington Square North.

This series of revivals will present the history of the motion picture through a representative collection of the best works of cinema creators throughout the world. It is designed to be of educational and cultural value to students of literature, photographic art, acting, direction, contemporary history, and sociology.

The film showings at each session will be preceded by a brief introductory comment by Robert Gessner, author and screen writer, who will direct the course. Class discussion will follow each screening. A different period of style or aim will be presented each Monday evening, thus making possible a comprehensive history and appreciation of the cinema. Actors, directors, and writers will speak at some of the revivals.

September 27. The Rise of the American Film. The New York Hat by D. W. Griffith, with Mary Pickford and Lionel Barrymore; the Fugitive by Thomas H. Ince, with William S. Hart; The Clever Dummy, a Mack Sennett comedy; A Fool There Was, with Theda Bara.

October 4. The Movies Come of Age. The Birth of a Nation by D. W. Griffith, with Lillian Gish.

October 11. The Comedies. His Bitter Pill, a Mack Sennett satire; The Freshman with Harold Lloyd; The Sex Life of the Polyp with Robert Benchley; The Skeleton Dance by Walt Disney.

October 18. The Early American Spectacle. Four Horsemen of the Apocalypse by Rex Ingram, with Rudolph Valentino.

October 25. Legend and Fantasy in Germany. Primitive German films, 1898. Don Juan's Wedding; Misunderstood; The Golem; The Cabinet of Dr. Caligari.

November 1. The Moving Camera in Germany. Hamlet; The Last Laugh, directed by F. W. Murnau, with Emil Jannings.

November 8. The Mass Film. Potemkin, directed by Sergei Eisenstein.

November 15. The Realistic Film. Greed, directed by Erich von Stroheim, with Zasu Pitts.

November 22. The Psychological Film. The Love of Jeanne Ney, directed by G. W. Pabst.

November 29. The End of the Silent Era. Plane Crazy, the first Mickey Mouse; The Last Command, directed by Josef von Sternberg, with Emil Jannings.

December 6. The Talkies. The Jazz Singer, with Al Jolson. Movietone newsreel with G. B. Shaw; Steam Boat Willie by Walt Disney; Anna Christie, with Greta Garbo.

December 13. Contemporary Soviet Naturalism. Chapayev, with Baboohkin.

December 20. The Film of Social Satire. A Nous La Liberté, directed by René Clair.

January 3. The American Film of Protest. Fury, with Sylvia Sidney and Spencer Tracy.

January 10. An American Classic. It Happened One Night, with Clark Gable and Claudette Colbert.

Robert Gessner's syllabus for his 1938–1939 "History and Appreciation of the Cinema" class at New York University. *It Happened One Night* is the last film scheduled, as "an American classic." (Wesleyan Cinema Archives)

N E W   Y O R K   U N I V E R S I T Y
DIVISION OF GENERAL EDUCATION

H I S T O R Y   A N D   A P P R E C I A T I O N   O F   C I N E M A

ROBERT GESSNER, Course Director

Session XV: January 10, 1938

AN AMERICAN CLASSIC

IT HAPPENED ONE NIGHT   1934

    Produced by Columbia Pictures Corporation. Directed by Frank Capra.
    Original Story by Samuel Hopkins Adams. Screen Play by Robert Riskin.
    Edited by Gene Havlick. Photographed by Joe Walker. Cast: Clark Gable,
    Claudette Colbert, Walter Connolly, Roscoe Karns, Jameson Thomas, Alan
    Hale, Ward Bond, Eddie Chandler, and others.

PROGRAM NOTES

    When some clean-shaven historian of the future comes to write the history of the
cinema during the fourth decade of the twentieth century, he probably will note the phenomenon of one film capturing five firsts awarded by the Academy of Motion Picture Art and
Sciences. What our fine feathered friend might not know is that IT HAPPENED ONE NIGHT not
only broke the bank at Monte Carlo (grossing over two million), but it broke the artistic
stranglehold of the producers who believed that a picture must be about passion in a pent-
house in order to make money. IT HAPPENED ONE NIGHT tapped the source of all truly great
art: it was about the ordinary, the common place, the average; it was about transcontinental
buses, bus stations, overnight camps, and hitch-hiking. Not all producers pet art theories,
however, have been revised, as we can witness daily on the screens. Darryl Zanuck tells
the New York press that nobody is interested in the life of a bookkeeper, but should be
(he hopes) in Stanley and Livingston. The performance of Charles Laughton in IF I HAD A
MILLION goes down the drain, and nothing is apparently learned from Emil Jannings's doorman
in THE LAST LAUGH, one of the screen's masterpieces. But a foreign-born, half-pint director
knows, and his pictures show it.

    Frank Capra's feeling for and knowledge of human interest may be attributed in part
to some of the following events: he arrived by steerage at the age of 3, at 5 sold newspapers, knew street gangs, at 19 was a graduate chemical engineer from the California Institute of Technology, was a fruit worker, did odd jobs, and was in the army. "Unable to
obtain work," Jim Tully wrote (N.Y. Herald-Tribune, November 14, 1937), "he wore his army
uniform for five months. 'It was all I had.'" It was a similar background which enabled
Stroheim to do GREED. Capra's work as an extra, around cameras and in labs, grounded him
in technical fundamentals. His short story writing, based on O. Henry, and his gag days
under Sennett and Hal Roach grounded him in story timing -- an essential in directing.
Capra began as a Poverty Row director at $20 a week, and did one of the best pictures of
1926, Harry Langdon in THE STRONG MAN. He directed Claudette Colbert in New York, but the
film failed; they clicked, nevertheless, later in IT HAPPENED ONE NIGHT.

    Capra has been one of the few directors to carry a technical kit which permits him
to utilize to a fuller extent the technical possibilities of the new art form. The film
has been superior to the film-makers, like a trans-oceanic airplane is superior to pilots
who only know how to fly if they can see the ground under them. But maturity is slowly
coming, via the film-makers, not the film-sellers. There are few writers and directors
with guts enough to make the pictures they want, like any other creative worker in another
art. But full independence will not be reached until films are sold like oils or books on
the open market, and the poor ones will sink to their level. Chaplin and Disney have done
their work in their way, and Capra has tried to and generally succeeded. It took guts to do
LOST HORIZON, but Capra was never quite at home in the escape-world. It took guts to do
the run-on-the-bank scenes in AMERICAN MADNESS, and the farmer's social criticism in DEEDS

Robert Gessner's program notes for the
screening of *It Happened One Night*.
(Wesleyan Cinema Archives)

Motion Pictures and Youth, *Children's Attendance at Motion Pictures*, *The Emotional Responses of Children to the Motion Picture Situation*, and *Getting Ideas from the Movies*, for instance.[9] Then, in 1939, Thorp published her sociological study. In something of the apotheosis of these various projects, Leo Handel published *Hollywood Looks at Its Audience* in 1950, a work that still stands out as perhaps the most thorough examination of reception in the United States.[10] Handel's highly detailed quantitative analysis of the composition of the audience for American films was based on data-collection technology such as the "Hopkins Electric Televoting Machine," the "Cirlin Reactograph," and other machinery with similarly frightening names. Just two years later, David Riesman and Evelyn T. Riesman's "Movies and Audiences" appeared in *American Quarterly*, the journal of the American Studies Association.[11] The Riesmans called for a much more thorough understanding of the manner in which various audiences interact with the movies they see, but the moment for this kind of research had already begun to pass.

Around this time the intellectual discourses about film started shifting decisively toward more literary concerns, and film studies came to occupy a place in the academy alongside humanities disciplines rather than those in the social sciences. The reasons for this development remain unclear, but they may have had something to do with the diversification of English departments during the period, with film becoming something of a staple in the English curriculum. In just one example of this disciplinary shift, the postwar period witnessed an extraordinary American studies movement. The professoriate finally started to include scholars—Jewish intellectuals, for instance, or those who had attended state universities rather than private institutions—whose connection to elite culture was somewhat tenuous and whose main interests were more regional, vernacular, and popular. The emergence of vast state systems of university education in Wisconsin, California, and elsewhere also led to a determination to study the regional, and to examine the ideological connection between artistic production and the project of building the nation. Most of this movement was literary, with much of it focused on finding distinctive American voices in Whitman, Stowe, Twain, and others. The movies, along with other such seemingly American aesthetic practices as jazz, seemed the perfect match for these interests, and thus the movies themselves, rather than their audiences (or other related institutional concerns), seemed to merit the most serious study.

In this narrative of disciplinary shift, as film became more and more the rival of literature and the other arts, the sociological impulse to study the audience came to be fixed on other popular media. The postwar period saw any number of studies of the effects that television had on its audiences, while Ruth Palter from the University of Chicago wrote "Radio's Attraction for Housewives," which remains a model for carrying out studies of gendered reception practices.[12] Of course, film studies still produced exemplary social science research, for instance Garth Jowett's *Film: The Democratic Art* in 1976.[13] But for better and for worse, with the expansion of film studies in English and other literature departments along with the development of graduate programs in cinema, the study of motion pictures remained primarily related to literary studies and art history, with an emphasis on the film text itself, at least through the late 1980s.

This lightning tour through the development of American film studies indicates that a thorough study of the discipline may yield similar findings to other significant historical examinations in the field. For at least the last twenty-five years film scholars have examined the possibility of alternative film histories. We cannot say with absolute certainty, for instance, why the feature-length narrative film became the dominant form, given the range of possibilities available around 1900. But we might also speak of the possibility of alternative film methodologies, that is, the prospect that in 1910 or 1925 or 1940 the study of cinema, at least in the United States, might have gone one way instead of another. Robert Gessner's approach, owing so much to art history and literary history, became the dominant mode for the practice of film scholarship in the United States. The coexistence of Gessner's method and that of Thorp in the late 1930s, however, and the ample scholarly precedents for each of them, indicate that the social science model of *America at the Movies*, or the Payne Fund studies, or *Hollywood Looks at Its Audience*, which deemphasized the film text and stressed issues of reception, might have become the primary model for organizing the study of the cinema.

There have been changes in material conditions that allow for this renewed interest in reception. Some of the requisite primary materials for audience studies have been available for a long time at such sites as the University of California at Los Angeles (papers from Twentieth Century-Fox and Paramount and such personal collections as that of animator Walter Lantz), the Library of Congress (invaluable motion picture copyright records), and the New York Public Library (the records of the National Board of Review). We have also seen the opening of a number of archival sources only since the early 1980s: the Hays Office censorship files at the Academy of Motion Picture Arts and Sciences Library and the extensive Warner Bros. files at the University of Southern California, the establishment of the Motion Picture Reading Room at the Library of Congress, and at least one studio—Disney—making many of its documents available to the public. Thus we now have records of industry censors, exhibitors, studio officials, and fans, all of which help us understand some of the complexities of reception. To the extent, then, that institutional attitudes toward collections of primary materials can influence intellectual work, these improvements have led to important shifts in film studies scholarship, particularly as they relate to issues of audience.

In part because of the extraordinary documentary evidence that now surrounds the American cinema, a number of film historians have adapted the recent work of such intellectual and cultural historians as Haydon White, Dominick LaCapra, and Natalie Zemon Davis, who have been instrumental in developing what can be called a theory of the textuality of the historical field. This makes it possible to treat all discursive practices—and for film studies this means fan magazines, theater manager reports, and studio memos, for instance, in addition to films—as worthy of being "read" as texts that create meaning through interrelationships rather than in isolation. In fact this method of reading has become part of a broad cultural studies project that includes film as well as other disciplines, with such practitioners as Eric Lott in American studies, John Bodnar and Mary Ryan in urban history, and Jane Gaines in such hybrid fields as critical legal theory and film studies.[14]

Applied to the audience this project allows for theorizing and historicizing how films, filmmakers, and the film industry were perceived, and in the case of this project about Capra, specifically during the classical period of Hollywood sound production, from about 1930 to 1960, roughly the period of Capra's career. My own research has been grounded in the everyday artifacts of material history that might provide evidence about audience—artifacts produced by fans, journalists, theater managers, industry censors, and government officials, among others. For film studies, this project and others like it shift the significant question from "What does a film mean?" to "To whom are certain interpretations available?" and "How might these interpretations vary among different spectators?" Guiding methodological principles were enunciated by Edward Buscombe more than twenty-five years ago; although, almost certainly because of a lack of available primary materials, film scholars tended to avoid dealing with Buscombe's concerns until fairly recently. In discussing some of the textual analyses performed on Hollywood films from the 1930s that claimed to establish the meaning of a film regardless of the interpretive gymnastics required, Buscombe quite reasonably wrote that "surely it would have to be demonstrated that such a reading was available to an audience at the time."[15] That is, these analyses tended to demonstrate the virtuosity of the scholar rather than the reactions of the film audience.

In adopting Buscombe's call for a different approach to interpretation, I do not mean to imply that we can ever conclusively reconstruct any film audience, just as we cannot chart all of the variations of an audience's interpretation of a film. But we can study a rhetoric of reception: the various discursive forms that articulate possible responses to a movie, such as fan letters and exhibitor reports, and also those forms that help to shape reception, such as advertising and movie star interviews. By following Thorp's 1939 assertion that films do not simply produce spectators but are also produced by them, I am not trying to indicate that meaning itself is endlessly deferred as we go from a film to a variety of audiences and then to a variety of sources describing both film and audience. Rather, following Ien Ang in her work on the television audience for *Dallas*, I plan to show that reports on response can be read "symptomatically" and that "we must search for what is behind the explicitly written, for the presuppositions and accepted attitudes concealed within them," so that they come to "be read as texts, as discourses." In Jackie Stacey's words, such a reading brings us to a methodology marking the "shift from the textually produced spectator . . . to the spectator as text."[16]

Practical Concerns

Of course, this interest in the viewer leads to some very practical problems. Most significant is the question of where to locate these audience texts, the reports of what viewers thought about movies. I suggest looking for materials in the sources described in the paragraphs below. These sources are by no means the only ones possible for evidence. Some of them allow us to go around the margins of the historical audience, while others bring us to the viewer much more directly. To a greater or lesser degree, these sources gave me the primary materials I used in this project.

Trade journals often provide excellent information. *Variety* and the *Hollywood Reporter* come immediately to mind, but for scholars working on the 1930s, 1940s, and 1950s, the *Motion Picture Herald* is particularly significant. The *Herald* was a journal for film exhibitors, and so it always dealt with aspects of the movie theater and movie publicity—architecture, lobby displays, merchandise tie-ins, newspaper gimmicks, etc.—thus giving us a sense of what it must have been like to go to the movies and to experience film culture more broadly in the everyday life of a city or town. And the *Herald* also gives us more direct information about audience. Every week the *Herald* ran a column called "What the Picture Did for Me," which has figured prominently in my research. In this column, theater managers wrote in to discuss how they advertised different movies, how long they played, who their audiences were, and what those audiences thought of the films they saw.

Nontrade journals and magazines also help us find out how films may have been understood and used. Magazines like *Time* and *Newsweek*, with their regular film reviews and features about movies, can be helpful. But there are also less obvious (and often less available) sources, such as fan magazines or *Parents* magazine, a publication from the 1930s that at times seemed fixated on the relationships between films and children. There are also journals that specialize in film but are not geared toward an industry audience: *Educational Screen*, for example, which was published in the 1940s and 1950s, dealt with movies in schools from kindergarten through high school, with most of its content devoted to issues of how, where, and to what effect films might be used in educational settings.

At least from the period under discussion here, there are more books by film experts than might be expected. As I discuss in chapter 2, the 1930s was something of a golden period in film textbook publication, and there were also those books of practical information written by people working in the industry. In 1938, for example, Frank Ricketson, who had spent a lifetime in the field, wrote the exhibitor's bible, *The Management of Motion Picture Theatres*.[17] As with the trade journals for exhibitors, Ricketson's book now stands out as a record of film culture from the period. Giving us a sense of the extraordinarily continuous showing of movies in most theaters, for example, Ricketson explains that the preferred time for the length of an entire program of films, from short subjects to feature, would be no more than two hours and two minutes. He then insists that the maximum length of time for an intermission, between the end of the feature and the beginning of the short film that marked the start of the next show, would only be two minutes.[18]

Newspapers offer superb records of exhibition and advertising. They provide the locations of theaters, show times, and often prices. The best of them for research purposes (the *Washington Post* stands out for the period under discussion here) also provide entire film bills, showcasing not just the feature but also the cartoon, shorts, and newsreels, and from this we can know exactly what audiences were watching.

Newspapers may be a self-evident source, but government documents are a less obvious choice. These documents, particularly those papers from the State Department, contain a surprising amount of information on films. Officials from the State Department, at least from the period of Capra's career, often spent a great deal of time making sure that American films faced no problems when they played overseas, in terms of censorship, embargo, or boycott. Thus issues of reception, and most often how foreign officials understood Hollywood movies, would intermittently preoccupy department bureaucrats. These documents tend to demonstrate the manner in which the federal government and the movie studio worked together. Other government documents, however, show some of the tensions between the government and, if not the studios, then the individuals who worked for them. The FBI, as is now commonly known, kept tabs on any number of film workers, ranging from leftists to conservatives like Capra. These documents, which are available through the Freedom of Information Act, were originally meant to track any possible dangers these workers may have posed to the country, but now they tell us about the ways a very specific audience of government workers understood films and filmmakers, and often about the relationships between film workers and a wide array of political and cultural movements, institutions, and consumers.

Private businesses as well as the government took an active interest in motion pictures, and their records often contain information about movies and consumers. Capra, for example, produced television shows for AT&T, so that company kept careful track of what he was doing and what audiences thought, and also made use of their connection with Capra in annual reports and various documents.

Similarly, the records of other institutions yield valuable information about movies. Research on reception demonstrates that audiences saw Hollywood feature films in addition to other kinds of movies in a variety of exhibition sites, not just conventional theaters. Schools, YMCAs, military barracks, and prisons typically showed movies during the period of Capra's career, and almost as often maintained useful information about audience response. In fact, whereas theaters have often discarded records about exhibition and spectators that might have been kept during the 1930s, 1940s, or 1950s, these alternative sites often have fairly thorough archives.

Personal paper collections can be the best source for information about audiences. Capra deposited his papers at the Wesleyan Cinema Archives, including documents from all of his films starting around 1930 and 1931. The collection includes production records, press books, contracts, scripts, and a wide range of correspondence, much of it from fans who wrote to Capra after seeing one of his movies during its initial release or after watching it in a college class or on television many years later. For all such collections, it is always impossible to tell how selective the individual may have been and thus what might be missing. In Capra's case, however, for virtually all of his post-1933 films there are ample numbers of unfavorable film reviews and critical fan letters, implying that early on the filmmaker was interested in being able to document his career as fully as possible. The collection at Wesleyan has been central to my research, and there are many more such collections open to scholars.

Reading through a director's fan mail is both something of a guilty pleasure and a wonderful way to reconstruct not so much the experience of going to the movies, but the tropes, genres, and terms that people used to describe that experience. A practice related to reading through this written record is talking directly to film viewers. Interviewing people who went to the movies provides information filtered through many years of memory, but these memories themselves stand out as valuable texts about the experience of seeing movies and also about the ways the sense of that experience might change. Examining fans' memories through extensive interviews was one of the objectives of Jackie Stacey's work on female viewers, and the practice stands out as a central means for understanding a wide range of audiences.

Thus we have source material for a number of different audiences, from the vast national and international audiences for Hollywood films to the very particular audience, such as government bureaucrats, prison inmates, and foreign censors. Once we acknowledge these plural audiences and then collect data about them, we must naturally make sense of the evidence, develop methodologies for understanding reception, and pose appropriate questions about audience. I would like now to bring Capra back into the discussion and explain some of the principles of this project and some ways of using this book.

Methodological Practices

After a brief try at filmmaking in 1922, and then a few years as a gag writer for Hal Roach and Mack Sennett, Capra began his directing career in 1926, making the first of two films with Harry Langdon. By the time of the astonishing success of *It Happened One Night* in 1934, Capra had already directed almost two-thirds of the thirty-six feature films he would make in Hollywood. His last film, *Pocketful of Miracles*, came out in 1961. In my examination of the responses to many of these movies, each chapter takes a case study approach to issues of audience, following Capra's career chronologically from early sound films like *Flight* and *Dirigible* to some of his last projects, such as the science programs he made for television in the late 1950s. My choices, both of the films and the audiences, have to do with practical concerns about available materials and also about the methodological and historical issues that they raise. There is, relatively speaking, less evidence for Capra's very early films, like the Harry Langdon silent comedies, than there is for those films from the sound era. The movies from Capra's most celebrated period of productivity, from *It Happened One Night* in 1934 to *It's a Wonderful Life* in 1946, receive the most attention here. These films almost certainly generated the most attention among viewers and they also allowed Capra to develop audiences—of teachers, social reformers, government officials, and fans of high culture—that paid scant attention to other filmmakers. A few of those films, however, such as *Lost Horizon* and *You Can't Take It with You*, make relatively brief appearances here because the audience issues that they raise tend to duplicate those for other movies, or because, as in the case of *Arsenic and Old Lace* or *Here Comes the Groom*, they generated relatively less attention than *Mr. Smith Goes to Washington* or *Meet John Doe*.

I begin this book with an examination of the exhibition and publicity strategies for *Flight*, *Dirigible*, *Ladies of Leisure*, and *Platinum Blonde* in order to understand the creation of a reception context for Capra's films. I then move to an analysis of foreign censorship and government intervention in the case of *The Bitter Tea of General Yen*. Returning to domestic reception, I look at the response of high school students to *It Happened One Night*, and then the manner in which *Mr. Deeds Goes to Town* came to be used by a range of educators. *Mr. Smith Goes to Washington* and *Meet John Doe* were Capra's most overtly political films from the period, and in chapter 4 I examine a variety of ideologically charged responses to *Mr. Smith*, followed by, for *Meet John Doe*, a fan discourse calling for a cinema more engaged with issues of national significance. During the war Capra shifted to documentary production with the *Why We Fight* series, and for those films I study the ways they entered into a social science discourse of education that was part of a project to shape the responses of two groups of captive audiences: the American recruits who were required to watch the films and the German prisoners of war who were made to view the documentaries as part of their de-Nazification program. A different set of prisoners watched *It's a Wonderful Life*—those men who saw a special screening at San Quentin in 1946 and then wrote to the warden about their responses. Here I show how that film participated in postwar programs of uplift and reform, and also how the movie's emphasis on loss and attempted suicide affected a few hundred men whose life experiences were almost certainly quite different from those of most audiences. Finally, I track fan response to Capra's return to political filmmaking with *State of the Union*, and then I examine how one corporation, AT&T, kept tabs on the responses to Capra's return to documentary filmmaking, the Bell Science Series.

Although the book proceeds from one case study to another, several narratives of reception run throughout the project. Capra's growing (and then diminishing) celebrity comes to be significant in terms of how typical moviegoers understood him and his films, and also how, at various times, government officials and film industry workers understood him. By 1941 and the production of *Meet John Doe*, Capra had come to be taken seriously, by at least some of his viewers, as a potential political force during very dangerous times; in other phases of his career he stood out as a consummate artist and an inspiration to other Italian Americans. Capra and his films tended to generate significant discourses of both enjoyment and disgust as his fans wrote to him about what they enjoyed in the cinema and also what they hated. Thus this project provides some of the empirical evidence of what different audiences desired in their popular culture. Furthermore, several of the studies here indicate that the cinema also produced displeasure for the everyday filmgoer and also for more specialized audiences; a kind of viewer response that has gone little noted, as the popular cinema is typically figured as a kind of pleasure machine. At least somewhat connected to this production of displeasure, a number of audiences often found themselves forced to watch movies, made by Capra and other filmmakers. In part because these viewers tended to be in institutional settings such as schools, the military, and prisons, extensive records exist recording their responses. Ranging from high school students in the 1930s to military recruits and German prisoners of war in World War II to San Quentin inmates in 1946, the story of Capra's audiences reveals how often filmgoing was completely or partially involuntary during the classical era of sound production, and also how frequently spectators watched films in nontheatrical settings.

The most sustained narrative here details the development of film studies as a discipline and also the shifting beliefs about motion pictures as teaching tools. Once again evidence exists because a number of educational institutions maintained effective records of film use and film audiences. But we also must take into account the centrality of film to so many educational projects from the early 1930s through the late 1950s. A specific goal of my work in this book is the recovery of an earlier era of academic film studies in which the audience stood out as the central object of study. But the case studies here also detail how different settings and media, from the high school to the library to radio, used the Hollywood motion picture to engage in programs of uplift and education directed at children and adolescents. Capra's films, particularly *It Happened One Night*, *Mr. Deeds Goes to Town*, *Lost Horizon*, and *Mr. Smith Goes to Washington*, took on particular prominence in these projects.

During World War II the cinema became part of a medicalized discourse of education and persuasion, with psychologists and other scientists certain that films might be used to indoctrinate vast audiences into an antiracist, antinationalist postwar liberal utopia. Once again Capra's films occupied the ground zero of these projects, with the success or failure of the *Why We Fight* films to influence recruits providing the data for future projects. At about the same time, Capra's cinema figured in significant reeducation projects aimed at ideological and social malcontents: in the first case, German POWs who ostensibly learned about American-style democracy from Capra's wartime documentaries; and in the second, San Quentin inmates who watched *It's a Wonderful Life* in order to reflect on the mistakes that had landed them in jail. More than a decade after the war Capra himself took on the role of educator with the production of four science television programs for AT&T that were designed for the junior high and high school audience. Capra, of course, had graduated from Caltech and at least occasionally lamented not pursing a career in science.[19] The television programs marked something of a return to a first love (as well as a decline in his career as a film director), and on a less personal level demonstrated some of the shifts in American science education and the hope that commercial television might take on a significant pedagogical role.

Narratives and case studies of audience desire, preference, and distaste give us broad insight into the cinema as an institution and film studies as a discipline. They help us ask the questions about meaning and interpretation that center on different viewers rather than on the films themselves. They can also give us a sense of the contours of film culture that extend beyond the theaters that people attended and the movies that they saw. In addition, they provide information about the multiple sites of film exhibition and the multiple audiences that went to films in so many different places. We can also gain from them a much fuller understanding of the relationships between the cinema and other institutions, such as the education system, the prison system, the government, and the military, and between the cinema and other media—for instance, print journalism and radio. And in a study of Capra's audiences we begin to understand the complicated interactions between the celebrity and the viewer, the expectations that audiences have of filmmakers, and, at least in the case of a famous director, the special status they grant him and also the familiarity they feel toward him.

Some examples from three periods in the director's career, from early success to solid celebrity status to decline, help delineate the goals of this project. These examples amply demonstrate the international reach of Capra's films, the ways in which fans felt comfortable "speaking" with him, and some of the issues that audience studies raise for the discipline—issues ranging from exhibition strategies to gendered reception practices, from the legacies of European colonialism to the nature of fans' debates about movies, and from the ways in which average fans thought about themselves to the manner in which some very specialized audiences thought about Capra and his films.

Capra made *It Happened One Night* in 1934 and, at least judging from his files, it was his first film to generate sustained fan response from around the world. He began receiving letters about the film from England in 1935, and the pace of this mail tells us something about global distribution systems. About a year and a half after the film came out in the United States a woman wrote to Capra from Manchester, saying "this film has only just reached our district," and then adding, "but I have seen it four times."[20] Another woman, from Shoreditch, called the film "the most entertaining picture I have ever seen," and praised it for showing "two great stars as they really are, Claudette Colbert and Clark Gable." She commended Capra for giving "us Clark Gable in a light role instead of a heavy lover which I have often heard him say that he hates playing."[21] Here, then, we see a very specific relationship between a female fan and a male star, and a certain sense of a fan's entrance into film culture. The woman knew—probably from fan magazines, but, in this letter, seemingly from Gable himself—that the actor didn't like playing heavies.

In 1937, now established as a preeminent director, Capra received a letter from Myrtle Beach, South Carolina: "Dear Mr. Capra: Today is my seventeenth birthday. I've just seen *Lost Horizon*. May I say that although I'm only a young girl, probably just another silly, prattling schoolgirl, I'm sure this picture is the greatest ever filmed. I sat through it twice. I intend to see it again."[22] Two weeks before, Capra had received a letter from Madras, India. "Dear Mr. Frank Capra: I am an Indian boy aged 20. I have taken courage to write to you. The reason for writing this letter is my seeing *Lost Horizon* yesterday. The picture is one of the greatest I have seen so far." The young man then asked Capra a question about the ending, saying, "I and many friends had a heated discussion about this and I decided to clear my doubt by writing to you."[23] Like so many other fans, he then asked for a signed photo.

The girl in Myrtle Beach watched films over and over again, itself an interesting and probably fairly common practice among fans. Despite being so avid about movies, however, she could not take her own seriousness seriously—she could only "prattle." For the young man in India, writing to Capra was itself an act of "courage," and the significance of the film extended beyond the theater. It occasioned serious and "heated" discussions among his friends, thereby giving us an idea of a film culture in India (at least among fans about the same age and background as the young man) in which the ideas in a film might be debated and argued over. These letters also seem gendered in terms of the self-presentation of the fans, the young woman somewhat diffident, the young man much more confident in his address to the director. In addition, from a distance of almost seventy years we can only wonder about the interest that this young man, himself a colonial subject, took in Capra's orientalist fantasy. And, of course, like so many of Capra's fans from around the world, this one asked for a photograph and an autograph, indicating that, perhaps, he was still caught between film cultures—one a more adolescent enthusiasm for celebrity, the other a more sophisticated interest in art and ideas. Finally, in all of these letters, from around the world and from men and women, from young people and from adults, there is a clear directorial discourse at work—fans in India, England, and elsewhere wrote to Capra as the "author" of the films they saw.

In 1952, well into Capra's professional decline, the FBI visited the director, probably as part of a background check after Capra became the director of motion picture production for the Defense Department's Project Vista, which concerned the study of air warfare in Western Europe.[24] Here we can see another kind of reading of the director, his films, and his career. The agents wanted information about some of Capra's coworkers, notably several of his screenwriters. Capra confirmed, for instance, that Sidney Buchman, who had written *Mr. Smith Goes to Washington*, had leftist politics, but that he did not know this at the time of their collaboration.[25] Capra did not have much information on the Hollywood Left, however, and so provided the FBI with little help. But the agents were also more than a little concerned with Capra himself, not so much with his films as with some of his past experiences and associations. Here, then, rather than a response to any of his films, we have an interpretation of Capra himself, almost certainly not indicative of the vast audience for movies but rather of a very small one that concerned itself disproportionately with the political inclinations of film industry workers.

Indeed, it was an episode of film exhibition and an agent's awareness of Southern California film culture that helped make the FBI suspicious of Capra. His file reports that "in June, 1945, an informant of the Los Angeles Office advised that the Russian-American Club of Los Angeles was showing certain films for benefit and that one of the films, *Operation Titanic*, . . . had been produced by the United States Army Signal Corps under the direction of Frank Capra." In their interrogation of Capra, agents grilled him about being "a member of a Communist inspired picket line" during a newspaper strike, of being a 1941 "sponsor and National Vice-Chairman of the Russian War Relief which was strongly Communist infiltrated," of being active in the same year in "the National Federation for Constitutional Liberties," of contributing in 1943 to the "Joint Anti-Fascist Refugee Committee," of associating for "a number of years" with "writers and other individuals reported to have been members of the Communist Party," and of receiving, during the war, "considerable propaganda literature direct from Russia."[26]

Capra denied the inferences of Communist sympathies behind these allegations. He insisted that in his charitable giving there was "a Catholic pattern, a California Institute of Technology pattern, but no red pattern." Then, clearly irritated over the claim that he worked too cozily with the Russians during World War II, Capra reminded the agents that Russia fought as an ally of the United States and that, while he received "unsolicited data from Russia," he had also been awarded the Order of the

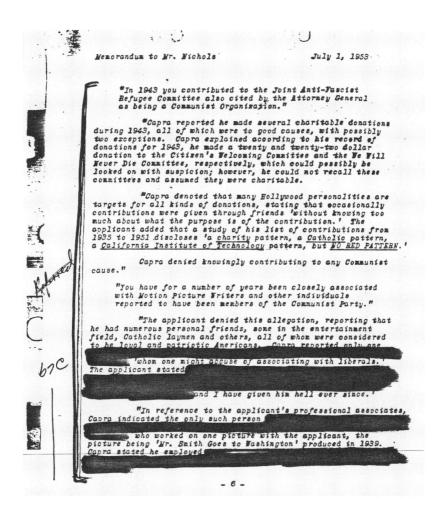

"In 1943 you contributed to the Joint Anti-Fascist
Refugee Committee also cited by the Attorney General
as being a Communist Organization."

"Capra reported he made several charitable donations
during 1943, all of which were to good causes, with possibly
two exceptions. Capra explained according to his record of
donations for 1943, he made a twenty and twenty-two dollar
donation to the Citizen's Welcoming Committee and the We Will
Never Die Committee, respectively, which could possibly be
looked on with suspicion; however, he could not recall these
committees and assumed they were charitable.

"Capra denoted that many Hollywood personalities are
targets for all kinds of donations, stating that occasionally
contributions were given through friends 'without knowing too
much about what the purpose is of the contribution.' The
applicant added that a study of his list of contributions from
1935 to 1951 discloses 'a charity pattern, a Catholic pattern,
a California Institute of Technology pattern, but NO RED PATTERN.'

                    Capra denied knowingly contributing to any Communist
cause."

"You have for a number of years been closely associated
with Motion Picture Writers and other individuals
reported to have been members of the Communist Party."

"The applicant denied this allegation, reporting that
he had numerous personal friends, some in the entertainment
field, Catholic laymen and others, all of whom were considered
to be loyal and patriotic Americans. Capra reported only one
▓▓▓▓▓▓▓▓▓▓ whom one might accuse of associating with liberals.'
The applicant stated▓▓▓▓▓▓▓▓▓▓▓▓▓▓▓▓▓▓▓▓▓▓▓▓▓▓▓▓
▓▓
▓▓▓▓▓▓▓▓▓▓▓▓▓▓▓▓and I have given him hell ever since.'

"In reference to the applicant's professional associates,
Capra indicated the only such person▓▓▓▓▓▓▓▓▓▓▓▓▓▓▓▓
▓▓▓▓▓▓▓▓▓▓▓ who worked on one picture with the applicant, the
picture being 'Mr. Smith Goes to Washington' produced in 1939.
Capra stated he employed▓▓▓▓▓▓▓▓▓▓▓▓▓▓▓▓▓▓▓▓▓▓▓▓▓▓

- 6 -

A page from Frank Capra's FBI file from 1953, reporting that the director "denied knowingly contributing to any Communist cause."

British Empire, "receiving the personal congratulations of Prime Minister Winston Churchill."[27]

The FBI agents were clearly on a fishing expedition, with no basis for doubting Capra's patriotism or his solid conservatism. Instead, this brief look at the director's FBI file shows the possibility of perverse readings of the director's career, and also that studies of audiences should consider not just their readings of films but also their readings of celebrities' lives. More broadly, this kind of reception study demonstrates the relationship between institutions, in this case the film industry and the FBI, and also adds to our understanding of the cultural history of the period. We know about the FBI's persecutions of leftists in Hollywood and elsewhere; the bureau was only slightly less enthusiastic, however, in its occasional pursuit of those on the Right.

Despite the surveillance by the FBI, those thousands of eyes and ears might not have been so ominous after all. Capra based his image of the audience on a theater full of people, but his movies were seen by many millions more, and in far more diverse places than the conventional first-run site or neighborhood theater. Even Capra himself might not have known about all of the prison screenings or the specialized clubs that showed his movies, in spite of his own interest in and seemingly deep connection with his viewers. Invoking the main character in one of his major works, Capra referred to the audiences for his movies as "my John Does, about whom and for whom I made my films."[28] Although the attitude here seems paternal, all of those John Does were hardly obedient children. They let Capra know exactly what they thought; and indeed part of their pleasure in his movies seemed to come after viewing them, when they could think about, argue over, and discuss what they had seen—either with Capra or with friends, family members, or professional colleagues. Because of the audiences' engagement with Capra's movies and with films in general, we are left with an extraordinary record of interpretation along with a more significant understanding of at least one small part of a much larger history of reading, listening, watching, and responding.

Chapter One

The National and the Local: Ballyhoo
and the U.S. Film Audience

To advertise *Flight*, Columbia Pictures's 1929 "all-talking roadshow sensation" about U.S. marine intervention in Nicaragua, the studio announced that technicians had "wired" all of the battle scenes "so that Director Frank R. Capra could talk to any point of the battlefield without leaving his directorial chair."[1] This information appeared in the studio's nationally distributed "Exhibitor's Campaign Book" for the film, which was designed to help theater managers advertise their programs in local newspapers and create ballyhoo in general. In writing about Capra the studio seemed to believe in his marketing potential as the panoptic overseer of U.S. intervention into a Central American civil war, able to have instant contact with any point of "battle" without ever being there. More specifically, the film corporation, with its production facility in Hollywood and its distribution office in New York, depicted Capra as an armchair general as a means of attracting audiences throughout the country, both in big cities and small towns as well as in various regions.

This militarized, omniscient Capra was one of the director's more significant public relations incarnations from the era—no surprise, perhaps, when one considers that his filmography during the period includes *Submarine* (1928) and *Dirigible* (1931) in addition to *Flight*. Throughout this early period of Capra's career, before the huge triumph of *It Happened One Night* in 1934, Columbia worked hard in orchestrating national campaigns to convince the public of the director's celebrity and to make audiences interpret Capra's movies as realizations of a filmmaker's vision and his smooth working relationships with his actors. To supplement these assertions of individual genius, the studio developed national publicity strategies that provided theater managers with less middle-brow forms of ballyhoo that had nothing to do with Capra, but rather extolled the fashion sense of his female stars, recommended marquee displays, and suggested contests that might be connected to the movies. In doing so, the studio crafted methods for linking the movies and the movie theater to varying modes of advertising and a variety of consumers, as well as to a range of consumer activities and leisure sites. Here ballyhoo, as proposed by the studio and practiced by the theaters, helped to build a modern public space of related products and technologies, entertainment and business institutions, and celebrities and fans.

As might be expected, studio-designed publicity sought quite actively to generate interest in and knowledge about Capra and his films, and to create audiences for those movies. Often Columbia developed its publicity and sought out audiences through specifically gendered appeals to women—appeals that rejected the martial approach to Capra's celebrity and instead stressed romance and chic clothes and the reading of novels. And in doing so the studio asserted its connection to other leisure industries such as publishing. Despite this advice and these campaigns from the corporate office, however, the actual ballyhoo for Capra's films, at theaters, in newspapers, in shops, and elsewhere, gives us a sense of the relationships between centrally organized national strategies and the local efforts to tailor publicity to relatively small audience groups. In light of this, in this chapter I look at studio suggestions for approaching audiences with publicity and advertising, and then I examine the publicity and advertising themselves as typically practiced by theater managers who followed corporate directives and also adapted them to local needs.

Capra's films from the mid-1920s to the early 1930s provide excellent case studies in movie advertising and in the ways that studios and local theaters attempted to reach and to create audiences for their films. Between 1926, when he began directing full-time, and 1933, Capra made twenty-two films that covered many of the familiar Hollywood genres from that era: immigration melodrama, newspaper comedy-drama, women's film, society comedy, working-class comedy, orientalist fantasy, and military action film. He also began his long association with screenwriter Robert Riskin with *American Madness*, a 1932 social conscience film that served as a prototype for the Deeds/Smith/Doe films of the late 1930s and early 1940s, and as a partial model for *It's a Wonderful Life* from 1946.[2] As I discuss in chapter 3 Capra himself became something of a celebrity during this period, making prestige pictures for a studio that, with few major stars under contract, was only too happy to publicize its leading director. Nevertheless, "Capra films" were not the sort of known products that they would become after *Lady for a Day* in 1933 and especially after *It Happened One Night* a year later, and so they required significant exploitation by the theaters showing them. And the variety of Capra films from the period helps us to examine the gamut of city and small-town ballyhoo practices from the late 1920s and early 1930s.

The period covered by the national distribution of these films marked a significant, transitional one for both film exhibition and advertising. In 1931, single-feature exhibition was still something of an industry standard. As Tino Balio has noted, "double features established a foothold in New England in 1930," and by "the middle of 1932, six thousand of the fourteen thousand theaters then operating, or 40 percent, had adopted the practice." For the next few years, that percentage would only increase.[3] Necessarily, theatrical advertising for single films, as in the cases studied here, differed at least somewhat from advertising strategies aimed at coaxing customers into seeing two movies. Moreover, throughout the 1930s movie advertising came increasingly to be coordinated nationally, with less leeway for input by individual theater managers. Janet Staiger, in what is still the best discussion of movie advertising, has detailed the long history of tension between New York film offices and local theater managers. By the end of the decade that tension may have remained, but advertising practices themselves had shifted, at least somewhat, to the film corporation rather than the theater.[4] But with Capra's films from the early 1930s we can study the specific, and quickly passing, advertising mode and exhibition practice of single films that was marked by a fair amount of local control, and that also would soon be changed considerably.

The recent historiography of advertising has emphasized, in different but complementary ways, precisely this merging of the national and the local. Some of the most significant examinations of advertising, such as Roland Marchand's groundbreaking *Advertising the American Dream*, emphasize the manner in which advertising as a practice and as a profession became increasingly nationalized over the course of the early twentieth century. The development of mass market magazines, such as the *Ladies Home Journal*, *Good Housekeeping*, and *Better Homes and Gardens*, made it much easier to reach national audiences (with the titles of these magazines also offering a good idea of the centrality of female consumers during this period, which, as we will see, was not lost on the film industry). Advertisers themselves used World War I to demonstrate what Marchand calls their national muscle, as they helped "the government raise funds and recruit military personnel," as well as "sell war bonds, enlist army and navy recruits . . . and promote conservation of food and resources." Developments in media technology and science also aided in the nationalization of advertising and products. The company AT&T sought to control telecommunications nationwide and engaged in national campaigns as early as 1908 in order to convince the public of the efficacy of such a plan. At around the same time, through a massive advertising program Proctor and Gamble turned its new product, Crisco, into something of a national craze. Many other companies developed national ambitions at this time, so that in 1909, as Marchand notes, even the aptly named "National Casket Company embarked on a national magazine campaign."[5]

Marchand is quick to point out, however, that the benefits of these national projects may have been difficult to determine. Advertisers themselves could never be sure that their campaigns worked, and Marchand himself admits that he could not "prove conclusively that the American people absorbed the values and ideas of the ads" that they saw.[6] Marchand's work becomes, finally, an examination of the representational systems of the ads of the first part of the twentieth century, and an analysis of the industrial structures of the agencies that created them and the production companies that, like AT&T and Proctor and Gamble, made use of them.

Other scholars, however, have taken a far less nuanced approach and have determined that, following Marchand, advertising and production activities came to be overwhelmingly nationalized during the late nineteenth and early twentieth centuries, so much so that the public—in cities, small towns, rural areas, and everywhere else—was helpless against this public relations onslaught. In this formulation, consumption practices also became fully national. Stuart Ewen and Elizabeth Ewen's work adopts this viewpoint while examining the manner in which "mass" images and products came to be aimed at a "mass" audience as a means of "shaping [the] American consciousness." Two other authors of fundamental works in the field, Jackson Lears and Stephen Fox, look at advertising from about the same angle. Indeed, the title of Fox's book, *The Mirror Makers*, implies a homogenizing, one-way transmission of advertising agency-created images that helped to craft an American national identity among tens of millions of consumers.[7] The approach of the Ewens, Lears, and Fox has all too often been adopted as a cultural studies paradigm for understanding twentieth-century American consumers and their relations to those products that they consumed. In this top-down model, as capitalism developed in the United States the local became engulfed by the national, and regional preferences and habits turned into American practices that were virtually the same across the country. The motion picture industry here thus becomes the new medium that fully levelled regional differences and produced a national consciousness.

Some American studies scholars, however, have concentrated on Marchand's uncertainties about the development of national markets and consumers and have studied quite local interpretations of advertising as well as local uses of the products advertised. Lizabeth Cohen, for instance, has written about the significance between the two world wars of the local "mom and pop" store for urban, working-class consumers. Kathy Newman, in her work on radio, has looked at local responses, particularly consumer boycotts, to national radio advertising campaigns.[8] Thus the work of Marchand covers the nationalization of advertising and the sophisticated networks that distributed products to all parts of the country, with Marchand's followers overstating the hegemony of these national projects. Concomitantly, the research of Cohen, Newman, and others indicates that local publicity and buying practices still must be considered of central importance to any understanding of the relationships between goods and the consumers for them. In this latter model, one that increasingly has been adopted in cultural studies, American studies, and film studies, the national and the local exist side by side, in tension with each other and also working cooperatively together. And it is the Hollywood film industry from the classical era that precisely demonstrates this mix of production and consumption activities, and the mixture of national and local approaches for reaching the audience in the United States.

Directorial Celebrity

In media studies, the understanding of the relationship between the national and the local has developed alongside an increased awareness of the mechanics of celebrity. The work of Richard deCordova, Kathryn Fuller, Gaylyn Studlar, and Shelley Stamp, among others, has demonstrated the efforts of the film industry in the United States to turn actors into stars, and has shown the exchanges between the movies, fan magazines, book publishing, radio, and other outlets to exploit that stardom as fully as possible to the benefit of the movies and a range of other products, and to create as well as fulfill the varied pleasures of the film audience.[9] This work also gives us a better sense of celebrity before the movies. As Richard Wightman Fox has shown, in his discussion of the fame of nineteenth-century preacher Henry Ward Beecher, "the culture of celebrity was one manifestation of the culture of publicity," with the latter developing quite fully and quickly in the years following the Civil War.[10] It should come as no surprise, then, that half a century after Beecher's greatest fame, movie stars would not be the only celebrities developed by the film industry. Indeed, there was ample room for film directors to become stars, and for the studios that employed them to cultivate that stardom and use it to promote their movies.

The 1930s produced a significant intellectual discourse about directing, one that appeared in a number of scholarly and educational sources. But along with this discourse (which I examine later in this book, especially in chapter 3), there was also a popular vocabulary for discussing many of the same issues of quality that interested the era's film scholars. With *Flight*, the studio configured Capra as a kind of technologized, militarized visionary. In an article in the campaign book designed for placement in newspapers, Capra weighed in authoritatively on the very nature of the contemporary cinema, as he was "inclined to doubt [that] the introduction of sound and dialogue has in any manner changed the wonders of screen entertainment." Then, in the same article, the director became nothing less than a great explorer: "Capra is the man who did the impossible a year ago when he made *Submarine* at the bottom of the sea," the article claimed, and now, "having conquered the ocean, [his] ambition was next centered upon the air." The studio had Capra conquering that space too, as the director filmed "above the clouds by using radio and airplanes." [11] Thus the ballyhoo represented Capra as a fully modern hero, one who invoked Charles Lindbergh and mastered new worlds largely by mastering new technologies.

Unlike Lindbergh, however, Capra was no lone eagle. The director apparently made *Flight* with cooperation from the federal government, which another article described as pledging the full support of the U.S. marines. The article stressed that the government never automatically cooperated with film studios, particularly after experiences with films that "were not always the kind that reflected credit to Uncle Sam's forces." However, when marine officers "learned that Frank R. Capra, director of Columbia's *Submarine*, was to handle the megaphone [on *Flight*] . . . the officers were ready to listen to Columbia's proposition." [12]

From this publicity, of course, it is difficult to tell the exact nature of the military's involvement, particularly given the industry's willingness to make things up for the sake of good ballyhoo. Other branches of the federal government had varied relationships with the film industry. For example, the judicial system during this period typically investigated such movie business practices as block booking, and in the next chapter I show how the State Department worked with the studios to make sure that foreign markets remained open for Hollywood films. In the case of *Flight*, we have evidence of very real cooperation—an officer who had actually seen service in Nicaragua allegedly supervised "every foot of the film"—and also a kind of metaphorical slippage.[13] In what might be called the discursive representation of Capra at work, the articles in the campaign book portrayed the labor of the director on the set as very much the work of the commander in the field, from his technologized oversight of all of the battle scenes to his control of the officers and others working with him.

Creating Viewers:
Studio Strategies and Gendered Appeals

Despite the emphasis on the patriotic virtues of the film, Columbia, in its publicity suggestions, did not simply imagine the audience in national and nationalist terms as an undifferentiated mass moved by the spectacle of American military strength. The construction of Capra as a movie studio military hero and the emphasis on government involvement would seem to cast *Flight* as a standard adventure film for boys and men. But Columbia's publicity recommendations for *Flight*, at least to the extent that they were indicative of broader industrial strategies, complicate our understanding of the studios' approach to audience during the early sound era. Throughout their publicity, Columbia stressed a distinctly gendered audience by emphasizing the particular appeal that *Flight* had for women.

On the first page of the campaign book Columbia seemed to speak directly to exhibitors. "Don't lose the thought that *Flight* is one of the greatest romance pictures of the year as well as being an aerial thriller," the studio claimed, and then went on to assure that "the women will love it!" The rest of the first page is filled with advertisements that could be placed in newspapers. In one, the address is directed precisely at a potential audience of women as it stresses a few of the film's more salient plot points: "What would you do if the man you loved wanted you to love his pal?" The advertisements on the page emphasize Lila Lee's role in the film, and, with exclamation marks, concentrate attention on the film's "Thrills! Romance! Adventure!" as well as its "Heavenly romance!" Once again speaking to exhibitors, the bottom of the page reminds them to "play up to the women with these special ads."[14]

We have only sketchy information about the composition of movie audiences during this period. Garth Jowett notes that, at the time, "it was

Advertisements for *Flight*, stressing the film's appeal to women. (Library of Congress)

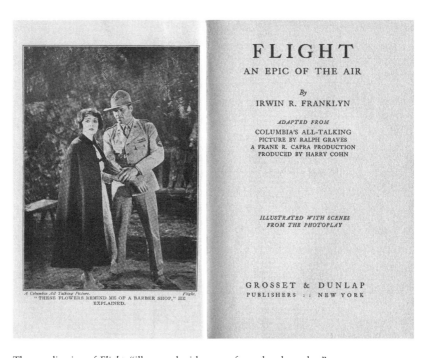

The novelization of *Flight*, "illustrated with scenes from the photoplay."

usually assumed that the content of films was largely determined by the female segment" of the audience, although it was never clear that women attended in greater numbers than men.[15] And although we have fairly precise overall attendance numbers from the period—75 million in 1931, declining to 60 million in 1932 and 1933, for instance—the ratio of girls and women to boys and men remains unclear.[16] Nevertheless, Columbia's proposed exhibitor strategy for *Flight* indicates the centrality of women to the film audience. Hollywood certainly created genre cycles for specific audiences: adventure films for men, love stories like Capra's *Ladies of Leisure* (1930) for women. As I show in chapter 2 in relation to *The Bitter Tea of General Yen* (1932), exhibitors themselves also understood fairly significant differences between small town and city audiences. But the U.S. film industry, both the studios and the theaters that used studio-generated publicity, also seemed to assume the necessity of directing all films to one fairly undifferentiated audience—women—either because they attended in greater numbers than men or because they were assumed to make the decisions about which movies to see with their husbands or boyfriends.

There also seems to have been an assumption on the part of the studio of other gendered leisure activities that might have a connection to film viewing. From this, we can see that the film industry understood the typical exhibition day as consisting of different audiences at different times. To coincide with the opening of Capra's film, Grosset and Dunlap published a novelization of *Flight* by screenwriter Irwin R. Franklyn that was "adapted from Columbia's all-talking picture."[17] The campaign book claimed that "for the past twenty years," Grosset and Dunlap had been "publishing photoplay editions of really great motion pictures, showing actual scenes from the screen play." At the suggestion of the campaign book, exhibitors might have wanted to place the current *Flight* volume in bookstore windows in order to generate publicity for the theater playing the movie.[18] Those same exhibitors were also encouraged to take it on themselves to put the novel into the hands of viewers.

The studio suggested that "here is a way to build extra matinee business," and added that exhibitors should "announce in your daily ads during the showing of the picture that to the first twenty-five women who hand their tickets to your doorman at each matinee performance . . . they will receive handsomely illustrated copies of the novelization of *Flight* absolutely free."[19] In the following chapters I show some of the connections between the "spaces" of film reception and very specific audiences, for example the theater and the classroom in the case of high school students, or the prison in the case of San Quentin inmates. There were also connections between entertainment and educational institutions—for instance, film, radio, schools, and public libraries—and once again with very specific audience groups in mind, most commonly children and adolescents. In the case of *Flight*, we can see another such connection—between the film and publishing industries. Implied as well is the understanding that women were more likely to be affected by that connection than men, as they seemed to be the targeted audience for the novel. The movie matinee also becomes the space, at least at this time, for a very specific viewing group. We know from the work of Richard deCordova that the industry actively sought an audience of often unescorted children and adolescents for its Saturday-afternoon showings.[20] But clearly the industry also assumed—and attempted to increase with the assistance of the publishing industry—an audience of women for its other daily showings, probably during the week when kids were in school and men were at work.

In this early period of Capra's career and of his celebrity, the director moved back and forth between the military melodrama—*Submarine*, *Dirigible*, and *Flight*—and the woman's film—*Forbidden* (1932) and *Ladies of Leisure*. And even more so than with *Flight*, Columbia insisted on the specifically gendered appeal of the movies that stressed maternal suffering (*Forbidden*, a version of the Fannie Hurst novel *Back Street*) and emotional turmoil. In *Ladies of Leisure*, Barbara Stanwyck plays a golddigger who falls in love with a wealthy man whose family objects to the romance. Love is, of course, triumphant by the end of the movie, with the studio publicity asserting the precisely gendered appeal of the formulaic narrative.

In its campaign book for the film, the studio advertised Capra very much as it had for *Flight* as the man in charge and as the ideal of the film artist capable of doing everything on the set. In an "advance feature" article for newspaper publication, headlined "Director Capra Expert At Every Phase of Talkie," the campaign book extolled the filmmaker's broad range of talent. "Capra is not only an expert at every phase of talking picture production," the article explained, "but is capable of rewriting portions of the script when it is necessary, and of introducing ad lib lines that add materially to the story." Moreover, "although he has never been on the stage, he seems to have an instinctive talent for reading lines and is able to give each actor just the intonation necessary," with the result that "there is a harmonious quality about the Capra productions that most other pictures lack."[21] Capra's control is not quite military here, as it was for *Flight*, but it is just as wide and all-encompassing. His authorship and his celebrity are

From the "Exhibitor's Campaign Book" for *Ladies of Leisure*, with Capra labeled an "expert" and "ace director" in separate articles. (Library of Congress)

marked by a mastery of everything that goes on during filming, the director as virtuoso rather than battlefield hero but still just as powerful.

Columbia, however, provided many other stories for newspapers and made many other publicity suggestions, and most of this recommended ballyhoo, rather than stressing Capra's astonishing abilities, instead seemed directly concerned with addressing the women in the film audience and explaining the pleasures that these viewers might get from Capra's new film.

The campaign book urged exhibitors to purchase a "3 Column Fashion Cut or Mat" from Columbia, one that could run in newspapers or be hung in store windows to provide viewers with a "fashion forecast."[22] In the cut, "Barbara Stanwyck, Juliette Compton and Marie Prevost display the stunning creations they wear in *Ladies of Leisure*, the sensational Columbia all-talking drama of night life," which would be followed by the name of the theater showing the picture. This is not quite the "Carole Lombard in Macy's window" that Charles Eckert wrote about, but like that department store display it is an extension of a certain kind of visual pleasure associated with the cinema, and likely very specifically gendered.[23] A woman's pleasure in examining the fashions in a movie turns into the female newspaper reader's pleasure, or that of the shopper browsing in a store carrying the advertisement.

With clothing and free books we can see the cinema's working out of the fiction and fashion appeal to women that began developing in the United States at the end of the nineteenth century. We know from the work of Kathy Peiss that nineteenth- and early-twentieth-century working women were not simply oppressed by the modern industrial system but instead took advantage of having at least a little disposable income. In short, working women did indeed have some fun away from work.[24] Following Peiss, Nan Enstad has written about the two industries from that period that "for the first time mass produced two types of commodities expressly targeted to a young working female audience; inexpensive fashion and formulaic fiction."[25] At least from the 1870s these women became avid consumers, and products that were ready to wear and pleasurable to read, as well as chic and exciting, seemed the perfect match for their incomes, desires, and class aspirations. Enstad is careful to point out that the working-class (and middle-class) women who bought the clothes and read the books were not simply dupes of bourgeois consumerist ideology but instead exercised choice and engaged critically with what they read and the fashions they encountered. And these same women fifty or sixty years later almost certainly became a central audience for movies, even for the kind of adventure fantasy afforded by *Flight* and other similar films. The "little shop girls" going to the movies may well have been distracted by the new medium, to borrow Siegfried Kracauer's term for this audience and the pleasures the cinema gave them.[26] But they were also discerning consumers: they had some income to spend on such things but not a lot. As a result, the cinema, publishing, and other entertainment industries competed with each other to attract this clientele, but they also worked together. Indeed, in the case of

Flight we can see the combination of literary fiction, fashion, film, and journalism. With newspaper ads, women got to study the dresses worn by the
stars and then see the stars in those dresses when they went to the movies.
Or, as they entered the theater, they were rewarded with free novels based
on the film they were about to see.

The pleasures in looking that were delivered by the cinema, as well as by
newspaper fashion advertisements and the novels illustrated with photos
from the films on which they were based, have become conventionalized
in cultural studies and film studies, particularly since Laura Mulvey first
fully proposed them in her famous essay "Visual Pleasure and Narrative
Cinema."[27] But the advertising for *Ladies of Leisure* and probably for other
movies from the period sought to replicate, or perhaps even induce, different pleasures as well, particularly for those same female fans who may have
studied Barbara Stanwyck's clothes, or read the novel about the woman
asked to love the pal of the man she really loved.

Jackie Stacey, in her groundbreaking work on reception, *Star Gazing*,
has noted the manner in which women remark on the intensity of their
identification with female stars while watching a movie, to the point of
imagining themselves as those stars.[28] At least some of the advertising suggested by Columbia for *Ladies of Leisure* attempted to provoke a similar
relationship, beginning outside the theater and, implicitly, continuing inside. The studio recommended a contest to be run in local newspapers that
like the free novelizations of *Flight*, was designed specifically to get women
into the theater. Columbia proposed a "How would you get back?" contest taken from the narrative of *Ladies of Leisure*, in which Barbara Stanwyck finds herself about to be compromised at a high society party aboard
a yacht. "If you were invited out on a yacht party located in the middle
of a ten mile wide river, and after you got there you were told that you
would have to pet," the contest began, "how would you get back?"[29] The
contest was meant as a joke, with women encouraged to "think of a funny
answer" and submit it to the theater showing the film. Nevertheless, this
advertisement asked women to imagine themselves in the same predicament as Stanwyck, constructing at least the possibility for an identification
with the star, as well as for her situation within the narrative, quite similar
to the one explored by Stacey.

It is likely, then, that a variety of relationships between spectator and
film, and in this case between a woman viewer and the film, actually began
to develop before a fan had watched the movie and well away from the film
and the theater, often through different modes of advertising. Thus the en-

tire institution of the cinema, including, in this case, affiliations between theaters, newspapers, and stores, produced viewers just as much as did the instance of watching a specific film.

But the studio never neglected the special significance of the space of the theater. In the campaign book for *Ladies of Leisure*, Columbia developed something of a theory of spectatorial psychology, connecting the potential for satisfied customers directly to the exhibition space. The studio suggested a three-part approach to linking all aspects of the theater, inside and outside, to the movie itself. Reminding theater managers that "the first thing your patron approaches is your box office," Columbia suggested painting it in "gaudy modernistic colors" for Capra's film, accompanied by "hot and jazzy numbers" playing over a loudspeaker. Above the box office the marquee was said to be "the selling eye of your theatre," and, in an enthusiastically mixed metaphor, also "the flame that attracts the audience." Columbia recommended placing "cardboard stars made in colors and on each side . . . the names of one of the players" in the film. "Toy balloons" also would help, "in small clusters tied near the [marquee] lamps where they can receive the illumination through them." Once drawn inside, audiences should walk through a lobby full of "confetti, streamers, balloons," with "art layouts in 40x60 easels showing the party life of *Ladies of Leisure*." Theater managers should thus "render a general atmosphere of gaiety" in the lobby, one that would "throw your audience into a receptive mood which will help them like the picture and go out raving about it to their friends." Here the space of the theater would replicate the "hot and peppy" atmosphere of Capra's film, preparing viewers for it and also making them more receptive to it. According to studio strategy, the entire theater as much as the movie being screened there worked to produce a satisfied viewer.[30]

Recently, scholars in film studies have examined the ways in which this kind of display and the linkage between cinema, other forms of industry, and leisure—publishing and shopping, for example—contributed to a transformation of the public sphere in the expanding urban spaces of Europe and the United States, a transformation that fully marks the modern era. Miriam Hansen, for example, has analyzed the ways in which these shifts were facilitated by the silent cinema, with that cinema helping to create "the gendered itineraries of everyday life and leisure."[31] Early cinema facilitated these itineraries through textual and industrial strategies—that is, through a form of address perfected by the films and filmmakers themselves; through modes of exhibition and reception connected to shopping in downtown areas and other forms of visual spectacle and also linked to dating, taking time off from work, or just walking through town.

In his work on melodrama and modernity, Ben Singer cites the proliferation of early-twentieth-century scholars and critics, most notably George Simmel, who equated the seemingly new public sphere of urban modernity with an "intensification of nervous stimulation," or "social and audio-visual (over) stimulation," or even hyperstimulation.[32] Kathy Peiss—less concerned with the advent of modernity while still concentrating on technologized forms of urban pleasure, especially for working-class women— has analyzed the development, from the end of the nineteenth century, of leisure amusement activities and spaces for people with at least some income to spend on such things. For Peiss, Coney Island stood out as just such a space, one marked by a sort of melodramatic realism with the park's re-enactments of slum fires in New York ghettos, as well as by escape through its tunnels of love and other rides.[33]

Scholars have paid less attention to the connection after the development of sound in motion pictures and other leisure and consumer activities available to the public sphere. But with the cases of *Flight* and *Ladies of Leisure*, we can see that these early sound films may have had significant impact on those everyday "itineraries" of modern life, doing so both somewhat quietly and also through the kind of hyperstimulation that so vexed earlier critics. When theater managers linked literature to cinema by giving out free copies of *Flight* to women in matinee audiences, they were certainly addressing one of the central issues of what we might call a gendered modernity—that is, the unchaperoned woman, the female flaneur, out in public either alone or in groups engaging in consumption practices and leisure activities like shopping and going to the movies.[34] And the marqee suggestions for *Ladies of Leisure* point to the hyperstimulation of the side-walk, to the impossibility of avoiding the technologies of the film industry even if one had no intention of going to the movies.

In these cases we can see a full corporate acknowledgment of this public sphere, of the wider culture at least partially engendered by cinema. These are, after all, the publicity suggestions of Columbia Pictures, suggestions that take advantage of women walking through cities and the ubiquity of advertising opportunities. Thus the full corporate manipulation of an early-twentieth-century hyper stimulus might further mark the modernity of these linked spaces, industries, and technologies. But we should also accept that, unlike many arguments stressing the connection between cinema and modernity, the phenomenon was not simply an urban one, and the modern era was as much signaled by the continuing importance of the small town as by the city.[35] Kathryn Fuller's varied projects on regional cinema from 1895 to the 1930s, for example, have shown the centrality of the small town as much as the metropolis to a developing twentieth-century modernity of wide leisure opportunities, consumption, and technology.[36] Moreover, the corporate projects in the rendering of modern space are, finally, only representations. At least through the period discussed here, theater managers could, to some extent, take or leave the ideas that the studio sent them in their campaign books. Thus it becomes important to move from the ideas of the studio for reaching the public and shaping public space to an examination of actual publicity—its address to film audiences and its relationships to a variety of institutions and practices in both cities and towns.

Implementing Studio Strategies

During the 1930s, theater managers understood the relationships between viewing pleasure and the complete space of the theater, even as they refined studio approaches to their own, local needs. Managers followed the advice of the campaign books while also adapting it to neighborhood markets, current events, and a movie's connections to other consumer activities. In the actual ballyhoo for Capra's films we can see, if not the tensions between local theaters and the national campaigns suggested by the studio, then certainly the manner in which different aspects of the film industry developed both different and overlapping strategies to attract audiences.

In one example, toward the end of 1931 theater manager Jay H. Guthrie of Urichsville, Ohio, decided to do what he could to help the poor during hard times. For matinee showings of Capra's then most recent film, *Dirigible*, Guthrie asked patrons for canned goods rather than money. Once the cans had been collected, but before they were distributed, Guthrie made a display of the contributions in the lobby of his State Theater, showing to the town's filmgoers the result of their own good deeds. While the canned goods clearly qualified as charitable giving, they also worked as good ballyhoo for Guthrie's movie house. Patrons now could view going to Guthrie's theater as something of a community service—an image reinforced by the display of all the food—and this would certainly help attendance at other screenings that required a paid admission. But Guthrie also made use of slightly more conventional publicity, that is, publicity tied directly to the subject of Capra's movie. Guthrie mounted a cardboard cutout of a dirigible on a truck and drove it through Urichsville's main streets. He also attached another cutout under the State Theater's marquee, with one-sheet posters for the film placed above. The exhibitor's trade journal, *Motion Picture Herald*, which always reported on successful and aesthetically pleasing examples of ballyhoo, commented that these displays "attracted a lot of attention, especially so in view of the new navy dirigible 'Akron' making flights over this territory" during the period of the screenings.[37]

Guthrie's exploitation campaigns for *Dirigible* point out some of the complexities of movie advertising during the early sound period, at least in those small-town, late-first-run or subsequent-run theaters detailed by the *Herald*. The *Dirigible* cutouts and one-sheets almost certainly came from the main office of Columbia Pictures, which typically supplied exhibitors with all manner of posters and other similar materials, and made suggestions, as described above, in their campaign books about how to use them. Guthrie's marquee use of these materials seems conventional enough, a tactic that could be found at any number of theaters. But his truck-related ballyhoo seems more of Guthrie's own invention, something he had tried before that had worked well to drum up business. Similarly, his canned goods drive was probably also his own idea as a response to conditions in his community. Thus we have an advertising practice both national and local in its coordination, with the same materials and general exploitation outlines made available to all exhibitors but also subject to much different uses once a movie played in places like Urichsville. In Guthrie's case, as well, we can isolate a kind of tie-in practice that exceeded the typical, at least for that time, connection of a film to various products available in stores. For Urichsville audiences, the viewing of *Dirigible* came to be aligned with the social conscience of the community through the canned goods drive and also through the actual display of military technology and preparedness, because the exhibition of the film happened to coincide with the maneuvers of the *Akron* over that part of the country.

By studying the display of canned goods at the State Theater and the construction of the marquee there, we can start to understand what might be called the "architecture" of reception. Indeed, if we include the event of driving the truck through the city streets in order to ballyhoo *Dirigible*, we might more properly refer to an entire "spectacle" of reception. That is, we would be studying the manner in which advertising, quite separate from a film itself and just as the studio hoped when it suggested marquees and contests for *Ladies of Leisure* and ballyhoo for other movies, helped to create ways for audiences and potential audiences to make sense of a film. *Dirigible*, for instance, may have meant something at least somewhat different to those audiences who did not pass by those canned goods in the lobby or who had not seen the navy dirigible before seeing Capra's film.

Almost a year before the canned goods drive in Urichsville, Columbia Pictures, showing that it did not necessarily seek to control publicity from a national office, established an incentive for creative, local advertising for *Dirigible*. In January 1931, a few weeks before the film's premiere, the production studio announced "cash prizes for ad ideas," and set aside a purse of $1,875 "for exhibitors and theater managers in the United States and Canada to shoot at in a nation-wide contest for the best exploitation and advertising ideas submitted" for Capra's film. Columbia divided the contest into five divisions, one each for newspaper advertising, newspaper publicity campaigns, lobby decorations, window displays, and merchandise tie-ins. Thus the studio created competition among the exhibitors showing its films—a competition designed first to make exhibitors eager to acquire Columbia's product, and then, even while showing the same film, to develop very different approaches for attracting the public.[38]

Perhaps at least in part as a result, exhibitors developed some interesting advertising campaigns for Capra's film. In Maynard, Massachusetts, Burt Coghlan mounted a model dirigible on an Austin automobile and had it driven through town by two men dressed in aviator outfits. Marshall Quint, from the Colonia Theater in Belfast, Maine, also used an automobile, but had his driver dress as a clown, and tied-in the entire stunt with a sale at a used-car dealership. Eric Paulson, in Juneau, Alaska, chose a tie-in with city government rather than local commerce by presenting Juneau's mayor with a model of the *Akron* and then giving free theater passes to members of the Coast Guard stationed nearby. The manager of the Iroquois Theater in Petrolia, Canada, concentrated on newspaper advertising and convinced the editor of the local paper to carry a "streamer head" advertising the film across the top of the front page. Jake Rosenthal in Waterloo, Iowa, placarded ads for the film "on everything that was circulating about town," and made tie-ins with department stores, drug stores, and novelty shops. Indeed, for the *Motion Picture Herald* this Iowa campaign signaled the absolute significance of theater publicity during the Depression, and the understanding that a film, at least during hard times, simply could not sell itself. According to the *Herald*, the success of *Dirigible* in Waterloo "justified Rosenthal's theory that there's still loose money even in these times, if one will make a worthwhile attempt to divert some of it to the theater box-office."[39]

To use a term taken from narrative studies, we can see here, in these advertising practices, the kind of repetition-with-a-difference that typically has been remarked on only in relation to the storytelling strategies of Hollywood films from the classical period.[40] Naturally enough, representations of dirigibles, particularly the *Akron*, were used in most of the ballyhoo efforts for Capra's film, but to a slightly different effect. Automobiles, too, turned up in several of the *Dirigible* campaigns, but with aviators as drivers in Maynard and a clown in Belfast. The different costumes may have been a result of a theater manager's personal taste, or may have had something to do with perceptions of community preferences. Nevertheless, the different strategies for *Dirigible*, as well as Columbia's contest for the best advertising ideas, serve to highlight what movie studios and theater managers thoroughly understood during this period: successful advertising campaigns for films required local angles.

Advertisers in other media and for other products eventually realized the same thing and started developing their publicity for target markets. Regarding radio Kathy Newman has pointed out how advertisers had come to understand at least by the 1950s that campaigns often had to be developed with extremely small audience units in mind, and that neighborhoods had distinctive consumption habits, as did areas organized around similar occupations or family structures. Newman points out, as well, that in the 1940s Paul Lazarsfeld determined that even in voting for national leaders Americans were most likely to be swayed by "the political climate of their small environment" rather than by broad-based, organized advertising campaigns.[41] The managers of movie theaters, however, who oversaw the neighborhood outlets par excellence for national products, understood the significance of the local at least as early as the 1930s. Fox Theater manager Frank Ricketson, in *The Management of Motion Picture Theaters*, a practical guide to the profession, stressed again and again the need to devise very particular publicity strategies connected to specific areas. With newspaper advertising, he reminded fellow managers that "an advertisement planned for the Kansas City Star would be out of place in the *New York Mirror*, and copy suitable to the *Los Angeles Herald-Express* would not conform to the type of readers of the *Cincinnati Inquirer*."[42]

Just one month after beginning the *Dirigible* contest that stressed local difference, however, Columbia announced a national campaign for Capra's film. The small-town ballyhoo for the film emphasized, understandably, theater marquees and lobbies, and also the potential for reaching people after they had left the house: the placards on goods around town, the clowns driving cars, the ceremonies honoring local politicians. Columbia's publicity, however, targeted a much smaller space—the home—and chose a specific medium—the radio. On 31 January 1931, *Motion Picture Herald* noted that "an exploitation plan calculated to go direct to the public via the radio will be launched by Columbia Feb. 8, to continue eight weeks, in connection with the national release of *Dirigible*, the aeronautics yarn produced in co-operation with the U.S. Navy."[43] This, then, gives us some sense of the strategy behind major studio publicity. For a film like *Dirigible*, a first run—with staggered openings throughout the country—might be planned to last about two months, during which time the studio generated national, mass-media publicity. At the same time, for both first run and subsequent runs, the studio helped to organize publicity at the local level and also encouraged the development of campaigns specific to each locale.

The proposed national advertising campaign for Capra's film also points to the manner in which Hollywood corporations sought to align their product with other institutions, particularly those related to government and education. In advertising for *Dirigible*, Columbia stressed the film's connection to the navy, a connection that the *Herald* dutifully repeated and one that was quite similar to the link between *Flight* and the marines that the studio emphasized. As I show in chapter 4, within a decade, of course, as Capra's films increasingly became allegories of American democracy, this connection to the governmental and the federal would become more prominent, not only in the films' advertising but also in audiences' responses to them. In 1931, however, the assertion of "co-operation" between the studio and the military seems less motivated by a specific understanding of a "Capra film" and more generically driven. Links to the armed forces served to guarantee the authenticity and public-mindedness of the military film, which then as now was something of a staple of Hollywood production.[44]

This connection to the military seems natural enough for a film about navy dirigibles. Perhaps more interesting is the manner in which Columbia tried to advertise the educational value of the film and to engage in a sort of public uplift through the advertising for the movie. The radio campaign would consist of "programs of not less than 15 minutes over stations throughout the U.S. and Canada," with this length itself conforming to much standard programming from the period, thereby making the *Dirigible* radio promotions seem much more like entertainment than advertising. The ostensible aim of the programs, however, was uplift rather than entertainment, as they were designed to elicit the "interest of the general public in writing essays of 500 words on some phase of the development of lighter-than-air craft." Columbia added that "the reading of the essays will form part of the radio programs," with cash prizes, including a $300 first prize, to be awarded "in each of the three classes arranged respectively for university students, high school pupils, and the general public."[45]

In chapter 3 I examine the manner in which the film education movement, separate from the studios, adopted motion pictures as a suitable area of study for adolescents and teenagers. But at least by the early 1930s the studios clearly were seeking the cultural capital associated with promoting the educational values in their films and also in the publicity that surrounded those films. From our position decades later it is impossible to judge the sincerity of Columbia's motives here, and it is also unclear just how many people actually wrote essays. Nevertheless, in a national strategy similar to the canned goods campaign in Urichsville, Columbia here used advertising to attempt to create at least something of an active, thoughtful consumer, one who would be encouraged to consider and then write about the history of aviation technology. This advertising program, designed to create and then disseminate public knowledge, also worked to turn the stars of the film and Capra himself into experts, with the roles played by the actors apparently corresponding to real-life capabilities and the director seemingly having a natural proclivity for a film about aviation.[46] Included among the judges of the essay contest were military men and professors, stars Jack Holt and Ralph Graves, along with Capra, the two men who played the aviators in the film, and also the man who oversaw the production.[47]

This national campaign for *Dirigible* also brings to mind Columbia's efforts to construct Capra as an all-seeing general in charge of men in the field during the filming of *Flight*. With the essay contest Capra's celebrity, and that of Holt and Graves, came to be marked by authority and expertise, and by the ability to judge the merits of writing about the development of technology. This may be an aspect of a gendered form of stardom, one of the differences between male and female celebrities. Fans, especially female fans, were asked to "identify" with Barbara Stanwyck in *Ladies of Leisure* in terms of her narrative predicament, as in the "How would you get back?" contest, as well as her clothing with the links to newspaper fashion advertisements. The fans of *Dirigible*, apparently both men and women and boys and girls, had the chance to assert a relationship with Capra based on shared knowledge, on entering into a discussion with him about air transportation. In chapter 4 I show the serious political interactions between Capra and his fans, especially after the release of *Meet John Doe* in 1941. Ten

years before *John Doe* however, Capra's military films and the studio representations of Capra demonstrate the possibility for relationships between
fans and stars—or at least male stars such as Capra, Graves, or Holt—based
not so much on glamour but on a sense of shared intellectual substance.

"These New Kind of Blondes" and the "Financially Lower Strata"

On the local level, though, for most of Capra's films from this period ballyhoo emphasized not so much the connections between a movie and public
uplift through education but rather the links between films and other commercial ventures. For example, the 1931 campaign for Capra's Jean Harlow vehicle, *Platinum Blonde*, in Brockton, Massachusetts, capitalized on
seemingly all of the city's major businesses, demonstrating the very fluid
relationships between them and the movie theater. During this period, and
similar to the novelizations of *Flight* and other films, studios often produced
written "serializations" of their films and distributed them to theater managers. At the end of 1931, Brockton theater manager Bill Adams placed in
a local newspaper over six days successive chapters of Columbia's adaptation of *Platinum Blonde*. Making sure that no one might assume that the
serialization was purely and simply a literary undertaking, at the end of the
story Columbia and Adams let readers know that they could see the whole
story all over again, at the theater. An advertisement following the conclusion stated that "everybody's talking about *Platinum Blonde*," and then
provided the theater name, playdates, and cast.[48]

This small-town connection between the theater and the newspaper was
absolutely central to movie advertising from the period, making the serialization of *Platinum Blonde* fairly standard stuff. But theater manager Adams
also made use of the paper to turn ballyhoo into a news story. With the
cooperation of the newspaper, he hired two "platinum" blondes, and as
the *Motion Picture Herald* admiringly described it, "turned [them] loose in
the business district at a stated time on a certain day." Members of the
public were invited to become "captors," and, once spotting the blondes,
bring them to the newspaper office for a five-dollar reward. The contest resulted in several stories in the newspaper as well as a photo of the blondes
and the man and woman who captured them.[49] In other words, the theater
and the newspaper constructed a public event that worked as advertising
for the former, and as a human interest feature for the latter.

Just as with several of the *Dirigible* campaigns ranging from canned goods to aviation essays, this mode of advertising sought to create something of an active audience for Capra's movie. In this case, viewers were assumed to be mobile rather than sitting in theaters, and were understood to be walking through town looking for someone who may or may not have been nearby. They were encouraged to scan outdoor space for the right blonde among all the women in the business district and then bring her in for money. These are, perhaps, different viewers from those imagined by much of contemporary film theory, which has concentrated on the act of watching movies and has tended to develop much more passive models of spectatorship. We might, then, as with the case of the contests and fashion tie-ins for *Flight*, have to investigate the possibility of film viewing taking shape from an overall film culture and not just from the experience of sitting in a theater and gazing at a screen. Of course, in the instance examined here, Adams's interests were practical rather than theoretical. The theater manager hoped that this extended "audience," the one looking for blondes outside of the theater, would then pay to watch Jean Harlow as the emblematic blonde in the more confined space of the movie theater. The practices and pleasures, then, of that first, business district, audience seem at least somewhat different from those of the audiences that eventually watched the movie. We know that the classical film text worked to mobilize a certain kind of voyeurism in its viewers. But if the case of *Platinum Blonde* in Brockton was a typical one, then the cinema as an institution, including advertising, also encouraged very different versions of watching and seeing, and different forms of interaction with the objects being seen.

In fact, in the Brockton campaign for Capra's film, blonde women became the objects of a sort of all-seeing advertising/consumer gaze, with the public invited to interact with them in various ways. On the Friday the film opened, Adams sponsored "a fashion show in a window of one of the foremost gown shops in town," but clothes seemed to receive second billing to the models themselves who were described as "two blondes." Apparently, interest in either the models or their clothes "ran so high that reserve police had to be sent from the station." Adams employed these same two blondes as decorations for his lobby, using them to distribute announcements about the upcoming film three days before *Platinum Blonde* opened. One of the blondes demonstrated Victor radios at the local dealer's store, while in a tie-in with a car dealer a chauffeur was hired "to drive blondes about town." [50]

Thus the Brockton ballyhoo for Capra's film connected all manner of spaces and businesses: from the theater lobby to the gown shop to the radio store to the car dealership to the newspaper. In virtually every case, Harlow surrogates certified the connection between the film and other products, with the *Motion Picture Herald* admiringly reminding readers to "note that the two platinum blondes were plugged in this campaign and there can be no doubt that this stunt offers many possibilities in the way of tie-ups with both newspapers and merchants." The title of the film, then, and Harlow's hair, created something of a ballyhoo bonanza. The entire reception spectacle for Capra's film turned the platinum blonde into a very rare species, one that the public might seek out, look at, and buy from, and then pay to see all over again at the theater. The *Herald* even cautioned that some exhibitors trying to duplicate Adams's success "may not be able to locate these new kind of blondes," but that, as the fad seemed to be spreading, theater folk should "cheer up if you already haven't a couple of these around right this minute."[51]

For another Capra film, though, no shortage existed of women qualified for a variety of promotions. *Lady for a Day*, from 1933, told the story of Apple Annie, a Depression-era apple seller transformed, through the largesse of a gangster, into the temporary lady of the title. The promotional strategy derived logically enough from the film's narrative, and in this case for the film's first run it came to be coordinated by the studio itself. Quite simply, the Columbia exploitation department alerted theater managers to the possibility of using impoverished women to ballyhoo Capra's film. In so doing, the film company helped to point out that relations between the theater and the newspaper may not have been as smooth in big cities as they were in the small towns that showed Capra's films. Further, the move also demonstrated the manner in which the individual exhibitors of small-town theaters adapted national publicity strategies.

Lady for a Day opened at Radio City Music Hall, and its placement in such an important exhibition site clearly signaled its significance to Columbia. As a result the studio seemed determined to attract as much attention as possible in the very competitive market of New York City. The *Motion Picture Herald* reported that "blasé Broadway ballyhooers perked up a bit early this week," and that even the city's tough newspapermen fell for the studio's publicity. The *Herald* continued by stating that "city editors all over New York, hardboiled . . . newspapermen that they are, for the first time in some years opened up their editorial pages and gave real space to an avowed exploitation departure conceived by Columbia Pictures Corporation." Reporters from all of the city's papers "actually were assigned to cover a press agent's 'gag,'" and this constituted an event "of such importance that many an exhibitor will be inspired to spend many sleepless nights thinking up campaigns to equal this one." [52]

Here, then, we get a sense of the differences between small towns and big cities during this period. In all of those campaigns for *Dirigible* and *Platinum Blonde*, newspapers and theaters worked fluidly together, each benefiting from the efforts of the other. In New York, however, there was at least the perception—among the very savvy editors of the *Motion Picture Herald*, for instance—that journalism and cinema were, at times, antagonistic institutions. Ballyhoo may have constituted news in Brockton but this was not necessarily true in New York, thus making the case of *Lady for a Day* so extraordinary.

The campaign that attracted so much attention exploited the very real issues of class, unemployment, and homelessness that Capra combined with the comedy and melodramatic fantasy of his film. Columbia instructed Radio City's manager to locate what the *Herald* euphemistically referred to as "a member of New York's financially lower strata to enact the part of the picture's heroine in real life . . . with photographs." Radio City selected Nellie McCarthy, a seventy-three-year-old apple seller in the city's theater district. The theater "snatched [Nellie] from her apple stand, [gave her] one glorious whirl for 24 hours, and then returned [her] to the stand." The "whirl" included a three-room suite in the Waldorf-Astoria. Columbia spent $500 on Nellie, but as the *Herald* reported, "the net free space [in newspapers] was worth ten times as much." [53]

This ballyhoo seems the precise opposite of the Urichsville canned goods drive during the run of *Dirigible*. There, the theater became the space of community consciousness, even though the film itself—a military fantasy—had virtually nothing to do with the country's economic problems. In that case, typically escapist entertainment nevertheless called attention to the Depression because viewers had to make a charitable gift in order to see the movie. Nor was this use of a "real" person to promote *Lady for a Day* the same as the ballyhoo for *Platinum Blonde*. In that instance, scarcity—the chance to see a "rare" blonde—became the point of publicity. With *Lady for a Day*, however, the publicity for this film about the effects of the Depression stressed a perverse sort of abundance in making connections between the movie and the city; clearly, impoverished women were everywhere. Columbia and Radio City reproduced the mise en scène of the film for an evening at the Waldorf, and the fluidity in this case was not so much between the theater and the department store or the auto dealership, but rather between the narrative of the movie and that of the publicity. Both could acknowledge the Depression, particularly its effects on elderly women, and both also could provide a "solution" that emphasized temporary excess before a return to impoverished routine.

Other exhibitors adapted Columbia's strategy to good effect. In Kansas City, not just any penniless woman would do. Instead, a local exhibitor advertised among the city's dispossessed for a "double" for the film's star, May Robson. The exhibitor found her "through local charity workers," used her "as atmosphere in the foyer" of his theater, and also wrote to Robson herself to tell her about the stunt. Robson, "that grand trouper," responded by sending $100 "for the relief of the woman."[54] Rather than sending his Apple Annie to the Waldorf, however, this exhibitor brought her to his theater as a celebrity double for someone who in Capra's film herself impersonated a woman just like this one. The foyer thus became the space of a "real" Annie, just as the film at the theater presented a "false" one, Robson, with the woman from Kansas city serving as something of an anthropological display, attesting to the verisimilitude of the movie.[55]

Poverty on display also did well for other exhibitors, with the boundaries between "real" Annies and pretend ones becoming more blurred. When *Lady for a Day* left Radio City and moved to other New York theaters, Nellie McCarthy, fresh from her evening at the Waldorf, reprised her Radio City role at the Audobon Theater. Manager Edgar Wallack collected stills from her day as a lady and placed her in front of them in his lobby. Nellie wore evening clothes for the event, but nevertheless still sold her apples to those coming to see the film. In this case, rather than finding a double for the star of the film, ballyhoo generated, in Nellie's apotheosis, its own celebrity and used her appearance to create interest in Capra's movie. While Nellie wasn't Robson's physical "double," as in the Kansas City case, Nellie-as-lobby-display certainly repeated Robson's role in the film, and we can only wonder about the effect of seeing Nellie's photos alongside the *Lady for a Day* lobby cards and publicity stills that also must have decorated the Audobon's lobby.[56]

In each of these cases, for *Flight*, *Dirigible*, *Platinum Blonde*, or *Lady for a Day*, exhibitors used a studio strategy, adapted it, or developed their own in order to create a vast space for the reception of films. This space included local business as well as other media, such as newspapers and radio. Indeed, this space could be so extensive that it might take in the business districts where the public hunted for the right blonde, or those parts of town where poor women sold apples on the street. Exhibitors and studios understood not only that "the show started on the sidewalk" but also that reception did, and that the public's understanding of a film might well precede the viewing of it.[57] Typically, the film itself and the story it told seemed not as significant, at least in initially attracting an audience, as did the celebrity of the director or star, the newspaper contests based on the film, or the product tie-ins. Studio executives and local theater managers believed that the description of Capra as an armchair general, or the appearance of the lighter-than-air *Akron* in the skies over Ohio, were more central to getting audiences to see *Flight* and *Dirigible* than anything about the films themselves.

In spite of the emphasis on ballyhoo and on the importance of the overall architecture and spectacle of film reception, the early 1930s was also a period marked by intense concern over film content; over the manner in which the films themselves, apart from any other elements of spectacle, might be viewed and might influence those watching them. This concern, while present from the beginning of the cinema as an entertainment industry, quickened with the development of sound film, and also with the development of social sciences apparently more capable of understanding the effects of the media.

Thus, interested groups sought regulatory control over that which they had some power. Exhibitors, of course, had absolutely no control over film content, and so sought to regulate the public spaces around movies in order to develop the connections between those public spaces and their theaters. Other groups, however, both within the Hollywood film industry and outside it, had little relation to ballyhoo, but might successfully negotiate changes in film content. In each case, reception came to be understood as both volatile and malleable. For exhibitors during the early sound period, reception contexts frequently were created in cooperation with national corporations, although not necessarily in lockstep with them.

Studio officials understood the benefits of advertising that was specially designed for local constituencies. In examples from Capra's films of the early 1930s we can see some of the varied relationships between the corporate headquarters and regional exhibition sites, and also realize that those in the film industry during this period knew that they made movies for a vast domestic audience that was at the same time divided by gender, location, and other factors. This back and forth of national production and much more narrow modes of consumption was one of the markers of early-twentieth-century corporate and leisure cultures. Indeed, rather than being notable for the imposition of a national culture on a coast-to-coast viewing public, the cinema during this period instead witnessed cohesiveness and tensions on at least two different axes, one purely local and the other both national and regional. The first was made up of the different industries, populations, cultural activities, and consumption possibilities in any single location. The second had the national headquarters of the film company and such local businesses as theaters developing both general and specific appeals to the tens of millions of people who went to the movies and who could themselves be addressed as members of an American audience and as viewers whose interests, preferences, and reception practices were in large part shaped by the neighborhoods or towns or cities in which they lived.

Along with issues of advertising and publicity, however, during this period there was another, much more vexing, relationship between the national and the local, the one that formed around censorship. This relationship did indeed involve film content, and consisted of conflicts between the film studio and the censoring boards of states and localities, particularly in the early 1930s before the full implementation of the industry's self-censoring Production Code. And if varied and complex links between the national and the local stood out among the signs of modernity from the period, so too did international systems of production, distribution, and consumption. Censorship itself functioned across national boundaries, often placing foreign governments against both the U.S. government and the Hollywood film studios. In the next chapter I turn to such an instance, the case of Capra's *The Bitter Tea of General Yen* (1933), in which the film text came to be viewed as all important and as the absolute ground zero of all meaning.

With the publicity campaign for *Flight*, Columbia depicted Capra, at least metaphorically, as a general in the U.S. military's intervention in Nicaragua. To reach an audience in the United States the studio counted on Capra's special status as a directorial celebrity and on the representation of his military command and vision as a means of selling the romance of fighting in a third-world civil war. But the director's films, of course, did not just play in the United States. With *Bitter Tea*, Capra's fantasy of yet another civil war, the director hardly counted when it came to determining the film's reception in China, where the film takes place. Rather than standing out as different and better, because of Capra's participation or Barbara Stanwyck's, *Bitter Tea*, at least to Chinese government officials, became just another Hollywood film, indistinguishable from many others and just as politically insensitive, and therefore undeserving of an international release.

Chapter Two

Regulating National Markets: Chinese
Censorship and *The Bitter Tea of General Yen*

After a series of complaints from the Chinese vice consul in Los Angeles, Frederick Herron wrote an irritated memo to Willys Peck, American consul general in Nanking. The Chinese vice consul hoped to make changes in the international version of Frank Capra's 1933 film *The Bitter Tea of General Yen*. As a result, Herron, foreign manager of the Motion Picture Producers and Distributors Association of America (MPPDA), contacted Peck on 31 May 1933. He claimed that if Capra's studio, Columbia Pictures, acquiesced in this case, "this Vice Consul just as sure as the sun will rise tomorrow, will 'go Hollywood' sooner or later" and cause no end of trouble. Insisting that the desire to meddle in movie production—to "go Hollywood"—leveled all national differences, Herron went on to say, "I don't believe the Chinese are any different from any others in the world," and that if Columbia and the MPPDA recognized the authority of the vice consul, they would simply be "getting ready for a squabble in which we will come off second best."[1]

Herron, a longtime diplomat and friend of MPPDA president Will Hays, had been the MPPDA foreign manager for ten years, ever since the movie industry trade association had opened a Foreign Department to deal with other countries' complaints about Hollywood movies and economic practices.[2] During that time, he had gotten used to smoothing over a variety of problems relating to Hollywood's international markets. But the *Bitter Tea* incident tested his mettle and his patience, because it was just the latest case in a series of very difficult censorship negotiations with the Chinese government.

By examining Herron's memo and the more than thirty other State Department documents about *Bitter Tea*, all of which are stored in the National Archive in Washington, D.C., we can come to understand what might be called an official reception of Capra's film by Hollywood executives like Herron but mostly by bureaucrats in the Chinese and U.S. governments. That is, we can combine a cultural diplomatic history of a specific case of international business relations with a study of some very particular audiences. Looking at this form of reception helps us to rethink the narrative of American film censorship during the classical period. That narrative would have it that the Hollywood film industry weathered a period of government censorship, typically from cities and states, that began with the development of the cinema as a commercial enterprise at the end of the nineteenth century. In the happy end to the narrative, at least from the standpoint of the film companies, this form of censorship was made more or less obsolete in the 1930s by the industry's adoption of the self-censoring Production Code. In fact, however, at least through the 1930s, the industry confronted intense government censorship, some of it domestic but most of it from the foreign markets on which Hollywood depended for a substantial amount of revenue.[3]

Through the work of Richard Maltby and others we know that Hollywood executives were far less concerned with the domestic regulation of representational and narrative practices—censorship—than with the regulation of trade practices relating to distribution and exhibition.[4] As a result, they were pleased to let public discourse through the 1930s emphasize film content rather than such industry practices as block booking and the major studios' ownership of most first-run theaters. Foreign censorship, however, posed very serious problems. Governments—and this was precisely the case with *Bitter Tea*—might threaten to prevent Hollywood films from even showing in their countries, thereby eliminating all possibility for revenue. In spite of this, historians have paid relatively little attention to Hollywood's foreign markets. Ruth Vasey, Kristin Thompson, Ian Jarvie, and Thomas J. Saunders have written exemplary studies, but for the most part, attention has been devoted to considerations of domestic practices and audiences.[5]

Based on a popular novel by Grace Zaring Stone, *The Bitter Tea of General Yen* "reportedly cost about $1 million," according to Capra biographer Joseph McBride, with Columbia counting on it being the kind of high-quality, top-grossing film around which the studio could market its other, lesser films.[6] As a sign of this high profile *Bitter Tea* was the first film to play at the newly finished Radio City Music Hall, and in part because of the novelty of the venue the film had an impressive opening at the box office. Nevertheless, overall the film proved to be a financial disappointment for Capra and Columbia, although the reasons for this are difficult to pinpoint.[7]

The film begins with the "burning of Chapei" in 1931, an event that the film situates as part of the Chinese "civil war" rather than as an act of Japanese aggression.[8] An American missionary, played by Barbara Stanwyck, falls in love with a Chinese warlord, played by white, Swedish actor Nils Asther, who kidnaps Stanwyck and eventually commits suicide. American audiences possibly had begun to tire of this kind of film, as the studios had produced quite a number of movies taking place in China. There is evidence, as well, that the film may have alienated audiences outside of major urban areas. One theater manager, writing in to the *Motion Picture Herald*, lamented that this was "not a small town picture," while another complained that *Bitter Tea* was "too deep for a small town." Barbara Stanwyck believed that the film's failure was due to its interracial romance, and she stated that "the women's clubs came out very strongly against it, because the white woman was in love with the yellow man and kissed his hand." It is also possible, of course, that a film coming out in the midst of the Depression, along with its winter premier date of 11 January, might have resulted in difficulty drawing an audience. Yet another theater manager, merging concerns about the Depression with those about audiences outside of big cities, complained that, despite the high quality of *Bitter Tea*, "the low wages and restricted income that is rife in the small towns just won't let even good pictures gross what they would in good times."[9]

Such primary sources as these theater manager reports provide wonderful anecdotal evidence about the interaction between domestic audiences and the films they enjoyed or disliked, attended in droves or avoided. With recent scholarship, however, a continuing problem in understanding the success or failure of any movie has been the tendency of textual critics to remove films from the complex systems, both domestic and international, that could play a major role in determining audience enthusiasm or disinterest. In perhaps the most thorough contemporary reading of *Bitter Tea*, for example, David Palumbo-Liu suggests that the failure of the film "may be attributed in part to the fact that it is unable to establish a stable identificatory position," and that the film's apparent inability to negotiate complicated racial, gendered, and class-based subject positions also made it unable to "satisfy the moviegoing public in the 1930's."[10] In very basic terms, this kind of text-based analysis implies that people who saw the film did not like it and, apparently through word of mouth, convinced others to stay away. I would suggest, however, that in addition to some of the reasons mentioned above, some of the difficulties of the film came from its foreign audiences. More properly, problems arose not so much from those foreign audiences who saw *Bitter Tea* but rather from those industry officials and government censors who attempted quite actively to prevent people outside of the United States from seeing it at all. In script form and then as a finished film *Bitter Tea* easily passed muster with the industry's self-censoring Production Code, but it had serious censorship problems in the British Commonwealth because of its interracial romance. Further, in the case that interests me here, the film apparently never played in China, and it faced Chinese lobbying efforts against it in several other countries and was removed from at least one other foreign market, Japan.[11]

Frank Capra, Hollywood Cinema, and Chinese Markets

Within the context of the director's career, *Bitter Tea* comes from the end of a period that might be called "Capra before Capra." That is, Capra already had become well known, as I show in the next chapter, but with the exception perhaps of *American Madness* (1932) he had not yet begun making the films that we think of as quintessential Capra: *It Happened One Night*, for instance, would come out more than a year after *Bitter Tea*. Interestingly, however, for a director known for his "American" themes, Capra made more movies about Far Eastern locales than did most other Hollywood directors from the period: not only *Bitter Tea* but also *Lost Horizon* (1937) and the World War II documentaries *The Battle of China* (1944) and *Know Your Enemy: Japan* (1945). As a product of a major American corporation *The Bitter Tea of General Yen* and, indeed, the struggle between Chinese censors on the one hand and Columbia Pictures and the State Department on the other, help to explain relationships between the government and business and between that business and its global audience. In addition, the fight over the film demonstrates the broad efforts on the part of the Chinese government to control its own domestic commercial sphere and to discipline those Western countries seeking to exploit a new, huge market.

By the time of *Bitter Tea*, American businessmen had come to consider China a significant and expanding market for U.S.-made goods.[12] There is, as well, anecdotal evidence that the possibility of converting the Chinese into consumers of U.S. products had become something of an interest to the American public in general. At least two major commercial publishing houses—Macmillan and Harper and Brothers—issued books about the matter: C. F. Remer's *Foreign Investments in China* in 1933, and advertising-man Carl Crow's *400 Million Customers* in 1937, the very title of which goes directly to the point.[13] Crow's book, with its conversational style and amusing illustrations, clearly was marketed for a mass audience, and early on the author states, "My work has naturally made my point of view that of one who looks on the Chinese as potential customers, to consider what articles they may purchase, how these articles should be packed, and what advertising methods will be most effective in producing sales." Crow also asserts the importance of movies in his line of work when he writes that his firm "induced all the Chinese moving-picture stars to use the toilet soap we advertised" and then acquired testimonials from them.[14] For Crow, Chinese stars were more effective salespersons in China than were Hollywood celebrities, but the significance of movies in general, as a product themselves and as a means of selling other goods, could not have been lost on American businessmen.

Indeed, the Hollywood movie studios found China a conducive market. Precise figures are difficult to come by, but if American films played no more frequently in China in the early 1930s than they had before, they were almost certainly generating more concern. In 1931, for example, at the fourth conference of the Institute of Pacific Relations, held in Hangchow and Shanghai, attendees "urged that a conference round table concern itself with the disruptive influence of Western moving pictures upon the morals and manners of Oriental peoples." This influence, however, could only be assumed rather than proved, and the round table apparently was called off because "it was pointed out that no studies had as yet been made of the exact nature or strength of that influence; and that possibly effects were attributed to it merely because it was the most visible and, indeed, spectacular of many forms of foreign influence upon the indigenous culture."[15]

While these studies seem not to have been conducted, the American government became convinced of the centrality of Hollywood motion pictures in China and of the necessity of making sure that China remained open to American movies. As a result, in August 1932, just a few months before the State Department became involved in the *Bitter Tea* case, Richard P. Butrick, a member of the American Consulate in Shanghai, supervised the production of a lengthy document titled "The Motion Picture Industry in China."[16] The document cautioned that, despite Chiang Kai-Shek's emergence as a national leader, "the generally unsettled condition of the country, with its numerous bandit-infested provinces, the vast number of illiterate Chinese and the very small purchasing power of the masses," all militated against any expansion of either Chinese or American film interests.[17] Nevertheless, all of the major Hollywood film companies had branch offices in China, with Columbia, which produced Capra's films, sharing one with Paramount.[18] The document insisted, furthermore, that sooner or later there would be a significant expansion in the number of theaters in China, which would "increase the demand for American pictures." Even if Chinese film production itself increased (according to the document, China had produced fifteen sound films in the last eighteen months), theaters still would need American movies, which in 1932 accounted for 75 percent of the footage shown in Chinese theaters.[19]

These theaters stood out as particularly important to American concerns. At this time, there were about 280 movie theaters in China, and undoubtedly some were owned or managed by U.S.-based companies.[20] Even more significant for U.S. business, of the 97 Chinese theaters capable of showing sound films, 70 had been wired with American equipment. Thus, as the number of sound theaters grew, so too would the outlets for American films as well as the revenues for American companies supplying sound equipment.[21]

The highest concentration of these theaters (28 sound and 21 silent) was in Shanghai, with other major cities, such as Canton (20 theaters) and Tientsin (15 theaters), also having a significant number of venues for seeing movies.[22] Residents of these cities, and in particular those in Shanghai, experienced flourishing film cultures. Along with Chinese films, they saw British, French, Italian, and Russian films, but never to the extent that they were exposed to American movies, which, in Shanghai and elsewhere in China, usually were shown in English accompanied by subtitles.[23] Frederic Wakeman, in his study of Shanghai between 1927 and 1937, has pointed out that "it is difficult to exaggerate the centrality of the cinema" to that city's mass culture; and that "movie actors and actresses were national celebrities and popular idols." As a means of following these performers, over one million readers regularly read the illustrated newspaper *Dianying huabao* ("Movies Illustrated").[24] Their tastes in movies seem to have been similar to those of American audiences, with Butrick's document extolling the recent successes of such films as Chaplin's *City Lights* and the Eddie Cantor vehicle *Whoopee!*, along with Ernst Lubitsch's *Love Parade* and Lewis Milestone's version of Erich Maria Remarque's international bestseller, *All Quiet on the Western Front*. The State Department document also recorded the star preferences of these viewers, indicating that they were fans of Maurice Chevalier, Laurel and Hardy, Ronald Colman, Jeannette Mac-

Donald, Greta Garbo, and Joan Crawford, among others, with Norma Shearer occupying a special place by having a "large following among the better class Chinese."[25]

Of course, not all of China, and not all Chinese officials, welcomed Hollywood movies or, more generally, Western goods and services. In 1927 Chinese Nationalists (the Guomindang) began a ten-year period of control marked by almost immediately disaffiliating themselves from the communists who had fought with them and by attempts to establish a party-republic led by Chiang Kai-shek. In trying to carry out the "program of national construction" begun by Sun Yat-sen, who had died in 1925, Chiang Kai-shek emphasized efforts to limit foreign business and culture and to impose Guomindang discipline in Shanghai on the Chinese there as well as on foreign nationals.[26] Shanghai was then the most significant metropolitan area in China as well as the site of perhaps the greatest Western influence (the very geography of the city emphasized this influence, as it was divided into the International Settlement, the French Concession, and the Chinese Municipality). As a result, for the new government the city came to signify both the problems and prospects of modernity, and also "the westernized world of commerce that now occupied China's shores."[27]

The new regime established a modern police force in Shanghai, which sought to crack down on crime and vice. In the latter category came the old standbys—gambling (greyhound racing, for instance) and prostitution. But entertainment also figured prominently, including cabarets and, occasionally, movies. More properly, authorities, most notably the Public Security Bureau, concerned themselves with movie theaters, which could become locations for gambling and prostitution. Attempts to control the cinema as an institution, however, also applied to film production and representation. Throughout the 1930s, members of the government-approved "New Life Movement" worked to purge Communists from the Chinese film industry (which was centered in Shanghai), while the Guomindang government itself, through censors working in Nanking, routinely rejected film scripts and shut down fourteen film studios in 1934 and 1935.[28]

For Chinese officials, though, and especially for the Chinese censors, the American cinema posed a very special problem, with the popularity of Hollywood movies standing out as the surest sign of cultural degeneration in China.[29] As a result, in 1931 the Chinese government passed a national film censorship law, mandating that all movies receive clearance from the National Board of Film Censors (which also was referred to as the Film Censorship Committee) before they could be exhibited in China. The law itself, according to Butrick's document, seems to have been rather cumbersome, with a complicated series of fines and permits. The Film Censorship Committee convened in the capital, Nanking, and all seven of its members were political appointees chosen by the Guomindang leadership of the Ministries of Education and the Interior. The censorship law gave committee members a good deal of interpretive leeway, requiring them to reject four kinds of films: those "derogatory to the dignity of the Chinese race"; those "injurious to good morals or the public order"; those "tending to foster superstition and heresy"; and those "contrary to the Three People's Principles," which Butrick's document defined rather obliquely as "a complicated code on the political, economic and social development of China." [30]

The committee examined all films including shorts and newsreels, but feature-length films naturally received special attention. It is difficult to determine just how many feature films Hollywood studios submitted to the censors, but by 1 July 1932 — a full year after the law took effect — the committee had rejected twenty-six American films. Some of these — *Lasca of the Rio Grande* and *Boudoir Diplomat*, for instance — are unknown today. Others, though, are some of the more famous films from the period: for example, *Dr. Jekyll and Mr. Hyde*, *Dracula*, *The Unholy Three*, and *In Old Arizona*. In addition, *An American Tragedy* also failed to pass the committee, marking just the first of director Josef von Sternberg's problems with the Nanking censors. Most of the banned films, both American and those from other countries, failed to receive exhibition permits because the censors deemed them to be "derogatory to the dignity of the Chinese race." This meant, typically, that they included Chinese characters who clearly conformed to Western racist stereotypes. Even more than banning films, however, the Nanking censors sought to cut them in order to remove offending scenes or lines of dialogue. Butrick, for instance, "believed that at least fifty per cent of the films submitted are subject to 'cuts.' " [31]

In setting up its disciplinary practices, the Chinese government did not pretend to be starting from scratch or to be inventing something absolutely different from systems in other countries. For its police force, for instance, China depended on Western and Japanese models of command hierarchies, patrol methods, training practices, and weaponry. Particularly in terms of policing Shanghai, Chinese officials believed that using such models would be the best way to compete with the Western and Japanese domination of the city.[32] Similarly, as their model of film censorship China looked to the United States. Apparently believing that the U.S. federal government controlled film censorship practices, the Chinese Film Censorship Committee in June 1931 contacted Willys Peck, the American consul general in Nanking who later would have to deal with Frederick Herron's complaints about the Chinese vice consul in Los Angeles. The committee informed Peck that it was anxious to "avail itself of the experience of other countries in the censorship of motion pictures," and that it sought to "collect copies of laws, etc. relating to the subject." A member of the committee then asked Peck to get him whatever material he could from the United States.[33]

Peck related this conversation to the secretary of state, suggesting that the State Department might act as a liaison between China and the MPPDA, which administered the self-censoring Production Code. Peck added that it was his impression that the Chinese were "especially interested in learning the methods employed in censoring films in the United States . . . on a national scale and . . . locally, and in learning the principles which govern the condemning of films or portions of films as unfit for exhibition." In the name of international relations, Peck suggested that the United States cooperate with the Chinese in this request for information.[34] As a result, the United States, besides at least partially controlling world film markets, also may have had at least some control over world censorship systems. Rather than working to the benefit of Hollywood filmmakers, however, their own regulatory system would work, at least in China, to weaken their hold on the market.

This became abundantly clear to at least one State Department employee, who composed an apparently anonymous memo on the subject. The memo acknowledged the Chinese request for information on American censorship laws and also, rather mysteriously, for information about state censorship regulations in Kansas. While suggesting that the department cooperate with the Chinese in providing this information, the memo writer warned that "there is a possibility that the Chinese authorities may include in their censorship regulations the provisions of the . . . 'production code' and laws of the state of Kansas which might make very difficult an effective protest if such regulations were unreasonably interpreted to the detriment of American films."[35] In other words, the Chinese may have intended to use American-style censorship regulations precisely to censor American films, and neither State Department bureaucrats nor Hollywood officials could complain too loudly if the MPPDA's own regulations were used against the MPPDA's product.

Just as in the United States, censorship in China was never universally agreed on or enforced. Even after the institution of the 1931 censorship law, there remained some "independent censorship areas," such as Canton, Hong Kong, and, in Shanghai, the French Concession and the International Settlement. In addition, independent groups agitated for better films, with the Shanghai American Women's Club, for instance, printing a bulletin of "films worth seeing." For the most part, however, the Film Censorship Committee exercised by far the most power, and provided the greatest irritation for American diplomats and film executives.[36]

Censoring Hollywood Films in China

The first significant censorship case in China that seems to have come to the attention not only of the MPPDA, but also of the State Department, concerned the 1930 Howard Hughes production *Hell's Angels*. The exact grounds of the objection are difficult to determine, but a complaint seems to have been lodged by the German Legation in China, probably because of the manner in which the film interpreted German participation in World War I.[37] Honoring this objection, Chinese officials refused to grant the film an exhibition permit unless certain changes were made. After some negotiations between the Film Censorship Committee, the State Department, and an American law firm in Shanghai (presumably representing Hughes's interests), some cuts in the film were agreed to, and an exhibition permit was granted in June 1932. This event constituted business as usual in relations between China and the Hollywood studios; the latter never seemed too concerned about making cuts in their films, as long as those films then could be exhibited. That is, the film studios concerned themselves with access, and film content became very much a secondary issue.

On a few occasions, however, access itself came to be threatened, and these cases turned into significant diplomatic events, to the extent that this was possible in the film business. At about the same time as the amicable resolution of the *Hell's Angels* case, Beh Chuan Peng, a member of the Film Censorship Committee, complained to Willys Peck about Josef von Sternberg's 1932 film *Shanghai Express*. Chinese students who had seen the film in Germany and the United States had contacted Chinese officials about it, with Peng then telling Peck, reasonably enough, that "the plot of the film was objectionable, in that it laid great emphasis on Chinese bandits, prostitutes, and other disreputable characters." He went on to say "that there was reason to believe that [the] Japanese had inspired the film . . . with a view to defaming China and thus lowering China in the esteem of Western

DEPARTMENT OF STATE

DIVISION OF FAR EASTERN AFFAIRS

August 10, 1932.

Subject: "The Shanghai Express".

Mr. Hornbeck:

A member of the Chinese Censorship
Bureau has asked Mr. Peck to do what he
could to bring about the suppression of the
film "The Shanghai Express". The film is
not now being shown in China.

Some weeks ago in the course of a call
at the Division, Mr. Kung, First Secretary
of the Chinese Legation, informed me that
the Legation had received letters from
Chinese in the United States protesting
against "The Shanghai Express" in that it
depicted China in an unfavorable light. I
asked him whether he or Dr. Yen, the Chargé,
had ever seen the film and he replied in
the negative. I said that I had seen it,
that while I had not observed it from the
point of view whether there was anything in
it which would be objectionable to the
Chinese, I had enjoyed the film as an
adventure story. I said that it was
inaccurate in some details but that I had
found it pleasant and diverting. I
suggested that Mr. Kung or Dr. Yen endeavor
to see the picture at some convenient time.

I concur with Mr. Mackay's view that

it

A Department of State report on
the problem of *Shanghai Express*
in China. (National Archives)

nations." Paramount, the company that produced *Shanghai Express*, apparently had decided not even to try to exhibit the film in China, probably
for some of the reasons Peng mentioned. But Peng asked that the film be
destroyed, and thereby removed from all non-U.S. markets.[38]

Peck argued with him, and their debate set the ground rules for the *Bitter
Tea* case one year later. In addition, it established the inability of American
and Chinese bureaucrats even to use the same terms in their discussions.
Peng stressed representational issues—the depiction of the Chinese as bandits and prostitutes. Peck, in his rebuttal, asserted narrative concerns, telling Peng that "in every exciting plot there must be a conflict, and that the
usual conflict was between good and evil." He continued by stating, "To
eliminate all bad characters from a movie film would, therefore, destroy
the plot of most exciting films," and that the Chinese should not "feel over
sensitive if the bad characters in a film were occasionally Chinese, just as

they often were Americans and persons of other nationalities."[39] Peck's argument failed to persuade the Film Censorship Committee, and Paramount hardly felt compelled to withdraw *Shanghai Express* from the international film marketplace.

To get Paramount's attention, however, the committee "passed a resolution barring all Paramount films from exhibition in China unless all copies of *Shanghai Express* throughout the world were destroyed." In other words, the entire output of the studio would be barred, a situation that Paramount's Chinese representative called an "emergency." Paramount finally consented to a token (and soon discontinued) effort to remove prints from international circulation. In response, the committee agreed to censor Paramount films once again, thereby clearing them for exhibition in China. The studio also produced an apology and a promise, which it sent on to the committee: "In producing *Shanghai Express*, Paramount had not the slightest intention to disparage the Chinese people and it regrets that the film has been so interpreted. It is the desire and intention of Paramount to refrain from producing any film which may be regarded as injurious to the dignity of the Chinese people."[40]

Despite having brokered the settlement, the State Department seems to have been convinced that the problem had more to do with intransigent Chinese attitudes than with reasonable differences between the American film industry and a foreign government. In writing to the secretary of state about the affair, Peck adopted a position of distanced academic interest, saying that the *Shanghai Express* incident "throws . . . light on modern Chinese official psychology." He then insisted that the case provided "an illustration of the mental attitude which the younger generation of Chinese officials takes toward international relations," an attitude that "may overlook forms of procedure and may display an inherited arrogance," while also exhibiting "hypersensitiveness to real or imagined insult and oppression."[41] Thus the modern Chinese state of rationalized, Western systems of discipline was being undone by unstable and irrational Chinese bureaucrats.

The Case of *The Bitter Tea of General Yen*

Despite what he called the "mechanical and artistic excellence" of *Bitter Tea*, J. B. Albeck, Columbia Picture's Far Eastern representative, "decided on no account to show it in China, because of the various difficulties which had arisen."[42] He was referring here, of course, to the problems experienced by *Shanghai Express*, and also to the complaints that Capra's film already had generated in other foreign markets. Objections to the film came to China from Cuba, Batavia, Java, Sumatra, Chicago, and—the site of the most troublesome comments—Los Angeles, from consul members rather than from students, as in the case of *Shanghai Express*. In Havana, for instance, the Chinese consul general had managed to have about a thousand feet of film eliminated from *Bitter Tea*, while the consul general in Chicago lobbied to have "eliminated some sixty-three words of dialogue which . . . [he] considered insulting to China."[43]

The Los Angeles vice consul remained, however, the most intractable of the critics. He had apparently been sent to Los Angeles specifically "to look after films," with Herron complaining in his memo to Peck that the vice consul had become "pugilistically inclined in his obstreperous approach to the studios," and that "his idea is to demand that he be allowed to do this, that and the other." Herron added that "this attitude, of course, has not been conducive to good relations and it has irritated every one of our people naturally." Herron complained that if the MPPDA gave in to the vice consul in the case of *Bitter Tea* and other films about China, then the organization would have to give in to representatives from all over the world. "The first thing we would know," Herron concluded rather ominously, "our industry would be run by a lot of foreign representatives."[44]

Just as the Chinese censorship apparatus somewhat mirrored Hollywood's Production Code, industry representative Herron, here registered a complaint about foreign influence in the studios that, typically, had been lodged against the industry itself. Throughout the 1920s and early 1930s, industry critics frequently associated the "salaciousness" of Hollywood films precisely with the influence of foreigners—namely the Eastern European Jews who ran several studios. As Richard Maltby has pointed out, demands for censorship often came to be "couched in moralistic terms and under the anti-Semitic expectation that a Jewish-dominated industry had to be intimidated into decency."[45] For Herron, however, the problem had nothing to do with the perceived foreignness of any of Hollywood's executives but rather with staving off constant foreign pressure for influence. This pressure came from foreign governments and, according to Herron, acceding to it finally would lead to an industry run not by the Louis B. Mayers, Harry Cohns, and Samuel Goldwyns whose own Americanism so often was called into question by U.S.-based critics, but by a hodgepodge of bureaucrats of varying nationalities, speaking various languages, and representing vastly different global interests.

This was bold talk from Herron. The development of sound film had

made the censorship of international prints of Hollywood films more difficult. Silent films usually only needed to have a title card reworded, but the
state of recording and editing technology made the elimination of lines of
dialogue more difficult, and also affected the continuity of scenes. Nevertheless, as Ruth Vasey has pointed out, the Hollywood studios, at least from
the end of World War I, typically "adapted [films] for release in overseas
markets wherever their potential revenue outweighed the cost of modi-
fying, distributing, and advertising them."[46] In addition, the studios frequently sought the advice of consular representatives and other foreign officials in the planning of films with foreign locales or themes.[47] Regardless
of Herron's feelings about the Chinese vice consul, this tendency toward
accommodation, when it came to film content, even applied to the case of
Bitter Tea.

The Los Angeles vice consul wrote to the Film Censorship Committee
that Capra's film "contained situations and dialogues reflecting discredit
on the Chinese race." To emphasize the point, the committee itself decided
not to examine any further Columbia films, thereby keeping them from
playing in China.[48] An alarmed Columbia representative wrote that, as a
result, the studio might have to refund $60,000 to Chinese theaters that
had already contracted to show the films that would be denied entry. As a
sign of the continuing expansion of American film interests in China, the
studio also had plans to open a branch office in Shanghai in early 1934,
and so hoped not to alienate the Chinese government. Columbia, therefore,
quickly volunteered to cut the offensive scenes and to apologize to the Chinese vice consul in Los Angeles, and then requested that the censors once
again begin considering Columbia's motion pictures.[49]

The exact nature of the vice consul's objections remain somewhat obscure. One memo from J. B. Albeck, Columbia's representative, claimed
that they amounted to only "eight sentences."[50] Yet another document, this
one a State Department dispatch that quoted rather roughly from the film,
detailed something less than two hundred words. According to this document, for example, the vice consul complained when in the first reel a missionary exclaims, "Rain and Fire! What a country! I pity him who devotes
himself to China." The vice consul further objected to the same character
complaining that some Chinese peasants, whom he had attempted to convert, were nothing but a bunch of "highway robbers," and that they were
interested in the story of Christ only to the extent that it inspired them to
crucify members of a desert caravan. In the sixth reel, the problem became
an American arms merchant who claims, with pride, "In the business of

raising dough I am a match for any Chinese." All things considered, however, the number of changes was relatively small for Columbia, and the studio readily agreed to the cuts.[51]

Of course, neither diplomatic nor business relations ever run so smoothly. The vice consul could not speak officially for the Chinese censors, and for them the cuts were not enough. Taking the complaints about the film very seriously, and invoking the precedent they set with *Shanghai Express*, the censors informed Albeck that they would "refuse to censor any further films brought to China by Columbia Pictures . . . until that firm had agreed to withdraw *Bitter Tea of General Yen* from circulation throughout the world."[52] Just as they had with *Shanghai Express*, the Film Censorship Committee insisted that access to the Chinese market for an entire body of films from one studio depended on the censors being able to control the international distribution of any individual film from the same studio. This was not lost on the various U.S. government officials and film industry representatives who weighed in on the incident, as they typically commented that the case of *Bitter Tea* served to continue the policy established with *Shanghai Express*.[53]

Compounding this very significant problem, but also somewhat separate from it, were the complaints that still came in from those areas where Columbia claimed that prints of the film already had been altered. The studio insisted that it had shown a reedited version to the Chinese censors and, for good measure, to those in Batavia. Nevertheless, Chinese consular officials insisted that the offending footage remained in Batavian prints, and also in those showing in Java and Sumatra. Similarly, in Cuba, although the reedited film had been shown in Havana, a complete original print circulated in other locales (resulting in a fine being levied by the Cuban authorities against "the persons responsible").[54]

These conflicts over the prints of *Bitter Tea* demonstrate some of the significant problems with global film markets and the attempts to regulate them. Just as censorship in China might vary between regions (for instance, the separate censorship committee in Shanghai, discussed above), so too might communications from a country's government officials vary considerably, even to the point of contradiction. Columbia apparently felt that, by acting on the Chinese vice consul's requests for a reedited version of the film, the studio would appease the censors in Nanking as well. Instead, the censors lobbied for the film's complete withdrawal from the global market. In addition, if it is to be believed that Columbia really did delete several passages from the film, the studio itself apparently could not assure that those new versions actually would be exhibited, or that, in the case of the Havana version, a print tailored for one Cuban city would necessarily be exhibited in another. Even though the Hollywood studios made a limited number of prints and attempted to control their distribution fairly vigorously, the documents on *Bitter Tea* indicate that different versions might well have circulated regardless of studio efforts.[55] Further, as Albeck pointed out in Columbia's defense, in some markets the studio sold its films outright rather than renting them, thereby losing any of its ability to enforce cuts and, as a result, its capacity to placate some of the demands of foreign censorship.[56]

The studio also maintained a somewhat loose relationship with its foreign distributors. Charles Roberts, assistant foreign manager for Columbia, wrote to Albeck, the studio's Far Eastern representative, about the problems of *Bitter Tea* in the Dutch East Indies. Columbia had never favored exhibiting the film there precisely because of the possibility of protest, but the studio's distributor in the Dutch East Indies and adjoining territories had insisted on placing the film in the theaters under his purview. He seems to have come to regret this decision, apparently because of Chinese consular objections, but Columbia wanted to wash its hands of him and his problems. "If we are successful in these arrangements we will take Mr. Samuel's print away from him and he will be rid of all his worries," Roberts wrote, but added that "if we are not successful . . . we must leave it up to him to get the situation straightened out." Roberts then insisted that the distributor had acted alone, because the studio "never favored the shipment of this picture to the Dutch East Indies," and gave in only because of the distributor's "insistence." Thus, the global distribution system seems to have been a diffuse one, initially coordinated by the studio's foreign office, but then very much left in the hands of individual territorial distributors with the power to act on their own.[57]

When it did play in these foreign territories *Bitter Tea* faced Chinese lobbying efforts designed to keep people away. In the Dutch East Indies, Batavia, Singapore, Manila, and Calcutta, Chinese consular officials advised Chinese citizens "not to patronize the film in question." The exact nature of this consular advice remains unclear, but it was apparently effective enough, according to Willys Peck, to have "resulted in loss to the American firm." Peck, the State Department official, urged China's Foreign Office to contact their consulates and tell them that *Bitter Tea* indeed had been amended according to consular recommendations, and that the reedited film had been screened for the National Board of Film Censors in Nanking.[58] However, indicating the confusion caused by the case, which may have been either willful or accidental, the Foreign Office, after contacting the National Board for instructions, "was told that the Board knew nothing about the merits of the film." As a result, "the Foreign Office . . . expresed its inability to take the action requested" by Peck.[59] Here, then, a kind of extragovernmental form of censorship—that is, one organized by individual diplomatic officials rather than the National Board of Film Censors, but nevertheless receiving the board's tacit approval—seems to have had an impact on the foreign revenues of Capra's film.

The continuing inability to reach an agreement by Columbia and the State Department on the one hand, and the Chinese government on the other, led to some fascinating discussions by all parties to justify their positions, justifications that point out certain governmental and corporate notions of reception and also of national difference. Both Columbia and the State Department invoked a sort of global reception practice to make the film seem harmless to the Chinese. Albeck, the studio's Far Eastern representative, argued that the film "portrayed the Chinese in a favorable light, since a Chinese bandit general was depicted as a hero." He used, as proof of his interpretation, the advice of Columbia's Japanese distributor, who recommended against showing the film in Japan, China's longtime enemy, precisely because of the sympathetic depiction of General Yen.[60] In a subsequent memo to the Film Censorship Committee, Albeck insisted that this representation constituted absolute proof of the film's fitness: "The fact that Columbia's buyer in Japan has objected to take delivery of this picture, because it shows a Chinese General as a hero and in general gives a friendly picturization of Chinese," Albeck wrote, "will convince you, that the picture in general can not be considered offensive to [the] Chinese."[61]

Again and again, Columbia and the State Department brought up the Japanese in order to make the film acceptable to Chinese officials. Willys Peck, for example, engaged in a lengthy debate with Chaucer Wu of the Chinese Foreign Office about the fitness of *Bitter Tea*, and about Wu's objections to the anti-Chinese dialogue in the film. Peck, reprising his logic in the *Shanghai Express* case, wrote that "I called his attention to the fact . . . that every country has its enemies and to represent such enemies in a play as praising the country in question would be ridiculous." He went on to say that "to reduce the matter to its simplest elements, I observed that every Japanese in a motion picture play, if he were to meet the view of the Chinese, must be represented as finding no fault whatever in China." In other words, the imperatives of the dramatic form made it impossible not to insult China in the film; disregarding this logic would lead to films in which even Japanese characters would be forbidden to criticize China. Peck seems to have felt quite satisfied with this lesson in film appreciation, narrative construction, and character motivation, and noted that "Mr. Wu admitted the force of this contention."[62]

To underscore the point that the film should be acceptable to the Chinese, both Peck and Albeck shifted from narrative to ideological grounds. In a discussion with Peck, Albeck claimed that, if nothing else, the "one feature of the film that ought to please the Chinese was the denunciation of American missionaries by the Chinese general." Peck then used this interpretation to turn the Chinese censors' argument around by insisting that "he did not think it would be a good idea to show such a film in China, because it would be harmful to American missionary interests, which constituted a very important American interest in China."[63] That is, Peck interpreted Capra's film (which he admitted he had not seen) as being critical of an American religious movement with global aspirations.[64] As a result, *Bitter Tea*, if shown either in China or in territories with large Chinese populations, would act only to bolster the new Chinese regime's anti-Westernism. By this logic, the Chinese censors should have welcomed the film, and the Chinese consular officials should have urged Chinese nationals to see it.

Practically missing, of course, from these rather thorough readings of the film is any mention of the romance between the white American missionary and the Chinese general. Indeed, in Peck's comments and those of others interested in the case, the relationship can only be hinted at, and then without any judgments being made, or made only obliquely. Neither the Film Censorship Committee nor the various vice consuls seem to have had any problem with this aspect of the film. All of the requests for dialogue cuts, for instance, concerned descriptions of China or the Chinese. In at least one of China's "independent censorship areas," however, the love story may have constituted grounds for banning the film. In Shanghai, censorship regulations clearly reflected the ongoing colonial status of the city, and the attempt of Westerners to maintain power and authority in part by controlling motion pictures. In that city's International Settlement, censors banned films that "prominently" featured "the color question," and also those that were "calculated directly to lower the moral prestige of women (especially white women)."[65] American officials, however, seem to have positioned themselves somewhere between the Chinese censors and those in Shanghai—that is, able to acknowledge the romance as an issue, but unable to state precisely just what kind of issue it may have been.

In his conversation with Peck, Albeck mentioned that "the Chinese general was represented as falling in love with the American heroine, but as deporting himself in an unexceptionable way." Thus, Yen's gentlemanliness—that which the film clearly posits as his European manners—seems, for Albeck, to exempt the film from any exploitation of "the color question." The memo then either recounts the same conversation again, or indicates that Peck wanted to clarify further the nature of the love story: "Mr. Peck inquired whether the American heroine was represented as falling in love with the Chinese general, and Mr. Albeck said that this phase was touched on very lightly."[66] The men then moved quickly to their very assured discussion of the film's antimissionary zeal. The romance, then, became something of a structuring absence in the official American discourse about the film. It could be mentioned but without any certainty as to what it might signify in terms of international censorship, and then it was to be quickly dismissed. The romance seems, potentially, to have posed problems for both Peck and Albeck, but they were unable to place it within the narrative of the negotiations between the Chinese censors, the Department of State, and Columbia.[67]

Chinese officials, rather than countering with their own interpretive strategies, instead invoked a desire for efficient, rational international relations. During his own discussion with Peck, Chaucer Wu of the Chinese Foreign Office "observed that the Chinese Government is often in receipt of requests from different nationalities asking that motion picture films objectionable to them be suppressed, action which the Chinese Government sometimes takes in the interest of the international good relations."[68] Thus, for the Chinese, the request to suppress, from one friendly government to another, should suffice. The Americans countered this assertion of Chinese diplomatic gentlemanliness with their own version of national, governmental superiority, based on film reception. Albeck, in his memo to An Shih Ju of the Film Censorship Committee wrote that "you will be aware, that American films often picturize Americans as all kinds of crooks and murderers and in this particular film the Chinese General Yen is making some very insulting remarks about American missionaries." He then added that all of this took place "without the American Government having raised any objections."[69] Thus while Peck, in his debate with Wu, tried to give a lesson in film appreciation, Albeck simply insisted that American authorities had a far more reasonable attitude about representational issues.

Peck himself seems to have come around to Albeck's point of view. After several months of discussions with the Chinese, Peck felt that there was little left that the government could do, and he suggested that Columbia's home office in New York take up the negotiations. He lamented that the censors in "Nanking are genuinely sympathetic with the efforts of Chinese abroad to put an end to what they all consider are insulting references to Chinese in motion picture films." Peck further complained that "the Chinese are unreasonable in these matters," and then invoked his argument from the *Shanghai Express* case that the Chinese, simply, were different from Americans. Rather than insisting on a kind of modernized, bureaucratic arrogance primarily afflicting younger Chinese, as he had in his dealings with von Sternberg's film, Peck this time claimed that the censors' objections to American representational practices were simply "matters of sentiment," and that in the case of *Bitter Tea* "logic," on the part of the Chinese, "does not seem to count for very much."[70]

Despite Peck's problems with the Chinese censors, however, the State Department finally found itself limited in its ability to formulate criticism of Chinese censorship policy. Overall, officials could find no fault with Chinese national practice but rather only with Chinese attempts to manipulate the world market for American films. Acting Secretary of State William Phillips weighed in on the matter, restating the United States's official policy of and support for self-determining national markets. According to Phillips, the United States "does not question the right of any government to prevent within that government's jurisdiction the exhibition of any motion picture which it may regard as contrary to its interests." Indeed, Phillips, who seems to have been the highest-ranking official to offer an opinion in the case, went so far as to assert the possibility of aligning the United States with Chinese efforts to ban all of a studio's product — as had been threatened with both Paramount and Columbia — pending the removal from international distribution of a single film. The Assistant Secretary of State wrote that the government would not "be disposed to object if permission to exhibit pictures of any particular company were made conditional on the suppression" of a specific film. In making this statement of policy, Phillips proposed a theory of the absolute readability of any film and of the possibility of scientific certainty about the meaning of a movie. A foreign government could only be justified in making demands similar to China's when, "following a dispassionate and unbiased study thereof, [a film] is found to contain features which vilify or hold up to ridicule the people or government of a friendly power or which are likely to affect adversely international relations."[71]

The government therefore acknowledged the disruptive potential of motion pictures in the global market, and also established limits as to how much it would assist any American business enterprise. Nevertheless, Phillips established an extremely difficult standard for any foreign government to meet in the assessment of film content. "Such extreme measures on the part of any government, however," Phillips wrote, "would be warranted only when there could be no reasonable doubt as to the seriously objectionable character of the picture and when the picture could not be revised so as to remove its objectionable elements, or when the producer refused to make such a revision."[72] Columbia, of course, had passed this test, and so by Phillips's calculation they could count on at least some government support.

As a further sign of the government's willingness to help, and as an indication of the compatibility between national and business interests, Phillips insisted on the United States's right to protect commercial access to what might be considered "neutral" territories. In response to China's demand that *Bitter Tea* be removed from the global market, Phillips insisted that "this government could not admit the right of any government to demand the suppression of an American picture outside the jurisdiction of the government making the demand, and any attempt to coerce American producers by unreasonable demands should be firmly opposed."[73] Almost certainly, Phillips stressed Chinese jurisdiction over its own markets in order to justify the same for the United States. For the movie business, with regard to the United States, this meant access to most of the world.

These, then, were the two battles being fought between Columbia and the State Department on one side, and the Chinese government on the other: the first, determining national rights in domestic markets and international ones, and the second, determining control of representational practice and interpretation. In terms of the latter, the State Department and Columbia argued for logical, "dispassionate" systems of reception. Japanese disapproval must lead to Chinese approval, and the critique of American missionaries in the film must soften any of the movie's criticism of the Chinese. The Chinese censors and consular officials were no less rigorous and narrow, despite the State Department's claim of their sentimentality. They argued, simultaneously, to ban the film and to delete sections of dialogue, with Columbia gladly agreeing to make the proposed cuts.

The Chinese government also seems to have proposed the most acceptable solution to the problem of the film, and in such a way that would make *Bitter Tea* readable, finally, as a kind of literary fantasy, with all of the disclaimers usually associated with Western historical novels. Chaucer Wu of the Chinese Foreign Office, who had had to submit to Willys Peck's lectures on film appreciation, alerted Peck that "the Foreign Office had devised a means to meet the needs of the situation." Wu proposed that Columbia add a prologue to the beginning of the international prints of *Bitter Tea*, one that would read: "The picture represents a mere literary fancy devised by its author, and it does not in any way pretend to depict actual conditions in the real life of China. Its setting is introduced merely to promote the story of the sentimental conflicts of two civilizations symbolized by a Chinese warrior and an American girl."[74] Wu wanted to create a reception context, through the prologue, in which the film must be read as allegory, or only as melodrama, rather than as faithfully reproducing current events. In the battle over the reception of the film, and over the representation of Chinese events, Wu and the other Chinese officials wanted a final version of *Bitter Tea* that emphasized the sentimental narrative and not the political one.

Peck liked the idea, calling it "ingenious," and also appreciated its literary quality, likening it to the prologues that preceded so many novels about "contemporary politics" and that denied the likeness of any characters to persons living or dead.[75] He passed the idea on to Albeck, who forwarded it to the Columbia home office, "asking them to get such [a] 'prologue' prepared for insertion in all the prints." Albeck added that he hoped this move would "clear up any misunderstandings which may exist with regard to this picture." Columbia apparently viewed this as the most practical solution, and although cautioning Peck that preparing prologues for all prints worldwide might take awhile, decided to implement Wu's idea. The studio further asked Peck to issue an apology, on its behalf, to the Chinese. Expressing its "desire to continue to do business in China," the studio asked Peck to "point out to the Chinese authorities that Columbia is doing everything possible to avoid in . . . future productions any scenes or dialogues which may be considered offensive to the Chinese."[76]

This seems to have solved the *Bitter Tea* crisis, and in somewhat the same way that Paramount brought closure to the case of *Shanghai Express*: through a formal apology and an assurance that the studio would not allow the situation to happen again. Columbia issued the apology and began inserting prologues in December 1933, and the next month the State Department closed its file on the case.[77] It is difficult to determine how many prints with prologues actually played throughout the world and also the expediency with which the Chinese censors once again began reviewing Columbia's films. In a struggle over the international film market, however, the Chinese government appears to have won the battle over the final cut of

COLUMBIA PICTURES
DISTRIBUTING CO. INC.
729 Seven Avenue New York City

Cable Address: Albeck, Yohohama.
6-B Bluff, Yokohama.

December 12th, 1933.

Mr. Willys R. Peck
Counselor of Legation,
Legation of the United States of America,
NANKING.

Sir,

Re: THE BITTER TEA OF GENERAL YEN.

In receipt of your letter of December 1st, I greatly
appreciate all your efforts in this matter and thank you
for passing on to me the suggestion of the Nanking Foreign
Office regarding the insertion of a "prologue" in this
picture.

I have forwarded copy of your letter to my home office,
recommending them to get such prologue inserted in this
film and hope that they will comply with this request,
but considerable time will, of-course, elapse before this
prologue is prepared and reaches distributors all over the
world.

In order to keep you fully advised of all developments
in this matter, I hand you herewith enclose copy of letter
from Puma Films Ltd., Shanghai, dated November 28th together with a copy of a brief translation of the Notice #175
of November 24th from the Nanking Board of Censors to said
firm. Furthermore, I enclose a copy of letter from my home
office dated October 10th, together with a copy of their
letter to Mr. Kiang, Chinese Consul at Los Angeles, dated
October 6th and also copy of my today's letter to Puma
Films Ltd., Shanghai.

As Puma Films Ltd., Shanghai, will still have a
considerable number of films to censor in the near future
and as it is, of-course, Columbia's desire to continue to
do business in China, I hope that you, when opportunity
offers, will point out to the Chinese authorities that
Columbia is doing everything possible to avoid in the
future productions any scenes or dialogues which may be
considered offensive to the Chinese.

Thanking you for your kind attention to this matter.

Respectfully yours,
Columbia Pictures Distributing Co. Inc.
Representative for the Far East
(Signed) Johs. Albeck
Johs. Albeck.

Letter from Columbia's representative for the Far East, to the
American Legation in China, about the addition of a prologue
to *The Bitter Tea of General Yen* that might make the film acceptable to Chinese authorities. (National Archives)

Bitter Tea, thereby amply demonstrating that even as late as the 1930s a studio's control over its own product was never as absolute as perhaps has been perceived.

The Case of *The Bitter Tea of General Yen* and Film History

The incidents surrounding *Bitter Tea* might provide a way to rethink the manner in which audiences understood the films they saw, as well as the logic on the part of studio executives that went into production decisions. First, and most narrowly, we can start to imagine an international reception context in which Josef von Sternberg, the director of *Shanghai Express*, and Capra, the director of *Bitter Tea*, might be placed together as filmmakers. Such a pairing makes little sense in terms of most modern auteurist practices, with Sternberg the director of European and orientalist exotica, and Capra the purveyor par excellence of homespun Americana. But their films about China were interpreted and dealt with in almost identical ways by the Chinese censors. More broadly, scholars might also be able to chart in increasingly complex terms the development of genres. Although more research is necessary to be sure of this point, Hollywood studios apparently slowed down their production of films about China in the late 1930s. The lavish version of *The Good Earth* by MGM in 1937, may well have been one of the final movies in the cycle, while in terms of international diplomacy such films as *Oil for the Lamps of China* (1935) and *The General Died at Dawn* (1936) seem to have been among the last of the American movies to raise the ire of Chinese censors in the manner of *Shanghai Express* and *Bitter Tea*.[78] This lessening of interest on the part of producers may have had to do with a small cycle of films running its course with the American audience, or with a shift toward movies related to World War II, or with an inability to find the dramatic interest, for domestic viewers at least, in the Sino-Japanese war that began in 1937. But the end of the cycle of films about China also may have been influenced quite significantly by the headache of dealing with Chinese censorship.

Understanding the issues of international censorship also helps us to understand, or at least to extend the possibilities for understanding, the success or failure of a film at the box office. *Bitter Tea* has been labeled a failure, with some justification. There may well have been reasons for this in the domestic market, but the imposition of foreign censorship restrictions, the threat of such restrictions, lobbying efforts by foreign officials, and the unavailability of certain markets also may help to explain the performance of *Bitter Tea*. China itself counted for a relatively small percentage of foreign income for Hollywood studios, but the Chinese censors' ability to slow down the distribution of Capra's film throughout the world (by insisting on cuts and on adding a prologue), along with consular efforts to keep audiences away in Cuba and other territories and Columbia's inability to show the film in Japan, certainly could not have helped the film's financial prospects.[79]

Most significant here is that the case of *Bitter Tea* demonstrates, at least in the 1930s, that individual Hollywood films did not take shape solely from discussions between the studios and the Hays Office or from debates between the MPPDA and American censors in various states and localities. Instead, these films also were the product of negotiations between studio officials, the federal government, and foreign governments. The global market and the international audience also become more complex in light of the documents on *Bitter Tea*. The American film industry may have controlled the world market, but the Hollywood studios simply could not impose their will on foreign theaters and viewers. Indeed, the studios might willingly avoid sections of the international audience (Columbia never intended to exhibit *Bitter Tea* in China), might approach other sections of it only unwillingly (as in the case of the Dutch East Indies), or might have been kept away from some audiences as a result of a rather diffuse chain of command (the Columbia distributor who decided not to show *Bitter Tea* in Japan). And often, unless the studios acquiesced to their demands, foreign censors could threaten to ban a film company's entire output. This is not to discount Hollywood hegemony but instead to call for a more nuanced understanding of the place of American movies in the world. By explicating the complex relation of Hollywood to the international market we can understand the connections between American film corporations and the American government, and also the relationships between governments—in this case the United States and China—that finally helped to determine Hollywood representational practices.

Chapter Three

Film Education and Quality Entertainment

for Children and Adolescents

On 8 May 1934 Nelle J. Brown, a high school student in Kannapolis, North Carolina, wrote a brief thank-you note to Fred Powell, business secretary of the local YMCA. The YMCA doubled as a movie theater in Kannapolis, and on 4 May Powell had coordinated a free screening for area high school students of Frank Capra's then-latest film, *It Happened One Night*. In her letter, Brown told Powell that she and the other students were "very appreciative" of the "kind invitation" to see the film. She included, as well, her own brief review of the movie that starred Claudette Colbert as a runaway heiress and Clark Gable as the down-on-his-luck reporter who finds her, travels with her, and finally marries her. "The picture," Brown said, "to my estimation, was just as good as they ever get," and then added that "the moral part of the story was great."[1] Brown could speak with some authority on this issue because at the time of the screening her English class had been studying film appreciation. In fact, the other students in the class also wrote to Powell about the screening and, similarly, mixed their thanks with their opinions about the film. Along with his own commendation of *It Happened One Night* ("I think it is one of the best pictures that has come out of Hollywood in many years"), Powell sent the students' letters on to Capra, who deposited them with the rest of his papers at Wesleyan University.[2]

The Kannapolis high school class that wrote to Powell was a small one. Only twelve students sent notes to the YMCA in what was almost certainly a class assignment (all of the letters were handwritten on standard issue, three-hole, lined paper and were composed on either the first or second school day—Monday or Tuesday—after the Friday screening). Nevertheless, they tell us something of the uses of Capra's films in schools during the

1930s and as part of what Lea Jacobs has called the film education move-
ment.³ We also can understand from these letters how Capra's films contributed to a discourse about quality entertainment suitable for children
and adolescents. This discourse, although never a monolithic one in relation to Capra's films from the period, can be traced through student and
teacher responses to the movies they saw, and the pronouncements of parents' groups, as well as the content of school textbooks, educational periodicals, film industry trade journals, and National Board of Review documents. These sources point out many of the tensions between a variety of
the institutions involved either centrally or tangentially with motion pictures, most notably the film business and the educational system. Perhaps
more than any other films (with the possible exception of those of Cecil B.
DeMille and Walt Disney), Capra's movies, and in particular *The Bitter Tea
of General Yen* (1933), *It Happened One Night* (1934), *Mr. Deeds Goes to
Town* (1936), *Lost Horizon* (1937), and *You Can't Take It with You* (1938),
entered directly into the era's discussions about Hollywood and the moral,
intellectual, and emotional uplift of the child and adolescent audiences in
the 1930s.

These audiences have only recently been rediscovered, theorized, and
historicized by film scholars, chiefly by Lea Jacobs and Richard deCordova.
Jacobs, for example, has examined some of the film appreciation manu-
als used in classrooms during the 1930s, and also the one-reel excerpts
from Hollywood films that were prepared by Teaching Film Custodians
in cooperation with the major movie studios. These shorts were designed
for classroom use, and typically to teach lessons about the costs of crime
and delinquency, or about the problems that might ensue from an over-
fondness for material goods or too keen an interest in social mobility.⁴ De-
Cordova's work has analyzed the relationships between the youthful audience, the movie theater, and the fan club, in particular the latter two as sites
of education, entertainment, and social control. In so doing deCordova
produced histories of the 1920s matinee movement, which was sponsored
by the Motion Picture Producers and Distributors Association (the film industry's trade association), and Walt Disney's development of nationwide
Mickey Mouse Clubs in the 1930s. Both the Saturday afternoon movies
and the clubs were designed specifically for children and young adolescents, and both also were meant to promote filmgoing, the consumption
of film-related products, and to instill patriotic virtues. At the matinees,
for example, audience members might sing "America the Beautiful" before

the films began, while participation in the Mickey Mouse Clubs always included the Mickey Mouse Club yell, the Mickey Mouse Club creed, and, as with the matinees, the singing of "America the Beautiful." [5]

The work of Jacobs, deCordova, and others, and the resultant new possibilities for historicizing young audiences, are all the more significant because of the compelling connections between the development of the American motion picture industry and modern notions of the adolescent. In contemporary film studies it has become something of a given to examine the interesting confluences of the end of the nineteenth century; the development of the cinema at the same time as such discourses of power and knowledge as psychoanalysis and anthropology, or such technologies of the visible as the X ray, or such manifestations of nationalism and global diplomacy as modern imperialism.[6] But the cinema also made its debut in the United States at about the same time as the "discovery" of the adolescent by G. Stanley Hall and other educational reformers, and the concomitant shift in American education toward prioritizing the needs of the teenaged student and, indeed, toward finding ways of keeping teenagers in schools, both through curricular reform (vocational courses, for example) and legal coercion (mandatory attendance laws).[7]

This change led to a significant shift in the American high school, the goals of which moved from "that of just teaching academic subjects to that of being an institution which encompassed the social life of youth," thereby eliminating some of the divide between the classroom and certain leisure activities.[8] As a result, in the first two decades of the century sports came to play a significant role in the high school curriculum. By the 1920s, however, a belief in physical education as the perfect means for channeling the interests and energies of the teenager waned somewhat, as sports seemed more likely to develop passive viewers than active participants.[9] In part because of this, reformers' enthusiasm moved by the late 1920s and early 1930s, to understanding, developing, and in many ways controlling another kind of spectatorship—the viewing of movies.[10]

The film education movement seemed to understand watching movies, as opposed to sports, as an extremely active exercise and sought to use moviegoing to activate and improve other skills deemed necessary to the adolescent—including those involved in taste, consumption practice, and even family relations—as children could now, at least in theory, have more informed discussions with their parents about the best ways to spend their leisure time.[11] There was also a distinctly practical reason for teaching film appreciation. William Lewin, in his 1934 study *Photoplay Appreciation in*

American High Schools, noted that "three out of four high-school students readily name movie-going as one of the leisure occupations they most enjoy." He then added that "the implications for the curriculum-maker are unmistakable," and that, as it was understood that "classroom procedures should begin with emphasis upon the natural interests of children, the current photoplay offers an opening of almost unmatched interest."[12]

During the 1930s, largely because of these interests and concerns, high schools in particular often offered classes in film appreciation. In 1935 the National Education Association reported that more than two thousand high schools gave students the chance to enroll in such courses, although it is almost certain that students took the greatest part of these as brief units in other classes, most typically English.[13] In fact, a cottage industry in film appreciation textbooks developed to meet the needs of the teachers and students in these classes: Edgar Dale's *How to Appreciate Motion Pictures* (1933), Sarah McLean Mullen's pamphlet "How to Judge Motion Pictures" (1935), Richard Lewis and Helen Rand's *Film and School* (1937), Barrett C. Kiesling's *Talking Pictures* (1937), and of course, Lewin's *Photoplay Appreciation in American High Schools*, among others.[14] Educators viewed film education as a way to modernize the curriculum as well as turn students into more-avid readers, because these classes tended to favor movies based on classic novels. In the testimonial of one teacher converted to film education, the movement "can be to the study of literature what the airplane is to transportation."[15]

According to educators, in addition to turning students into better readers film appreciation courses would make them better movie consumers, which then would change the film industry for the better. The double bill stood out as the special pet peeve of film educators because of the manner in which this form of "mixed program," in William Lewin's term, worked to "appeal in part to adults and in part to children." Film education reformers wanted to build an audience that would "insist on stratifying programs or theaters so that some may serve the needs of children, some the needs of adults, and some the needs of family groups."[16] Thus, film education would teach adolescents that the "balanced" program—a bill designed to appeal to all ages—served the needs of no one. Changing the public demand for these programs would, in turn, change the practices of the industry that produced them.

Along with making the connection between film appreciation, the movie audience, and industrial practice, educational reformers also planned to teach viewers to insist on antiwar, antiimperialist films that dealt realistically with issues of class and race. In the textbook *Film and School*, for instance, Lewis and Rand suggest that students consider whether "we should not have pictures that make any one ridiculous because of his race or country," and ask, as well, if "moving pictures give a fair picture of economic conditions as they exist." Their chief concerns, however, were with war films. They write: "Because we know that wars do not just happen, that they are made, we want, in dealing with war pictures, to be sure that the strength of our influence is not on the side of the war-makers," and then go on to ask students a series of questions about the manner in which movies glamorized war or showed its horrors. Finally, in proposing the formation of an active, mobilized audience, they urge students to write letters to producers in order to "help build peace."[17] Groups that extended beyond the classroom shared Lewis and Rand's concerns. The Association of Film Audiences, for example, which represented "church, social, racial, labor . . . and youth groups" in addition to educational ones, screened films for their appropriateness for a variety of audiences. When rating war films, the association asked quite directly in its questionnaire: "Does it glorify . . . imperialism?"[18]

This popular-front sensibility about the possibilities for film to build better, more-informed, and enlightened citizens makes it clear that the supporters of the movement to teach film appreciation in schools had been influenced by the progressivism of such educational reformers as G. Stanley Hall, John Dewey, Sidney Hook, George Counts, and Harold Rugg.[19] That progressivism, which probably made its greatest impact on American schooling during the Depression, stressed a child-centered curriculum that rejected "rote learning and authoritarian discipline."[20] Progressives emphasized, instead, the "natural" interests of children and adolescents (like the movies), while arguing for extending education beyond the classroom, into the home, for instance, or the backyard, or even the movie theater. At the same time, these educators understood the importance of individual development, and called for "a recognition that the activities of children could be valuable in themselves, for their own sake, without reference to later life."[21] This notion of maturation may well have been taken, by at least some educators, to include such activities as going to the movies, the kind of leisure pursuit that may have seemed at first glance to have little to do with educational rigor or intellectual growth but that with the proper guidance might be brought effectively into the curriculum.

The architecture of the progressive classroom differed dramatically from that of the movie theater. In one of their most practical and long-lasting classroom improvements, progressive educators insisted on chairs and desks that could be moved around instead of being bolted to the floor—the precise opposite of the fixed position of the theater seat.[22] But this possibility for movement in the classroom also metaphorized a fluid space for progressive education, one that could extend beyond the walls of the school and beyond the formal curriculum. Dewey and others acknowledged the importance of "the traditional . . . three R's curriculum," but they also sought to foster the "active cooperation" of their students, which included using as educational tools those student interests and activities that typically had seemed beyond the range of traditional pedagogical practice.[23]

Although progressivism implemented some significant changes that are still with us today, such as portable classroom furniture, the movement itself never coalesced into a monolithic system of reform. If film appreciation was in fact connected to progressivism, it seems to have had the most in common with the less politically radical—rather than more overtly socialist—wing of the movement.[24] Further, as Arthur Zilversmit has pointed out, the effects and impact of progressive education have been overstated. The movement to bring film appreciation to the schools, then, almost certainly had as much to do with the problem of dealing with bored students often all too willing to drop out of school as with a commitment to vast curricular and social change.[25]

The Gender of Film Education

By the early 1930s Frank Capra had started to become a directorial star, one of the very few filmmakers whom the public recognized as readily as many of the celebrities who appeared in movies. Because of the quality of his movies and through the publicity efforts of Columbia Pictures, Capra had emerged as a director to be reckoned with, and as one whose films did credit to the motion picture industry.[26] At the same time, Capra established a significant role in the movement to teach film appreciation, which itself helped to produce and maintain his celebrity.

In 1933 Capra played an important role in a discourse of film quality, of masters of the craft, and, indeed, of the masculinization of the craft, when he became part of a test for high school students in Edgar Dale's textbook, *How to Appreciate Motion Pictures*. In a chapter titled "Direction: The Importance of the Director," Dale asked, "Do you think that Helen Hayes and Norma Shearer are great actresses? If you do, can you tell me who directed their latest pictures? If you are unable to answer this question, then your understanding of motion pictures is quite elementary, because one of the most important persons in the making of a motion picture is the director." Dale then proposed that students match film titles with their directors, whose photos appeared on a two-page spread.[27] Among the ten films— *A Farewell to Arms*, *A Nous la Liberté*, *Dishonored*, *Oliver Twist*, *Abraham Lincoln*, *City Lights*, *Street Scene*, *Thunder over Mexico*, and *Broken Lullaby*—was Capra's *Dirigible* from 1931. Knowing Capra the director, then, and, more broadly, knowing Capra as well as the other directors on the list—Ernst Lubitsch, Herbert Brenon, Cecil B. DeMille, King Vidor, Lewis Milestone, Josef von Sternberg, D. W. Griffith, Frank Borzage, René Clair, Charles Chaplin, and Sergei Eisenstein—had come to mark the educated film viewer rather than the movie fan, the student who appreciated the men who made the movies rather than the enthusiast who admired women like Hayes and Shearer.[28] Thus, along with an early auteurist discourse, the movement to teach film in schools produced a strictly gendered form of film appreciation. The interests of the newly discerning adolescent viewer would shift, from Shearer to Capra.

Educators understood that this shift applied mostly to girls, because boys already realized the importance of the men behind the camera. William Lewin, for instance, wrote authoritatively in his study of film appreciation in high schools that "girls admire chiefly story values as such, with less regard to details of directorial skill," while "boys admire chiefly the work of the director."[29] The necessity for girls to masculinize their understanding of film, however, was matched by the certainty that adult expertise in film, at least in schools, would be passed on to students by women. Educational reformers assumed that women would be the teachers in film appreciation classes, and insisted that this was preferable to men controlling the film classroom. Lewin discussed the manner in which movie study might lead students to other areas of interest, and wrote that, "beginning with movies as the subject of *her* story, the teacher can lead *her* pupils joyfully whither *she* will" (my emphasis).[30]

This was no idle acceptance of high school teaching as woman's work. Instead, it marked an understanding on Lewin's part of sexual difference that, if not taken into consideration, might well preclude any of the benefits promised by film education. In addition to finding differences between girls and boys, Lewin also found some striking similarities. "Pupils without guidance or instruction of any kind find all photoplays indiscriminately good," he wrote, while "pupils with guidance begin to become critical." He then added that "men teachers are less critical of movies than are women

CHAPTER XI

DIRECTION

The Importance of the Director

Do you think that Helen Hayes and Norma Shearer are great actresses? If you do, can you tell me who directed their latest pictures? If you are unable to answer this question, then your understanding of motion pictures is quite elementary, because one of the most important persons in the making of a motion picture is the director. Now I am going to try a simple test on you. Get paper and pencil and see whether you can match the names of the directors, whose photographs appear on pages 182–183, with the films which they directed in the following list:

1. "Farewell to Arms"
2. "Street Scene"
3. "Thunder over Mexico"
4. "A Nous la Liberté"
5. "Dishonored"
6. "Oliver Twist"
7. "City Lights"
8. "Broken Lullaby"
9. "Dirigible"
10. "Abraham Lincoln"

If you are like most high-school students and most adults to whom I have put this problem, you have not succeeded well at this task. The fact that you know much about motion-picture stars and but little about motion-picture directors shows that you have not thought seriously about the different phases of motion pictures.

As a matter of fact, a knowledge of a star's director is more important to you from the standpoint of an understanding of motion pictures than is a knowledge of what the star wears in the afternoon, whether she likes buttered toast,

179

Top: Edgar Dale, in *How to Appreciate Motion Pictures*, on "the importance of the director," asking high school students to match films with the photographs of their directors, with Capra's *Dirigible* one of the ten movies on the list. *Bottom*: The photos for Dale's test, showing Capra along with Borzage, Brenon, Chaplin, Clair, DeMille, Eisenstein, Griffith, Lubitsch, Milestone, Vidor, and von Sternberg.

Courtesy of Motion-Picture Herald
A GROUP OF OUTSTANDING
1. Frank Borzage; 2. Herbert Brenon; 3. Frank Capra; 4. Charles Chaplin; 5. René Clair; 6. Cecil B. De Mille.

Courtesy of Motion-Picture Herald
MOTION-PICTURE DIRECTORS
1. Sergei Eisenstein; 2. D. W. Griffith; 3. Ernst Lubitsch; 4. Lewis Milestone; 5. King Vidor; 6. Josef von Sternberg.

teachers." For students to go from indiscriminate enjoyment to discerning taste—from Shearer, as it were, to Capra—required the mediation of a highly skilled teacher. And men simply were not up to the job.[31]

Race, Religion, and *The Bitter Tea of General Yen*

In spite of the best efforts of the women who taught film appreciation, the movement itself never fully generated a universal understanding of what, precisely, constituted quality in motion pictures, or developed an educated, aware national audience of astute consumers united by their shared tastes and knowledge of social value. Instead, the study of film in high schools typically indicated the volatility of film reception, the possibilities for differences of opinion even among experts, particularly around issues of race and religion. In the early 1930s, the same William Lewin who had spoken so decisively about boys and girls, men and women, and the differences between them, devised a test to determine differences in appreciation and whether, during or after a course of study, students in grades seven through twelve and their teachers would react in similar ways to the same films. Lewin constructed a complicated system of scoring for a group of films shown in most parts of the country, with a smaller group of twenty-five films being seen by the greatest number of classes in the experiment. He then asked students and teachers to allot points to each film in such areas as main idea, story, value to humanity, value to society, direction, enjoyment, photography, fundamental idea, dialogue, and acting. No film could receive more than 300 points. Among teachers, *Cavalcade*, an adaptation of the Noel Coward play, ranked higher than any other film, with an average score of 250, indicating that the experts were more or less unanimous in their opinion of this 1933 Oscar winner for best picture and best director (Frank Lloyd).[32]

Some films, however, generated distinctly opposite scores. Among those with the biggest swing in score was Capra's 1933 film *The Bitter Tea of General Yen*, which averaged a score of 105 among teachers. But Miss Mary Olson in Colorado rated it 165, while Mrs. Nicholas in Virginia gave it a minus 5.[33] This disparity points out the problem of instructing students in taste and quality; there existed no necessary agreement among teachers about what constituted either term. Even more significant, given the desire of the educators who supported film education to teach primarily white students about tolerance and prejudice, the difference in scores for Capra's film indicates the difficulty in teaching about and evaluating issues of racial difference.

The 1932 film *Madame Butterfly*, directed by Marion Gehring, also appeared on Lewin's list of films. This nonmusical version of Puccini's opera scored quite well in high schools in West Virginia and Georgia, meriting a 190 from Sara M. Ferree's class in Williamstown, and a 145 from Virginia Ballard's group of students in Atlanta. At Abraham Lincoln High School in Los Angeles, however, Mrs. Mullen's group gave the film a median score of minus 5, while giving the story structure a minus 20, "as being very illogical." Further, they rated the film's social value a minus 20, "as being very destructive to society." Mrs. Mullen herself gave the film a score almost as low as that of her students. In explaining these low totals, Mrs. Mullen said that they were "doubtless due to racial feeling developed by class discussion," and added that "intermarriage between Japanese and Californians is recognized as disgraceful." [34]

These results, and this insistence on the absolute difference between a national (and racially "other") group and a local (presumably white) one, problematize any belief that educational reformers had about teaching racial tolerance through films. In this case, the low scores, if Mrs. Mullen can be believed, were in fact largely a result of the "racial feeling" that grew out of "class discussion" rather than impressions formed before the students had a chance to talk about the movie. It is also quite possible that *The Bitter Tea of General Yen*, about a romance between a white missionary and a Chinese warlord, generated at least some similar feelings in Mrs. Nicholas (and quite likely her students), who gave Capra's film such a low score. Indeed, Nicholas herself cannot simply be dismissed as an anti-Hollywood grouch, because she gave two other films the highest scores they received: 145 points for *Forty-Second Street* (1933) and 200 points for Cecil B. DeMille's *The Sign of the Cross* (1932).[35]

This invocation of DeMille as a director of quality seems particularly interesting in comparison to opinions about Capra, for as much as Capra, DeMille played a prominent (and frequently contradictory) role in the film education movement. In 1934, for example, the Photographic History Service of Hollywood (which was almost certainly connected to the major film studios)[36] released a new study unit for film classes, one that covered "ancient Egyptian life." In this unit, described approvingly by the *Educational Screen*, an academic magazine committed to bringing film into the schoolroom, classes could examine still photographs from two DeMille films, *The Ten Commandments* (1925) and *Cleopatra* (1934), as well as from

Karl Freund's *The Mummy* (1932).[37] In spite of this effort to make DeMille films educational, however, the movie reviewer for the *Educational Screen*, just two months after the units had been announced, dismissed *Cleopatra* as virtually worthless for adolescents: "So overdone that luxury becomes grotesque, history absurd."[38]

Both *The Sign of the Cross* and *The Bitter Tea of General Yen* serve to point out some of the tensions from the period in the film audience, or at least the adolescent one, and perhaps also some of the differences between that audience and the contemporary one. To the modern viewer, except for period differences (the early-Christian era and the Chinese civil war), *The Sign of the Cross* and *Bitter Tea* might seem like similar films that could have been grouped together by Depression audiences. Both movies use Christianity as a backdrop for a fairly racy sexual situation and for significant elements of spectacle (indeed, in mocking Lewin's findings in *Photoplay Appreciation*, the *Nation*, then as now the mass market liberal magazine of record, referred with heavy irony to DeMille's film as "that tasteful and reverent masterpiece").[39] For the student audiences in the 1930s, however, we have evidence that religion, rather than being a subtext, generated the primary level of meaning in these films, and the primary area of difference.

In examining the written responses of students to the films they watched, Lewin noted that *The Sign of the Cross* was mentioned more than any other as a movie that had "influenced" them in "specific ways." As representative examples, he cited a twelfth-grade girl in Los Angeles who said the film "made me glad I was a Christian; it made me stronger in my faith; it made me hold to my religion." Insisting once again on the gendered differences between high school viewers, Lewin further noted that "all the reactions to this picture except one were from girls, indicating the powerful appeal that religious pictures make to girls." He then added that "the trend was overwhelmingly in the direction of increased faith in whatever religion the individual happened to have." As a representative response to *The Bitter Tea of General Yen*, however, Lewin quoted the Lynchburg, Virginia, student (and made no mention of gender) who said that the film "shook my belief in the value of foreign missions." Even though the sexual content of *The Sign of the Cross* had so vexed the Hays Office, which enforced Hollywood's system of self-censorship, these high school students interpreted DeMille's film as an admirably religious one.[40] Capra's film, on the other hand, stood out as a provocative representation of the role of Western religion in the world, particularly in the context of post–World War I imperialism.[41]

It Happened One Night in Kannapolis

During the mid 1930s, Capra came to be known increasingly as a director of important pictures that were, nevertheless, exceedingly entertaining. As a result, educators' views shifted from thinking of his films as being high quality but potentially volatile (as in the case of *Bitter Tea*) to being absolutely perfect for classroom use. Capra's next two films after *Bitter Tea*, *Lady for a Day* (1933) and *It Happened One Night*, were canonized as two of the four screenplays—along with *Little Women* (1933) and *The Story of Louis Pasteur* (1936)—in the 1936 edition of *Four Star Scripts*, a volume designed in part for classroom use.[42] *It Happened One Night* in particular stands out as the first of Capra's films to be certified as a great motion picture by a variety of educational institutions, including, by the end of the decade, the university, when Robert Gessner placed it on his "History and Appreciation of Cinema" class syllabus at New York University in 1937–1938.[43]

Gessner's film list is itself remarkably consistent with the curriculum of many contemporary university film classes (as well as with those lists of worthy films that appeared in 1930s textbooks): *The Cabinet of Dr. Caligari*, *Potemkin*, *A Nous la Liberté*, and some early American silent films, for instance. On the syllabus, these films were screened under a variety of rubrics: "The Psychological Film," "The Realistic Film," and "The Moving Camera in Germany," as just a few examples. Gessner showed *It Happened One Night* the last week of class, and in the syllabus labeled it simply as "an American classic." Capra's film, then, at least in this class, marked the coming of age of cinema in the United States and stood as the film that showed the possibilities for works out of Hollywood to equal those produced in France, Germany, and the Soviet Union.[44]

At the time of the free screening for high school students in Kannapolis in May 1934, however, *It Happened One Night* had not yet achieved the status of an enduringly great motion picture. It is also difficult to determine the extent to which students there knew about the film's box office and critical success since its March opening. Kannapolis itself was a small town, but it was by no means an isolated outpost. Located about thirty miles northeast of Charlotte, Kannapolis seems to have been a 1930s North Carolina community of about average size, with the YMCA's double duty as a recreational center and movie theater telling us something about the kind of public buildings in the town and the manner in which leisure came to be organized. Information on Kannapolis during the 1930s is scarce, but its county, Cabarrus, contained mostly towns of fewer than five thousand people. Industrialization had come to Cabarrus more forcefully than to other counties in the primarily agricultural state, with about half of the population employed in manufacturing and mechanical occupations, and only 30 percent working in farming.[45]

Like the rest of the state, Cabarrus County segregated its population between "whites" and "coloreds." The white population there had grown dramatically since 1890 but the "colored" population far less so, so that by 1930 about 80 percent of the county residents were white.[46] A little more than a year after the screening, during the 1935–1936 school year, 599 students were enrolled in Kannapolis's lone white high school, which employed a faculty of 6 white men and 10 white women. The "colored" high school was attended by 66 students, who were taught by 6 African American faculty members: 3 men and 3 women.[47] Because there is no mention of race in the correspondence between the YMCA and Capra, it seems safe to assume that the students writing about *It Happened One Night* were white.

Cabarrus county spent only $17 to $22 per year on those students, matching most of the counties in the state but remaining far below expenditures of a number of counties, several of which surrounded Cabarrus, which spent between $22 and $36.[48] This funding affected all students, but white students in Kannapolis almost certainly would have had more access to the materials necessary to study film appreciation, in particular the instructional textbooks and other printed materials: the value of all library books in the five white schools there (including elementary) was $5,600; in the single black school it was $200.[49] At least in theory, though, North Carolina educators considered film appreciation a fit subject for all of its high school students. A brief history of secondary school education published in a 1937 North Carolina Department of Public Instruction brochure, for instance, explained that in the last quarter century, the mission of the high school curriculum had changed from college preparation to that of a more "practical nature." North Carolina introduced vocational subjects into the curriculum in 1917, and shortly after this time the state added other subjects that served to "meet the needs of the adolescent boys and girls, giving to them the education that would make them intelligent, happy, useful and vocationally efficient citizens." As a result, the curriculum had been "broadened and deepened."[50]

Because of this broadening and deepening, students in Kannapolis and elsewhere in the state learned about "ethical character, worthy home membership, intelligent citizenship . . . [and] health." In addition, they studied the "proper use of leisure."[51] Clearly, adolescent leisure constituted something of a problem in North Carolina, at least to those in charge of the educational system. In fact, a 1940 Work Projects Administration study of North Carolina adolescents, titled *Paths to Maturity*, lamented that "it is discouraging to probe . . . into the ways of [*sic*] which the high school youths spend most of their leisure time, for when we do so we find that pitifully small numbers of them are devoting leisure time to music, art or dancing lessons, or to private instruction in subjects not included in the school curriculum." High school students needed no prodding to go to the movies, but the apparent excess of their attendance may have encouraged educators to seek to teach them how to appreciate and demand only the best in motion pictures. Two-thirds of the white boys of high school age went to the movies anywhere from one to more than four times a week; African American boys and girls and white girls of the same age went slightly less frequently.[52]

High school film study in Kannapolis must necessarily have developed from a concern with these numbers, which then became part of a strategy to educate adolescents about leisure and to teach them about the "proper" way to choose movies and then watch them. As such, film appreciation, at least in North Carolina (despite some of the intellectual pretensions evident in the letters from Kannapolis), had as its goal not to prepare students for the university but rather to make them better consumers and more efficient members of their communities and even of their families. Indeed, the Kannapolis students who saw Capra's film already had advantages in this respect over many others in their age group. Most of the Kannapolis film appreciation students were seniors in a state in which the dropout rate constituted one of the major problems in education. "The most frequent North Carolina youth," according to *Paths to Maturity*, "left school before sixteen years of age."[53]

The Kannapolis screening itself typified one of the major projects of the film education movement. William Lewin, who devised the nationwide test about *Bitter Tea*, *Sign of the Cross*, and other films, also wrote about the significance of the exhibition venue. For Lewin and other educational reformers, film content seemed no more important than the space of viewing. Lewin predicted a school of the future with a fully modern theater along with assembly hall, classrooms, and other buildings. Until then, though, he claimed that "the democratization of educational opportunities can begin —in fact, has already begun—with the friendly use of neighborhood theaters for educational purposes," and added that, "indeed, such cooperation should logically continue even when schools are equipped to show talking pictures."[54]

The educators in the movement hoped to build better citizens through film appreciation. But reformers also called for a fluidity, facilitated by movies, between a number of different spaces, with this fluidity itself improving the lives of citizens in a democracy. By teaching film appreciation, the schoolroom could be connected to the home, where, at least according to educators, discussions of movies typically took place. The theater figured to become an extension of the schoolroom, especially when the theater volunteered its space for educational uses, as in the case of the YMCA special screening of *It Happened One Night*.

As education historians have noted, however, once we deal specifically with the activities in the traditional classroom, analyzing the school experience becomes very difficult, largely because it is so hard to know what happened during the school day. It is difficult, as well, to determine what else the Kannapolis students may have been learning and what other interests their school may have been trying to promote. In general, English classes throughout the United States in the 1920s and 1930s (and these were precisely the classes where students were most likely to learn about film) attempted to foster the elevation of taste through the reading of great works, with a canon that included Hawthorne, Shakespeare, George Eliot, Dickens, Carlyle, and the English historian Thomas Babington Macaulay. This curriculum served to instruct and improve that which was lamented as "the Saturday Evening Post mind" of so many students, whose favorite authors, at least in a 1922 survey, were Zane Grey, Arthur Conan Doyle, and adventure novelist Harold Bell Wright. Some teachers, though, did include popular and contemporary works in their classes, including Zane Grey novels and the Tom Swift series, as well as novelists who since then have earned a secure place in the canon but whose status as great writers was, at the time, more problematic: for example, Joseph Conrad, Sinclair Lewis, and George Bernard Shaw.[55] But it is impossible to determine precisely what the Kannapolis youngsters studied in their English class in addition to motion pictures, and what their attitudes and tastes may have been.

A further problem in reading the letters is that of knowing whether the sentiments conveyed were composed primarily with the teacher in mind, because after all, this appears to have been a class assignment. That is, many of these letters may well simply mimic the movie discourse that had come to be officially sanctioned by the film education movement. The letters about *It Happened One Night* are highly mediated documents rather than pure expressions of adolescent desire, knowledge, preference, or taste. They do not necessarily indicate how students talked about movies in other contexts—with each other, for instance, or with their families. Thus, the contemporary reader can only make cautious guesses about the students who wrote these letters more than seventy years ago. Nevertheless, from these letters we can come to understand some significant information about the film education movement in Kannapolis and perhaps elsewhere; the manner in which students were being taught to think about the movies they saw; and their success in mastering the discourse of film appreciation.

Some of the letters written after the screening of Capra's film actually tell us little about the place of movies in the classroom. One student produced virtually a form letter: "I enjoyed the picture very much and I wish there were more like [it]. Seeing the picture helped us in our study of motion pictures. Sincerely yours."[56] Even the letters that reveal little about classroom practice, though, can hint at some interesting things about individual preferences. One young woman wrote: "I thoroughly enjoyed seeing the picture. The story was a good one and many of the scenes were of the sort that I will remember them for a long time." She ended on a more personal note, giving us a sense of the pleasures of a small-town resident seeing *It Happened One Night*'s tale of a Florida-to-New York bus ride: "I enjoy shows which depict travels," she wrote.[57]

Several of the student letters about the screening do, however, give us a sense of the film appreciation unit in high school. One student wrote: "*It Happened One Night* was a very interesting show and was thoroughly enjoyed by all who saw it. The show was of a high class and seemed so real that I just lived in the picture. The costuming was very appropriate, as well as the photography which was very natural. The director's ability was appreciated very much. The music was suitable for the picture and the acting was simply grand."[58] Clearly, these students received aesthetic instruction in their film appreciation course, and they learned, just as Edgar Dale urged in his textbook's chapter on the student's necessary shift in appreciation from Norma Shearer to Capra, Lubitsch, Clair, and other filmmakers, to examine what this student called "the director's ability." A similar discourse on quality appears in other class letters; one student wrote, for instance, "I think that the direction, action, and the photography all were excellent in that picture. The story was unusually well planned."[59]

Film appreciation educators certainly stressed structure, action, character, and the like. But the movement also emphasized the social importance of films, often, as mentioned above, in terms of a film's attitudes toward war, race, and class. These concerns do not appear in the class letters from Kannapolis, but there is an interest on the part of several students in what we might call the social significance of film, or at least in the relationships between a film and the "real life" of the audience members. The same student who commended the costuming, the photography, and the director's ability, ended her letter by saying, "referring to criticisms no outstanding ones can be given. However there was no real moral in it, it served as good enjoyment and that is what we went to see." Another student more or less agreed, saying, "It was an excellent picture, although it didn't offer any lesson it was very entertaining." And, of course, Nelle Brown disagreed, but in similar terms, when she wrote about the film that "the moral part of the story was great."[60]

The first two students made distinctions between high-quality escapist films like *It Happened One Night*, and serious, important, "moral" films with social significance, and they almost certainly learned this great chain of film quality in their class. Indeed, these students seem to be paraphrasing one of the film appreciation sources from the period—Sarah McLean Mullen's "How to Judge Motion Pictures." Mullen, the Los Angeles teacher who had noted the "racial feeling" in her students generated by their discussion of *The Bitter Tea of General Yen*, ended her pamphlet with "the most important question of all," and went on to ask, "Does the [photo] play have any social value? Does it leave some part of its meaning in the minds of those who saw it, and will it govern their thoughts and actions after they have left the theater?" She also made sure to acknowledge the pleasures of the relatively frivolous film, saying that "we need not expect all moving pictures to carry a social message," and "entertainment for its own sake needs no defense." But she asserted, nevertheless, that "we do have the right to demand that a force appealing to so many millions of people accept a deep sense of public responsibility."[61]

Just like *The Bitter Tea of General Yen*, however, *It Happened One Night* polarized some high school students, as they interpreted it in at least two ways. The two Kannapolis students, following Mullen and other experts in the film education movement, found much to admire in Capra's film but also found it lacking when compared to films of "public responsibility" (typically, in the movement's literature, such films as *All Quiet on the Western Front* and *I Am a Fugitive from a Chain Gang*). Nelle Brown, though, impressed perhaps by the relative chastity of the film (the blanket serving as a "wall of Jericho" that separates Gable's and Colbert's beds in motels and tourist camps), or by its representation of the problems of the Depression, stressed the film's moral significance and implied that it was, indeed, an important and serious motion picture. In any event the emphasis, however contradictory, in these letters on the lessons learned from *It Happened One Night*, and indeed on whether the film taught any lessons at all, indicates that the film education movement tried to teach students to appreciate what Mullen called "social value" as an equal to any aesthetic category, and as that which required serious consideration and evaluation.

By teaching students how to weigh the social and the aesthetic, the film education movement planned on making students better movie consumers. Mullen herself insisted that by being "discerning and discriminating in our tastes," 1930s moviegoers "may help raise the standards of American motion pictures."[62] In fact, the letters from Kannapolis provide some evidence that, perhaps in part because of what went on in the classroom, students already had come to demand better product. One student made a direct link between her enjoyment of Capra's film and her time in the classroom: "The Movie Appreciation Course that we have been taking in school," she said, "has caused us to demand better pictures such as *It Happened One Night*."[63] The film education movement, according to this student, had very much accomplished its mission of activating and collectivizing spectatorship; that is, turning the passive individual viewer into the mobilized one, who, along with others so educated, now made "demands" on the film industry.

In studying the improvement of the student viewer, however, we can come to understand not just the formation of taste and discernment, but also something of the cooperation and connections between film education and the film industry, and the reasons why the industry typically sought to foster the interest of teachers and students in movies. For this special screening of *It Happened One Night*, the YMCA had invited the students to attend free of charge. One of the boys in the class wrote, however, that "I enjoyed the picture so much that I came back Friday night," the evening of the free matinee screening.[64] Thus in addition to trying to create discriminating customers, the film education movement, in spite of itself, encouraged movie consumption in general, and in a group of spectators who already constituted a major market for motion pictures. This student not only turned into a repeat viewer but also almost certainly brought friends or family with him the second time, with the cooperation between neighborhood theaters and schools working not just to benefit education but the box office as well.

Capra was delighted to receive the letters from the high school students.

He wrote back to Fred Powell at the YMCA and told him that "it was with genuine interest that I read your letter and the indorsed (*sic*) criticisms from the high school pupils." He added that these student opinions were "more liable to point out the real fault or merit in a picture than the more technical blasé reviews of professional critics," and that "your method of asking opinions from actual movie goers should certainly give us a truer insight on what the public wants."[65] Capra wrote personalized responses to much of the unsolicited mail he received about his films, and with the Kannapolis letters he made an effort to show that he had read the student letters and had given them careful consideration. But he also seems to have chosen to interpret the letters as constituting a kind of immediate, unmediated voice of a public unconcerned with the more intellectual and formal interests of bored, hard-to-please critics. In this case, Capra appears to have been mistaken, as these students' ideas were at least in part the product of a local, small-town application of a national movement to reshape adolescent movie fans into a vanguard of film experts determined to raise the level of the Hollywood product.

Constructing the Young Viewer

This model of a potential adolescent spectator works to complicate our understanding of the young viewer during the 1930s, or at least the manner in which a variety of experts came to understand that viewer. The most common and most cited construction of the child or teenager watching movies derived from the Payne Fund studies, a collection of works, indebted to modern social science and in particular to sociology, designed largely to gauge the effects of movies on kids. Kathryn Fuller, Ian Jarvie, and Garth Jowett have shown that the Payne Fund studies decidedly did not simply give a scientific imprimatur to antimovie hysteria; instead, Henry Forman's condensation of the studies, published as *Our Movie-Made Children*, did that job.[66] Nevertheless, the Payne Fund studies tended toward a notion of childhood and adolescent spectatorial passivity, of a mass audience that because of its immaturity could generate little resistance to that which they saw on the screen.

The Hollywood studios' self-regulating Production Code, the censorship document administered by the Hays Office and adopted in 1930, made many of the same assumptions about kids at the movies. In the "Reasons Supporting the Preamble of the Code," the document insisted on the special status and responsibility of movies, because of how they appealed to the "mature and the immature."[67] Particularly because of the latter—because of a large movie audience that, typically, did not frequent the serious, legitimate theater and might have its reading monitored by parents and teachers—the film industry had a special responsibility to police the content of its own films. Popular journalism, many church groups, and other institutions concerned with the well-being of young people echoed these sentiments and assumed that movies posed a kind of reflective danger to this audience. Put somewhat reductively, young people who witnessed criminal or sexual behavior in movies might well begin to engage in the same behavior themselves.

But there was at least one other view, and another construction of the youthful audience as an extremely active one. In fact, this audience consisted not of the "immature," as the Production Code would have it, but rather of incipient adults who, with the proper training, might make the same judgments as adults. Of course, these views were not mutually exclusive, and many held both at once, a belief in the dangers movies posed to children and adolescents and the potential of young viewers to have reasoned, mature, adult opinions about the films they saw. Still, less than half a century after the "discovery" of the adolescent mentioned above, and the understanding that children were different from teenagers and that both were absolutely different from adults, there also developed, in particular around motion pictures, the idea of the adult child and of a family made up of equal members—at least when it came to discussing leisure activity.

Capra's films from the mid-to-late 1930s—*Mr. Deeds Goes to Town* (1936), *Lost Horizon* (1937), and *You Can't Take It with You* (1938)—played a fundamental role in the discussions about these modern children and adolescents, the modern family, and the place of the filmgoing experience for all of them. The National Board of Review generated many of these discussions, while promoting and also designing the apparatus for an active and engaged youthful audience. But other sources, in particular certain aspects of both mass market and more specialized journalism, catered to a readership of enlightened adults, children, and adolescents. These sources, while typically concerned about the effects of movies, also viewed the motion picture industry as provoking important discussions about, for instance, politics and morality. The film experts considering these issues were almost all women, just as they often had been in the classroom, in keeping with a post–World War I tradition of white, middle-class female reformers.[68]

The National Board of Review, originally called the New York Board of Motion Picture Censorship, formed in 1909 as something of a reformist combination made up of a number of civic, religious, educational, and women's groups. The board, with the film industry's approval and co-operation, previewed films before they opened in order, in the words of Gregory D. Black, to "identify offending material, and 'suggest' cuts."[69] The board operated in this capacity for many years, including the period, the 1930s, under discussion here. As Garth Jowett has pointed out, the board had no direct authority to demand cuts, but producers apparently went along with its suggestions, at the very least to make it appear that they were interested in moral uplift and community standards, as well as to prevent attacks from institutions with more regulatory power (local, state, and federal governments, for instance). The board never officially affiliated itself with the industry, but it did depend on it for financial support, and, of course, this connection may have affected the manner in which board literature and activity imagined and constructed the movie audience.[70]

Like most groups concerned with film content, the National Board of Review took a special interest in children and adolescents. By the mid-1930s, and as something of a corollary to the film education movement, the board had established its Young Reviewers and 4-Star clubs, both nation-wide groups of children and adolescents between ages nine and seventeen, designed to encourage critical film viewing habits in a central audience for Hollywood movies. The exact extent of the clubs is difficult to determine, but typically during the period of one year between 350 and 400 members would cast votes for their ten favorite films of the year. Besides sponsor-ing these clubs, the board used its own council members as publicists for "clean" films and for the interests of young viewers. Later in this chapter, for instance, I examine an appearance by council secretary Bettina Gunczy to discuss "Children as Movie-Critics" on the radio program *Your Child*, broadcast in New York over station WNYC on 6 December 1939.

Far more so than radio, however, magazines and newspapers of varying circulations and interests, and with both disparate and overlapping audi-ences, were preoccupied with movies and children (as just one example among many, Henry Forman first published his condensation of the Payne Fund materials in *McCalls*).[71] *Parents* magazine, for instance, a mass market publication with a circulation of around 330,000 during the period, and which presented articles and advice seemingly designed for young, white, mildly affluent couples with small children, devoted a monthly column to rating movies and included a number of other essays about the media in general. Much more specifically, the monthly tabloid *The Motion Picture and the Family* provided articles precisely about the appropriate viewing practices of parents and children, and about furthering enlightened discussions between parents and children and teachers and students about movies they could see together. The exact provenance of the tabloid is difficult to determine, although the periodical itself advertised a connection to the Motion Picture Producers and Distributors Association of America which apparently helped in distribution. This link to the film industry's trade organization, or Hays Office, indicates that *The Motion Picture and the Family* was at least a small part of a public relations effort seeking to convince audiences that the studios were indeed concerned about film quality and uplift through movies.[72] Philosophically and methodologically, the newspaper also had a direct relationship to the film education movement, with the masthead announcing its "comment on current films by teachers, educators, [and] community leaders." Authors with bylines included many of the movement's major voices, and so beyond public relations *The Motion Picture and the Family* also seemed part of a sincere effort by teachers and other experts to improve the country's viewing habits and raise the quality of movies. Among the newspaper's main contributors, almost all of whom were women, Sarah McLean Mullen, author of "How to Judge Motion Pictures," wrote a regular column, "Films for the Pupil and Teacher," that made explicit the connection between tabloid and classroom.

Capra and High-Quality Entertainment

The materials from the National Board of Review, *Parents* magazine, and *The Motion Picture and the Family* all invoked Capra and his films as standards against which all of Hollywood's filmmakers and products could be measured. In so doing, they merely echoed a seemingly unanimous appraisal by educators, critics, and Hollywood itself. The student exercise in Edgar Dale's 1933 textbook, that of matching a movie to the photo of its director, made Capra stand out as one of many significant filmmakers. But by 1937, film educators included Capra's films in a select list of the absolute best the studios had to offer, a sign that sound films had come of age. Barret C. Kiesling, for example, in *Talking Pictures: How They Are Made, How to Appreciate Them*, lauded the sound film in general by pointing out some particular "accomplishments," and included Capra's *Mr. Deeds Goes to Town* among them.[73]

The film tells the story of Longfellow Deeds (played by Gary Cooper), who inherits twenty million dollars from an eccentric uncle and then moves from Mandrake Falls to New York City. Following a confrontation with a destitute farmer, Longfellow decides to give his money away to the country's needy, after which the lawyers for his uncle's estate have him brought to trial on an insanity charge. Deeds wins his case and triumphantly leaves the court, ready to marry Babe Bennett (Jean Arthur), the reporter who had been covering him since his arrival in New York.

Mr. Deeds is full of the hokum and homespun populism that many later critics would deride as "Capracorn." In spite of this, Kiesling places the film in some very high-toned company. In his list of significant movies from the sound period, Kiesling named films based on the works of Shakespeare (*A Midsummer Night's Dream* [Max Reinhardt, 1935], and *Romeo and Juliet* [George Cukor, 1936]) and Dickens (*David Copperfield* [Cukor, 1935]); films based on modern classic literature (*The Good Earth* [Sidney Franklin, 1937]); films about significant historical subjects (*The Private Life of Henry the Eighth* [Alexander Korda, 1933], *The House of Rothschild* [Alfred L. Werker, 1934], and *Rembrandt* [Korda, 1936]); and operetta films (*Naughty Marietta* [W. S. Van Dyke, 1935], with its score by Victor Herbert).[74] Only *Mr. Deeds* was derived from a virtually unknown source (a short story with a different title), taught no lessons about the great men of history, or made any claim to the (albeit limited) cultural cachet of a Jeannette MacDonald–Nelson Eddy light opera. Thus, Capra's contribution to the elevation of the sound film matched that of great playwrights and novelists, and his more or less original, contemporary stories merited the same attention as the great historical narratives.

The media apparatus of the motion picture industry also looked to Capra and *Mr. Deeds* as evidence of Hollywood's potential. In 1936, writing in the *Motion Picture Herald*, the trade journal that he edited, Terry Ramsaye, who was also one of the first serious historians of the American film industry, lamented that the "sex lure looms again," and continued that " 'The curse of Eve' lies heavily across movieland."[75] Ramsaye hyperventilated about this "curse" throughout his editorial, but he also pointed to *Mr. Deeds* as the kind of film that the American public really wanted to see, a film that "depicted wholesome American life." This is an interesting antifilm-industry discourse coming from a trade journal that itself was very much a part of that industry, and was read by people (primarily exhibitors) who worked in it. By Ramsaye's logic, the film industry gave the public precisely what it did not want except in very rare instances, as with the production of *Mr. Deeds*. After 1936, as I show in the next chapter with *Mr. Smith Goes to Washington*, Capra often came to be posited, frequently by members of the film industry, as the best Hollywood had to offer precisely because his films seemed antithetical to the typical Hollywood product. Here, in Ramsaye's editorial about a rebirth of Hollywood prurience, *Mr. Deeds* stood out not so much for greatness on a par with the major novelists, playwrights, and others mentioned in Kiesling's textbook, but instead as a perfect expression of a kind of American vernacular, and as a representation of national norms, desires, and characters.[76]

Ramsaye lauded *Mr. Deeds* for its unproblematically wholesome content. But for the Hollywood studios *Mr. Deeds* represented a kind of enlightened mode of production and exhibition that itself guaranteed quality and indicated an awareness of a discerning audience. Those industry practices from the 1930s that typically interest historians today — block booking, for instance, or self censorship, or a vertically integrated system of production, distribution, and exhibition — of course were of concern to film educators, parents' groups, and even politicians. But contemporary scholarship tends to have lost any sense of the fervor caused by double bills, which, as I mentioned above, came to be singled out by those in the film education movement as one of the primary evils of the film business. Possibly concerned about the perceived problem of showing two films back to back, the industry itself by the mid-1930s began its own anti–double bill discourse and, in moderation at least, production strategies that mitigated against the practice. Here, the measure of *Mr. Deeds*' greatness had less to do with its depiction of "wholesome American life" than with a mode of exhibition — that is, showing a single film rather than two.

The 11 April 1936 issue of the *Motion Picture Herald* ran a lengthy story on "The Case for and against Longer Feature Pictures," and reported that the best recent films, and those films currently in production that showed the most promise, were quite long, in some cases up to three hours (*The Great Ziegfeld*, for example).[77] In the story, producer Samuel Goldwyn claimed quite practically that "if the public will sit through two bad pictures that consume three hours of time, there is no reason why it shouldn't sit through one good picture that will run that length," and then pledged himself to making films that would exceed the "normal length." The story also quoted Joseph Bernhard, an executive for the Warners Bros. theater chain, as making an explicit connection between lengthier movies and the problem decried by film educators. Longer films, he said, "will eliminate one of the greatest evils of the entertainment world today — double feature bills."[78] Of course, movie executives like Bernhard were mostly thinking in terms of box office revenue, but his absolute condemnation of the "evils" of the double bill at least hints that the discourse of film reformers regarding the practice had entered into the industry's thinking about the best way of discussing the matter. To underscore the industry's commitment to getting rid of the practice, the *Herald* listed thirty recent, successful films of considerable length. Capra had directed three of them (*It Happened One Night*, *Broadway Bill*, and *Mr. Deeds Goes to Town*), a number greater than that of any other director (George Cukor, Sidney Franklin, Henry Hathaway, and DeMille had directed two each).[79]

Capra and his films thus became part of the proof of a kind of industry self-regulatory practice far less well known than the system of censorship administered by the Hays Office. In carrying out this practice, even though films designed specifically for double bills would continue to be produced in great numbers, the studios would see to it that they made enough films of such a length that they could only be shown alone, so as to blunt criticism of the more typical exhibition practice. As the article in the *Herald* pointed out, for the industry, running time in and of itself often signified "augmented prestige," a cachet more difficult for an eighty or ninety minute film to acquire.[80] Educators, on the other hand, looked for other qualities before anointing a given film. But by the late 1930s the film industry and film educators, so often at odds, agreed, although largely for different reasons, that Capra's films stood out as entertainment of the highest quality and as an extraordinary brand of filmmaking that the rest of the industry seldom could match.

Largely as a result, those organizations and media outlets catering to parents and committed to the general improvement of children and adolescents paid particular attention to Capra's films. In spite of a broad reception context in which those films signified quality, however, there remained at least some room for different interpretive strategies and different attitudes about the fitness of the films for all audiences. *Parents* magazine, for instance, in its July 1936 "Family Movie Guide" listing of abbreviated opinions about current releases, gave general praise to *Mr. Deeds Goes to Town*, calling it a "unique comedy" with "deep human interest." The appeal of that human interest, however, might only go so far. In the same issue, in a rating of the fitness of a number of films according to age group, the magazine found that *Mr. Deeds* would be excellent for adults and for those twelve to eighteen years old. It was given only a rating of "possible" for children eight to twelve years old.[81]

"Suppose You Had Twenty Million Dollars Dropped into Your Lap"

Just a few months later, in September, Agnes Benedict, one of *Parents'* film experts, discussed her views in an article titled "What's Ahead in the Movies."[82] Benedict praised the improvement in movies over the last few years, singling out the "screen versions of works by Shakespeare, Dickens, Tolstoy, Hugo, [and] O'Neill," and celebrating, as well, a new tendency on the part of the industry to "take chances" with such films as *The Informer* and *The Story of Louis Pasteur*. Then Benedict lauded the way in which "history is coming alive" with *The Private Life of Henry VIII* and the various biographical films starring George Arliss. In a final exultation of the new spirit in the film business, Benedict applauded the industry's apparent commitment to examining pressing contemporary problems by saying that "social propaganda films such as *I Am a Fugitive from a Chain Gang*, *Fury*, [and] *Black Fury* . . . are handling social problems in a more moving way, as well as more frankly and honestly."[83]

In keeping with the usual discourse from film reformers about the necessity for both enrichment and escapism, Benedict claimed that "certainly, no one would wish all films to be 'uplifting,' or even educational." To prove the point, she continued by stating, "a rousingly good comedy such as *Mr. Deeds Goes to Town*, such mysteries as the Charlie Chan series, thrilling travel pictures like *Fang and Claw*, certainly deserve all the popularity they have had with children and adults alike." This constitutes the precise opposite of much of the educational discourse about Capra. In Kiesling's formulation, *Mr. Deeds* stood out as a rough equivalent to film versions of Shakespeare or the works of the major novelists. For Benedict, *Mr. Deeds* represented the high end of what Hollywood had always done, that is, turn out matchless glossy entertainment. Along with praising *Mr. Deeds*, Charlie Chan, and *Fang and Claw*, she claimed that "the phenomenally successful musicals of Rogers and Astaire should have a niche all their own," and that "Walt Disney might be called the Hans Christian Andersen of pictures." In this widely circulated guide for parents, then, *Mr. Deeds* provided hope against the "over-sophisticated sex dramas and lurid crime dramas" that came in for special scorn from Benedict.[84] Finally, however, for the benefit of those parents and their concerns for the kinds of films their children saw, Benedict seemed determined to interpret *Mr. Deeds* not as a "social propaganda" film, despite its handling of questions of wealth and responsibility during the Depression. Instead, she grouped the film with the fairy tale fluff of Astaire and Rogers (whose own films were inferior to "the beautifully screened version of the immortal *Show Boat*"), and the cartoons of the heir to Andersen himself, Walt Disney.[85]

Clearly, as the examples from Kiesling and Mullen show, there existed no necessary consensus about the meaning and use of various productions of unquestioned quality. This made for a range of opinions about such films as *Mr. Deeds*, which, for Benedict, stood out as terrific fluff, while for those who might have shared most of her ideas and goals it emerged as an intensely political motion picture, intimately tied to the economic context of the Depression. *The Motion Picture and the Family* devoted at least two columns to Capra's film in spring 1936. In April, Sarah McLean Mullen, in her column "Films for the Pupil and Teacher," proposed to discuss "the noteworthy accomplishments of the directors" of recent significant motion pictures, and then proceeded to examine not only *Mr. Deeds* but also *Two in Revolt* (Glenn Tryon), *The Great Ziegfeld* (Robert Z. Leonard), and *These Three* (William Wyler). The analysis of the films tended toward the aesthetic: the "carefully photographed backgrounds" in *Two in Revolt*, the "prodigious number of persons, sets, and incidents" in the spectacular *Ziegfeld*, and the "fastidiously" told story of *These Three*. Capra, too, came in for praise for the "rich humor" of his film, and for its effective mixture of the "ludicrous and the pathetic." But Mullen ended her discussion of *Mr. Deeds* by calling it "a caustic commentary upon the foibles of mankind."[86]

Mullen's analysis provides a 1930s auteurist discourse that matches that of Edgar Dale in his textbook's discussion of the significance of the director (and his downplaying of the contributions of such performers as Shearer and Hayes). Like Dale, she stresses story construction and technique, but Mullen also clearly valued *Mr. Deeds* as something of a political and moral document about contemporary "foibles." Just as in her own work on film appreciation, then, which itself seemingly echoed the letters from the Kannapolis students, Mullen here saw social commentary as very much a part of a film's value and as very much a part of the director's, or at least Capra's, stock-in-trade.

The experts who wrote for *The Motion Picture and the Family* favored many of the same films as did Benedict: *Show Boat* and *Romeo and Juliet*, for instance, in addition to *Mr. Deeds*.[87] At least in terms of Capra, however, and unlike Ruth Benedict, the tabloid stressed the possibility, and even the educational benefits, of an overtly political reading of *Mr. Deeds*. In the May 1936 edition, Howard Le Sourd, dean of the Boston University

Graduate School, contributed an article titled "Lessons Learned from the Movies."[88] He began with a poem pointing out how "the horizons of young people are broadened by the movies," and then moved on to *Mr. Deeds*. "Suppose you had twenty million dollars dropped into your lap," he asked, "What would you do?" This sounds very much like an exercise being proposed for the classroom and addressed directly to students studying either film appreciation or the general effects of the Depression.

In summarizing the film, Le Sourd wrote that "the case against [Deeds] was based principally upon his plan to give his fortune away, for money-mad people always think that there is something radically wrong with one who is not in complete control of his generous impulses." The author went on to cite Deeds's well-known speech from his sanity trial, about cars that can go up a hill "lickety split" and those that "sputter and shake and slip back to the bottom," and about the necessity of helping those cars that "cannot make the hill." In commenting on this use of the automobile as metaphor for the problems of the Depression, Le Sourd concluded by saying, "This philosophy of Mr. Deeds', however, is not the philosophy of many of the so-called hard-headed business men of America," and then added that "the theory of these and other supporters of 'rugged individualism' is that the cars that cannot make the hill can lie at the foot and rot—there will be just that much less traffic ahead."[89]

This constitutes an extremely interesting political reading of the movie that is absolutely different from Benedict's insistence on the film's fluff. Le Sourd moves from using *Mr. Deeds* to ask a question about personal responsibility in the face of receiving a huge inheritance to adapting Capra's film to a progressive-era-style critique of modern capitalism, in which businessmen have only exacerbated the problems of the Depression. Implicitly, too, Le Sourd answers the question he posed at the beginning of his article, thereby using his essay about the film, rather than the film itself, to instruct students in proper behavior during periods of economic crisis. Naturally, if they inherited twenty million, in spite of pressure from "rugged individualists," they should act just as Deeds did and give much of the money away.

Through his editorializing about wealth, charity, and capital, Le Sourd seemed actively to be trying to produce a politicized reception for *Mr. Deeds* on the part of students and also those teachers who may be using the film in class. This matches the reception context that at least some aspects of the film industry attempted to create for the film. During the Jersey City run of *Mr. Deeds* in 1936, for example, the manager and publicist of the Stanley Theater cooperated with a local newspaper on a publicity stunt.

According to the *Motion Picture Herald*, a "photographer covered [the] streets stopping folks at random and distributing cards with space allotted to answer . . . [the] question, 'What would you do if you inherited 20 million dollars?'" In this stunt, those who devised the best answers had their pictures in the paper and also received free tickets, which was clearly intended to increase public awareness of and interest in Capra's film.[90] While its goal may have been different, the discourse of the stunt matched almost precisely that of Le Sourd, who posed the same question. As a result of gimmicks like the card distribution and of educational instruction like Le Sourd's, it might have become difficult to see *Mr. Deeds*, in spite of the best efforts of such experts as Benedict, without also asking oneself significant questions about wealth and responsibility during the Depression. In a rare instance, educational discourse matched industry ballyhoo to help construct *Mr. Deeds* for young people and adults as a significant social document that posed a question that, for Depression audiences, must have been a deeply charged one.

The National Board of Review and the Adult Child

This virtually identical usage by educators and publicists of *Mr. Deeds*— the same question being posed to students and to people on the street— indicates that at this time Capra's films might have been thought to break down any perceived differences between young audiences and older ones, and might even have been invoked to support the wisdom of the film industry's dominant production practice. During this period, and in the midst of significant debates about film censorship between the industry and a variety of organizations (church groups, educational groups, women's organizations, etc.), the motion picture industry opted for a code uniformly covering all of its films, in theory making every movie available and suitable to a mass audience. In opposition to much of the discourse of the film education movement, then, the industry decided not to separate its audience by age and make films that could only be seen, for instance, by children over twelve or by adults (a strategy that would be adopted in the 1960s and after, with such designations as GP, R, and NC17). The National Board of Review, perhaps because of its connection to the film business, or because of a particularly modern conception of children as fully rational citizens in an urban, technologized, consumer-driven democracy, directly supported the industry's approach, and at least tacitly confirmed the wisdom of asking kids and grownups the same question about *Mr. Deeds.*

In its announcement of the results of its nationwide 4-Star and Young Reviewer clubs voting on film preferences for 1936, the board applauded the independence of these youngsters between eight and seventeen from know-it-all adults. "Quite oblivious to the solicitations of older people who claim to know exactly what children should like in the way of movies," the board claimed, "the young people of America have just finished choosing the ten pictures they consider the best made in 1936." Then the board quickly did away with any audience divide based on age, with the choices representing "a highly critical attitude on the part of the younger generation to its motion picture entertainment, and in variety and intelligence of selection [ranking] very respectably with any similar list selected by adults." Following this assertion came the list of the voters' top-ten films: *The Great Ziegfeld* (Robert Z. Leonard), *Anthony Adverse* (Mervyn LeRoy), *San Francisco* (W. S. Van Dyke), *Romeo and Juliet* (George Cukor), *The Charge of the Light Brigade* (Michael Curtiz), *Mr. Deeds Goes to Town*, *The Story of Louis Pasteur* (William Dieterle), *The Devil Is a Sissy* (W. S. Van Dyke), *The Last of the Mohicans* (George B. Seitz), and *Mary of Scotland* (John Ford).[91]

After this cataloging of 4-Star and Young Reviewer preferences, the board engaged in more of the anti-industry discourse that seemed to mark much of the movie discussion produced by the industry itself, whether from Terry Ramsaye writing in a prominent trade journal, film exhibitors (as in the examination in the next chapter of the reception of *Mr. Smith Goes to Washington*), or, as in this case, the National Board of Review. Implying that the film industry had no understanding of the preferences and desires of the child audience, or even of the best ways to represent children, the board made much of the fact that "for the second year in succession, Shirley Temple is conspicuously absent from the 'best ten' list," and that so too were "all other cute kids, who usually annoy, rather than entertain, young audiences."[92] Further underscoring the apparent strangeness of members of the child audience—that is, their seeming refusal to act like children—the board then insisted that they had even more sense than adults in some instances, or at least than the women in the adult audience: "Love, as usual, took a pretty severe battering from youthful hands," the board noted, "and Robert Taylor, who set many a female heart a-beating during the past year, has not a single picture listed among the first twenty."[93]

Showing their eminent, mature good sense, the 4-Star and Young Re-

The National Board of Review
of Motion Pictures
ESTABLISHED BY THE PEOPLE'S INSTITUTE
70 FIFTH AVENUE
NEW YORK CITY, N. Y.
TELEPHONE ALGONQUIN 4-6344

*other copies in
4 Star Clubs Publication share*

Box 172

FOR IMMEDIATE RELEASE

Over 300 Boys and Girls Choose Their 10 Best Films of 1936

From as far West as California and as far South as Louisiana the Votes Come In

Quite oblivious to the solicitations of older people who claim to know exactly what children should like in the way of movies, the young people of America have just finished choosing the ten pictures they consider the best made in 1936. As gathered by the National Board of Review of Motion Pictures through its Young Reviewers and 4-Star Clubs, groups of boys and girls ranging in age from 8 to 17 years, the list represents a highly critical attitude on the part of the younger generation to its motion picture entertainment, and in variety and intelligence of selection ranks very respectably with any similar list selected by adults.

In their order of preference, the ten pictures are:

THE GREAT ZIEGFELD

ANTHONY ADVERSE

SAN FRANCISCO

ROMEO AND JULIET

THE CHARGE OF THE LIGHT BRIGADE

MR. DEEDS GOES TO TOWN

STORY OF LOUIS PASTEUR

THE DEVIL IS A SISSY

THE LAST OF THE MOHICANS

MARY OF SCOTLAND

Ranking just below the first ten and grouped closely together in votes are THE GREEN PASTURES, FURY, SWING TIME, RAMONA, MODERN TIMES, THE GENERAL DIED AT DAWN and TEXAS RANGERS.

For the second year in succession, Shirley Temple is conspicuously absent from

The National Board of Review announcing that its Young Reviewers and 4-Star clubs had chosen the ten best films of 1936. *Mr. Deeds Goes to Town* finished in sixth place.
(New York Public Library)

viewer audience only "found favor in [the] love scenes" in *Romeo and Juliet*, and these kids, though they "didn't expect to rush out and read Shakespeare avidly," still hoped "to see more of his works on the screen." The announcement continues as something of a scientific document, reporting on a dominant but previously completely misunderstood section of the audience. Implying the success of the antiracist mission of the film education movement, the board revealed that "one of the stranger results of the balloting was that in the small town of Welsh, Louisiana, *The Green Pastures*, which ranked eleventh nationally, was considered second only to *Romeo and Juliet*," in spite of the fact that the film featured "an all-Negro cast."[94] Thus the markers of the maturity of the child audience, and even, perhaps, its superiority to the adult audience, were the literariness of their preferences, their disdain for sugar-sweet child stars, their dislike of the mushiness so favored by female fans of Robert Taylor, and their rejection of racism in their judgments of film quality. Clearly, the logic of the announcement was twofold: first, adults needed to learn a great deal about the child audience; and second, adults indeed could learn a great deal from that audience.

There is a social science certainty to the pronouncements of the National Board of Review, in spite of the fact that the data had not been gathered scientifically. Among a variety of expert opinions about children and adolescents in the 1930s, however, many of them focusing on the seemingly new problem of young people as consumers on a massive scale, there is at least some support given to the notion of the child as a protogrownup, as capable of mature, rational choices and desires. These findings only truly become possible in the 1920s and 1930s, the first time that educational theorists turned their attention fully to child development rather than to the field of "educational hygiene," that is, improving the lighting in classrooms, making sure students had eyeglasses if they needed them, raising the quality of school nutrition, and getting rid of the drinking cup and hand towel that serviced all of the kids in a classroom.[95]

In 1939, with this new interest in the intellectual and emotional status of young people, Edna Bailey, Anita Laton, and Elizabeth Bishop, all professors of education or psychology, quantified with seemingly absolute precision the developments of children from two years of age to eighteen. They found that the "emotional life" of the teenager was "rich and varied," and that these same subjects had already reached an "adult level of intellectual abilities." Perhaps most significant, in terms of movie preferences, Bailey, Laton, and Bishop determined that these same young people were able to "establish their own moral codes and their own relation to the established order." Even much younger children, those between eight and twelve, were notable for their "elaborately organized" playgroups, complete with "rituals [and] pass words," and were also fully able to "apply . . . moral precepts."[96]

Of course, experts pointed out significant differences between young people and adults, and noted that even among children and adolescents, intellectual, emotional, and moral development varied dramatically. Experts during the period did tend to agree, however, on the previously unacknowledged complexity of young people and on the nuances of their thought processes and actions. Now aware of all of this, modern parents might change their relationships with their children, stressing equality rather than absolute difference. Agnes Benedict, for instance, who wrote so authoritatively about film for *Parents* magazine, also cowrote a book the title of which, *Your Best Friends are Your Children*, indicated the "adultness" of the child and the possibility for new, mature interactions between parents and children.[97]

These "friends" of their parents, these very modern children—or at least those who voted in the National Board of Review balloting—had a very special sense of the importance of *Mr. Deeds Goes to Town*. Of the ten films they preferred, five dealt with historical figures or subjects (*Ziegfeld*, *Light Brigade*, *Pasteur*, *San Francisco*, and *Mary of Scotland*); three came from major literary sources (*Adverse*, *Mohicans*, and *Romeo and Juliet*, and, additionally, in a blurring of the two categories, *The Charge of the Light Brigade*); and one dealt directly with a significant problem facing young people (*The Devil Is a Sissy*, about juvenile delinquency). These, of course, were always the favored categories of film reformers—history, literature, and contemporary dramas about major social problems. Only *Mr. Deeds*, a more or less original comedy-drama, stood out as something of a separate category—as, in fact, a Capra film—thereby signifying unproblematic and adult quality even though it could not be pigeonholed generically into one of the typically favored film groups.

Mr. Deeds appealed to all groups in the Young Reviewers and 4-Star clubs. Continuing to show a sort of scientific impulse, the announcement broke up the voting by age and gender, indicating the point at which, for the board at least, children turned into adolescents, with each needing to be measured as a separate audience. Boys between eight and thirteen liked Capra's film well enough, placing it tenth, but ultimately far preferred the crime and excitement of *The Devil Is a Sissy*, which they put in first place, while also valuing westerns (*Texas Rangers*) and sports films (*The Big Game*). Girls of the same age made *Mr. Deeds* the fourth best film of the year, while in general favoring musicals (*The Great Ziegfeld*, which they placed first, then *Show Boat* and *Swing Time*). Boys and girls between fourteen and seventeen showed the real maturity of the incipient adult, as these groups were the only ones to appreciate fully *Romeo and Juliet*, which placed first and third in each age group. These boys and girls were the most literary and historical of the bunch, with each enjoying, in addition to Shakespeare, *Anthony Adverse*, *The Charge of the Light Brigade*, and *The Story of Louis Pasteur*, with boys also favoring *The Last of the Mohicans* while the girls chose a film based on a recent literary achievement, *Dodsworth*. In spite of the presumed racial tolerance of the young viewer, only girls between fourteen and seventeen placed *Green Pastures*, with its "all-Negro cast," on their top-ten list (it finished eighth), while both teenage boys and girls named *Mr. Deeds* their seventh favorite film of the year.[98]

The following year, the boys and girls taking part in the balloting chose Capra's utopian fantasy, *Lost Horizon*, as the fourth best film of the year. In another display of adult literary taste, the voters chose films based either roughly or directly on significant novels or plays, or in one case the biography of a great writer, as their top six: *The Good Earth*, *Dead End*, *Captains Courageous*, *The Prisoner of Zenda*, and *The Life of Emile Zola*, in addition to Capra's adaptation of James Hilton's novel. Even more than the year before, the age and gender groups demonstrated a high degree of consensus in terms of favorite films, with the board's press release underscoring the maturity of the choices. "Past years have shown a close parallel between these young people's selections and the adult lists," the board claimed, alluding to a variety of ten-best lists made by critics, and then continued that "this year's choice would seem to uphold the Board's belief that children have as discriminating an attitude toward the motion picture as their elders."[99]

Because of its connection to the motion picture industry, the board had, of course, at least some vested interest in promoting a belief in the adult child, the better to counteract the various calls from different groups for stricter movie censorship in order to protect the young, unaware viewer. But other groups, unrelated to the industry, seemed at least somewhat to second the board's construction of the child and adolescent spectator, with *Lost Horizon* emerging as one of the test cases of a young audience's good judgment. In November 1938, for example, Joseph Mersand, director of the Institute of Adult Education in Brooklyn, wrote an article titled "Facts and Fiction about the Educational Values of the Cinema" for the *Educational Screen*. Mersand called for a much keener understanding of the young viewer on the part of educators, asking, "How many of us know the movies which our pupils see?" He then posed questions that scholars would do well to consider even now: "What do they think of [these movies]? Why do they see one movie rather than another? What do they think of double features?" As part of an attempt to answer these questions, Mersand reviewed the results of a project in which 173 students were asked to rate all of the films they saw in September and October 1937 (because of the "star" rating system used these results almost certainly came from the National Board of Review's 4-Star Clubs). Looking at the results, particularly at the students' praise for *Captains Courageous* and *Dead End*, Mersand claimed that "certainly, teachers need not be pessimistic about the tastes of their pupils when the majority prefer such pictures."[100]

Lost Horizon also performed remarkably well in this student poll, particularly considering that even though the film still played in some first-run theaters in fall 1937, it had premiered the previous February (*Dead End*, for instance, had opened in August, just in time for the two-month test). Of the 173 students involved in the project 27 saw *Lost Horizon* in either September or October, and 25 gave the film the highest possible rating of four stars (the other two students awarded it three stars). No film seen by more than two students could match this percentage. In contrast, 49 out of 69 students gave *Captains Courageous* four stars, while 55 out of 75 gave *Dead End* the highest rating. To the students in this control group of viewers, then, *Lost Horizon* more than any other film signified superior entertainment and helped provide the proof of Mersand's faith in young viewers.[101]

Professional educators who should have known better, like Mersand, displayed a scientific certainty in some very partial and highly suspect numbers. By believing the statistics about *Lost Horizon* and other films, Mersand and others developed not only a notion of the child viewer as incipient adult but also as superadult, at least if some equally unscientific though compelling theater manager reports are to be believed. In the "What the Picture Did for Me" column in the *Motion Picture Herald*, local exhibitors, typically of subsequent-run theaters, sent in their opinions about movies they had shown in order to act as guides to other theater managers who may have been considering booking certain films or devising specific advertising strategies. Of course, these opinions about films were never unanimous. But *Lost Horizon*, which proved to be a significant box office disappointment, generated criticism indicating that many adult viewers neither appreciated nor understood it.

From Conway, New Hampshire, for instance, an exhibitor wrote that the film would only "please the people who are fussy about their movie fare." From another New Hampshire theater, in Penacook, where "audience reaction was bad," the exhibitor claimed that Capra's film would "be best appreciated by the class trade." The manager at the Princess Theater in Lincoln, Kansas, called the movie "one of the biggest and best pictures that has ever come out of Hollywood," but warned, as well, that "the picture is not a small town picture," and so his business was "just fair." The theater manager at the Rialto in Paynesville, Minnesota, where business "was average," bluntly assessed his clientele by saying, "they couldn't make heads or tails of it," and that it was "just a little above the heads of the general run of patrons, as many asked me what it was all about." [102]

These adult audiences rejected *Lost Horizon*, and in each case the exhibitor insisted that the film only appealed to a specific type of person ("fussy"), a particular social stratum ("the class trade"), specific demographic areas ("not a small town picture") and precise intelligence levels ("just a little above the heads of the general run"). If this constituted the received opinion about the film, that its appeal was very partial and that this was comprehensible largely in social and economic terms, then we can begin to understand more about the construction, on the part of experts, of the child and adolescent audiences. Dr. Mersand, the members of the National Board of Review, and others used findings from a few hundred students about *Lost Horizon* and other pictures to depict a nationwide audience of youngsters as fully mature, urban, educated, and, at the very least, middle-class consumers, who appreciated the finer aspects of American culture far more fully than many of the adult bumpkins in the hinterlands. For many, then, in both education and the film industry, this "modern" child or adolescent clearly signaled a shift in American culture and demographics and pointed to a future dominated by a "class trade" of enlightened grownups.

This child would be the product of a combination of institutional forces. Will Hays, president of the Motion Picture Producers and Distributors Association (MPPDA), in a "state of the industry" message in 1936, proclaimed that films such as *Lost Horizon*, *Romeo and Juliet*, *Green Pastures*, and *Mary of Scotland* indicated continuing "upward trends in motion picture standards." [103] This certainly marked part of a continuing trend, throughout the 1930s, on the part of the motion picture industry to align its product with

New Research Exhibits Lend Added Interest To Film Study

The central panel for the exhibit on Columbia's "Lost Horizon," filmed from the Hilton novel.

Traveling exhibits of research stills to lend additional interest to the study of feature films have caught on. The popularity of the *Romeo and Juliet* exhibit has answered once and for all the question as to whether these exhibits are worthwhile adjuncts to film programs. Clubs, libraries and schools are clamoring for more of them. To meet the demand three additional exhibits have been assembled this month.

One of the most fascinating is the series of research panels on Warner Brothers' *Anthony Adverse*. With a rich field to draft on in the combined romance, travel and historical setting of the book, the exhibit-makers have made the most of their material. The panels take us from the slave quarters at Felicity Hall and the author's study through Anthony's devious wanderings to the day when he and his small son set sail for America. Particularly effective is the panel

(Continued on Page 5)

From *The Motion Picture and the Family*, news in 1936 of the "traveling exhibit of research stills" from *Lost Horizon* and other prominent films. (Margaret Herrick Library, Academy of Motion Picture Arts and Sciences)

canonical literature and cultural uplift in order to demonstrate that self-censorship worked perfectly to regulate the studios' product, with no requirement for any kind of local or national intervention. Indeed, as part of this program of improvement, the motion picture industry released "traveling exhibits of research stills" for clubs, libraries, and schools, so that children might learn more about the finer aspects of motion pictures.[104]

The Motion Picture and the Family considered this such an extraordinary development, that the tabloid published a front-page story about the exhibits, and for the accompanying photograph chose a still from *Lost Horizon* (one of the first four films chosen for exhibition) showing the hypermodernist architecture of Shangri-La. The *Lost Horizon* exhibit worked to guarantee the authenticity of the production, and also to introduce students to a sort of ethnography of the Orient. As *The Motion Picture and the Family* pointed out, "color plates of native Tibetan costumes, from which the artists and costume designers worked in costuming the film, are sure to be coveted by teachers and librarians everywhere for their permanent collections," while also adding that there were "many beautiful stills of scenes actually in the production."[105] Thus, the film *Lost Horizon* became not just the adaptation of a significant novel from the period but also an ethnographic document, one perfect for teaching students about the customs and costumes of an "exotic" locale.

Educational Uplift and Institutional Affiliations

In so extending the site where young people might encounter *Lost Horizon*, from the theater to the schoolroom, the motion picture industry, under the auspices of the MPPDA, markedly aligned itself with the country's educational institutions and underscored its concern with creating worldly, knowledgeable young people. Other educational settings also came to be connected with the movies, and, in fact, advertised their own wares as well as those of local theaters. In 1936, for instance, the Cleveland Library instituted its "Bookmarks of the Month" program, giving their patrons markers that promoted both education and commerce.[106] In October of that year the library highlighted four films from literary sources: *Ramona*, *Come and Get It*, *Dodsworth*, and *Lost Horizon*. In the case of Capra's film, as with the other movies, the bookmark first provided a summary ("Mysteriously abducted by aeroplane in India . . ."), and then suggested related reading materials ("The lure and mystery of the Orient recreated in these books . . ."). For *Lost Horizon* the library categorized this reading as "Mystic Tales of the East" (including Hilton's novel), "The Roof of the World" (oriental travel writing by Westerners), and "The Philosophy of the East" (again, books by Westerners). At the bottom of the bookmark came the commercial payoff: "Printed through the courtesy of the [name of theater] presenting *Lost Horizon*."

Here, then, the library and the motion picture industry, both often competing for the same young clientele (with the movies, of course, usually having the better of it), cooperated with each other on the one hand to promote "quality" reading, and on the other to develop a community's sense of a theater's good citizenship, commitment to a high-toned product, and concern with children's education. Just as in Kannapolis, with the fluidity between classroom, YMCA, and movie theater, here in Cleveland the young person would be confronted by sites in seeming contradiction—the library and the movie theater—that instead worked together for the ostensible benefit of children and adolescents. And, of course, the film education movement came to confirm all of these connections, extolling the manner in which important films could turn young viewers into more avid readers, and the ways in which those films themselves might teach those viewers important literary lessons (in the textbook *Film and School*, for example, Lewis and Rand single out *Lost Horizon* as an exemplary movie for studying proper story construction).[107]

Film historians have spent a great deal of time studying the vertical integration of the film industry during the classical period: the manner in which a few companies controlled film production, distribution, and exhibition. But the evidence from *It Happened One Night*, *Mr. Deeds Goes to Town*, and other Capra films demonstrates the importance of studying a sort of horizontal integration—that is, the connections between institutions bound by no formal corporate agreements. In this case, the film industry, education, and the library established a partnership in producing "quality" for a specific audience and distributing it to them (at various times religious institutions also took part in this relationship). In addition to film, another modern communications technology also came to be a part of this group: radio. Here too we may have to rethink our understanding of cooperation between industries. The film and radio businesses did, of course, cross-pollinate: by the late 1930s stars might go from one medium to the other, and even narratives "traveled" (Orson Welles, for instance, who himself would go from one medium to the other, produced radio versions of three Capra films—*It Happened One Night*, *Mr. Deeds Goes to Town*, and *Lost Horizon*).[108] But the two media also commented on each other, and this was particularly true in both network and local radio, which, as part of their presumed responsibility in public affairs and education, frequently aired programs about all manner of media; for instance, literature, music, and the movies.

On 6 December 1939 station WNYC in New York broadcast an installment of the *Your Child* series, covering the topic, "children as movie critics." The program, "intended to help parents and children work together toward the building of a better world," was sponsored by Youthbuilders, Inc., a club designed to encourage good citizenship in young people and one that seems to have been a New York rather than a national organization. This did not stop the club from some impressive claims, however, among them converting German-American children from Nazism to acceptable American values, and convincing some other local youngsters to give up their growing faith in communism. Elizabeth Seiferheld and Sabra Holbrook, the latter an adult leader of Youthbuilders, hosted the program, and their guest on 6 December was Bettina Gunczy, the council secretry of the National Board of Review of Motion Pictures.[109]

New York City owned and operated WNYC, and by the late 1930s a variety of city council members and borough presidents had lobbied, unsuccessfully, to have the station taken off the air for broadcasting "communistic propaganda," or for refusing to provide enough time for airing a "Sunday morning communion breakfast of the Police Department's Holy Name Society."[110] On the day of the *Your Child* broadcast, however, the station seemed to provide New Yorkers with fairly safe programming: a "sunrise symphony" at seven in the morning followed by more classical music, a late-morning discussion called "Turkey Faces West," afternoon music and educational programs, and then news before the station signed off at 5:30 in the evening. *Your Child* aired at 10 A.M.[111]

Like so much of the film education movement, this program, on which all of the participants spoke with authority (broadcast transcriptions have been preserved in the National Board of Review files), certified the manner in which expertise in the cinema had come to be feminized. In addition, as Michele Hilmes has shown, early programmers assumed (often incorrectly) that the audience for daytime radio was, primarily, made up of women.[112] This program, then, hosted by women, was designed for a New York audience of women, and more precisely, given the information and classical-music dominated programming on WNYC, a more or less middle-class, educated female audience.

For the women on this program, children, "with their fresh viewpoints, their way of bringing to everything a judgment uncolored by too much experience, or too many biases," actually were the ideal movie critics.[113] Indeed, according to Gunczy, children had become better movie critics than adults, because children concentrated on the "motion" in motion pictures and paid less attention to the dialogue. "This dislike for dialogue," according to Gunczy, "makes the children real motion picture critics."[114] And these critics, if left alone, would display extremely adult preferences. Gunczy commented on the 4-Star Club selections for 1938, among them Capra's *You Can't Take It with You* and also such serious films as *Marie Antoinette*, *The Citadel*, *Boystown*, and *Suez*, as well as such unarguably high-quality films as *Snow White*. "I'd like to point out to our audience," program host Seiferheld stated, "that this is quite a mature list, and a discriminating one too," with the real lesson being that "it is possible for parents to rely on their children's own sense of values far more than most parents suppose."[115]

These discriminating children, in their radio listening as well as in their movie viewing, preferred realism over "super-man" stuff, and they had learned their lessons about naturalness, in acting and also in dialogue and in setting, from a careful study of film in school. Gunczy advised that this very special, adult child might not necessarily be the average child but rather the one "who is probably studying motion pictures in his school English classes."[116] For this young but highly informed film critic, Capra's films held a special position as those that signified absolutely the highest quality. Gunczy indicated that these students paid more attention to film directing "than the majority of adults," and they were careful to watch for the "directorial touch."[117] As Gunczy recalled, in one questionnaire about preferences in movies, and demonstrating the acquired taste for the master director, one student claimed that "when Frank Capra makes a picture you feel that the people are natural, that you could be put in their place."[118]

Neither the guest nor the hosts of the program mentioned any other director. In citing the opinions of children, only Walt Disney came to be mentioned in terms approximating (or, actually, exceeding) those used for Capra, with one student, according to Gunczy, judging the cartoon producer "wonderful enough to rank among the great geniuses of all time."[119] Clearly, by the late 1930s, the filmmakers of quality, the ones who indicated the success of the film education movement and the potential of young people to make mature, informed judgments about their leisure activities, were Frank Capra and Walt Disney. The presumed female audience listening to *Your Child* could rest assured that despite the shortcomings of so much of the product from the film studios, their children, if given the proper guidance in school as well as in the home, would gravitate toward the best Hollywood had to offer, toward the producer of *Snow White*, and the director of *It Happened One Night*, *Mr. Deeds Goes to Town*, *Lost Horizon*, and *You Can't Take It with You*.

By the time of the radio program, however, the uses of Capra's films in schools, and the perception of Capra as an educational director whose films were perfectly suited to the needs of young people, had begun to shift. Within a few years, the place of Hollywood films in high schools appears to have changed, although, once again, precise information on curricula can be hard to come by. As the next chapter shows, Capra's films from the end of the decade and the beginning of the next—*Mr. Smith Goes to Wash-*

ington (1939) and *Meet John Doe* (1941)—certainly seemed to have special appeal to students. In a mark of a possible transition in schools, however, this appeal apparently derived only in part from film appreciation units, while also coming equally from lessons learned in classes in civics and history that had nothing to do with film. This may have had something to do with the subject matter of Capra's movies from the period just after *It Happened One Night* and before the entrance of the United States into World War II. Most of the films, including *Mr. Deeds Goes to Town* as well as *You Can't Take It with You*, *Mr. Smith*, and *John Doe*, can easily be interpreted as extended lessons in the promises and problems of American-style democracy and capitalism. Indeed, perhaps because the civics lesson elements of these films were so overdetermined, a broad national audience made up of all age groups viewed these films as both entertaining and educational. If anything, then, the perception of Capra-as-pedagogue had only grown. High schools may have been teaching fewer class units in film appreciation, but now Capra's films seemed perfectly suited to the educational needs of a national audience of children, adolescents, and adults.

At the same time as this apparent expansion of Capra's role in education, the possibilities for studying films in schools appear to have contracted. The early-to-mid 1930s boomlet in film education textbooks was over by the end of the decade, indicating, perhaps, that the Hollywood film had lost some of its significance in the curriculum. In addition, progressive education itself, which included at least some aspects of the film education movement but which had never become nearly as widespread as John Dewey and other adherents had hoped, no longer seemed capable of transforming American education. In part, progressivism met its match in the education for victory programs of the World War II era, with American education changing dramatically in 1942 as a result of the United States entering the war and the subsequent lowering of the draft age.

As Richard M. Ugland has explained: "Government estimates [from this period] forecast that 80 percent of the nation's 1,300,000 high school boys between 16 and 18 would enter the armed forces shortly after graduation," while many of the remaining 20 percent, as well as a significant number of recently graduated girls, would enter war-related industrial work or obtain "essential community occupations." [120] To prepare for such activity, many government officials and school administrators understood that students would need a different kind of education. As a result, the federal government established the "High School Victory Corps" in order "to encourage and coordinate preinduction training for students in the high schools" and to spearhead the schools' response to the national emergency of wartime.[121] The corps had land, sea, air, production, and community service divisions (the latter mostly for girls), and in order to become members of the corps, students "had to participate in a physical fitness program, study subjects useful to the war effort and be active in at least one wartime service activity such as farm labor, salvage, or child care." By July, 1943, around 70 percent of the country's high schools had adopted the program.[122]

Such a Victory Corps program would seem to leave little room for units in film appreciation, in particular given the antiwar stance of so much of the film education movement. If, however, after 1942 Hollywood films no longer were used in the classroom nearly as much as just a few years before, Capra's role as a film educator continued to increase. In the same year as the introduction of the Victory Corps in high schools, Capra officially became one of the principal "teachers" of millions of men beyond high school age—wartime inductees—when he began production for the Army Signal Corps of the *Why We Fight* and *Know Your Ally* films, which sought to educate viewers about the enemies facing the United States and the reasons for going to war against them, as well as about the fighting forces that were going into combat on the side of the United States. In addition to the average age of this new student audience being different from the one that analyzed Capra's films in the 1930s, so too was its gender, as it remains unclear just how many women involved in the war effort saw the Signal Corps documentaries. In a number of ways, though—and this would have horrified many of the educational reformers and film appreciation teachers from the 1930s who hoped to use the cinema to promote a national antiwar movement—the foundation for this wartime use of cinema was built a decade before, when Capra's films first played a significant role in teaching students to understand film as something other than mindless, unproductive entertainment.

Chapter Four

This Business of America: Mr. Smith,

John Doe, and the Politicized Viewer

In defending his 1987 nomination of Robert Bork to the Supreme Court, Ronald Reagan invoked another battle against all odds: "You may remember," his speech ran, "in the movie *Mr. Smith Goes to Washington*, when Jimmy Stewart stands in the well of the Senate and says that lost causes are 'the only causes worth fighting for . . . I'm going to stay right here and fight for this lost cause even if this room . . . is filled with lies.'" Casting himself in Stewart's role, Reagan then asserted, "So will I." Five years later, discussing a politician who himself seemed to be playing a role popularized by Reagan, the *Wall Street Journal* likened presidential candidate Ross Perot to "Jimmy Stewart in *Mr. Smith Goes to Washington*, the pure idealist who triumphs over corrupt insiders." One year after this, in the Los Angeles mayoral race, candidate (and eventual victor) Richard Riordan used his campaign material to characterize his position in the contest "as the Southern California equivalent of *Mr. Smith Goes to Washington*."[1]

Half a century after its 1939 release, then, Frank Capra's film had become a cinematic allusion par excellence in both local and national politics. The story of the ultimate political outsider served as the inspiration for a phenomenally popular president, for one of the richest men in the country, and for a lawyer/investor with a fortune of one hundred million dollars.[2] In other words, in this 1980s and 1990s incarnation, Capra's film would be appropriated by powerful mainstream politicians seeking to make voters believe that they were, in reality, virtuous but defenseless Don Quixotes jousting at monolithic institutional windmills.

My point here is not to argue with this use of *Mr. Smith*; rather, what I find interesting is the absolutely unproblematic interpretation of the film. This same reading is echoed in numerous movie reviews that use Capra as a kind of shorthand to indicate either the strength or deficiencies of a current film, or in newspaper arts-page features that discuss Capra's films, Jimmy Stewart's acting style, and Norman Rockwell's paintings as a sort of 1930s American school of representation. In each case, the film becomes an eloquent if somewhat utopian assertion of universally recognized and understood democratic values.[3]

When the film first appeared in 1939 this was hardly the case. In fact, perhaps more than any other Hollywood film from the period, *Mr. Smith Goes to Washington* had a deeply charged history in terms of how a variety of audiences interpreted it and also appropriated it. Few other films so interested the federal government. As much as any other movie, *Mr. Smith* had a place in debates about junior high and high school curricula. The subject matter of very few Hollywood products so tied into a growing national awareness of the links between history and representation—in this case because this story of the proper exercise of government appeared during an era of major public displays of patriotism and the value of American-style democracy, such as the 1937–1939 celebration of the 150th anniversary of the ratification of the Constitution. During a period when even Eleanor Roosevelt entered the debate over the propriety of playing "The Star-Spangled Banner" at movie screenings, *Mr. Smith* helped define the changing relationship between theaters and the filmgoers who went to them.[4] Finally, to my knowledge, no film from the period elicited anything near the response from motion picture exhibitors themselves when it came to describing audience reaction.

In this chapter I want to study the very charged reception of *Mr. Smith* and of Capra's next film, *Meet John Doe*. In each case there is evidence that, at least during certain periods, the cinema came to be seen both by "average" viewers and by some who were not so average (theater managers and government officials, for instance) as contributing directly to regional, national, or international discussions about political issues. For *John Doe*, my primary material is the fan mail that Capra received right after the opening of the film. For *Mr. Smith*, the primary evidence comes from a variety of industrial, educational, and governmental sources that cover two reception phases: the film's initial domestic release and then its distribution overseas.

When *Mr. Smith Goes to Washington* was released during the fall and winter of 1939–1940, the trade journal *Motion Picture Herald* provided at least a cautious guide to domestic audience response. Every week, the *Herald* ran a column called "What the Picture Did for Me." There, exhibitors would write in and say how their clientele responded to movies. This column was meant as a guide for exhibitors on how to advertise films and what kind of business to expect, and so the demographic information was fairly precise. The column provided the location of the theater and the kind of audience that came to it. Race did not seem to register as a category, but profession often was explicitly stated, and class and ethnicity typically were strongly implied or occasionally clearly expressed (an audience might be listed as "general," "rural," "mining," or "prisoners," for instance). As Kathryn Fuller has explained, we can get something of a regional, small-town sense of a film's reception from these columns. Fuller has written that "the overwhelming majority of contributors to the column were independent movie theater owners who operated 200–500 seat houses in towns of 5,000 or fewer people." In terms of location, most of the correspondents wrote from "the Midwest, Plains and Mountain states, and others were from the Mid-South and northern New England, but very few were from the populous East Coast."[5] Typically, descriptions of audience response might run seventy-five to one hundred words. It is a mark of the special reaction to *Mr. Smith* that many of the entries, sent in by pretty hard-boiled industry types, run several hundred words. As I explained in chapter 1, the *Herald* also offered detailed reports on film ballyhoo, helping us to understand the gimmicks that familiarized people with movies before they saw them.

Coinciding with the 1939 release of the film, Educational and Recreational Guides, Inc., published an edition of *Photoplay Studies* on *Mr. Smith*.[6] These studies were designed for use in junior high and high school film appreciation classes and came out regularly, typically covering films based on classic literature or detailing a particularly significant historical period (to my knowledge, the guide to *Mr. Smith* stands out as the only one of its kind; based neither on a famous literary source, nor a momentous event, nor the life of a well-known individual). Officially "recommended by the Motion-Picture Committee of the Department of Secondary Teachers of the National Educational Association," these guides functioned in several ways in relation to reception and its regulation. They helped certify the educational value of a film at a time when, as I mention in chapter 3, many high schools were teaching motion picture courses or film units in other courses. In addition, the guides worked to equate film study with aesthetic enjoyment; as the masthead states, the publication was intended as "a magazine devoted to photoplay appreciation." By so stressing issues of cinematic form and quality, the guides also sought to assure a reading of

Mr. Smith on the part of students that made a critique of political systems far less important than narrative plausibility or character motivation.

State Department documents from 1940 and 1941 that deal with the overseas exhibition of *Mr. Smith Goes to Washington* indicate how a group of government bureaucrats viewed the film. These documents also show how those same bureaucrats imagined that a foreign, perhaps anti–United States audience might receive the film, and then how department officials debated the possibilities for controlling this reception.[7] Indeed, State Department papers point out the perceived problems involved in showing Capra's film to this arguably mythological and almost completely hostile foreign audience. Probably only one other film from the period just after the beginning of the war in Europe but still prior to U.S. involvement generated as much governmental concern—Charles Chaplin's *The Great Dictator*, from 1940.

"I Am Filled with Song and Tears"

Some of our most detailed indications of audience response appear in the "What the Picture Did for Me" column in the *Motion Picture Herald*. According to that column, one of the standard responses to *Mr. Smith* was that of having a transcendental experience, of having life in the United States explained. A theater manager in Waldoboro, Maine, showing movies to a general audience, wrote: "I have just seen one of the greatest emotion [*sic*] pictures of my life . . . I am filled with song and tears and I am sitting on a mountain peak watching a new sun rising over this land . . . with a new insight on kindness, greatness—a new realization of the meaning of truth and freedom." Similarly, from a theater in Newark, Ohio, catering once again to a general audience, the exhibitor implied that audiences were already tired of the kind of superpatriotic spectacle that we associate with the war years and often assume that audiences were eager to watch. *Mr. Smith*, he wrote, "sells more sermon-pure Americanism the hard way than all the star-spangled purpose pictures of the period have managed to instill," and he added that "the picture will bring to your patrons a spirit of patriotism they never thought they would ever have."[8]

This constitutes an extraordinary discussion of how theater managers and their clientele viewed the film. Further, this sense of being a spectator in front of "history" and "patriotism" had, by the time of *Mr. Smith*, become an especially important aspect of both American citizenship and participation in all manner of cultural activity. For at least a seventy-five-year period

MR. SMITH GOES TO WASHINGTON: James
Stewart, Jean Arthur, Edward Arnold, Claude Rains,
Guy Kibbee, Eugene Pallette, Beulah Bondi, Ruth
Donnelly—I have just seen one of the greatest emotion
pictures of my life. It is a film called "Mr. Smith
Goes to Washington." I am filled with song and
tears and I am sitting on a mountain peak watching a
new run rising over this land, States with a new insight on kindness, greatness—a new realization of
the meaning of truth and freedom. For once, and it
is a rare occasion indeed, I am proud to be connected
with the cinema industry; thankful of the privilege to
be one of that army of theatre managers whose duty
it now is to make certain that every citizen in his
community is on hand when "Mr. Smith" comes to
town. My one regret at this moment is that a lack of
foresight and of faith—however excusable because of
Hollywood's notoriously high percentage of disappoint-
ments—caused critics of motion pictures to exhaust
all of the superlatives in our language, so that when
a truly great film arrives, sincere praise cannot be
properly bestowed.
The tears were in my eyes when the picture closed,
and, all during, the power of the production caused
the back of my neck to crawl. I am just as tough as
any of you, possibly as sophisticated. Perhaps it is all
done mechanically out there in Hollywood; perhaps
you will cross this off as another rave and start lick-
ing your fat thumbs to count dollar bills, but some day
you will wander in and see it and if it doesn't get you,
doesn't make you all Stars and Stripes Forever inside,
it is not because you are "superior" and British, or
heartless and Nazi; it is because you are stupid and
lost.
"Mr. Smith Goes to Washington" should be shown
to every member of the Senate and Congress, and if
the outcome of this exhibition were a law making
it compulsory for every citizen of the U. S. to see it,
then I should be satisfied—even if an extra 10 per cent
of the gross were exacted by the Government to go
toward supporting not only those nearsighted men of
movies who continue to feel the public must be treated
as though possessing their own ignorance, but also
those who, failures and in poverty, have attempted
poison the roots of our democracy. Played October
20-5.—C. T. Cooney, Jr., Waldo Theatre Corp., Waldoboro, Maine. General patronage.

"I am filled with song and tears." An exhibitor reports on *Mr. Smith
Goes to Washington* in the *Motion Picture Herald*, 4 November 1939.

before Capra's film, as John Bodnar has shown, public memory (that is,
commemorative and patriotic activity) had become increasingly nationalized and increasingly tied to strategies of representation. At least since the
end of the Civil War, expanding business interests in conjunction with the
government made cultural production the "natural" place to depict the nation's history, to explain its government, and to promote unproblematic
loyalty to its institutions. Thus was created an official culture that could be
shared by all Americans despite deep ethnic, regional, racial, religious, and
class differences.[9]

Among other evidence of the construction of history and patriotism in such a way as to support a corporate and governmental status quo, Bodnar cites the national monuments built in the 1890s to celebrate Civil War soldiers; the emergence of Abraham Lincoln as a symbol of the country's unity during the same period; and also the various celebrations in 1892 of Columbus's landing, celebrations that tended to be organized by businessmen and civic leaders and that stressed the connections between the quadricentennial, military readiness, and social order. Many of these late-nineteenth-century spectacles, however, were as much a tribute to technological progress as to the possibilities for a national culture and shared national history. By the early twentieth century, particularly during World War I, there was a shift to an official culture that sought to construct consensus in the service primarily of democratic forms, with technology taking a decidedly secondary role.[10] Throughout this period, the central theme of American history, as conceived by parades, Fourth-of-July celebrations, Civil War commemorations, and other city, state, and countrywide festivities, was the evolution of a unified nation rather than the development of competing local interests.

Concentrating specifically on the 1930s, Warren Susman has analyzed the construction of a national symbolism aided and abetted by massive technological and communication systems, and with dominant notions of history and patriotism now extending from national monuments and public parks to such everyday entertainments as movies and radio shows.[11] For Susman, the New Deal achieved its success largely from the manipulation of a nationalized signifying practice that dominated not just government documents and activities but popular culture as well: for instance, the National Recovery Administration eagle, reproduced in the credits of so many movies, functioned as a symbol of restored economic stability, and President Roosevelt's fireside chats, broadcast over national radio networks, created a kind of national living room. Thus, Bodnar and Susman both suggest that by the late 1930s, largely because of the convergence of ideological concern and technological possibility, issues relating to citizenship, history, and the country's system of government had consolidated themselves around issues of representation, issues that exhibitors expressed in their commentary on *Mr. Smith Goes to Washington* and that also marked numerous forms of public display, leisure activity, and popular entertainment.

The 150th anniversary celebration of the ratification of the Constitution, for example, held between 1937 and 1939, undoubtedly helped people equate momentous historical events with parades and ceremonial paintings and even with postage stamps, as the commemorative imprintings of a number of countries made for frequent news items. Indicating a fully modern mobilization of mass media, advertising, technology, government purpose, and corporate enthusiasm, these celebrations maintained high visibility and effectively reached millions of people in department stores, schools, museums, and other public gathering places (in contrast, the centennial celebration of 1887 to 1889 had been a bust).[12] The 1939 New York World's Fair performed much the same function of using representational practice to create an official history shared by all citizens by featuring gigantic statues of great Americans like George Washington and regularly screening the film industry's contribution to the fair—Cecil B. DeMille's pastiche of great moments from the country's past, *Land of Liberty*.[13]

In keeping with those efforts described by Susman to sell the New Deal to the American public, the federal government added to this notion of legitimation through representation by finalizing its plans for the mall in Washington, D.C., with the construction of the Jefferson Memorial. So important had this project become to arbiters of American culture that in 1939 a work stoppage at the memorial turned into a major news story, with journalists worrying over the prospect of an unfinished representation of the third president.[14] Along with the government, most branches of the entertainment industry also engaged in the conflation of culture, democracy, and history. They did so in part because the public often indicated that it could not get enough of this sort of media edification and uplift, at least when the effort seemed serious and sincere, rather than the kind of mindlessly "star-spangled" spectacle that the Newark exhibitor dismissed as tiresome and ineffective. Of course, Kate Smith's radio program was extremely popular. But also, when CBS radio on its aptly named *Pursuit of Happiness* program broadcast Paul Robeson's version of "A Ballad of All Americans," a folk epic quoting liberally from the Gettysburg Address and the Declaration of Independence, *Newsweek* reported that "the results were startling. The demonstration in the studio continued for twenty minutes . . . switchboards . . . were deluged with calls; letters poured in."[15]

Finally, merging modern technology and a kind of representational mania, Mount Rushmore neared completion during this period with the unveiling in summer 1939 of the fourth and final presidential head, that of Theodore Roosevelt. This unveiling turned Mount Rushmore into an icon that contained all of American history, as *Newsweek* reported that "Indians performed a pageant depicting the white man's arrival in the Northwest, and Rough Riders who served with Theodore Roosevelt looked on."

In addition, the monument itself served to negotiate both modernity and the ancient, with the magazine measuring the mountain sculptures against the Capitol dome as well as the Egyptian Sphinx.[16] Thus Mount Rushmore typified a 1930s cultural and political context in which it seemed that democracy could in fact be depicted and that representational practice might not simply signify the historical but actually present it, virtually unmediated, to the public.

One motion picture exhibitor, showing films to a general patronage, typified this slippage between the monumental, the historical, and the real and the importance of how all of this got represented, and he did so while providing his fellow managers with advice on how to sell the patriotism in *Mr. Smith*: "The Lincoln Memorial scenes alone will sell more America to them than any book or story ever published . . . The crackpots with a torch to burn may have the situation a little foggy, and to offset that just exploit [the film] as though it were [an] actual dramatization of the Declaration of Independence itself."[17] The film, then, practically became an actual historical artifact, providing a representation of the signing of one of the sacred documents of the United States.

Some exhibitors did indeed promote this angle in their ballyhoo for Capra's film.[18] The manager of a theater in Buffalo, "tying in with the local election . . . built an election booth, ballot boxes, etc., for his lobby display" for *Mr. Smith*. "Standings of local candidates were changed daily on the blackboard," and the display "also consisted of [a] regulation voting machine which was loaned by [the] local election board for the occasion." Similarly, for a Chicago showing, "campaign headquarters were set up" advertising the film, with a banner proclaiming: "The people's choice—put Smith in Washington for life!" For another Chicago showing, an exhibitor distributed *Mr. Smith* "business cards . . . with [a] handwritten message on the back reading 'Sorry you were out when I called. Just wanted to say Goodbye before going to Washington, but you can see me at the Avalon [Theater]."[19]

Through this brand of advertising, theaters stressed the realism of the film, with Jeff Smith himself passing out business cards; with campaign headquarters being established; and with a blurring of the electioneering in the film and in local neighborhoods. As a result, before ever seeing the film, audiences might be prone not so much to believe unproblematically that which they would see on screen but to view the film as signifying the real, both in terms of a fictional character seeming like an actual one and the film itself embodying the prized values of democracy: the right to vote and to have one's opinion count. By serving as a message board about local elections or by simply implying the importance of voting through the establishment of campaign headquarters, these theaters established their own civic spirit and their importance to the community.

Thus the entire viewing context for *Mr. Smith*—including advertising gimmicks and lobby displays—worked to create a specific kind of relationship between the spectator and both the film and the theater, a relationship that assisted in the legitimation of a national culture of patriotism. Typically, film studies has resisted analyzing the kind of spectatorship that extends well beyond the time spent viewing a film. Simultaneous to helping construct a reading of the film, the advertising campaigns for *Mr. Smith* worked to create a response to the very act of going to the movies. Through advertising, the theater came to be equated with yet another private space where people could feel themselves to be both part of a greater community and also alone—the voting booth. The viewing context for *Mr. Smith* helped to establish a kind of democratic relationship between viewer and film in which watching the movie became the equivalent of exercising the rights of citizenship.

Several managers, marveling at the apparent universal appeal of the film, used variations of such stock phrases as *Mr. Smith* "will click with the masses 100 percent" and do great business in the smallest town or the biggest city. One theater manager, writing from Canada, also stressed the special class appeal of the film, saying that business was "big" and that this fact was especially telling because his theater was "strictly a class house." These comments stand out as unusual in audience reports from the period. Throughout the decade, many managers emphasized the splits between small-town and big-city entertainments, as well as high-class and working-class films.[20] Many of these same reports also stressed Capra's skills as an artist: "Here is proven that the director is the picture," for instance, or "How can you beat that Capra? If there is anyone I would like to meet and talk to in Hollywood, it is Frank Capra!"[21] At this stage in his career, a little more than a year after *Time* magazine certified his celebrity by featuring him on the cover of the issue from 8 August 1938, Capra was being perceived as someone who spoke for the people (indeed, as someone a viewer might "like to meet" and "talk to"). His work seemed to transcend class and regional differences and to create consensus (a trait he shared with very few other filmmakers from this period, perhaps only with Walt Disney).

These reports from exhibitors give a clear indication that audiences wanted more motion pictures like *Mr. Smith* but also that they certainly did not expect them, primarily because of the motion picture industry itself. Despite the triumph of the nationalized representational practices described by both Bodnar and Susman and manipulated by business and government interests, Capra's film shows how the conflation of popular culture, history, and patriotism could in fact mobilize audiences to voice displeasure with corporate and elected leaders. For many viewers, *Mr. Smith* emerged not as a triumph for the film business but as a triumph in spite of it. One exhibitor wrote: "For once, and it is a rare occasion indeed, I am proud to be connected with the cinema industry; thankful of the privilege to be one of that army of theater managers whose duty it now is to make certain that every citizen in his community is on hand when *Mr. Smith* comes to town." [22]

Thus the reception of the film points out the manner in which low-level members of the industry—exhibitors—and probably many audiences, too, felt deeply dissatisfied with the industry. This dissatisfaction was different from the one historians associate with perhaps the dominant antimovie movement of the 1930s, that of the Catholic Legion of Decency, and fueled by such studies as those commissioned by the Payne Fund. [23] This 1939-style sensibility about the cinema had nothing to do with the perceived licentiousness of movies or with their deleterious effects on children. Rather, it implied that the film industry should play a role as liaison between citizens and government and had been derelict in its civic duty to the American public. But the attitude toward *Mr. Smith* also shows the level to which many members of the industry sought to mobilize around products they believed in, to the extent that they could consider themselves a kind of people's "army," in the exhibitor's words, bringing light to the masses. Capra's film, which itself typified the manner in which issues of government and of representation merged, also became a symbolic call to arms, demonstrating the possibilities during the period for a kind of evangelical merging of governmental purpose and industrial practice.

Just as the reception of *Mr. Smith* evidenced unhappiness with what the film industry had become, so too did it show dissatisfaction with what the federal government had turned into. Responses also indicated how representational issues seemed to crystalize, for the audience, their own uneasy relations with their national leaders. One exhibitor praised Jimmy Stewart for "pitching *Mr. Smith* down the throats of frantic Washington." Another lumped Washington, the film industry, and the rest of the media together as

FIFTEEN CENTS   August 8, 1938

TIME

The Weekly Newsmagazine

Color photograph for Time by Paul Dorsey

Volume XXXII	DIRECTOR FRANK CAPRA	Number 6
	His stories cannot match his story.	
	(See Cinema)	

Circulation Office: 330 East 22nd Street, Chicago.   (Reg. U. S. Pat. Off.)   Editorial and Advertising Offices: Time & Life Building, Rockefeller Center, New York, N. Y.

Capra on the cover of *Time* magazine, 8 August 1938, one of the surest
indications of the director's celebrity. The pipe, woolen plaid jacket, and
vest indicate a professorial seriousness and intellect, but the partially open
script is the sign of the hardworking Hollywood professional. The caption
offers a hint of an extraordinary life: "His stories cannot match his story."

the combined enemy of the people: "*Mr. Smith Goes to Washington* should
be shown to every member of the Senate and Congress," and there should
be a law making it "compulsory" viewing for every citizen, "even if an extra
10 percent of the gross were exacted by the Government to go toward supporting not only those nearsighted men of movies who continue to feel the
public must be treated as though possessing their own ignorance, but also
those who . . . have attempted to poison the roots of our democracy."[24]
He added that no one saw any insult to the United States in this film until
newspapers started complaining about it (he referred here to newspaper
criticism of the representation of journalists in the film and to coverage of
the Senate's own disapprobation after a special screening).[25] So even within
the industry itself there existed a sense of a conspiracy of which movies

and the other mass media were all a part, with *Mr. Smith* standing out as something of a miracle, as that which got made in spite of a governmental/media monolith that opposed the common person.

Education for Democracy

Besides the hyperbole of proposing laws to make the film compulsory viewing, exhibitors made some very practical suggestions for ensuring the largest audience possible for *Mr. Smith*. One exhibitor wrote: "Play it and plug it 100 per cent over your usual budget. It will come back with interest. Your school teachers will send their pupils for one of the greatest lessons in the 'American Way of Thinking' they will ever get anywhere." Similarly, the review of the film in the *Motion Picture Herald* stressed the educational value of *Mr. Smith*, turning the film into an exhibitor's dream come true because of how it functioned as "a spectacle, a lesson and an entertainment" all at the same time.[26] Throughout this period, exhibitors typically tried to tie motion pictures into educational concerns, but the connection rarely seemed as self-evident as it did with *Mr. Smith*, and the exhibitors' conviction rarely so heartfelt.

By asserting the educational value of Capra's film, exhibitors were in fact entering a much larger debate about the practicality and efficacy of teaching democratic values to adolescents and children. Between August 1939 and January 1940, the national media made significant news stories out of Columbia University's Congress on Education for Democracy; a highbrow journal's special issue on "the challenge of democracy to education"; the White House Conference on Children in a Democracy; and the potential of the National Council for the Social Studies to devise a method of building better citizens through education.[27] In addition, just as the media during this period became a site for depicting democracy, so too were they expected not simply to entertain the masses but to educate them as well, frequently about issues of perceived particular importance to Americans. In 1939, for instance, both the CBS and NBC radio networks began ambitious art appreciation programs, *What's Art to Me?* and *Art for Your Sake*. A program on the NBC Blue Network, *America's Town Meeting of the Air*, regularly broadcast programs around such special issues as "How Can We Defend Democracy in America Now?" while composer and public intellectual Deems Taylor broadcast a weekly NBC program, *Musical Americana*, which *Newsweek* said "flourishes a frank bias in favor of musical nationalism."[28]

In the late 1930s, specialized journals aimed at educators engaged in a serious discussion of the possibility of teaching democratic values to young children. Articles such as "Educational Planning in a Democracy," "Education for Democracy," "The Unique Function of Education in American Democracy," and "Propaganda, Democracy and Education" generally supported the notion of education-as-indoctrination with regard to American values, and even President Roosevelt weighed in on the issue. In an address to the National Education Association in 1938, he said that "for many years I, like you, have been a pedagogue, striving to inculcate in the youth of America a greater knowledge of and interest in the problems which, with such force, strike the whole world in the face to-day."[29] Certainly the exhibitors who stressed the educational value of *Mr. Smith*, in particular its lessons for youngsters in "The American Way of Thinking," were interested in the box-office possibilities of selling the film to students. But they participated in a project that could seemingly be shared by all Americans and by all forms of cultural production. All adults, from film exhibitors to presidents, had a responsibility to instruct kids in the marvel of democracy, and all popular culture entertainments could be judged and enjoyed in relation to the political lessons that they taught.

The *Photoplay Studies* guide for *Mr. Smith Goes to Washington*, however, shows that the discourse about education at this time did not unproblematically concern itself with the necessity of teaching democracy to the masses. In its seventeen pages the guide introduced students to the plot of the film and its production history, and provided "Questions for Classes in Civics" as well as "Questions about Washington" and "Questions on Cinematic Treatment." All of the sections were prepared by experts—a high school principal, the president of the New York City Association of Civics Teachers, and National Education Association officials. Immediately, in its opening paragraphs, the guide sought to persuade students not to view the film politically: "*Mr. Smith Goes to Washington* . . . stands or falls . . . solely on its cinema merits . . . even the dialogue should be considered first of all as a contribution to cinematographic qualities: and so too should be judged the complications and interweavings of the plot, the motivation of the characters, the realistic truth of the background. To classes and students of movie enjoyment and appreciation, consequently, this first advice should be given: consider *Mr. Smith Goes to Washington* as a movie."[30]

Then, in an implicit critique of the film's apparent ideological position (and of the more overtly political projects of the film education movement from earlier in the decade, which I discussed in chapter 3), the guide instructed each student to disregard any possible link between *Mr. Smith* and

PHOTOPLAY STUDIES
A MAGAZINE DEVOTED TO PHOTOPLAY APPRECIATION
Copyright, 1939, by Educational and Recreational Guides, Inc.

VOLUME V   SERIES OF 1939   NUMBER 21

FRANK CAPRA, DIRECTOR OF "MR. SMITH GOES TO WASHINGTON," AND JAMES STEWART

Capra and James Stewart on the cover of the *Photoplay Studies* guide to *Mr. Smith Goes to Washington*. (Margaret Herrick Library, Academy of Motion Picture Arts and Sciences)

contemporary events. The film undoubtedly had a basis in "many recent occurrences enacted on the American scene and reported in newspapers." But students should ask themselves "whether the process of highlighting [these occurrences] has been carried too far, whether the total result is plausible, whether a wrong impression of American political life is given, and whether the total effect has been exaggeration rather than a truly artistic effect."[31] For the study guide, the film's criticism of governmental systems could only be judged aesthetically, with students learning about narrative plausibility and with the language of the guide itself suggesting that *Mr. Smith* had indeed gone "too far."

The study guide's questions inspired by the film seem dryly informational ("Why was a successor to the late Senator Foley not elected immediately by the people?" "Who is the Senior Senator from your state?" "How did it happen that Washington was made the nation's capital?" "In what noted but still unfinished cathedral is Woodrow Wilson, the World War president, buried?").[32] Other parts of the guide pose an early auteurist discourse about the film's director ("more important than the presence of a competent acting cast is the fact that the whole production has been under the guidance of Frank Capra").[33] The project of the guide, then, anticipates Lauren Berlant's thesis on Washington discourse in general. In her analysis of a 1990s appropriation of *Mr. Smith*—an episode of *The Simpsons* television program called "Mr. Lisa Goes to Washington"—Berlant writes that this discourse "is already all about the activity of national pedagogy, the production of national culture, and the constitution of competent citizens," particularly among young children and adolescents.[34] *Photoplay Studies* provided just this kind of training (although, of course, it is impossible to tell how seriously any student took this instruction). The guide to *Mr. Smith* gave students a seemingly thorough lesson in citizenship—who senators are, for instance, and how they are elected—and in the history that all citizens needed to know. But the guide also added an aesthetic dimension to that citizenship with its questions and commentary about cathedral architecture and Capra's direction. In this "construction of a patriotic youth culture," to use Berlant's phrase,[35] the study guide insisted that the nation's capital and American history and aesthetic accomplishment were in fact complementary categories that created a logical, nonthreatening, smoothly working system of power relations between people and institutions.

The Problem "Below the Rio Grande"

In reviewing *Mr. Smith* for overseas exhibition, particularly in Latin America, State Department officials also expressed an interest in the educational value of the film. They concentrated, however, much more on what the film might teach a national body politic rather than an adolescent one. But first I need to point out here that the very fact of the State Department's interest indicates a special status for *Mr. Smith*. Of course, the federal government regularly looked for ways to use the film industry to further foreign policy (arranging star tours of various countries, for instance, or producing propaganda films for countries perceived to be within the United States's "sphere of influence").[36] And, as I showed in chapter 2, the State Department worked in particularly fraught exhibition cases as a liaison between the American movie studios and foreign governments. On a film-by-film basis, however, the State Department did not involve itself in the overseas details of the U.S. film business. Only when a private citizen or govern-

ment bureaucrat brought a problem to the department's attention did officials start to weigh in on the merits of an individual movie. In the case of
Capra's film the documents provide an indication of how the State Department assumed the film would be received, but they also give a much more
thorough account of how department officials themselves interpreted the
film. Further, their language in discussing *Mr. Smith* indicates their own
anxiety about the place of the United States in global politics.

The documents show much of the same anti-Washington tension that
the exhibitors wrote about in "What the Picture Did for Me." The issue,
though, was not that of Washington versus typical U.S. citizens but rather
Washington against the world and, more specifically, those developing
countries in Latin America that may not have made the kind of commitment to democracy that the U.S. government would have liked. In this debate about relations with Latin America, *Mr. Smith* became a lightning rod
through which State Department officials could register concerns with the
film industry and censorship and about exporting U.S.-style capitalism and
political systems.

In March 1940 Thomas Burke, chief of the Division of International
Communications, composed a memo that discussed the problems facing
the film industry and the federal government, and the contradictions that
emerged from these difficulties. He wrote that motion picture markets overseas had dried up considerably, largely because of the war and of foreign
censorship restrictions. He went on to say that "censorship is one of the
main threats that confronts the motion picture industry on the western
hemisphere" and that the industry had "called upon the [State] Department
for assistance perhaps more frequently than ever before in its history." He
added that "it seems reasonable to say that our ability to ride successfully
through the morass of censorship is in no small measure based upon the
respect and confidence which we have instilled in the minds of both governments and governed in the Latin American area . . . [where] democracy
is ridiculed as an impractical device by certain of the totalitarian governments." Then the memo cautioned that "it seems incredibly inconsistent for
any American commercial enterprise which thrives on United States prestige to abet the hostile propagandists by ridiculing" democratic systems.[37]

Thus the State Department's perception of Latin America created a
puzzle. Censorship was an evil that threatened the film industry. But in
places where democracy was ridiculed, why allow U.S.-made, arguably
antidemocratic, artifacts to flourish? And this was where Capra's film came
to the department's attention and where different kinds of reception prac-

DEPARTMENT OF STATE

DIVISION OF
INTERNATIONAL COMMUNICATIONS

MAY 8 - 1940
DEPARTMENT OF STATE

March 21, 1940

DIVISION OF
APR 17 1940
THE AMERICAN REPUBLICS
DEPARTMENT OF STATE

A-L - Mr. Long
RA - Mr. Briggs
Mr. Bonsal
Mr. Duggan

Reference is made to Mr. Duggan's memorandum of March 21, 1940, and the comments of earlier dates made by Mr. Briggs and Mr. Bonsal.

Unfortunately I was a bit obscure in my memorandum of March 15 with reference to the suggestion to confer with Mr. Hays.

Although I am firmly convinced that the motion picture - Mr. Smith Goes to Washington - should be discussed specifically with Mr. Hays (along the line indicated in my memorandum), I agree that we would be badly out of role if we attempted to set up - even remotely - anything suggesting the "suitability" or "censorship" of individual American pictures. That, of course, was not intended in my accompanying memorandum. I assumed that the entire matter could be handled on the basis of indicating to Mr. Hays the reactions which we have obtained to date, and the effect which such reactions might conceivably have on the very problems

which

The Department of State weighs in on the "suitability" of *Mr. Smith Goes to Washington*. (National Archives) tices would be acknowledged. The author of the memo and his associates saw the film as "a bit of buffoonery." But they were not convinced that the film would be received in this manner in Latin America. In fact, the memo pointed out "the serious damage that might result from showing such a film outside the United States and particularly below the Rio Grande."[38]

The same sentiments turned up in a number of memos. In September, for instance, the chargé d'affaires in Bangkok wrote that while *Mr. Smith* constituted excellent entertainment "for home consumption . . . [it] should never be permitted to be shown outside of the borders of the United States."[39] Even when officials decided to oppose censoring the film, they viewed *Mr. Smith* as a dangerous movie, and their language shows how the film spoke quite directly to nationalist, masculinist concerns. A few days after he wrote his first memo about *Mr. Smith* (and subsequently had a department official question his call for banning the film), Burke reversed his resistance to Capra's movie.[40] Nevertheless, he added that "in order to establish our national virility," the United States need not go out of its way "to establish our susceptibility to sin," as *Mr. Smith* seemed to do. For Burke, the film demonstrated to "our neighbors the fact that we are 'muy hombre,'" but did so in the worst possible way, by implying that the United States was "basically corrupt."[41]

What I find especially interesting here is not so much a concern with how "natives" might receive the film but with how the United States itself would be "received" in Latin America. The entire Southern Hemisphere seemed to mobilize northern fears of being feminized among the Latinos, of not being quite virile enough. In this instance, the discourse of at least some government officials created a kind of homosocial sphere of influence, where "our" men must be shown to be more manly than "theirs." If this were true, it might give us a better understanding of the discomfort with Capra's film, which takes the shape of an oedipal drama about sons slaying fathers and ends with the male hero having passed out, and then, a few moments later, Clarissa Saunders—the woman who acts as Senator Smith's political mentor—screaming "yippee."

Anticensorship sentiment prevailed at the State Department, although most of the memos discussed sitting down and talking with Will Hays about how such a movie could have been made in the first place. Typically, the tone was friendly but firm: "It is my understanding that it has been our policy to bring to the attention of Mr. Hays instances where the Department . . . considered that the susceptibilities of our friends south of the Rio Grande have been offended by American-made motion pictures. I believe that this policy is absolutely sound and should be continued."[42] State Department and diplomatic officials generally disapproved of the film, citing, among other things, its "malicious ridicule" of U.S. governmental institutions and the manner in which it worked to "distort the facts in regard to American life."[43] But most of these officials also tended to doubt that they should routinely "express views concerning specific commercial pictures."[44] Moreover, they worried whether it would not be "highly undesirable if a member of the Congress used the personal opinions of our officers as the main basis for an arraignment of the motion picture industry?"[45] Many members of Congress criticized the film industry for everything ranging from block-booking practices to producing interventionist propaganda to moral lapses, and official State Department action against *Mr. Smith* may have allowed them to assume that they had the backing of the federal government in their attacks against Hollywood (indeed, after the 1939 Washington preview of *Mr. Smith*, a number of senators vowed to pursue with new interest a variety of antitrust measures against the film studios).[46]

Thus the case of *Mr. Smith* pointed out the delicate balance between various segments of the industry and the government and the strains caused by conflicting goals: promoting the film industry versus promoting the United States's interests around the world. The Hollywood studios needed the State Department's help in dealing with overseas markets and so might have been susceptible to pressure concerning film content. But the department itself had to be careful to maintain the appearance of a hands-off relationship rather than a regulatory one with private corporate production. Indeed, one of the sustaining myths of American capitalism has been that of the laissez-faire attitude of the government toward business, even during a century of increasing regulation. Furthermore, the State Department, at least in 1940, sought to separate itself from those members of Congress who vigorously agitated for increased government supervision of film production. And besides, in 1940 the department had better ways to spend its time than monitoring individual movies.

Even so, the decision to permit the overseas exhibition of *Mr. Smith* was a difficult one for department officials. Much of the evidence that convinced them came from the American Consulate in Switzerland, where the reception of the film demonstrated its potential for promoting democracy rather than the opposite. The American consul general there (felicitously named James Stewart) wrote to the State Department, saying that the film had been playing to packed houses and had "achieved a position as a symbol of democracy in this country, probably never enjoyed by any other character originating in the United States." In fact, progressive leaders in Switzerland had decided to use the film "to attack . . . the antiquated principles of the Federal Parliament" and to work for "parliamentary reform."[47] In the State Department's understanding of reception, then, *Mr. Smith* functioned to criticize the United States only in "uncivilized" places. But in "civilized" ones like Switzerland, the film served to posit the United States as a model of the possibility for democratic reform.

Assessing Reception

How can we make sense out of these multiple discourses? Two of them seem in absolute opposition to each other: the exhibitors' discussion of the film, which primarily detailed a domestic response; and the analyses from the federal government, which speculated on a potential global reception of the film. Clearly, both demonstrated a deeply felt, though contradictory, antagonism toward the motion picture industry. Exhibitors were furious that this kind of film rarely got made; State Department officials were upset that this type of film got made at all. Everyone felt that the film raised issues of the efficacy of democracy, but in different ways in different places and to different ends.

All of the discussions about *Mr. Smith* demonstrated a consensus in terms of method and goal. That is, motion pictures possessed a powerful ability to indoctrinate, and the spread of democratic institutions constituted a fitting national project. But they demonstrated absolute fracture when it came to determining the best way to indoctrinate and discern the meaning of democracy. That break became apparent in the tension between the industry and "the people." But it was no less evident in the interactions between those institutions that we might tend to think of as monolithically conforming to a dominant ideology—the motion picture industry and the federal government—even as the country moved toward a period of war marked by increased efforts on the part of government and business to build consensus.

In the final analysis, this rhetoric of *Mr. Smith*'s reception may well construct interpretations that are "false"—simple binary oppositions between the "little people" and the federal government, as in the case of the film exhibitors, or irrational concerns about degrees of manliness, which we find in the State Department documents. But these interpretations are themselves nonetheless "real," that is, deeply felt and capable of mobilizing a great deal of activity. Here we might follow Paul Virilio and keep in mind that the conflation of representation and government that held such a central role in the exhibitors' reports had its full effect in a devastating global war that started in the same year that *Mr. Smith* was released.[48] And certainly, concerns about U.S. virility versus that of the Third World continue to be played out, not only discursively, as in the memos about *Mr. Smith*, but also in the implementation of U.S. global policy.

"This Business of America": Fan Mail and "Meet John Doe"

In contemporary film studies, the voices of "average" moviegoers typically have been lost. Consider the voice of Mrs. E. Coate, who wrote the following letter to Frank Capra in June 1941: "Yesterday morning at 2 A.M. we were seeing our eldest son Denny, with 45 others, off for an Army Camp somewhere. At 2 P.M. of the same day, we were seeing our first Frank Capra picture, *Meet John Doe*. My! What a picture, just what this old world needs."[49] For Mrs. Coate, seeing Capra's latest film marked an intense conflation of real-life problems—losing a son to military service and an almost certain war—with the fictional ones of the film. In addition, such highly personal concerns combined with those that were, in fact, global. The film not only helped Mrs. Coate through a difficult period but was precisely "what this old world needs." This letter to Capra indicates a need to thank the film director and to tell him that, rather than allowing Mrs. Coate to forget about her difficulties for two hours, *Meet John Doe* helped her to contextualize them and to see them in relation to the issues that his film addressed.

We have very little understanding of this kind of complex and deeply felt response to films from this period, largely because the study of the audience of which Mrs. Coate was a part presents such serious problems, both methodologically and practically. It is impossible, for example, to produce any reasonable kind of ethnography of the 1940s film audience to match the one that David Morley has constructed, through interviews and a careful process of selection, for the contemporary British television audience.[50] Moreover, the evidence of the historical audience's responses to films, probably ephemeral in the first place (preview cards, diary entries, and so on), is exceedingly difficult to come by.

As I hope to show with this project, however, although methodological constraints remain, film studies has begun in earnest the project of historicizing the film spectator. Among the most compelling work is that which indicates an interest, on the part of certain audiences, in a cinema that addressed concerns of political importance. For instance, Janet Staiger has examined the mixture of spectatorial and political desire as it became apparent in a very specific group of viewers—film critics of the 1920s. Staiger has found that reviewers for ostensibly nonideological periodicals, such as the trade journal *Variety*, quite explicitly developed an aesthetic based as much on a film's expression of hyperpatriotic nationalism as on its manipulation of such formal categories as narrative or visual style. In perhaps the most detailed analysis of an audience's political expectations and pleasures, Steven Ross has shown that in the years leading up to World War I a wide audience existed, in New York and perhaps elsewhere, for labor union–produced feature films about unfair economic practices.[51]

Thus we have evidence that, at least during certain periods, the cinema came to be seen by many average viewers as contributing directly to regional or national discussions about political issues. In the following section I examine film spectatorship from just such a period, the very early 1940s. My primary source of information here is the fan mail—and I use this term loosely to include both enthusiastic and critical letters—that Capra received in 1941 just after the opening of *Meet John Doe*. Several significant questions arise from these fan-generated texts about the film: When, why, and in what manner did audiences perceive that a major Hollywood production spoke to national concerns or embodied a national consensus? What were viewers' expectations of a Capra film, and what pleasures did his work generate? Finally, what role did certain segments of the audience expect a film celebrity of Capra's status to play within the national political scene?

The letters about *Meet John Doe* indicate that for many film viewers the Hollywood cinema needed to engage more directly with issues of perceived importance. Even more broadly, for reasons that are not altogether self-evident but that may have had something to do with the era's economic collapse, during this period there seems to have existed no necessary contradiction between consuming all manner of popular culture for entertainment and escape, and consuming it for at least a degree of political edification. By the time of *Doe*'s release, as Barbara Foley has pointed out, the proletarian novel had become an accepted (and occasionally best-selling) literary genre, one even occasionally spoken of admiringly by such arbiters of middle-class taste as the *New York Herald Tribune* and the *Saturday Review of Literature*.[52] During the same period, the populism of the previous cen-

Left: A fan writes to the director: "Mr. Capra, why not make another picture somewhat like *Meet John Doe*? Have it based on Defense and our Morale." (Wesleyan Cinema Archives). *Right*: Another letter about Capra's film: "I enjoyed *Meet John Doe* very very much and feel we need more pictures like it." (Wesleyan Cinema Archives)

tury received its first serious scholarly attention with the 1931 publication of John D. Hicks's *The Populist Revolt*, and at least some limited popular success with C. Vann Woodward's 1938 biography *Tom Watson: Agrarian Rebel*, which told the story of the populist hero. This interest in a politicized popular culture came from both the Left and the Right, from those who made Upton Sinclair's *I, Governor of California* a best-seller, to those who listened to Father Coughlin's weekly national radio broadsides against Jews and Communists.

This is not to imply that the readers of proletarian novels, or those with an interest in nineteenth-century political history, or those who sympathized with the socialist Sinclair formed the central audience for Capra's films. But by 1941, as I will show, there was a broad field of cultural production aligning not only literature, history, and political tracts, but also school textbooks, radio music programs, public assemblies, and even the occasional gossip column, with discussions of pressing national issues. As the case of *Mr. Smith Goes to Washington* made clear, by the end of the 1930s at least some fairly large segments of the motion picture audience hoped for Hollywood to deal more realistically with pressing political issues, and these audiences celebrated Capra for standing out from the rank and file of film directors because of his willingness to interrogate issues of wealth, corporate power, and government corruption.

The era's discourse on Capra himself demonstrates that a popular culture that stressed politics over pure escape, and that attempted a critique of capitalism and the fabulously rich, might attract any number of eager viewers. By the late 1930s, Capra was one of the few Hollywood directors to have emerged as a major celebrity, one who attracted a great deal of attention from media and from fans. This attention, in Capra's case, typically centered as much on his politics as on his filmmaking abilities.

In 1938, even the magazine of homespun Americana, the *Saturday Evening Post*, wrote admiringly of Capra's reception in the Soviet Union and implied that a Communist audience understood democratic values far better than government officials in the United States: "For painting America as he sees it, [Capra] is regarded in Moscow as a Utopian dreamer . . . Travelling in Russia after *Mr Deeds [Goes to Town]* appeared, he was hailed as a comrade, a world improver and a Red propagandist. In their enthusiasm over Capra's portrait of an American philanthropist [in *Mr. Deeds*], the Soviet critics showed themselves far behind the advanced thinkers of Washington, who want to abolish the American philanthropist because his money is needed to buy votes with."[53] While the *Post* certified the filmmaker's patriotism ("Capra likes American institutions"), the magazine posited him as a version of one of his own heroes, battling against institutional forces that have a knee-jerk response to all social criticism and political debate: "Capra says the best thing he ever worked on was *Soviet*, an unborn photoplay. He was getting ready to shoot it for Metro-Goldwyn-Mayer, when the company decided it was full of controversial dynamite and put it on the shelf."[54]

In 1940 the *New Yorker*, a magazine with a decidedly more intellectual and elitist approach than the *Post*, titled a profile on Capra "Thinker in Hollywood," and referred to him as "the most thoughtful man in the industry." The magazine also admiringly stressed the connection between Capra and Communist ideology, saying that, "in Russia, the point of view he had displayed in *Mr. Deeds* caused him to be well received by Soviet officials."[55] Writers for mainstream magazines apparently saw no problem in constructing Capra as someone who embodied the best in the United States by incorporating that which was best about the Soviet Union. Almost certainly, part of the enthusiasm for Capra's films came from the audience's willingness to have their own political institutions criticized, and to have solutions posited that could, in some sense at least, be labeled "Communist," but that still posed no conflict with perceived basic American values, and that of course signaled no endorsement of Stalin or the Soviet Union.

Indeed, this position formed one of the defining characteristics of the 1930s-style populism embodied not only by Capra but by, among others, such disparate characters as Father Coughlin; advocate for the elderly, Francis Townsend; Louisiana governor Huey Long, and even Franklin Roosevelt—that is, a serious critique of wealth and class inequality and a concomitant belief in a mixture of egalitarianism and the kind of activist Christianity endorsed by Pope Pius XI's 1931 encyclical, "On Reconstructing the Social Order." [56] The fan mail for *Meet John Doe* exhibits the same kind of commitment, but beyond this, and beyond the conviction that the cinema should address significant issues, the letters show no necessary formal or ideological consistency and range from Mrs. Coate's family melodrama to more overtly political tracts, from religious allegory to discussions of the problems of nosy neighbors in small towns.

Capra deposited at least one hundred *Meet John Doe* letters with his papers at Wesleyan University, and I have transcribed approximately two-thirds of them.[57] The letters are often critical as well as favorable, and some offer praise as well as suggestions for ways in which the film could have been better. So Capra seems to have saved a wide range of fan response. But in spite of this apparent inclusiveness, interpreting the letters about *Meet John Doe* raises the issue of typicality, both in terms of the general response to Capra's movies and to those made by other filmmakers. Because of his celebrity, Capra undoubtedly received more fan mail than most directors, and because his films were frequently so overdetermined as narratives of nationalism, fan mail about his movies probably differed significantly from the fan mail generated by the more typical Hollywood product. And, of course, most viewers, whatever they may have thought about the movies they saw, chose to write no fan mail at all. Despite these limitations on interpretation, it seems at least plausible to assume that the mail Capra received tells us something about a variety of the subgroups and subcultures, to use Morley's terms, that made up the film audience in 1941. The letters certainly provide information about segments of what might be called the "Capra audience," those fans who took a special interest in such films as *Mr. Deeds Goes to Town*, *Mr. Smith Goes to Washington*, and *Meet John Doe*. Further, given the widespread popularity of Capra's films during the period, and the general desire of so many consumers for a politicized popular culture, it figures that we can at least cautiously assume that the opinions expressed in the letters were shared by a great many movie fans.

The most extensive holdings in the Capra collection at Wesleyan, including fan mail, begin around 1933 and 1934 with the production of *Lady for a Day* and *It Happened One Night*. At the same time, at least according to his autobiography, Capra became more and more concerned about his status as a filmmaker with a social consciousness, claiming that in his post-1932 movies he "took a hard look at life from the eye level of the hard-pressed Smiths and Joneses." Arguably, then, starting at about this time, Capra used his mail as something of a barometer to determine whether he was in touch with what he called "the *real* lot of American citizens."[58] Thus Capra himself may have believed in the reliability of a relatively small number of letters to indicate a more broadly experienced response to his movies.

There are several reasons for studying viewers' responses to *Meet John Doe* as well as the relationships between this reception and the period's popular political discourses. Most obviously, the film comes from a period in U.S. history that perched precariously between domestic economic collapse and entrance into World War II. In the context of Capra's career, *Meet John Doe* was the director's first film as an independent producer, and it also appeared more or less in the middle of what generally is considered Capra's most productive period—1934 to 1946. *Meet John Doe* also comes from that cycle of films—*Mr. Deeds Goes to Town* (1936), *You Can't Take It with You* (1938), *Mr. Smith Goes to Washington* (1939), the *Why We Fight* film series (1942–1945), and *It's a Wonderful Life* (1946)—that typically have been considered the most reflective of the U.S. body politic. In film studies, however, in spite of a general acknowledgment of the social impact of the films, there has been very little effort made to examine just how that impact was felt, by whom, or in fact, if it was felt at all. As a result, we are left with little understanding of the tensions within the mass audience, of the different kinds of pleasure that the Hollywood cinema could generate, and of the often intense interaction between viewers and the films they watched.

"All This Talk of Pessimism":
The Educational Discourse

The experience of seeing Capra's film in 1941, at least as expressed on the conscious level of fan letters, indicates a diverse range of interpretive possibilities. But the constant trope in the letters is the extent to which the film itself became something of a national document at a particularly crucial period in the country's history, when the effects of the Depression had hardly lessened, a war in Europe threatened to come to the United States, and Franklin Roosevelt's unprecedented election to a third term as president in 1940 raised concerns, at least among a significant minority of the electorate, about the possibilities of domestic dictatorship. Capra himself hoped that the film would depict "the hard-nosed brutality" of the era, as well as reflect the manner in which "Hitler's strong-arm success against democracy" was spreading, with "little 'führers' . . . springing up in America, to proclaim that freedom was weak, sterile, passé." [59]

Meet John Doe depicts the production of a "forgotten man" by journalist Ann Mitchell (Barbara Stanwyck). Washed-up baseball player John Willoughby (Gary Cooper) "becomes" John Doe, and with Ann as his coach he protests the condition of all the John Does in the country. As a sign of his seriousness Doe pledges to commit suicide on Christmas Eve, after which he becomes a national celebrity. Newspaper magnate D. B. Norton (Edward Arnold), who commands a personal army of storm troopers, senses the possibility of using Doe and his followers to promote his own dictatorial ambitions, and thus actively promotes Doe's celebrity and the John Doe clubs being formed across the country. Doe finally finds out about Norton's machinations and tries to expose them, but at a mass rally for Doe, Norton manipulates the crowd into turning on their hero. A despondent Doe tries to fulfill his promise to commit suicide, but Ann and the repentant members of the John Doe clubs convince him not to. In the original ending, which Capra changed after the film's opening and to which many of the letter writers responded, Norton himself repents and helps convince Doe not to take his own life. [60]

A number of fans, in the manner of Mrs. Coate, spoke of *Meet John Doe* —which so clearly narrativized concerns about poverty, leadership, democracy, and the possibilities for collective action—in terms of its significant connection to major personal events, with at least three of the letter writers aligning the action in the film with their own graduation from high school. One recent graduate was up until three in the morning writing his letter, and he told Capra that if he did not get to bed soon he would not be able to get to work by eight and would certainly lose his job. The film made him realize "that all this talk of pessimism that all high school graduates get must be wrong . . . We are told that we go out to meet a cruel, hard, debasing world, of men that will cut your heart to sunders if they possibly can. There must be something else in the world." [61] Yet another eighteen year old, who said she was graduating in a week, viewed the film as a state-ment directly from Capra and took the occasion to admonish him. For her, spectatorship meant a kind of direct discussion with filmmakers and im-plied contracts between Hollywood and filmgoers: "I am very serious about this business of America," she wrote. "I am hoping with all my heart that the message you gave *to me* . . . is sincere. I am hoping that you are not a D. B. Norton" (emphasis mine).[62]

Despite the emphasis on graduating from high school and the common denominator of the viewers' age, these examples represent differing experi-ences of *Meet John Doe*: one about the possibilities and problems confront-ing young people, and another that delineated an extraordinary kind of spectatorship that stressed a personal and very political conversation with Capra. Both letter writers, however, aligned the film with varying notions of the national—"this business of America," in the words of the second stu-dent—and about the responsibility of the cinema during times of perceived national crisis. For the first letter writer, motion pictures needed to pro-vide an antidote to pessimism. For the second, movies had to offer both a serious message and a commitment to continuing to spread that message.

The high school seniors or recent graduates who wrote to Capra (an-other told him "I have often had ideas [like those in the movie], but never had the nerve to write them on paper for fear that someone would laugh at me") may in fact have been responding to more texts than just Capra's film.[63] On 3 March 1941 *Time* magazine put Gary Cooper as John Doe on its cover. In the same issue several columns were devoted to the current textbook controversy in which high school social science texts were being challenged by such institutions as the New York State Economic Coun-cil for being "New Dealish in tone . . . critical of big business . . . [and] against unequal distribution of wealth and unequal opportunities in the U.S." The National Association of Manufacturers decided to examine the texts, hiring "a liberal, a conservative and a Marxist" to look for objectivity and bias, with particular concentration on the texts' views of the U.S. gov-ernment and "free business enterprise."[64] In other words, a battle waged over the possible interpretations of educational rather than motion picture texts, but many of the issues were precisely the same. The textbooks them-selves apparently engaged in the same kind of mildly progressive politics as Capra's film, which arguably equates big-time corporate capitalism with incipient fascism, and also tries to expose the plight of the "forgotten men," the army of John Does. Moreover, the specific concerns about the text-

Gary Cooper as John Doe on the cover of *Time* magazine,
3 March 1941. Rather than a Hollywood glamour photo of a
great star, this is a shot of a very serious character in a serious
film, *Meet John Doe*, just the kind of politically engaged motion
picture that many fans had come to expect from Capra.

books centered on issues of representation, on the manner in which they
depicted government and business and created a portrait of the nation.

If even *Time* took notice, then the textbook controversy probably had
some currency among Americans generally. Indeed, education leaders at
this time seem to have been almost obsessively, and quite publicly, interested in national, political projects. As just one example among many, in
March 1941, a few days before *Doe* premiered in Los Angeles, a Pasadena,
California, school district official, speaking at a "Youth and Democracy"
rally, offered a five hundred dollar prize for the student who wrote the
best essay on the topic, "Why I Believe in America."[65] It seems reasonable to argue, then, that the students watching *Doe* and writing to Capra
were in fact responding to a textual field that, in 1941 at least, could con-

tain both movies and school books. Their intense reaction to Capra's film, and their stress on the connection between the movie and their own high school graduations, might well show that their experience as film viewers was deeply influenced by their experience as members of the classroom audience. For these students, *Meet John Doe*, if not other films, provoked a similar kind of national and political sensibility to the one being constructed in schools and encouraged its teenage viewers to respond as if they were listening to a teacher or reading a class text. In this case two kinds of spectatorship—in movie theaters and in schoolrooms—merged, particularly around issues of government and business and the best ways to represent each.

"I Am Just a Dum Person": The Domestic Threat

Most of the letters that Capra deposited in the Wesleyan collection came from people whose frame of reference was not contemporary educational practice in secondary schools. In fact, some letter writers, through their spelling or grammatical practice, or through their own descriptions of themselves, stressed their uneven negotiations with educational discourse but nevertheless read *Meet John Doe* in relation to complex national problems, often critiquing it for not dealing with them in a sufficiently sophisticated fashion. As with the high school graduates, these letter writers show that spectatorship, in 1941, constituted an extremely nuanced and varied relationship between viewer and film text, and also between consumer and film industry.

One such letter writer, indicating her difference from those fans who confidently philosophized for Capra, told the director "I am just a dum [sic] person in your estimation." But she also provided information about her and her husband's filmgoing habits and attitudes, both of which problematize notions of an audience eager for escape and viewing motion pictures as the ideal instrument of that escape. "We go to a movie once in awhile," she wrote, "once a month or so that is at night when I can get a tired husband to go." Then she added that typically, they "come home dripping with disgust and so mad that we have wasted our time energy and money, the money is the last you notice."[66] If these sentiments were in any way common, perhaps among adult, working audiences, then the cinema of the period constructed, along with other kinds of viewers, a sort of antispectator for whom the cinema provided displeasure (in fact, generated "disgust"). This viewer hated films generally and considered moviegoing a waste of time and money, but at least occasionally, went to the movies anyway.

Capra films, however, stood out from the routine Hollywood product and, for this dissatisfied audience at least, constituted a kind of special, quality, adult viewing experience, one worth the effort. The letter writer told Capra that despite her and her husband's low opinion of movies, "we have always looked to you to do the right thing." She proceeded to criticize the film, particularly for its ending (a constant complaint in the letters and in much subsequent Capra literature). She wanted Doe to commit suicide and thought that Ann "should have egged him on to jump." This final narrative failure particularly bothered her, because until then the film was "just right for the times." Then she told Capra something that had "been smoldering in my heart for some time," and that his film had had the chance to address: "Why don't the Motion Pictures do something to help our country from the Hitlers within. The time is ripe for big things to be done."[67]

In other words, the letter writer interpreted *Meet John Doe* as detailing the possibility of a fascist takeover of the United States, from domestic enemies rather than foreign ones. By far the greatest number of letter writers in the Wesleyan collection interpreted Capra's film in just the same way, as a document detailing the potential ruin of the United States from within, as a national allegory produced during perilous times. One viewer wrote that she "was certainly made familiar by said picture with the unscrupulous political machines working in our country today to undermind [sic] American principles and ideals." Another wrote that until the problematic ending the film showed him the possibility to "beat the pants off all the crooked politicians and lick all the hard luck and 'isms' in this cockeyed world of ours." Yet another insisted that "the spirit that is awakened in people through seeing *Meet John Doe* must be related somehow to the need for national unity." A viewer from New York wrote of the responsibility of the entire motion picture industry to uphold democratic institutions, and thus of the exemplary status of Capra's film: "As one who regards democracy as the strongest theme the movie makers can use now and forever . . . I should like to congratulate you on your achievement."[68]

For these viewers the Hollywood cinema typically was not sufficiently concerned with the nation's welfare, in that movies tended not to promote or embody the country's values or protect its institutions. As a result, *Meet John Doe* deserved special mention because of the way it ably reflected, at least according to these viewers, both spectatorial desire and political reality. At least twenty fans (almost one-third of the sample that I have been able to study carefully) wrote to Capra to talk about the film's timeliness and its defense of democracy, implying that for many spectators, viewing pleasure by 1941 meant not being allowed to forget, even for two hours, a perceived threat to the United States from domestic fascism and political corruption. I do not intend to imply here that most viewers completely eschewed escapism—there were certainly plenty of movies made in 1941 that amply provided it. But the *Doe* letters indicate a desire for a kind of viewing practice that addressed the audience as a nation and that audience members could apply outside the theater, particularly in the development of the "national unity" and the regard for democracy that so many fans stressed should be the primary goals of motion pictures.

The concerns of these letter writers were not isolated ones. Their readings of the film can in fact be placed against numerous texts from different sources that emphasized the national implications of Capra's film. In her gossip column in the *Los Angeles Times*, for example, Hedda Hopper, hardly a defender of politicized cinema, wrote that people had been waiting for *Meet John Doe* ever since Capra's previous film, *Mr. Smith Goes to Washington*, had critiqued government so effectively. She was hardly disappointed in the follow-up effort, calling *Meet John Doe* "a much-needed dose of optimism to lift us out of the slough of defeatism everyone's wallowing in." In a more detailed analysis of the film's relation to current events, Edwin Schallert, in his *Los Angeles Times* review, praised the film's "social significance" and insisted that the picture would "give a new turn to the thoughts of a nation." The Communist newspaper the *Daily Worker* discussed throughout its review the connection between the film (and, indeed, Capra's entire oeuvre) and contemporary politics. Even aspects of the studio-generated publicity for the film sought to produce something of a nationalist response by stressing, for instance, the score by Dmitri Tiomkin, which "will describe in musical terms the daily life of an average American family of four" and which "blends the folk music of every section of the nation."[69]

Of course, the texts surrounding any film are never so unanimous. While some of the advertising emphasized the romanticized U.S. folk tradition reflected in the score, other publicity stressed the film's relation to consumption practice rather than to issues of national unity or any perceived urgency to the body politic. Exhibitors across the country concocted tie-ins between the movie and newspapers, department stores, transit systems and radio shows, thus using *Meet John Doe* to support the same mass media and economic practices that Capra's film ostensibly critiques.[70] Even the events of the film's gala Los Angeles premiere exemplified a kind of fascist aesthetic that seems antithetical to the film's political project, at least as the letter writers interpreted it. Reporting on the premiere, the *Los Angeles Times* noted that the security staff that evening "was augmented by . . . 40 members of the Vic McLaglen motorcycle troop," reprising their role as D. B. Norton's private storm troopers in the film, with the difference that these Hollywood vigilantes were viewed as keepers of the peace at the premiere rather than as threats to it, as in the film.[71]

Even the viewers, while focusing on the political implications of the film, interpreted them in different ways. Rather than concentrating on the threat of domestic fascism and the erosion of democratic institutions, at least eight fans fixed on the manner in which the film conflated national values with spiritual ones. One viewer wrote to Capra stating, "I really had a feeling that I had seen a picture that was destined not only to make a name for itself . . . but a picture that actually would start the country in a movement toward the Golden Rule." Another "commended" Capra "for the redblooded patriotism and the spiritual atmosphere that permeates the entire picture," while a teenager who claimed that she was "not a specially serious minded person" nevertheless told Capra that "people know this picture stands for everything Christ stood for," and that "America is a grand country, but it needs more of this."[72]

In fact, several of these viewers seemed to seek these values and also find them in a range of films, indicating that for at least one group of filmgoers there might have been little difference between that which today we would probably consider typically escapist and that which, like *Doe*, seems like serious entertainment. One viewer asked Capra for a series of *Doe* films, saying that "a continuity of pictures in this theme might be possible, just as the *Andy Hardy* series has been in its concept." The letter writer went on to say that at "the center of these [*Hardy*] pictures is the spiritual value, but in my estimation *Meet John Doe* was more penetrating and practical."[73] If some of *Meet John Doe*'s viewers desired a cinema that refused to provide them with escape, others clearly went to the movies primarily to see a reflection of religious values and did not make the distinction between films that were or were not escapist, realistic or nonrealistic, frivolous or high minded. Rather, there were only spiritual and nonspiritual films, so that *Meet John Doe* and an *Andy Hardy* film, despite the generic, production, authorial, political, and other differences we might point out today, could be seen as providing virtually identical viewing experiences.

"You Had a John Doe Club Right There in the Theater": Audiences and Political Action

The fan mail about *Meet John Doe* indicates that many viewers believed in the possibility of a kind of participatory spectatorship and looked to Hollywood to make films to promote civic action and even to create politically motivated audiences outside of the theater. Capra received no less than a dozen letters telling him that his film had indeed started a John Doe movement, with John Doe Clubs across the country trying to create a local and then national response to national problems (other than the testimony of the letters, however, I have found no evidence in newspapers and magazines from the period that John Doe Clubs actually formed or, if they did, created much of a following).

Letter writers discussed the film as well as these attempts to create the clubs in relation to the perceived dangerous route taken by Depression-era democracy. One person complained, for example, that there had been limited response to her clubs and to her theory of a "people's democracy," because "the people have been doped for so long it's awfully hard for the poor devils to see the light."[74] Another viewer, in a letter deeply critical of the end of the film, asserted nevertheless that *Meet John Doe* virtually formed the clubs spontaneously, and in describing this phenomenon the viewer alluded to the construction of a spectator motivated to political, collective action by the movie but also virtually helpless against the workings of the film text: "By the time you had the band play the Star Spangled Banner," he wrote, "we were about ready to turn around and give away anything we had to anybody that needed it. You *had* a John Doe Club right there in the theater."[75]

Of course the viewer exaggerated; no John Doe Club actually formed during the movie that night. Nevertheless, despite the hyperbole, this statement stands out as an extraordinary assertion of a kind of spectatorship that has not been theorized fully, if at all: viewers who are simultaneously completely passive (apparently ready to do anything the film tells them) and absolutely active (seemingly mobilized to engage in collective action while still in the theater). More broadly, the letter points up the astonishing political power that many audiences wanted the cinema to exercise, and the deep disappointment they felt when movies seemed to refuse this responsibility.

Viewers of *Meet John Doe* typically extended this power to Capra himself, with the director emerging as a potential hero of national rehabilitation, and just the man to mobilize the masses.

Nine viewers told Capra he was a "genius," or compared him to such disparate national heroes as General Pershing and Walter Winchell.[76] And at least another seven viewers expressed their admiration for Capra by urging him to continue, and to take control of, the incipient John Doe movement. One letter writer insisted that "the responsibility falls on your shoulder; to you will come the plea to carry through that which you have started." By fulfilling this responsibility Capra would help "raise the motion picture industry to the height which it deserves—that of being a bearer of the simple truth to all people who seek it."[77] Capra's special status comes out in many of the letters, as well as the belief that the film industry had not nearly reached its potential as a political force, a potential that also, at least in part, was like a religious calling.

Echoing those viewers who conflated nationalism with spirituality and who viewed the film in deeply religious terms, one letter writer implicitly looked to Capra as a kind of evangelical leader. "This isn't a picture," the viewer insisted, "it's one of the most powerful sermons since the one on the mount," and he continued that "there are millions of more John Does who believe the same thing, but who are waiting for someone to bring it to their attention." Indeed, Capra's leadership was necessary because of crushing national and even global problems. "I'm just one of the millions of John Does," the letter writer continued, "who are sick of wars . . . and the eventual taxes that are piled on us; of the cheap petty politics with their intrigue and selfishness." Then, in a final assertion of Capra's influence and the power of the film text to mobilize people, the writer suggested a sequel to *Doe*, at the end of which Capra himself would appear and urge "those in the audience to get together on the John Doe principle."[78] In other words, this viewer proposed a direct-address appeal by Capra as director/star/national leader, thereby invoking, while not mentioning, the model of Charles Chaplin at the end of *The Great Dictator* when Chaplin steps out of character to address the audience about tolerance and world peace.

To his credit, it appears that Capra responded to many of the viewers who wrote to him (these responses are included in the Wesleyan collection). To those who virtually demanded his leadership he always demurred, citing his own limited organizational skills and the possibility for critics to detect a conflict of interest. Running the John Doe Clubs "would be cynically taken in many places as a publicity stunt for the picture," he wrote to

April 8, 1941

Mr. M. Gluck
6726 Milner Road
Hollywood, California

My dear Mr. Gluck:

I am extremely grateful to you for writing me that interesting letter about your reactions to "MEET JOHN DOE."

The end of the picture is my own -- that is, I'm responsible for it. You evidently missed the point I was trying to make, and it's not your fault, it's mine.

Briefly, my point was this. The Golden Rule is the only law or commandment that can make for happiness. Up to the convention the John Does were following it and their lives were happier. By contrast I wanted to show them what happened when they listened and followed human leadership, the greedy men after power whom people are wont to listen to. Also I wanted to show them an example of what was happening in the world when people listened and believed in this type. They were turned into a howling mob, their peace and happiness shot to pieces. And then I wanted to hold out hope for them at the end, if they understood and were willing to follow spiritual leadership.

Your point is that the John Does wouldn't have turned on John Doe. You say you wouldn't do it, and neither would any other John Does. I say the world today is a pretty good example that they do do it.

People have urged me to let John Doe jump off the roof. My argument against that is that his blood would be on the souls of the John Does.

Capra answered most of his fan mail: Shown here is the first page of his response to a letter critical of *Meet John Doe*. (Wesleyan Cinema Archives) one fan, adding that "my job and my talents and my hope is to continue to make pictures" rather than direct a national movement.[79]

The number of letter writers who so admired Capra, who requested his help, and who asked him to be their leader, at least implies, without making any direct link between the fans who wrote and those who did not, that a significant portion of the audience wished to be spoken to by someone they could trust, to be addressed as a mass audience eager to implement the John Doe philosophy. In an invaluable discussion of the complexity of contextualizing Hollywood products, Nick Browne has pointed out that the discursive strategies of *Meet John Doe*—the use the narrative makes of mass rallies and radio networks, the constant invocations of "the people"— work to address the audience "as a congregation," as "America."[80] Indeed, if the letters in the Wesleyan collection are any indication, the audiences of the film clearly wanted to be addressed in just this way, and felt the strongest identification not so much with any major characters in *Meet John Doe* but with the audience within the film, the audience that Doe exhorts.

"We John Does Are Made to Look Like Judases": The National Spectator

If the cinema can be read in terms of audience desire, then we must keep in mind, at least for the period covered by *Meet John Doe*'s release, the desire to be addressed as an audience, and indeed as a national audience needing to be called to action around national concerns. In fact, one of the perceived problems with the film had to do with the intensity of the identification with the audience within the film. At least nine of the letter writers were harshly critical of the scene toward the end of the movie when the members of the John Doe Clubs turn on their leader, expressing a sense of personal betrayal at the portrait of themselves as mean spirited and unforgiving. A letter from "six John and Jane Does" told Capra, "You showed us that you *don't* believe in us," and insisted that "you think we're a lot of silly sheep." Yet another viewer complained to Capra: "We John Does are made to look like Judases who would sell out their leader."[81] Indeed, the most common criticism in the fan mail that Capra saved dealt with the representation of a featureless national audience, of a mass that for many viewers constituted the real star in the film, directly mirrored the audience in the theater, and finally appeared as nothing more than a mob. Individual spectators viewed the film as speaking to a national spectator, and their most intense reactions came from their understanding of how that national spectator was both depicted and addressed.

In stressing their own status as members of a national audience, viewers showed themselves to be adopting a subject position that had seemingly come to be required by the growing number of entertainment activities that were overtly nationalist or political in nature, or by 1941 had come to be considered so. In 1941 on network radio alone, for example, "the time had come for U.S. Writers to fill the air full of the cause of democracy," stated an article in *Time* magazine, with CBS broadcasting *The Free Company*, a weekly program dwelling on those freedoms guaranteed by the Bill of Rights. Three times a week the same network broadcast *Back Where I Come From*, devoted to U.S. folk songs, while other shows, like *America's Town Meeting of the Air* and MBS's *American Forum of the Air*, broadcast discussions about the New Deal or the dangers of domestic Communism. Even the popular media's discussion of cultural production emphasized the political systems that might lead to certain aesthetic forms. In the same issue of *Time* that discussed *The Free Company*, for example, an art critic reviewed a display of European sculpture in New York, and opined that "under paternalistic governments, artists produce the kind of art that government likes," while "under a democracy, artists produce the kind of art they themselves like." [82]

By the time of the release of *Meet John Doe*, it had become difficult to read about popular culture or to experience it without being made aware of being addressed as a spectator or listener whose primary identity had to be that of U.S. citizen, or at least that of active participant in a political system. In an acknowledgment of this kind of audience, national leaders, before the widespread availability and use of television, frequently took their shows on the road, just as Doe does in Capra's film. In doing so, they developed one of the significant forms of popular entertainment in the 1930s and 1940s, the mass rally, which self-consciously collapsed the distinctions between politics, patriotism, audience participation, and spectatorial pleasure. Los Angeles alone hosted several of these rallies in March 1941, at the same time that it served as one of the sites of the initial, limited release of *Meet John Doe*. News analyst H. V. Kaltenborn, himself something of a Capra hero after appearing in a small part (as himself) in *Mr. Smith Goes to Washington*, addressed a crowd of five thousand, despite a threatened demonstration by the isolationist America First Committee. Similarly, journalist and author Eve Curie spoke to a large audience about the war in Europe, while the same America First Committee that had challenged

Kaltenborn's right to an audience sponsored a mass antiwar rally featuring the exgovernor of Wisconsin, Philip LaFollette. Demonstrating the era's easy slippage, at least publicly, between government and entertainment, a group of actors along with federal and Los Angeles city officials announced the formation of the "I Am an American Foundation," with plans to organize a rally to "welcome . . . and instruct new citizens before a Shrine of the Constitution."[83]

In March of the same year, in New York, the Communist Party sponsored a rally for eighteen thousand people in Madison Square Garden to celebrate the birthday of party leader William Foster "in song, pageant, banners and tributes," with the audience urged to "rally and demonstrate for freedom and peace."[84] Clearly, by 1941, politics, celebrity, entertainment, education, and spectacle had coalesced in the mass rally, with audiences expected to take part in the proceedings by asserting their status as citizens, as in the case of the "I Am an American" extravaganza, or their commitment to nonintervention, as in the Communist rally or, as in the case of the Kaltenborn or Curie addresses, their concern with national and world affairs. The audiences of *Meet John Doe* that were so critical of the representation of the audience within the film were in fact acting like the mass rally audience, judging and then responding to the message Doe gives at his own rally, and then chastising Capra for misunderstanding that response.

The National Audience in 1941

I do not mean here to romanticize a kind of politically motivated, now-long-gone movie audience that tried to interact politically and collectively with a broad range of popular entertainments. Such an audience would provide no guarantee of progressive politics, as a few of the most enthusiastic fans of *Meet John Doe* displayed an all-too-eager nativism, thanking Capra for making a film for "real Americans."[85] Rather, my point is that in 1941 there existed at least a significant section of the audience that was organized around issues of perceived national importance, was ready to participate in debates about those issues, and that expected the popular culture industries to take their interests and desires into consideration. Even the federal government apparently recognized the significance of that audience and Capra's ability to reach out to it. Only a year after *Meet John Doe*, army chief of staff General George Marshall made the newly enlisted Capra the director of a massive military propaganda project that resulted in the

Why We Fight films and in other documentaries that proselytized for the war effort and sought to create a political consensus among the millions of armed forces personnel who were compelled to watch those movies.

There is ample evidence in the fan mail that the nationalized and politicized audience for *Meet John Doe* definitely was not a monolithic one. Capra received a number of letters that had nothing to do with the connection between his film and any perceived national emergency. Some letter writers asked him for jobs, sent him ideas for movies, shared the poems or songs they had written, or just made general gripes. There were also several letters that complained about Capra's commitment since 1936 to "message" films and implored him to return to the more escapist fantasies of *It Happened One Night* and *Broadway Bill* (both from 1934).[86] At a distance from the letters of more than sixty years, and because writers tended to speak of themselves primarily as "John Does," it is also extremely difficult to categorize responses to the film that might be class- or race-based. Finally, I know of no reliable method of determining whether the dominant sentiments expressed in the fan letters accurately represented the opinions of the millions of viewers who did not write to Capra.

What emerges from the letters, however, are concerns both at odds with and sympathetic to much of the discourse of the New Deal. Rather than reflecting the need for economic reorganization, which so many Roosevelt bureaucrats stressed, the letters indicate a belief in a disjunction between traditional U.S. values of neighborliness and participatory democracy and an individualized, segmented modernity. In this, the letters closely followed the general findings of Robert Lynd and Helen Merrell Lynd's 1929 study of Muncie, Indiana, *Middletown*, except that while the Lynds blamed developments in capitalism for the demise of long-held values, the letter writers cast a larger net and worried about the effects of "isms" in general.[87]

The issues relating to a politicized, nationalized popular culture, and the relations between the people and their political systems, cannot be settled purely by an analysis of a sample of the fan mail sent to one director about just one of his films. But such an analysis does allow us to study the cinema at the point of consumption by looking at the varied reception strategies of movie audiences. This kind of project also forces us to complicate a tendency to consider Hollywood production from the studio era as unproblematically constituting a national cinema. Evidence such as the Capra fan mail demonstrates that formations such as the nation and the national audience are never static or unchanging. Instead, the letters indicate the possibility of tracking the formation of perceptions about the nation in particular periods through the interaction of audiences and the products of their popular culture. In doing so we might, in fact, have to proceed on a case-by-case basis. *Meet John Doe*, then, may well stand out as a nationalist film and political tract produced by a cinema that many in the audience from the period believed to be derelict precisely in its production of national, politically significant artifacts.

Although the information can be difficult to locate, there exists a fair amount of evidence from the period of the release of both *Mr. Smith Goes to Washington* and *Meet John Doe* of the interactive nature of film production and film viewing, of the manner in which those making films solicited and made use of audience response—among other things, exhibitors' reports, preview cards, poll results, box-office figures, and, of course, fan mail. Capra himself claimed in his autobiography that the mail he received about *Meet John Doe* after its initial, limited release helped him decide to modify the ending of the film for national distribution.[88] Thus we need to place any study of Hollywood production alongside an analysis of the reception texts produced by historically specific audiences. In particular, these texts help us understand not just the interpretations that some spectators made of the films that they saw, but also the charged, dynamic relationships between spectators and the film industry, the film celebrity, and, perhaps most interesting, other spectators.

Chapter Five

Coercive Viewings: Soldiers
and Prisoners Watch Movies

From the 1930s through the 1950s, more captive audiences saw Frank Capra's films than those of any other Hollywood director.[1] In December, 1939, for example, Capra received a fan letter from an inmate at Folsom State Prison in California, telling him that *Mr. Deeds Goes to Town* had been the first film shown there in twelve years. The inmate described a rapt audience of film-starved fellow prisoners, "those surprised thousands" for whom "the picture turned from entertainment to reality," and who felt that "the master scripter had suddenly given us the words with which to voice our inarticulate despair."[2] Twenty years later, as I will discuss in chapter 6, a far more privileged nationwide audience whose movements and activities were, nonetheless, constrained—junior high and high school students—watched Capra's series of AT&T science documentaries. In between, Capra's World War II instructional and morale-building Army Signal Corps films along with his own, independently produced *It's a Wonderful Life* (1946), became not so much the films of choice but the films chosen for a variety of audiences living in various degrees of confinement: American enlisted men, German prisoners of war, and San Quentin prison inmates. As such, these Capra films participated in projects that attempted to construct preferred forms of masculinity and, in the cases of the POWs and inmates, to rehabilitate men thought to be marked by histories of deviant behavior.

Studying these uses of the World War II films and *It's a Wonderful Life* furthers my project in the last chapter, that of understanding the development of film studies as a discipline. Through this work we can come to understand the professional classes—of teachers, psychologists, military personnel, film industry executives, and prison administrators—who by the early 1940s had come to believe in the potential of cinema to persuade, educate, and, indeed, reeducate all manner of audiences. In addition, these instances of film education show the smooth relationships and also the tensions between institutions, or even the contradictory practices within any one of those institutions. Most significantly, however, for the purposes of my overall project, the responses of the captive audiences for these films help indicate the relationships between men and the films that were imposed on them, the forms of reception specific to situations of confinement, and the success or failure of programs designed to accomplish nothing less than change the ways that certain populations thought and lived.

Captivity and coercion bring to mind the Foucauldian disciplinary paradigms, and we can indeed see them at work here. By World War II, the architecture of military observation and control had changed or, rather, been enhanced. Foucault writes about the construction of the military camp and the ways that barracks and other facilities came to be built in order to maximize the ability of authorities to observe all of the men contained within them. In the case of Capra's *Why We Fight*, observation was practiced by psychological experts rather than generals. Instead of having unlimited access to the men themselves, here the experts examined all of the men's judgments on the movies they had seen and their responses to examination questions about the documentaries they had watched. The goal was not so much "to qualify, to classify and to punish," to employ Foucault's terminology about the uses of the examination, but rather to qualify, classify, and to reconstruct: the men into fighters and the coming postwar period into a model of tolerance that would prevent future wars. This shift marks not only the treatment of the prisoners of war but also the prisoners at San Quentin, and shows how these uses of Capra's films during the 1940s participated in the period's developing liberal program of personal and social uplift and improvement through science and education.[3]

With the prisoner viewers, the German POWs and San Quentin inmates, and their engagement with Capra's films, we can see the enactment of Foucault's shift in disciplinary enforcement, and also its reversal. According to Foucault, punishment had ceased to be a public spectacle by the early nineteenth century. The extended, open-air 1757 execution with which Foucault begins *Discipline and Punish* would by 1840 be unthinkable in Europe or the United States.[4] This was just as true in the 1940s. Moreover, during this period, with the enlightened social science that attended to the prisoners of war and the progressive penal system that worked with San Quentin inmates, the prisoners themselves were presented with spectacle. That is, the prisoners attended the theatrical spectacle, and were not themselves the unlucky stars of it. This theatrical spectacle—the films—would serve to educate and edify the prisoners, rather than an audience of law-abiding citizens who would be both horrified and entertained by the sight of criminals being punished.

For American soldiers during World War II, Capra's *Why We Fight* documentaries were designed to turn individuals into an effective fighting force for the duration of hostilities, and then to make them part of an enlightened citizenry during peacetime. For German prisoners of war, government officials hoped that Capra's films might make fascists into supporters of American-style democracy. In San Quentin just after the war, Capra's first Hollywood film following his discharge from the army, *It's a Wonderful Life*, served as part of a project to make inmates functioning members of society after their sentences were served. In each case, Capra's movies took part in a project designed to construct a certain kind of masculinity—cohesive, or democratic, or noncriminal. And also in each case, at least in part to chart the progress of these projects, government officials and prison authorities carefully monitored the reception practices of the men involved.

The 1930s progressive discourse of childhood and adolescent uplift surrounding *Mr. Deeds Goes to Town*, examined in chapter 4, showed that for some parent and teacher groups the adolescent's apparent ability to analyze films demonstrated that young people were, really, incipient adults. Other, more concerted, efforts at film education in secondary schools—when students were asked to think about *The Bitter Tea of General Yen* or *It Happened One Night*—detailed a New Deal sensibility at least among some teachers that their students might be turned into properly liberal grownups in part through the study of worthwhile Hollywood movies. At the same time, however, film studies had become the province not just of parental, educational, and other related groups but also of such disciplinary institutions as the military and the prison. In the different settings, varying notions of audience aptitude and ability came to organize the ways that films were used. For film educators in secondary schools, the results of supervised film viewing provided evidence of the maturity and judgment of young people. For the military and the prison, at least in the case of Capra's war documentaries, the careful viewing of films became one of the solutions to difficult problems: the perceived intellectual shortcomings of the typical American fighting man and the perverse ideological education of the average Nazi.

Capra's army career has been well documented. Shortly after Pearl Harbor, Capra, who also had served during World War I, enlisted in the military as a major. There ensued a fair amount of army infighting for Capra's services, between the Signal Corps and the newly formed Morale Branch. This struggle ended in May 1942 with the creation of the 834th Signal Service Photographic Detachment, with Capra as commanding officer. Just after the entry of the United States into the war, the War Department's Bureau of Public Relations, in the words of the Office of the Chief of Military History, "had a corps of speakers busy traveling over the country delivering lectures to troops on the general theme of why they were being called upon to fight." [5] Audiences seemed to find these lectures less than compelling, however, and so army chief of staff General George C. Marshall, a film enthusiast, put into motion the plan that led to Capra's military films. Working first in Washington, D.C., and then in Los Angeles, Capra oversaw a group of military men and Hollywood professionals who worked to produce seven *Why We Fight* films, a series of *Know Your Enemy* and *Know Your Ally* films, and a regular troop newsreel called *The Army-Navy Screen Magazine*, in addition to other films. All of these productions had wide military (and even some civilian) audiences. General Marshall himself ordered that soldiers had to see the *Why We Fight* series.[6]

The success of the series can be marked by the manner in which its title became, by 1945, something of a signifier of selfless, patriotic activity. That year, the opening article in the initial issue of the *Hollywood Quarterly*, one of the first important, long running scholarly film journals in the United States, was Dorothy Jones's "The Hollywood War Film: 1942–1944." Jones discussed "Films about the Home Front," "Films about Our Fighting Forces," "Films on American Production," and other war-related genres. Among these, and in a direct reference to Capra's movies, she included "Films Telling Why We Fought," a category encompassing movies about "the American way of life," either allegorically or directly: *The Ox-Bow Incident*, for example, and also *Joe Smith, American* and *The Human Comedy*.[7] Almost fifty years later, in his study of homosexuality in the military during World War II, Allan Bérubé titled his introduction, in which he sketched out the vast contributions of homosexuals to the war effort, simply and without irony, "Why We Fight."[8]

Within a few years of their production, the *Why We Fight* films also came to be understood as representing the possibilities for postwar film studies. In 1946, Iris Barry, from the Museum of Modern Art Film Library, extolled the cooperation between the film studios and the academy, and the placement of film alongside "painting, sculpture, architecture . . . primitive and folk art, industrial design and the like." Merely for the cost of making the print, the studios agreed to deposit copies "of important older films" in the museum library, so that they could "be seen and studied." Writing about the museum's initial series of thirty-six foreign films and sixty-eight from the United States, Barry said that the selections ran the gamut "from Louis Lumière and Edison's films of 1895 to John Huston's *Maltese Falcon* and Capra's *Why We Fight* series."[9] Here, then, Capra's documentaries had entered a canon of great works that merited the same serious consideration as those from the other arts, and that also marked Barry's belief in a post-war fluidity between the corporate and the educational that could lead only to intellectual and aesthetic uplift.

Barry, of course, was writing about film studies as film appreciation and historical understanding; the acknowledgment of the highest achievements of film art and the placement of motion pictures within their social contexts. In this sense she was bringing to the museum audiences the pedagogical practices that had so marked the high school film education movement of the previous decade. But Capra's films also provided the possibility for a different kind of postwar film study, one much closer to General Marshall's concerns when he commissioned the series in the first place. In the fully technologized classroom of the postwar period, films would be used just like books and teachers to instruct students in a variety of subjects. Writing in 1947 about the shift from—and connections between—a wartime and peacetime culture, Robert Rahtz explained that the wartime instructional films, "like those in the *Why We Fight* series," had "proved their effectiveness as teaching aids, to the satisfaction of even the most skeptical." These films were instrumental "in reducing learning time," and so could become pedagogical models for the streamlined, modern classroom.[10]

Shortly after the war, then, the *Why We Fight* films were viewed both as art and as educational models for future films covering a variety of subjects. At the time of their production, though, Capra's films marked the development of a different kind of film studies. By the early 1940s film studies, at least in the case of the *Why We Fight* project, had moved from the humanities emphasis of the previous decade—thematic analysis, aesthetic understanding, and so forth—squarely into the social sciences, in which cinema became the tool par excellence of intellectual and psychological persuasion. And this film pedagogy would be administered not by the high school teachers of the 1930s but by a larger culture of experts—psychologists, sociologists, and college professors, among others. While those in the film education movement hoped to use films to create progressive action and critical thinking, those involved with Capra's projects had different goals for their different audiences. For the millions of American fighting men, the *Why*

We Fight filmmakers and administrators planned to create consensus, both about the facts of the war and the moral imperative of fighting it. That is, they sought to turn a civilian audience into a militarized one. The goal for the German prisoners of war was just the opposite: the desired effect was to change the fascist fighting man into a pastoral supporter of democracy. Just as with the students involved in the film education movement, however, the military viewers for *Why We Fight* came to be considered the perfect audiences for research purposes, the better to understand their reception practices and the success or failure of the films they watched.

Military Aesthetics and the Militarized Civilian

Of course, before the researchers fully got ahold of *Why We Fight*, the film series was a military project. And the various military brass who weighed in on the documentaries understood them and wrote about them in somewhat contradictory ways—in a high modernist mode that anticipated Iris Barry and also in strictly disciplinary terms. In October 1943, for example, Robert Lord, a lieutenant colonel in the Signal Corps, wrote an extended memo on the history and progress of Capra's various film series. Lord's understanding of the films, while they were still being made, anticipated the postwar canonization of the *Why We Fight* movies by nonmilitary experts. Capra's documentaries were "of a special, highly personal nature," comparing favorably to the best films of the American studio system produced by the likes of David O. Selznick and Samuel Goldwyn. Moreover, these films would fully "reflect the personalities of Col. Capra" and his assistant, Anatol Litvak, and "the artistic result" would be high.[11]

The army, then, amply appreciated Capra's talents and produced a sort of auteurist discourse around the director and his films, stressing personality, artistry, and individual virtuosity. But this was a directorial appreciation different from that of the film education movement of the 1930s or that of Iris Barry and others in the late 1940s and 1950s. Rather than sounding like appreciative critics, the army actually responded to Capra like frustrated studio chiefs. All of this artistry really only meant that Capra, in the view of military authorities, worked incredibly slowly. According to Lord, Capra felt determined to "do and re-do and re-re-do every step of every operation," and was generally "lacking in the ability to make . . . subordinates understand exactly what is desired."[12] If Lord could be considered representative of army thinking—and his memo very much has the feeling of an official history of the projects, complete with budgets, production schedules, and dates of scenarios and answer prints—then military officials clearly considered Capra an artist, and just as certainly believed that his artistry could not be made fully compatible with wartime production methods. The army invoked something of the discourse of aesthetic modernism to demonstrate that Capra could not work effectively in the contemporary, fully Taylorized military.

Of course, Capra may have acted like the auteur at times. But he also acted like the devoted, anonymous military man. In this instance, at least if we trust his own understanding of his role and of the films he produced for the military, Capra became the standard-bearer of a wartime effort to make civilian and military cultures merge, however uneasily. Robert B. Westbrook, among others, has written about the mobilization of civilian life during World War II, a mobilization marked by everything from rationing to loan drives to Norman Rockwell's *Four Freedoms* paintings for the *Saturday Evening Post*.[13] Unlike some of the military officials writing about him, Capra saw no conflict between the corporate and the artistic. Rather, he believed in the possibility of a fluidity between Hollywood-style film production and military objective.

In August 1942, Capra wrote a memo to all officers involved in *Why We Fight* production. His nine-point program covered such areas as relations with the press ("absolutely no interviews"), relations with other civilians ("absolutely no discussion"), drinking in public ("prohibited"), and attention to military detail (uniforms required during working hours). For Capra, the primary mission was to convince studio workers far away from other members of the military, let alone combat, that "at all times," they were "officers of the U.S. Army." "Most of you were individuals in civilian life," Capra wrote, and then added, "Forget that," because they were now "working for a common cause," in which their "personal egos and idiosyncrasies [were] unimportant." Sounding less and less like an artist, Capra warned that there would be "no personal credit for [their] work," and indeed even Capra's name appeared nowhere on the films he made. In capital letters at the end of the memo, Capra reminded his troops that "the greatest glory that can come to any man is to join the service when his country is in danger."[14]

Enlisted Men Watching Movies

Comments from soldiers tended to suggest the success of Capra's films. The men at various posts apparently needed to fill out attendance reports verifying that they had seen the required training films, with these reports also providing the space for optional comments. Typically, few men made comments of any kind. But those comments that were made were collected and summarized, and these summaries were sent to Capra. In addition, in the manner of the "What the Picture Did for Me" entries for *Mr. Smith Goes to Washington* examined in chapter 4, camp officers attempted to gauge the response of their viewers, whether they wrote comments or not. The recruits at Fort Screven, Georgia, for instance, felt that *Divide and Conquer* was a "very good film" and "all personnel [were] very interested." At the army air base in Richmond, Virginia, "98% of the reports were lacking in criticisms of either adverse or complementary nature," but the film nevertheless "was enthusiastically received by all officers and Enlisted Personnel." At an unspecified marine barracks, *Divide and Conquer* stood out as "the best we have seen with a terrific emotional impact that left a marked effect on the men." The officer assessing reception called the film "far superior to the former 'lecture' orientation" and ended by insisting, simply, "just show it to everyone in the armed forces."[15] This duplicated, of course, much of the discussion about *Mr. Smith Goes to Washington*. Like the exhibitor who wanted to make that film "compulsory" viewing for all citizens, this marine officer suggested that *Divide and Conquer*, which was in fact required viewing of new recruits, simply be shown once and for all to everyone in the military.

From *Mr. Smith* to *Why We Fight*, the pressing need for lessons in democracy remained constant, at least for some viewers, and Capra still seemed the man best able to provide those lessons. Only the site of those lessons had changed, from civilian theaters to military ones. In this case, then, rather than speak of the militarization of World War II civilian culture, we might speak of the use and apparent reception of the *Why We Fight* films as examples of just the opposite. If these exhibition reports can be believed, the military—which, after all, enlisted millions of men with no previous armed forces experience—successfully adapted civilian representational forms and modes of address, with Capra acting as liaison between private industry and government practice. And the viewers themselves, some of them perhaps the same high school seniors who wrote to Capra concerning *Meet John Doe*, seemed to shift quite easily from viewers seeing movies alone or with friends or families to soldiers watching movies together.

Some of these soldiers provided evidence of an audience mobilized to action by the *Why We Fight* films. A private at Camp Mackall, North Carolina, weighed in quite seriously on the series, seeing it as proof that "the moving pictures [*sic*] is the best possible medium for getting over to these fellows the idea that all this training and hell that they are going through now is with good purpose and intent." He added that the films had a definite, positive effect on behavior, turning disgruntled recruits into a cohesive unit. When the men "see those tanks, planes and infantrymen putting all they have into it over there," the private wrote, "it sure cuts down on the bitching and goldbricking." Another soldier, a sergeant stationed overseas, wrote of intent audience members all focused on the same thing despite the conditions of combat theaters: "The scenes were truly stirring and throughout the picture (even though we were sitting on hard wooden seats) our attention never shifted from the main theme." From Miami Beach a recruit reported rather perfunctorily on such films as *Sex Hygiene*, *Military Courtesy*, and *Articles of War* ("These were all good and served their intended purpose very well"). Capra's films were different, however, and actually seemed able to change civilians into combat-ready soldiers. The recruit wrote that "one of my best friends said as we left the theater, 'after seeing that I really want to fight.' " The same soldier added that "on every occasion that I have attended these shows there has always been an uproarious applause at the finish of the film." [16]

This constitutes an extraordinary reception discourse. In comments from different camps and different parts of the world, certain remarks and certain perceptions of the military audience remain constant. The men concentrated intently on the films and then were moved to applause when the movies ended. Moreover, the films changed behavior, both in minor ways, by cutting down on "bitching," and very significantly, as the movies made the men want to fight. But of course, reception is never so unanimous, and perceptions of audience response never achieve such perfect consensus.

Watching Recruits Watch Films

Capra's *Why We Fight* films probably were more significant than any others to developments in film studies during the 1940s. Of course, the military used the films to train millions of recruits. More broadly, an entire group of scientific experts viewed both the films and the audiences that watched them as ideal objects of study in order to determine the effects of the cinema as a medium of persuasion. This marked at least something of a shift in modes of studying cinema. In the 1930s film studies became the province of

WAR DEPARTMENT
SERVICES OF SUPPLY
Office of the Chief of Special Service

Initials of
Officer Who
Prepared   JWH:js
Memo

FILE NO. _____   DATE ___June 1, 1943.___

FROM __Distribution Branch, ASF__ BLDG "G", ROOM __2E56L__ TELEPHONE NO __5325__

SUBJECT __WHY WE FIGHT Films.__

SERVICES OF SUPPLY

TO ___C.G., S.O.S.   ___MIL PERSONNEL DIV.   ___ TRAINING DIV.   ___ Q M G
   ___ADM. BRANCH   ___CIV PERSONNEL DIV.   ___ FISCAL DIV.   ___ C. OF E.
   ___CONTROL BRANCH   ___OPERATIONS DIV   ___ PUB. REL BRANCH   ___ SURG. GEN

For Attention of _____

ADMINISTRATIVE SERVICES

TO ___CH., ADM. SERVICES   ___CH. OF FIN.   ___ P. M. G.   ___ ARMY EXCH SERV.
   ___A.G.   ___J.A.G.   ___ CH. OF CHAP.   ___ STATISTICAL SER

For Attention of _____

SPECIAL SERVICE   Attention of Lt. Colonel Frank Capra.

TO ___CH. OF SPEC. SERV.   ___ PERSONNEL OFFICER   _X_ INFORMATION DIV   ___ S. S SCHOOL
   ___ASST. CHIEF, S. S.   ___ PLANNING DIV   ___ W & R. DIV.   ___ ARMY INSTITUTE
   ___EXECUTIVE   ___ BUD & FISC DIV.   ___ FACILITIES DIV   ___ ADM. ASST
   ___ASST. EXECUTIVE   ___ RESEARCH DIV.   ___ A M. P S   ___ MAIL & FILES

FOR ___ PREPARATION OF REPLY   ___ APPROVAL OR DISAPPROVAL   ___STUDY AND REPORT
    ___DIRECT REPLY   ___ REMARK & RECOMMENDATION   _X_YOUR INFORMATION
    ___COMPLIANCE   ___ CONCURRENCE OR COMMENT   ___FILE
    ___APPROPRIATE ACTION   ___ NOTATION AND RETURN   ___ _____

(Informal reply in available space and on reverse side, turning bottom edge up)

Here is an extract from a note from a recently inducted buck private
at Camp Mackall, North Carolina:

"We saw another WHY WE FIGHT film recently. It was a great deal
like the invasion of Poland but I think it was presented in much
better style and all the boys were quite impressed. Personally, I
firmly believe that the moving pictures is the best possible medium
for getting over to these fellows the idea that all this training
and hell that they are going through now is with good purpose and
intent. When they see those tanks, planes and infantrymen putting
all they have into it over there it sure cuts down on the bitching
and goldbricking. We also saw a British film about General Montgomery
in Africa called "Desert Victory". It was put on with a feature film
at a regular showing and some of the fellows paid two and three admissions in order to see those British do the job. I thought it was
a fine picture of the campaign and would like to see certain parts
of it many more times myself."

"It sure cuts down on the bitching and goldbricking." The War Department's attempt to monitor the reception of the *Why We Fight* films. (National Archives)

the humanities-oriented film education movement and also of the sociologists and psychologists involved in the Payne Fund and other studies. The
two groups often acknowledged each other, with Edgar Dale, for instance,
in *How to Appreciate Motion Pictures*, approvingly discussing the scientists
who had demonstrated the effects on children of certain kinds of film.[17]
By the 1940s, though, a film studies coalition had developed not so much

between psychologists and humanities teachers but between psychologists and psychiatrists, with the serious study of motion pictures moving quite significantly into the field of "hard" scientific research.

A new class of experts—psychiatrists, psychologists, and sociologists as well as other social scientists such as economists—had been given a significant boost by the New Deal and its various projects aimed at merging social theory and federal operations. Then, as Ellen Herman has written, the post-1940 period, with its increased "atmosphere of international military crisis and conflict," fully allowed these "social experts" to become important and influential government functionaries.[18] Herman refers to the "romance of American psychology" in order to identify the period's belief in an organized class of scientific experts working for the social good. And, indeed, it was very much the perceived needs of World War II that first mobilized the psychological and psychiatric professions, many members of which initially worked in the government-sponsored Emergency Committee in Psychology, begun in 1939. Later, they aided the military in determining issues of enemy morale, the effective running of Japanese American internment camps, and the manipulation of U.S. public opinion toward the support of certain war aims. Thus these experts worked as human management specialists. As such, they had no more important group of humans to manage and understand than the millions of men who either were volunteering for or being conscripted into the American armed forces.[19]

These were not the first soldiers to be used as experimental subjects. The results of tests from World War I had made prodding, poking, and quantifying World War II recruits seem all the more important. Intelligence tests from the first war revealed that "the mental age of the average native-born recruit [was] slightly over thirteen years."[20] Assuming that the general public at least somewhat matched these results, scientists, as well as government officials and even advertisers, realized that public opinion was, in fact, frighteningly unpredictable and subject to all manner of persuasion. In the years after World War I, psychological experts came to comprehend public opinion, in Herman's words, as "a real threat to rational planning, even to moral order itself."[21] By the time the United States entered World War II, these experts were at the ready, and were prepared to make sure that the American military had men in it who understood precisely why they were fighting and who were free from any influences that might undermine their commitment to their country's cause.

This meant that recruits required indoctrination, and that the effects of this indoctrination needed to be carefully monitored. In terms of the training and propaganda films that the armed forces produced, this meant further that the experts in charge of indoctrination understood the necessity of studying film reception. To analyze the effectiveness of these films, with special emphasis on Capra's movies, which were, after all, required viewing of all enlisted men, the armed forces called upon the Experimental Section of the Research Branch in the War Department's Information and Education Division. These researchers developed two primary goals: "To study the effectiveness of the films in imparting information about the background of the war and in effecting changes in attitudes towards the war that were related to the objectives of the Army's orientation program"; and "to insure against the possibility of any undesirable effects that might result from the films." For the scientists involved, the tests they developed were among the signs of psychology and psychiatry's absolute indispensability to the creation of a rational, comprehensible modernity, utilizing as they did all of the "modern socio-psychological techniques" currently at their disposal.[22]

From these experiments, we can learn something about the reception context for Capra's films. The scientists conducting the research viewed the films as ideal for their purposes because the manner in which the films were shown was not directly connected to military educational efforts. "The films were shown during training hours," the scientists noted, "but they were not presented as part of any courses of training on which the men would be tested." Because of this, the films could be "distinguished from instructional films that are integrated into a regular teaching program in that little or no external motivation is applied as an incentive for learning the material presented." In other words, and in a further link between civilian and military film viewing, these films were shown in such a way as to emphasize their entertainment value rather than their educational impulses. The men knew they would not be tested on the content of the movies or have to apply anything they saw into direct daily practice. Like Hollywood films, these, as the scientists noted, needed to "sell themselves" to the men watching them precisely because the military screened them in such a way as to separate them from the standard training film experience.[23]

Researchers also understood the differences between military and civilian audiences, and these very differences made enlisted men ideal objects of study. Only men, of course, watched these films at the army camps, and their age range, unlike that of audiences in civilian theaters, varied only slightly. The researchers noted, however, that these arbitrarily thrown together military viewers ranged widely in terms of "regional and socioeconomic factors." Clearly, social scientists from the period understood typical, local movie audiences as too homogeneous for effective study, making the situation of World War II an all too rare research opportunity. Apparently assuming further difference because of these regional and class variations, the army researchers also commented on the "wide range with respect to intellectual ability" among the servicemen.[24] Understanding the *Why We Fight* project as "the largest-scale attempt yet made in this country to use films as a means of influencing public opinion," these same scientists almost certainly understood the study of the audiences for the movies as having significance beyond the war effort. The chance to examine an extraordinarily heterogeneous group of servicemen allowed scientists to plan more fully for a postwar modernity in which the workings of public opinion might first be understood and then more competently manipulated.

The experiments took place in two camps, in February and April 1943. Slightly more than two thousand men were questioned, half who had seen the film and half who had not. Researchers told all of the men that they were participating in a War Department survey to discern the opinions of a cross-section of soldiers. Those men watching the movies as part of the experiment saw the first four films in the *Why We Fight* series: *The Battle of Britain*, *Prelude to War*, *The Nazis Strike*, and *Divide and Conquer*. In conducting the experiments, researchers hoped to determine the films' usefulness in two central areas, one geopolitical and the other quite personal — improving the men's attitudes about the U.S. role in the war and increasing their own motivation for fighting in it.

In general, the films seemed to enhance the men's factual knowledge about the war. From *The Battle of Britain*, for instance, they learned of the superior size of the German air force and of the number of modern guns in the United Kingdom.[25] They also seemed to understand from the film that British resistance gave the United States a little more time to prepare for entering the war as well as saved the United States from attack. More than one-third of the men who saw the film (as opposed to around one-quarter of those who had not) believed that had Germany won the battle "the U.S. was next on Hitler's list" of countries to be invaded.[26] Nevertheless, the film did a relatively poor job of improving the men's attitudes toward the British, and it hardly changed anyone's motivation to get into battle. When asked, "If you had your choice when you finish your training, which would you choose," 38 percent of the group that had not seen the film answered, "Duty in an outfit overseas" rather than "Duty in an outfit in the United States." The response barely differed from the men in the viewing group:

Only 41 percent of them claimed they would seek overseas duty after seeing the film.[27]

For each of the *Why We Fight* films under consideration, results stayed about the same. The men's factual knowledge about the war seemed to improve. Their "opinions"—aggression toward the enemy, sympathy for the Allies, motivation for fighting—generally did not.[28] For the researchers, then, the very problem with the army's educational films was that they were, in fact, too educational. They reliably increased knowledge but were far less dependable when it came to changing attitudes. The researchers noted, however, that at least in some cases there was, in fact, little room for improvement. About 78 percent of the men who had not yet seen the films already believed that "we should see to it that the Germans and Japs suffer plenty for all the trouble they are causing us." In the group that had seen the films, precisely the same percentage shared that belief.[29]

The social scientists conducting these experiments were assessing the possibilities for creating a wartime fighting force through military propaganda. Rather than having an interest in creating critical thinking—ostensibly the goal of the film education movement—they hoped to find the best way of creating the certainty of specific influence. These same scientists, however, also knew that the war would end, and that their *Why We Fight* experiments might really demonstrate the possibilities for a postwar progressive modernity, one fully in keeping with the desires of the film educators of the 1930s.

In writing up their findings the researchers posed two sets of questions, one about the present and one about the future. Did the films "benefit the morale of the men," the researchers wondered, thus making "the soldiers more willing to serve in the Army?" By asking such a question, they were actually asking "the still more general question"; that is, "Can motivations of this sort be influenced by documentary films," those that they described as "films with a purely educational approach." This war experience provided the testing ground for those interested in such questions, because of the "possibility of using documentary films as a mass education medium for producing desired changes in motivations—as, for example, overcoming racial or national prejudices."[30] For the experts working for the military during the war, the documentary film might well be considered part of the postwar conjunction of science, cinema, and governmental will, directed at nothing less than changing the ways that Americans thought, and in particular aimed at teaching a vast population how to be neither racist nor nationalist.

The sort of United Nations liberalism espoused here seemed both possible and implausible because of the scientists' belief in a culture of indoctrination. An apparently only partial shift in attitude among recent recruits after watching the *Why We Fight* films, for instance, probably was attributable to beliefs that already had been shaped by "all of the civilian information media." Scientists noted that, before the entry of the United States into the war, "religious intolerance under Hitler was highly publicized," and that probably because of this, most men believed even before they watched *Prelude to War*, from the *Why We Fight* series, that if Germany won "Hitler would close all of our churches . . . [and] persecute Jews and other minority groups."[31] The army researchers continued, stating that "it might be argued that sizable changes in motivation as a result of a single 50-minute film are very unlikely simply because the film is such a small influence relative to perhaps years of exposure to points of view contrary to material presented in the film."[32]

This produced the paradox for the scientists in their study of reception. There could be no doubt that a variety of media had an absolute influence on opinion. But because of this there could be no guarantee that even the most systematically developed series of educational films would ever have much of an effect. For the scientists, with their own self-image as members of a rationalist vanguard, the most reasoned scientific educational program might only work on men such as themselves. "Such a program," they wrote, "may be effective with only a small percentage of individuals whose attitudes are primarily determined by rational analysis of the relevant facts." Thus their utopianism was only matched by their feelings that scientific reason might actually have no postwar future at all. "For the majority of individuals," they lamented, "it may be true that motivations and attitudes are generally acquired without regard to rational considerations and are practically impregnable to new rational considerations."[33]

Operation Celluloid: The POW Viewer

The government's research experts in the end questioned the usefulness of the films to change attitudes. The military, however, as well as others among the experts they employed, maintained their faith in *Why We Fight*. In fact, the military believed in the worth of the films not only for the American soldier but for the German one as well. In this case, they understood the films as ideal for conditioning, in different ways, two very different groups of men. Capra's superiors hoped that the documentaries would serve to militarize American men. But they also were just as determined that the films could be used to pastoralize the German soldier.

At least, the films could be used in this manner on those German soldiers captured by American forces. Around 380,000 Germans were held in the United States as POWs during the war and just after, in about five hundred camps located mostly in rural parts of the country.[34] At first, President Roosevelt and many in his inner circle rejected any notion of rehabilitating seemingly incorrigible Nazis. Eventually, after much debate, Secretary of War Henry Stimson, Secretary of State Cordell Hull, and others convincingly proposed that many German soldiers might be able to unlearn the ideological lessons of Nazism through logical persuasion.[35] As a result, American authorities, under the auspices of the Special Projects Division, began a program of reeducation for these prisoners, a "barbed-wire college," to use a term from Ron Robin, and one that he has likened to a freshman undergraduate curriculum in the liberal arts.[36]

To facilitate the reeducation of the potentially "normal" German, authorities placed perceived Nazi ideologues in separate camps. They also enlisted the help of "friendly" and well-educated German prisoners to help them prepare their curriculum. By late 1943 the program had begun, with a strong emphasis on courses in German and American history and also on language and literature. By spring 1945 camp authorities started using movies for instructional purposes.[37] The military developed a fairly elaborate system of film distribution and exhibition for the camps and selected movies carefully. The major studios apparently made a selection of their movies available, and the choices came from all significant Hollywood genres, with an emphasis on biopics and other period films: *The Life of Emile Zola* and *The Story of Louis Pasteur* from Warner Bros., for instance, and *Madame Curie* and *The Great Waltz* from MGM.[38] From accounts by military officials we have, at least, a sense of how screenings worked in the camps, and also some understanding of the prisoners' responses to the films that they saw.

In 1947 Jaye E. Gordon, who as Visual Aids Coordinator for the Sixth Army oversaw film distribution and exhibition for camps in the western United States, described the film system in the *Hollywood Quarterly*. The very title of the article, "Operation Celluloid," amply demonstrates the significance for the military of the film viewings, and the importance of entertainment as reprogramming. Gordon had charge of 106 16mm feature films, with camps showing movies twice a week. None of the camps had theaters, so prisoners usually watched movies in mess halls, after being charged a fifteen-cent admission fee—paid in camp canteen coupons. Before a showing, camp officials posted German-language synopses of the film being screened, synopses that typically would be prepared by army linguists. In addition, at least on occasion according to Gordon, "artists among the prisoners would make posters for added publicity." Gordon also wrote that "motion pictures were reported by the prisoners to be the most favored source of diversion," with many paying "to see the same film several times."[39]

In part through these repeat viewings Gordon made some tentative assessments of film reception among the prisoners, ranking film preference by figuring the average number of viewers. In terms of sheer numbers, the most popular film was one of the two German-language movies distributed to the camps, *Dream of Spring*, a biography of Franz Schubert that drew on average 230 viewers per screening (exact prison populations are difficult to determine, but the camps seemed to vary from a few hundred men to around four thousand).[40] Among Hollywood films, though (all of which were shown without German subtitles), prisoners were particularly enthusiastic about the Rita Hayworth musical *You Were Never Lovelier* (with 171 viewers, on average); an MGM film with a "German" theme, *The Great Waltz* (167 viewers); *Captains Courageous*, with Spencer Tracy (165 viewers), and two war films, *A Guy Named Joe*, also with Tracy (145 viewers) and *Thirty Seconds over Tokyo* (141 viewers). Another war film, however, stood out as the prisoners' least favorite: *Operation Burma*, with Errol Flynn, attracted only 101 viewers on average. *Purple Heart*, about American POWs, hardly did better (115 viewers), and neither did three other war films: *Guadalcanal Diary* (120 viewers); *Back to Bataan*, with John Wayne (132 viewers); and the Edward G. Robinson comedy *Mr. Winkle Goes to War* (134 viewers).[41]

Gordon himself proposed some theories of prisoner preference. The two favorite war films, *A Guy Named Joe* and *Thirty Seconds over Tokyo*, both had screenplays by Dalton Trumbo, who included "a maximum of expressive action and a minimum of dialogue as a matter of principle," a potentially important difference for an audience of men who spoke little English. Gordon also pointed out that *Captains Courageous* had been made in Germany in 1937 as *Manuel*, and had been extremely popular in Hitler Youth Camps all over the country.[42]

Thus the average German POW seems to have been a fairly avid viewer who enjoyed the same pinup—Rita Hayworth—as did American GIs, while also appreciating quality war films (Trumbo's), and taking a certain nation-

FILMS FOR THE PRISONER OF WAR MOTION PICTURE CIRCUIT

OWI Documentaries

O - 1 COWBOY
O - 2 SWEDES IN AMERICA
O - 3 CITY HARVEST
O - 4 STEELTOWN
O - 5 PIPELINE
O - 6 THE TOWN
O - 7 AUTOBIOGRAPHY OF A JEEP
O - 8 POWER AND THE LAND
O - 9 SAND AND FLAME
O - 10 HARVEST FOR TOMORROW

Warner Brothers

W - 101 HOLLYWOOD CANTEEN
W - 102 DESTINATION TOKYO
W - 103 ADVENTURES OF MARK TWAIN
W - 104 OBJECTIVE BURMA
W - 105 OKLAHOMA KID
W - 106 ROUGHLY SPEAKING
W - 107 FRISCO KID
W - 108 DR. EHRLICH'S MAGIC BULLET
W - 109 EMILE ZOLA
W - 110 ONE FOOT IN HEAVEN
W - 111 JUAREZ
W - 112 LOUIS PASTEUR
W - 113 GENTLEMAN JIM

M G M

M - 201 DRAGON SEED
M - 202 CAPTAINS COURAGEOUS
M - 203 A GUY NAMED JOE
M - 204 HUMAN COMEDY, THE
M - 205 MADAME CURIE
M - 206 PRESENTING LILY MARS
M - 207 THE CLOCK
M - 208 THE GREAT WALTZ
M - 209 THIRTY SECONDS OVER TOKYO
M - 210 WITHOUT LOVE

Paramount

P - 301 A GREAT MAN'S LADY
P - 302 BISCUIT EATER
P - 303 CHRISTMAS IN JULY
P - 304 GOING MY WAY
P - 305 GREAT VICTOR HERBERT

P - 306 HOLD BACK THE DAWN
P - 307 HOLIDAY INN
P - 308 OUR HEARTS WERE YOUNG AND GAY
P - 309 SO PROUDLY WE HAIL
P - 310 THERE'S MAGIC IN MUSIC
P - 311 UNION PACIFIC
P - 312 WELLS FARGO
P - 313 BIRTH OF THE BLUES
P - 314 ALDRICH FAMILY, THE
       (Life with Henry)
P - 315 DISPUTED PASSAGE
P - 316 OUR NEIGHBORS, THE CARTERS
P - 317 PARSON OF PANAMINT, THE

Columbia

C - 401 DESTROYER
C - 402 HERE COMES MR. LINCOLN
C - 403 THE IMPATIENT YEARS
C - 404 LOST HORIZON
C - 405 PENNY SERENADE
C - 406 TOGETHER AGAIN
C - 407 WHAT A WOMAN
C - 408 OUR WIFE
C - 409 MR. WINKLE GOES TO WAR
C - 410 YOU WERE NEVER LOVELIER

Twentieth Century Fox

F - 501 EVE OF ST. MARK
F - 502 GUADALCANAL DIARY
F - 503 HAPPY LAND
F - 504 HOW GREEN WAS MY VALLEY
F - 505 PURPLE HEART, THE
F - 506 STORY OF ALEXANDER GRAHAM BELL
F - 507 SULLIVANS, THE
F - 508 WILD GEESE CALLING
F - 509 WING AND A PRAYER
F - 510 YOUNG MR. LINCOLN
F - 511 KEYS OF THE KINGDOM
F - 512 SONG OF BERNADETTE
F - 513 HOLY MATRIMONY
F - 514 ALEXANDER'S RAGTIME BAND
F - 515 WESTERN UNION

The list of films on the German prisoner of war circuit. *Lost Horizon* was one of ten Columbia films in distribution. (National Archives)

alist and nostalgic pleasure in films that reminded him of home (*The Great Waltz, Captains Courageous*). But the camp context for all of these films was also overtly educational, with the synopses themselves, which were both posted and also read to the men before screenings, attempting to shape reception practices.

Columbia Pictures placed ten films in camp distribution, among them Capra's *Lost Horizon* (as well as the camp favorite, *You Were Never Lovelier*). The foreword to the synopsis for *Lost Horizon*, both posted and spoken, stressed the need to understand the film as a prophetic one about World War II, and about the necessity of saving "civilization." "In the early 1930's," the synopsis began, "shadows of a future war could be discerned by far-seeing men. Many wondered what would become of Civilization, man's cultural achievements, the treasures of Art he had created . . . Another world-war, and Civilization, as man had known it, would be wiped off the face of the earth."[43] Here the audience was taught a very specific kind of textual analysis, one that stressed interpreting the film as an anti-war tract, and that also, at least implicitly, blamed the spectators themselves for the destruction of "civilization." Viewing *Lost Horizon* and the other camp feature films was voluntary; nevertheless, entertainment became education or, more precisely, de-Nazification, with the men being encouraged to understand Capra's 1930s utopianism as a warning against German aggression.

The blame hinted at with *Lost Horizon* came to be stated overtly in the *Why We Fight* films. In the POW camps, military officials hoped to use entertainment in the form of Hollywood movies as education. This is precisely the manner in which the *Why We Fight* documentaries were used in U.S. military bases. As the researchers in charge of the experiments pointed out, the fact that the men saw the documentaries outside of the usual army educational context may well have made recruits less resistant to the overt pedagogy of Capra's movies. But in the POW camps, the *Why We Fight* series was clearly marked as educational, both in terms of the practical matter of repatriation after the war and in terms of understanding German responsibility for the war.

The POWs had to sit through lectures in German before the screenings of Capra's documentaries, and English-version transcripts of some of these still exist. At the Indiantown Gap Military Reservation in Pennsylvania, for example, the speaker's opening comments tell us something about exhibition practices at the camp. "First of all," he began, "I will answer some questions which you have submitted and when it becomes dark enough, we will show the second film of the *Why We Fight* series."[44] Here the men were either watching the film in a building in which windows could not be covered or, more likely, they had to watch outdoors, and hence only well after sundown.

The speaker, either a prisoner himself or an American competent in German, then answered questions that had been submitted by POWs. Almost all of them had to do with the goods that prisoners would be allowed to bring back to Germany after the war. "There are no restrictions on the types of articles of personal property," the speaker informed the men, except for "government issued property in excess of that authorized." The men also would be permitted to bring back "photographs, diaries, personal manuscripts, books, letters, and other written material," as long as it had been "censored, packaged, sealed and stamped 'approved' at the camp level." Overall, prisoners would be allowed a maximum of fifty-five pounds of material, "plus a special ten pounds allowance of publications purchased in prisoner of war canteens or distributed by the War Department."[45] In this case the educational evening began with an assertion of a kind of watchful benevolence on the part of the United States, which allowed the men significant leeway to bring back anything they wanted, as long as the military itself reserved the right to censor such personal items as diaries and letters.

The lesson then moved from the local to the global as the speaker intoned, "For the next few minutes, we will consider the results of the Potsdam Conference which President Truman, Prime Minister Atlee, and Generalissimo Stalin attended a few days ago." Here the Allied nations became the benevolent overseers of global stability, as the results of Potsdam would lead to "speedier, more orderly, more cooperative and efficient peace settlements than could otherwise be obtained."[46] Only after this discussion of repatriation and world affairs did the speaker even mention the film for that evening, *The Nazis Strike*. And in the narrative of the evening's education, the lecture preceding the film fell between the very personal interests of the opening comments and the abstractly global aspects of the lesson about Potsdam. In preparing the audience for Capra's film, the speaker tried to prepare them to accept Germany's national guilt for the war. This guilt also became, in particular, that of Hitler rather than the prisoners because the men in the Indiantown audience—just like the men in most of the POW camps—were not considered among those hardened Nazis who all had been squirreled away in separate camps.

About the film, the speaker noted that it "shows in detail how the German Reich, under the leadership of the fanatic Hitler, secretly built up an army while insisting to the world that Germany's only aim was peace." He went on to say that "we will show how Hitler's plan was to bite off little pieces of Europe," and then he assured the men that "this is a factual film" and urged them to "note the consequences which Hitler imposed in countries he conquered, namely, hunger, pestilence, famine, rape, stark terror and wholesale wanton destruction."[47] In American army camps the point of *Why We Fight* was to use the film series to create fighting men out of civilians. In the POW camps, through the same films and through the lectures that accompanied them, lectures that asserted the disaster of German military authority, the goal came to be to create a very different kind of masculinity. To U.S. military authorities the Germans needed to be turned into men who understood not the necessity of fighting but the importance of peace, and a peace as far as possible from German influence.

There was, at least, one other difference in the uses of the programs in the different sites, at least if we believe the rhetoric of the officials involved. Rather than inspiring the men as in the American camps, the *Why We Fight* films were meant to make the POWs accept a kind of national guilt and also to make them physically ill over the horrors of the Third Reich. Jaye Gordon, the army's visual aids coordinator, stressed that the Hollywood "feature-film program was sold as entertainment," and, in fact, they indeed were "sold," as the prisoners had to use camp coupons to gain admission. Capra's films, however, as well as other compulsory documentaries about Germany's concentration camps, "cost the prisoners nothing," in Gordon's words, "except maybe their dinner."[48]

With the fan mail for *Meet John Doe*, there seemed to be the possibility of a segment of the audience that was left virtually sickened by the films they saw. Remember, for example, the woman who, with her husband, usually came home from the movies "dripping with disgust." In the prison camps, the construction of this kind of spectator came to be precisely the point; that is, spectators who would feel the need to avert their eyes, because they could not bear the images before them. Of course, Hollywood did not seek to create viewers who felt, mostly, "disgust." But the prison camps did want to use Capra's films to construct an aversive viewer—a viewer suffused with shame and coerced into watching what Gordon and other officials hoped would be unwatchable.

We have scant direct evidence of POW response, sickened or otherwise.[49] We do, however, have an extraordinary document assessing Capra's films, written by a POW. Oskar Wintergerst worked in a camp called "the Factory" at Fort Kearney in Rhode Island. Factory workers, as Ron Robin has written, generally were chosen because they were the prisoners who were "alienated . . . intellectuals, disillusioned Communists, writers, and journalists."[50] Military authorities hoped to use them to design a reeducation program fit for rank-and-file German soldiers. Reviewing *Why We Fight* as a tool of reeducation, Wintergerst developed a reception aesthetic based on national difference, varying notions of realism, and even camp politics in order to question the value of the films for POWs.[51]

Wintergerst complained of the "trick" photography and fanciful editing in some of the films, and he made a direct comparison between American and German indoctrination methods. Complaining about a scene in *Prelude to War* in which the German military appears to be firing on German civilians, Wintergerst wrote that "if a documentary film shall be addressed to the prisoners it must be free of hatred and falsifications." He added that "this kind of propaganda was used by Goebbels, because the Nazis could not work with facts and arguments founded on reason." In an attempt to delineate the specific differences between Americans and Germans as persuadable subjects, Wintergerst moved right to the issue of Hitler's global desires. The researchers examining the usefulness of the films among Americans noted a 33 percent increase in the number of men who, after seeing *The Battle of Britain*, believed that Germany would have invaded the United States had it only been able to defeat England.[52] Wintergerst, however, explained that "the prisoner of war will not accept the German expansion to America as credible reason for war with the U.S.A.," with this kind of imperial enterprise simply the province of a few "primitive [German] politicians who had no idea of military possibilities." Again and again Wintergerst emphasized the relationship between national difference and reception practice. "The *Why We Fight* series cannot fill [the] demand" for reeducation, he wrote, "because those films are cut for the orientation of the American soldier only." Capra's films were designed "to explain the causes of war to the American soldiers," but now the military planned to show these films to German POWs. Because of the original intention behind the films, Wintergerst wrote, "it cannot be expected that the films are fit as educational remedy." Along with national considerations, camp culture itself probably affected reception. Wintergerst suggested that some prisoners still might be "strongly impressed," but only "if they are not under pressure of the camp-Gestapo," those hardline Nazis who had not been successfully segregated from the rest. Later in his report Wintergerst lamented that "the majority of prisoners have not yet [had] the opportunity for re-education, because the Nazi fanatics in the camps control the whole intellectual life."[53]

Wintergerst's POW viewer appears to be markedly different from Jaye Gordon's: either disbelieving or still too much under Nazi influence rather than physically ill. Both Wintergerst and American officials, however, agreed that there were differences between American and German soldiers, and that the same films would produce different effects. Thus in the United States film education, at this time and at least in the military context, meant acknowledging the volatility of reception and also attempting—via scientific studies and through "native informants" like Wintergerst—to understand reception practices and finally to control them. For *Why We Fight*, control meant realizing how to use specific kinds of film in the construction of specific kinds of male subjects. In the United States during World War II, military officials and other professionals connected to the military understood the imperatives of American and German masculinity in very different ways. German and American soldiers watched the same films and often in camps just a few miles apart. The desired results, however, were absolutely at odds with each other. Nevertheless, both social scientists and government officials viewed the possibility of achieving those varied results as essential to guaranteeing a liberal, scientific postwar modernity at home, and lasting peace throughout the world.

Rehabilitation through Film:
The Case of *It's a Wonderful Life*

San Quentin warden Clinton T. Duffy began his 1951 prison memoir with a story about a movie. "One evening not very long ago I went to the movies to see a prison picture," he wrote, and then goes on to say that "the film was advertised as a 'shocker' " because of its depiction of life in a jail ostensibly modeled after San Quentin. Continuing his first-person narrative, Duffy states "I got quite an education that night," and then described the warden "who was a pawn in the hands of a scheming chief guard," all of the prisoners who, with the exception of the hero, "were cruel, moronic characters . . . plotting all sorts of violence," and the "vicious" guards who "clubbed prisoners whenever they felt like it." Although unnamed, the movie obviously was Robert Rossen's 1947 docu-noir *Brute Force*, which starred Burt Lancaster.[54]

For Duffy, the movie did indeed provide an "education" about the apparent corruption of the postwar prison system, in complete contradiction to his own experience. To the warden's alarm, the cinema provided the public with dubious information about inmates and the potential for their rehabilitation. To counter this narrative Duffy offered another one, which seemed practically to be taken from a Frank Capra film. Duffy's father had been a guard at San Quentin, and one day, confronted by an angry prisoner armed with a dagger made from a file, the elder Duffy said, "I am ashamed of you," and then, "give me the shiv." The prisoner acquiesced, saying, "I wouldn't do this for any other man alive." To the younger Duffy the lesson was a significant one, providing the "reminder that even the most savage of men need and appreciate a friend." Duffy added that "my father, in truth, was more of a friend than jailer to hundreds of San Quentin's men."[55] From his father, the future warden learned the same lesson about the inestimable value of friendship and trust as did George Bailey in *It's a Wonderful Life*.

One of the marks of Duffy's postwar progressivism in prison issues was his belief in the possibility of rehabilitating his inmates through stern kindness and common sense rather than punishment. He understood, as well, the educative potential of motion pictures. In the case of *Brute Force*, he realized that the cinema actually hindered the cause of spreading the word about the possibilities of prison reform in the world outside of prison walls. But he believed quite strongly in reversing this process, in showing movies on the "inside" to prisoners in order to entertain them and also to teach them certain truths. It was in this context that Duffy arranged a screening of *It's a Wonderful Life* at San Quentin in January 1947, and then asked his inmates to tell him what they had learned.

Before Duffy took over at San Quentin, the prisoners there never saw any movies. In 1941 Duffy mentioned this to his friend, movie executive Harry Warner, who according to the warden seemed incredulous "that there could be anywhere in the world an audience of five thousand men that had somehow eluded Warner Bros." Warner promptly provided San Quentin with projectors and some films, and Duffy began weekly showings of movies lent to him by the Hollywood studios, despite warnings against allowing thousands of criminals to gather together in a room with the lights down so that "every sorehead in the place [could] take care of his beefs in the dark."[56] Duffy showed the movies in the prison mess hall, and he only allowed attendance to those whose conduct and work records had been exemplary. Duffy understood very specific modes of prisoner reception. The movies were educational, allowing the men to keep up "with the world, its fashions and fads, its politics and preachings."[57] The movies also offered the men at least partial escape from prison routine, and because of this Duffy decided in 1943 to bring 16mm projectors onto death row, where the prisoners needed that type of escape more than did the other men.

The belief in the educational and psychological benefits of movies in prison had a relatively recent history when Duffy took over at San Quentin in 1941. Indeed, education in general had been a low priority at most penal institutions. According to one educational journal from the period, for much of the early part of the twentieth century prison chaplains had been encouraged to "provide a limited amount of formal academic instruction,"

THE NOTICEABLE LACK OF FANFARE HERALDING THE ARRIVAL OF
"IT'S A WONDERFUL LIFE" AT S.Q. GAVE ME A FEELING OF
PERSONAL DISCOVERY, HAVING READ THE "RAVE" NOTICES IN THE
LOCAL PAPERS AND ITS SELECTION AS "THE-MOVIE-OF-THE-WEEK"
IN THE CURRENT ISSUE OF "LIFE MAGAZINE." THE FACT
THAT WE WERE BEING TREATED TO A "WORLD PREMIERE"
MADE US, THE ONES WITH BRUISED KNUCKLES FROM
GRABBING FOR THE "BRASS RING" ON LIFE'S MERRY-GO-ROUND,
ASK "WHAT IS THE CATCH?"

    THERE WAS NO "CATCH!" DIRECTOR FRANK CAPRA
PLAYED ON EVERY EMOTION IN THE MAKEUP. I HATED OLD
MAN POTTER; LOVED DONA REED; SYMPATHIZED WITH JIMMIE
STEWART; CRIED WHEN HIS FATHER DIED; LAUGHED WITH THE
ANGELS, AND WAS "READY-FOR-THE-RIVER" AT THE CLIMAX.

    THE MORAL OF THE STORY, SO BEAUTIFULLY BLENDED INTO
FINE ENTERTAINMENT, WILL EFFECT EVERYONE WHO SEES
THE PICTURE. NO ONE COMES INTO THE WORLD, OR S.Q.
BY INVITATION, BUT EACH ONE OF US WILL LEAVE
THE WORLD, OR S.Q. A DIFFERENT PLACE FROM WHAT
IT WOULD HAVE BEEN WITHOUT US.

    SO, TO THE FEELING OF "PERSONAL-DISCOVERY" MAY I
ADD A LITTLE "SELF-RESPECT" - THAT SCARCE COMMODITY
TO A CONVICTED CRIMINAL? WHO KNOWS? A KIND WORD
FROM ME, TO A GUY WHO IS "READY-FOR-THE-RIVER" MAY GUIDE
HIM TO SUCCESS WHICH MY GRAND-CHILDREN WILL ENJOY!

One of the lengthier San Quentin prisoner reports made to warden Duffy on *It's a Wonderful Life*. (Wesleyan Cinema Archives)

but as late as 1930 "no correctional institution in the country had a well formulated educational program as an integral part of its routine."[58] At around that time—in keeping with several decades worth of developments in progressive education, the professionalization and bureaucratization of teaching, and general increases in the availability of all levels of education—prisons began providing full instructional programs. Experiments in Elmira, New York, soon moved to other states, and these programs at least in part marked an era in which prison authorities viewed education as the means for the social and economic rehabilitation of prisoners.[59]

Of course, literature played a prominent role in these efforts. The press from the period occasionally told the public about the various Great Books programs in prisons, in which, in one instance, inmates "for two hours critically discussed Aristophanes's *Lysistrata*, *Birds*, and *Clouds*."[60] Inmates also had the option of studying other academic subjects or taking on vocational training, and after such courses of study men might earn their grammar school or high school diplomas or even receive college credit.[61] As part of the educational and rehabilitative initiative, prison authorities understood that along with other kinds of training inmates needed the "stimulating of interest in wholesome leisure-time activities." Implicitly this was because their pleasures had been less than "wholesome" before prison, but also, after their releases, it would allow them to mingle more easily in acceptable spaces of popular culture—the concert hall, the theater, and the movie house, for example.[62] To further this form of education some prisons brought professional theater to their inmates, in the form of plays or vaudeville acts, and also encouraged prisoners to produce and perform in shows.[63] In addition, movies came increasingly to be used in prison settings. These films were often educational rather than the Hollywood product, and the rationale behind showing them sounds a great deal like that directing the use of the *Why We Fight* films for soldiers. A 1942 essay titled "Prison Education and the Sound Film" intoned that "motion pictures when used intelligently can impart more factual information; bring about longer retention; develop better relationship understandings; stimulate pupil description, explanation, analytical thinking, imagination, and interest, and help the mentally retarded acquire more understandings."[64] Just as important, movies helped offset the problems of one of the great difficulties among prisoners: illiteracy.

Part of the intelligent use of motion pictures included Hollywood movies. While precise information can be difficult to come by, it seems likely that this, too, was a function of the changing attitudes during the 1930s of prison authorities toward the needs of inmates.[65] As the prisoner wrote to Capra in 1939, *Mr. Deeds Goes to Town* was the first film shown in Folsom since the late 1920s. Other prisons adopted film viewing as an ideal modern and potentially productive form of leisure activity. The New Jersey State Prison seems to have been particularly active, hiring J. A. Reynolds as the director of recreation who oversaw film viewing. Along with other theater managers, Reynolds wrote in to the "What the Picture Did For Me" column in the trade weekly *Motion Picture Herald* to discuss the success or failure of different films. *Three Cheers for Love*, for example, a Paramount musical with Bob Cummings, proved to be a "good amusement" for the prison viewers in 1937. A year later, the men also liked *Hula Heaven*, with Reynolds urging fellow exhibitors to "book it and feature it." *The Citadel*, a much more serious project that screened in 1939, demonstrates some of the connections between film and literature in the prison education program. Reynolds wrote that most of the inmates had read the novel before seeing the movie (which sounds very much like part of a classroom project fitting in well with a Great Books syllabus), and were then impressed by the direction of the film and by the performances. Inmates there also enjoyed the less-high-brow *Honolulu* with Eleanor Powell, as well as *Reap the Wild Wind* with Ray Milland and Paulette Goddard.[66]

Duffy showed films, too, with the warden and his prison emerging in popular discourse from the period as models of progressive prison reform. *Life* magazine featured San Quentin in October 1947, with a ten-page spread of pictures and text. The magazine explained that the practice of prison administrators, "under California's progressive penal system, is an earnest attempt to treat criminals like what they are—human beings, not much different from those outside the walls by any measurable standards . . . who have got into trouble through some flaw of the spirit." Duffy, like his father, worked to become the inmates' confidant and advocate, offering them "friendly counsel over the prison radio," trying to lessen the ill effects of a deadly daily routine of activities, and developing art classes and hobby shops, prison orchestras and gymnastic teams. Significant for my project in this chapter, Duffy also encouraged the men to write up to "three letters a week to . . . family or friends," a marked increase from the one letter per week "on a single piece of paper" allowed by most prisons. *Life* marveled that "strangely, many prisoners would rather write than receive letters—it gives them a chance for self-expression and for feeling important."[67]

Correspondence classes had been offered at San Quentin at least since the 1920s.[68] Warden Duffy, however, brought the classroom to the prison in 1943 when he began an affiliation between the prison and the College of Marin, which supplied instructors in a number of subjects. Between 1946 and 1947, slightly over six hundred men were enrolled in the prison's day school, and more than eighteen hundred in its night school—for a total, in all probability, of nearly half the men in San Quentin. By 1947 thirty-two of these prisoners had received high school degrees and eleven earned elementary school diplomas. For Duffy and many other progressive wardens like him, education came to be seen as the surest method of rehabilitation, with "cultural development," which included exposure to Hollywood films, having a central role in prison pedagogy, along with vocational training, instruction in citizenship, physical education, academic subjects, and training for family life.[69]

The project of having convicts watch movies at least somewhat reversed the typical relationship between the prisoner and the photographic image, with inmates probably far more used to being the subjects for the camera rather than the viewers of motion pictures. John Tagg has written of the manner in which photography served as a means of surveillance and evidence gathering in the prison and the asylum in the nineteenth century, a process that led to the development of the mug shot, with new photographic technologies providing new opportunities to document and control inmate behavior.[70] In 1948, for example, eighteen months after the San Quentin screening of *It's a Wonderful Life*, prisoners viewing films gave officials at Colorado State Penitentiary in Canon City, in cooperation with *Life* magazine, a chance to use modern developments in photography to record inmates in the act of being spectators.[71]

Eagle Lion Films produced a movie that year called *Canon City*, about an actual jail break at the prison there. Brian Foy, who produced the film, sponsored a special screening of the movie for the prisoners, including the recaptured escapees. "While they watched," *Life* reported, "photographer J. R. Eyerman . . . set up a battery of automatic cameras pointing at them, [and] used infrared film to catch their expressions in the darkness." The extraordinary photographs show one escapee, "James Sherbondy, a lifer in for murder," as he "hides his face in embarrassment from his fellow convicts when [his] screen counterpart shows remorse, gratitude, pity and other normal emotions." Another of the participants, R. L. Freeman, "a 21-year old kidnapper with a 25-year sentence, simply laughs." A third viewer, "Billy New, the baby of the desperadoes, looks on unconcerned," being "chiefly interested in meeting the actress who plays [the] role of his girlfriend."[72] In this rather extreme example, as the men got the chance to watch themselves in the movie the camera that was trained on them could record their responses, with the result proving that the captured escapees remained incorrigible—either embarrassed or amused by the representation of "normal emotions."

When Warden Duffy spoke over the San Quentin radio system to tell the men to write their responses to Capra's film, he almost certainly had nothing so extreme in mind as the Canon City exercise in photographing prisoners. But he probably did want to gauge the reception practices of his inmates in the same manner as the *Life* photographs. Thus watching movies in prison provided different kinds of education: the inmates might witness good models for various forms of behavior, while prison officials could get some sense of the success or failure of their efforts toward rehabilitation.

Duffy's request may have been somewhat unusual, but the screening itself formed part of an extensive interaction with mainstream popular culture for the men in San Quentin. Just a few days before the film screening, the prison had sponsored its thirty-second annual New Year's Day show, with four thousand inmates cramming into a mess hall auditorium that seated only three thousand. The entertainers were singers and dancers from the San Francisco area, including a "Copacabana chorus," acrobats, and jazz ensembles. The show seems to have been a big hit, with several of the inmates mentioning it in their comments to Duffy about *It's a Wonderful Life*. Apparently echoing the enthusiasm of so many of the men, one of them told Duffy, "here is also thanking you for that grand, which is putting it mild, New Years show." [73]

There were also speeches at the prison, which were typically uplifting and educational. The same week as the screening, for example, Mrs. Maud Ballington Booth, the founder of the Prison Department of the Volunteers of America, spoke to the inmates on "her favorite theme—'Men Can Be Trusted.'" The prisoners also took part in all kinds of sporting events, with baseball and basketball teams competing with other local squads, and boxers fighting for prison championships. Inmates also formed a San Quentin orchestra with an "accompanying complement of vocalists, instrumentalists, dancers, comedians, and tumblers." [74]

We know about entertainment at San Quentin largely through the *San Quentin News*, the eight-page newspaper published by the prison every two weeks, with contributions from prison officials, the prisoners themselves, some outsiders, and various wire services. Along with general news, the paper provided information about high- and middle-brow culture, from reviews of John Hersey's *Hiroshima* and Robinson Jeffers's free adaptation of *Medea*, to Billy Rose's regular columns about gossip and nightlife. The *News* also had complete radio listings, so the men must have been able to listen to their favorite programs. The dates and times for shows were usually accompanied by photos of radio actresses: Ann Blyth, for instance, who "broke her back in a tobogganing accident" but had finally recovered; or the "lovely Joan Barton, one of the fastest rising young actresses in radio."[75]

But mostly, there were movies. Duffy sponsored a full schedule of educational and training films with the usual tedious titles: *Story of Metal Bellows*, *Working Lathe*, and *Hay*.[76] And the men also saw Hollywood films: in the weeks following *It's a Wonderful Life* they watched a double bill of *Gentleman Joe Palooka* and *Bringing up Father*; Jeanne Crain and Cornell Wilde in *Centennial Summer* (along with a cartoon and an episode of *March of Time*); Rosalind Russell in *Sister Kenny* (accompanied by an MGM newsreel and a Walt Disney cartoon); and Jack Carson in *Two Guys from Milwaukee*, along with a travelogue called *South of Monterey* and a Bugs Bunny cartoon (*Hare-Raising Hare*).[77]

If the newspaper serves as an indication, none of these films generated the excitement of that for *It's a Wonderful Life*. On the front page of the *San Quentin News* from 3 January 1947, next to an article headlined "Calls for Unskilled Men Drop," an announcement told the men about "a movie 'treat,'" under which appeared a photograph of Donna Reed. The caption for the photo read: "One of the best motion pictures to be shown here in many a month will bring lovely Donna Reed, above, to the auditorium screen over the weekend in the showing of *It's a Wonderful Life*."[78] Indeed, given the recurring pictures of radio and movie actresses, the men seem to have had a greater interest in female rather than male stars, and Reed may have been a far greater attraction for the men than any possible educational benefit in Capra's film (an image of James Stewart appeared in the same issue of the *News*, but not until page 5, above a story detailing the actor's return to movies after the war).[79]

"A Warm Good Type of Sadness"

After the screening of *It's a Wonderful Life*, the inmates' interest seemed far more focused on the emotional, moral, and intellectual impact of Capra's film than on Donna Reed's performance. Some of the responses, along with passing judgment on the film, provide a fuller understanding of the assignment that the warden gave the inmates. Fred McDermott prefaced his remarks by telling Duffy: "You have asked over the radio hook-up, what our personal opinion was and what we got out of most in the recent picture," indicating that the warden sought individual opinions of Capra's film and also something larger about character development.[80] Most of the men were

Donna Reed on the front page of the *San Quentin News*, advertising the screening of *It's a Wonderful Life*, "a movie treat" for the prisoners.

willing to oblige, but the film also made them judge not just their own reactions but those of their fellow inmates, giving us an overall sense of the
men who saw the film and of their general response to Capra's movie. One
of the men, for instance, felt the full burden of speaking for all of those
men unable to respond to the warden's request, praising Duffy for showing the film and then saying to him, "thanking you for myself, and [for]
the many men who can not write." Several of the inmates mentioned that
the film remained a topic of conversation for a few days after the screening: "Men are still talking about it and will for some time to come," one
inmate wrote, while another said, "I have heard a lot of comments on it
in the yard and all of them were for it." Still another letter, signed by four

men but written in the first-person singular, claimed that "coming out of the theatre I heard nothing but absolute praise from all sides." The letter went from this description of prisoner reaction, based on what the inmates heard, to a more psychologized, more difficult to demonstrate assertion of the men's response. "Everyone I am sure had a feeling of sadness," the letter continued, "but a warm good type of sadness and silent reflection of our own loved ones at home."[81]

Most of the letter writers, while often thanking the warden on behalf of all the men, responded primarily in personal terms. Some of the prisoners read the film as a political allegory ("To me it brought out the two extremes in democracy"); or in relation to class issues ("It illustrates the everyday life of the many Rich and underdog classes"). Others provided their thoughts on the film business ("The movie industry seems to be able to produce only an occasional picture of this caliber"); on the performances of the film's stars ("James Stewart and Donna Reed deserve unlimited credit for doing a wonderful job of acting"); or on the director ("the Capra touch").[82] For the most part, though, the inmates openly told Duffy about their own highly charged reactions to the film. Other evidence from San Quentin during the period indicates that the prisoners were emotional men. In the *Life* magazine article about the prison, for instance, one inmate, telling the reporter about the importance of visitors, said "I cry when they come and I cry when they leave."[83] Moreover, despite the Canon City photographs of remorseless criminals, the reception of *It's a Wonderful Life* at the prison demonstrates that the inmates could be deeply moved, even to tears, by at least some films.

For one inmate, the movie "made me realize I could still cry, and after all a good cry is good for anyone." Another said that at "some parts I would laugh and other parts it would bring the tears to my eyes," and yet another claimed that "parts of the picture started tears and again some parts I thought were very deep." Other inmates "shed a tear or two" or "wept," while one prisoner sought to confide in Duffy about the reaction of many men. "Warden I will tell you a little secret," he wrote. "I looked around me in the show and through my tears I could see several more with wet eyes." He concluded by saying that "it's no disgrace to cry when we see such a wonderful picture as that was."[84]

For all of the interest in reception studies over the last fifteen years, we still have very little understanding of, or knowledge about, crying in the cinema. Perhaps the best work, which we know about from the contemporary scholarship of Sue Harper and Vincent Porter, was conducted in Great

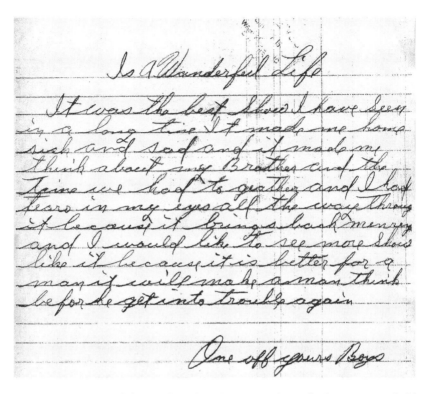

Is A Wonderful Life

It was the best Show I have seen in a long time. It made me home sick and sad and it made me think about my Brother and the Time we had to gather and I had tears in my eyes all the way throu it because it brings back memory and I would like to see more Show like it because it is better for a man it will make a man think befor he get into trouble again

One off yours Boys

"I had tears in my eyes all the way through." A letter to warden Duffy about *It's a Wonderful Life*, signed by "one off yours boys." (Wesleyan Cinema Archives)

Britain in 1950 by the Mass Observation group of social scientists.[85] They asked both men and women about crying at the movies, and their findings tended to confirm notions of gender difference. That is, men much more than women sought emotional reserve in their film responses, although they might acknowledge crying. Most typically this occurred when they watched films about World War II, and they would often admit to having the ability to cry only since the war.

These findings come from about the same time as the San Quentin screening, and they seem to indicate the possibility for men to cry while watching films that mirrored their own intensely emotional experiences. For the men in Great Britain, this meant being reminded of their own activities during the war. For the prisoners at San Quentin, just like many of the men in the Mass Observation studies whose combat experiences were still fresh in their memories, crying seemed directly related to the manner in which narrative events corresponded to past personal trauma. One of the inmates who cried wrote that, like George Bailey, "I have experienced some very desperate times," while another saw a direct link between George's family crisis and his own. He wrote in rather abstract terms, but seemed to be talking about himself when he said that he cried because the film was "heart breaking," making a married man "feel very bad that is if he was a fellow that didn't take care of his home."[86]

In the broadest use of the term, then, these men who cried, and many of the others who responded to Warden Duffy, "identified" with the narrative events of *It's a Wonderful Life* and with James Stewart as George Bailey. The film made them reflect directly on their own experiences with family and friends, with religion, and with alcohol, and they did so by asserting a direct link between themselves and George. There is some empirical data about forms of identification like this, but it is primarily about women. Jackie Stacey has produced the most detailed work, and in her analyses of female film viewers and their relationships with female movie stars, she has noted several variations. Women might, in fact, worship these stars, or develop virtually romantic sensibilities toward them. They might also engage in what Stacey calls "transcendence," that is, the "pleasure in imagining themselves taking on the roles and identities of the stars whilst in the cinema." As one of Stacey's respondents put it, "I was no longer in my seat but right up there fleeing for my life from chasing gangsters, skimming effortlessly over silver ice, or singing high and sweet like a lark."[87]

We see a form of this response with the men at San Quentin, with a difference that seems not so much gender based as it is dependent on the conditions of viewing and on the pedagogical project of showing movies in prison; that is, teaching the men to be responsible citizens. For Stacey's women, seeing themselves on screen constituted a kind of escapism from the theater and into the screen itself. The prison inmates, however, did not imagine themselves transcending the material experience of viewing. Rather, in "seeing" themselves on the screen they seemed to understand both the circumstances that helped get them into jail and also the necessity and possibility of rehabilitation.

The men at San Quentin experienced with particular power their own form of identification. One inmate explained that "the feeling was so intense it made one almost live the part by watching," while another wrote, speaking for all the men, that "one in here couldn't possibly help feeling that he was the central character, facing the troubles [and] worries of life and winning out in the end."[88] Most of the men, along with these general assertions of their own interchangeability with George, also located specific aspects of the film that made it possible for them to see their own lives on screen. Indeed, many of the prisoners focused on one aspect of George Bailey's character that, quite possibly, may have gone more or less unnoticed by other groups of viewers. Aware that he is now in Pottersville and needing to calm his nerves, Bailey drags his angel, Clarence, into a bar for a drink. To the men at San Quentin, this was the sign of Bailey's descent into alcoholism, and thus the mark of his desperation.

One prisoner turned this scene into the lesson of the film: "The picture shown last week had a *good moral*," he wrote, adding emphasis. He then stated that the movie "proves that alcohol does destroy the marital and moral fiber of all who drink, moderately or otherwise." Some of the prisoners took a less distanced approach to the issue and used Bailey's drinking as a means of speaking autobiographically. For one of them, the film "showed it did not pay to worry and then try and hide them with a bottle of liquor, or anything else as some people do and I also have done." And still another wrote, somewhat ruefully, that the surest lesson of the film was to "*leave liquor alone*" because "it is *never* our friend." As a postscript he wrote, "I know."[89]

From the remarks about alcohol, we can learn something of the culture of San Quentin. One prisoner wrote, for instance, that films like *It's a Wonderful Life* "would work hand in glove with the weekly A.A. Broadcast" at the prison.[90] The introduction of Alcoholics Anonymous to San Quentin sounds like one of Duffy's innovations, and it also indicates the extent to which alcoholism was a problem among the inmates. But the responses about drinking most often stressed the perceived direct link between Bailey and the inmates, thus presenting us with a less artificial rendering of the viewing situation recorded in *Life* about the Colorado prison. At Canon City, the inmates witnessed their own escape on screen. At San Quentin, prisoners configured a minor moment in George Bailey's life into significant scenes from their own lives.

One such viewer showed the possibility for moving back and forth, between acknowledging a personal relationship with the film and also a more abstract, political one. The same viewer who wrote "I know" about the problems of alcohol also placed the film in a far broader context. Making an economic analysis of Capra's film, he said that the movie showed "the fight the 'small' business man has on its hands when fighting 'capital' & organized business."[91] For at least one of the viewers, though, the likeness between Bailey and himself blocked any other reading, and seemed so intense as to make the movie unwatchable. "Being an Alcoholic myself," he wrote, "I remember too many fool things I did and they greave (*sic*) me so I can't stand to see much of those things any more." We have seen before, in some of the responses to *Meet John Doe*, that the cinema might create disgust in viewers, both a compulsion to watch and a shame at having continued to watch, in that case because the quality of Hollywood films seemed so low. In the instance of Capra at San Quentin, however, those films depicting drinking made this prisoner "grieve" so significantly that he found it virtually impossible to go on watching. That same prisoner concluded his letter to Duffy by saying, "We have had two horse pictures lately that I like better than any of the others."[92] A great many of the prisoners seemed to value the opportunity to watch a movie like Capra's with what seemed to them to be positive messages. For at least this inmate, however, the motion picture in prison had to function purely as escape rather than as a reminder about one's life or as a means of rehabilitation. In this case viewing pleasure came directly in inverse proportion to the intensity of the viewer's identification with events and characters.

Most of the men, of course, were able to watch the movie without this kind of discomfort, and for them the connections between their own lives and the action in the film tended to produce a kind of contemplative identification, linked most directly with Bailey's desire never to have been born. One prisoner enjoyed the film, and afterward thought his "pleasure came from the quality of the production and unusually capable acting performances." His appreciation moved from the aesthetic to the philosophical and personal as he added that "later I thought about the movie and knew that several times in my own life I have sincerely (or so I thought at the time) wished I had never been born." Capra's film "convinced" him that he had "been of some help to various people when they needed help."[93]

Similar sentiments occur in many of the responses, and most of them indicate that the prisoners had done a good deal of thinking about *It's a Wonderful Life*, even well after the screening had ended. "After seeing it I thought what good or bad has come to people through contact with me," one prisoner wrote. He then asked, "If I hadn't been born what would the life of people I have come in contact with have been like?"[94] The film impressed one prisoner as "the best picture I've ever seen," and he said that "I have been thinking about it ever since I saw it." He added, "Many times I wished I'd never been born or that I was dead just like the main character in the picture." The inmate told the warden that "the picture has caused me to think a lot of my own life."[95] Another prisoner, however, made it clear that the men really did not need the film to make them contemplate their past. "Most of us who are in places like San Quentin," the inmate wrote, "have time to sit back and think of what might have happened had we taken a different course in life."[96] Thus San Quentin, and the events that put the inmates there, seem to have produced a reception context in which Bailey's desire never to have been born entered into an ongoing autobiographical and philosophical dilemma among the men. Capra's film seemed to have provoked even further thinking about the issue, and perhaps motivated new conclusions for the prisoners about the worth of their lives.

"Believe Me Warden, It Hit Home"

While the film moved the men to philosophize about the value of their lives, it also mobilized serious consideration of the responsibilities they carried for the problems they had caused and the pleasures they had lost. In these responses the men typically referred to a domestic discourse, both metaphorically and actually, with home and the family becoming dominant terms. One prisoner wrote that the film made him "realize the unhappiness I caused . . . by being a fool and getting into trouble." He then told Duffy, "Believe me, Warden, it hit home." Another inmate, who enjoyed the film "for the simple reason [that] it was human and down to earth," agreed that "it hit so close to home."[97] For most of the men, though, the link to home was not so metaphorical. They were moved most strongly, and identified most clearly, with the depiction of the Bailey family—George, his wife, and their children. The inmates frequently framed their responses in terms of familial memory: the damage they had done to their loved ones and also the manner in which the film made them nostalgic for the family pleasures that they remembered.

Some of the men felt compelled to talk about the film with their families. "I told my wife to see it," one said, because Capra's film would "bring back a lot of home life."[98] For another inmate, the nostalgia generated by the film was for that which he could not get back, because of divorce or separation or death, and rather than imagine himself as George Bailey, he saw in Mary Bailey his own exwife. "I had a wonderful wife," he wrote, "whose patience, understanding, love and help when times were tough, was on par with the part Donna Reed played in the picture." He then extended his familial reading of the film to the warden and even the warden's wife, and interpreted Bailey as the kind of father figure that Duffy seemed to be for at least some of the men. He thanked the warden for the picture and hoped that, "for all the good you have done . . . you and Mrs. Duffy will be rewarded . . . in the fact that you, like Mr. Stewart, have done so much that only a life long career of happiness could repay your kindness."[99] Still another inmate talked about his "four and a half year old daughter that I love very dearly and it is my desire to make up as much as possible to her for what I am causing now." One of the men told Duffy that "I have a wife and two children whom I love as much as Jimmy Stewart loved his wife and family, and I know they feel the same way towards me." He concluded by assuring the warden that "when I am fortunate enough to be reunited with them I know that I can give them the happiness they have always wanted and deserved."[100]

For so many of the inmates, then, the film generated identification with Bailey as a husband and father, and provided melancholic fantasies of a home life that would be forever deprived to them or that might some day be attainable. In the latter instance the film indeed functioned, as Duffy hoped it might, as a metaphor of recuperation and rehabilitation, with the men apparently coming to understand the proper ways to return to their families after their sentences had ended. We cannot, of course, ever know if the men rejoined their families or if they did so successfully. Indeed, reading the letters now, at more than a fifty-year remove, one cannot help but be struck by the sadness of the men's hopes for families like George's and at the seeming difficulty of ever finding Bedford Falls–style happiness after prison. But at least in the context of life at San Quentin, the film motivated very specific responses about wives and children and very precise forms of spectatorial desire regarding families. For the inmates, the fantasy generated by *It's a Wonderful Life* concerned love and stability—typically with a return to the location where the men had already experienced these feelings and, in most cases, felt responsible for losing them.

This desire to go back to the family constitutes a rehabilitative discourse in the literal sense of the word, a restoration to a condition of stability and well-being. But the film also motivated another sort of rehabilitative reception that detailed the religious lessons that the men claimed to have learned from or had reinforced by *It's a Wonderful Life*. One inmate seems to have experienced a religious epiphany from the movie, telling the warden that Capra's film had "something to do with a scripture that I read in the Bible and never was able to understand [that] the lips of the righteous shall feed many, but the lips of the wicked shall die, from want of wisdom." In similar fashion, another inmate wrote that "I believe a fitting moral to the picture would be the scripture, 'whatsoever a man soweth, that also shall he reap.'" Aligning himself with Bailey and speaking autobiographically rather than scripturally, one prisoner claimed that "once I felt the same way he did, had no friends and thought that all was lost[,] but one thing I found out [is] a prayer can always be answered if you really pray." For another inmate, "This picture . . . brought out the fact that God is ever near, and surely I must have a guardian angel or I should long ago have been dead."[101]

The film seemed so transparently spiritual to so many men that in their responses they barely referred to *It's a Wonderful Life* but instead used the occasion to explain their religious philosophies. "I am a firm believer in the Golden Rule," one wrote, and then continued, "as a man thinketh so is he, and all things work together for good to those who love The Lord." Continuing to use the responses as a means of praising Duffy, and in addition to likening him to Bailey, the men sought to compare him to George's savior. One inmate said, simply, "You Warden Duffy are our Guarding [*sic*] Angel." Others enjoyed the picture not so much for themselves, but for the other men and the lessons they may have learned, with one inmate writing that "I am always glad to see pictures with connections of our Heavenly Father," adding that "I know it was a very good picture for the morals of the inmates."[102]

In seemingly overwhelming terms, the men interpreted the film as a religious allegory and as a means of speaking of their own religious beliefs. We have seen before, in the case of *Meet John Doe*, that a Capra film might provoke discussion about the Golden Rule or about the spirituality of Hollywood films generally. Of course, *It's a Wonderful Life* has a more specifically religious narrative than any other Capra film, and it seems to have been used by the men as a means of telling Duffy about the spiritual rehabilitation they had already begun, or about a religious education to which the film contributed. These men had a clear sense that the cinema needed to have a moral mission, and that films like Capra's and leadership like Duffy's might combine to provide both uplift and enlightenment. At least implicitly, the modern prison and the current cinema were combined in the men's thoughts about the film as potential locations and institutions of religious conversion and education.

In responding to the religious dimension of *It's a Wonderful Life*, the men at San Quentin apparently wanted to let Warden Duffy know that they were already on their way to a spiritual rehabilitation, and that the movie served to confirm the correctness of the path they had chosen. Moreover, many of the discussions of family indicated the manner in which the film provoked a kind of nostalgic response, most typically for families and for a past domestic happiness that was either real or imagined. But Capra's film also motivated what might be called a prospective response, an autobiographical reading not about the men's past lives or current rehabilitation program but rather based on what they hoped their lives might look like once they were out of jail. Rather than identifying themselves strongly with George's situation at the time of viewing the film, these men in fact aspired to imitate George and to replicate the movie's narrative sometime in the future.

One inmate, who told Duffy that he had been in jail for only nine months, said "that is how I would like to be in the 'Free World' to be so popular with my friends." Another prisoner, who found the film just "a little eccentric," nevertheless told Duffy, almost certainly reflecting on his own situation, "wouldn't it be wonderful if a person really could wake up from a nightmare of dreams and find himself happiness and reality instead?" Another inmate wrote that the film "just shows that no matter how dark life looks to one, there's always a brighter side," and then insisted that "I myself I know I am going to see the brighter side someday." [103] Thus in some cases the film gave the men a vocabulary for dealing with their own incarceration—the "nightmare" from which one might awaken. But for many more of them the film developed an imitative fantasy, in which the men seemed to sense that their own lives had at least somewhat matched the trajectory of Bailey's through some of the film, and so they hoped to use Bailey's eventual triumph as their model for a life outside of prison, in the "Free World." For these men the film generated pleasures that were not so much about mirroring past and present but were instead based on providing a sort of narrative closure to their own lives that might match the one that Capra provided for George Bailey.

"Made Me Feel Sort of Wistful"

Not all of the men discussed the film uncritically. Two of them, for instance, disputed Capra's ending and felt that Lionel Barrymore's evil Mr. Potter should have been redeemed. "I think," one of them wrote, "seeing as there was so much xmas spirit and good feeling towards Jimmy [Stewart] and family that Potter should have followed suit by bringing back the $8,000, confessing, asking forgiveness, so there would have been the real happy ending for the picture." Another wanted to put himself in Capra's place, saying "I wish I could have been the one to put an ending, I would have had the old rich man to be at the end and make him give up the money he had stolen from the old man who was his uncle I think." [104] This constitutes a critical discourse both common to Capra fans of the period and also different. The viewers who wrote letters to the director after seeing *Meet John Doe* tended also to complain about the ending, in that case because Edward Arnold's evil media magnate did indeed undergo too much of a conversion in the final scene. Here, though, at least some of the prisoners sought an absolutely happy ending, even down to Mr. Potter understanding and making amends for the error of his ways.

There also were comments that were more fully dismissive. "To me the Picture itself did not interest me," one inmate told the warden. But he went on to say that "the part I enjoyed most was the good fellowship and home-like atmosphere the two brothers were raised up in." The prisoner explained that "there [*sic*] Mother [and] Father were ideal Parents, it brought back to me little insidents [*sic*] in my youth [and] made me feel sort of wistfull [*sic*]."[105] This constitutes a complicated kind of response, one that combines both a distance from the film and an attraction to it. In so doing, it acknowledges the film's ability, and quite possibly that of the cinema in general, to mobilize powerful and pleasurable identificatory fantasies in spite of aesthetic or intellectual distaste. For this prisoner, despite his lack of interest in Capra's film, *It's a Wonderful Life* nevertheless had an impact similar to that experienced by so many of the men, producing nostalgia for a time before prison when families could be together.

These responses from the inmates at San Quentin may well demonstrate the possibility of reception practices unique to the confined spectator. One inmate wrote that Capra's film "made us stop and think about others" and then referred directly to the manner in which the site of exhibition—San Quentin—affected viewer reaction. "It is hard to express our suppressed feelings toward others in here," he said, "but it did make us feel better inside." He added that all viewers would have "those feelings," but that these sentiments were much more "relaxed . . . on the outside" rather than in prison.[106] Watching *It Happened One Night* as a high school student in a film appreciation class, or the *Why We Fight* films as draftees, almost certainly influenced viewer response. But the Canon City experiment may have been right about one aspect of prison viewing. There was, indeed, something particularly significant about inmates watching movies, with the men's status as prisoners having a determinant effect on reception greater than that of any Capra audience examined here so far.

The men in San Quentin believed that while watching *It's a Wonderful Life* they saw their own lives on screen, yet at the same time the film allowed them to imagine what their lives might be like. That is, Capra's movie seemed to develop a kind of duplicative response (George's life was like those of the inmates) as well as an imitative one (the inmates hoped that they could be more like George). Because of their confinement, these viewers were denied some of the usual means of imitation; they could not, for instance, buy any of the products associated with the film or dress like any of the stars. As Stacey has pointed out, in just these ways imitation usually comes to be linked to various forms of consumption.[107] For the prison viewers of Capra's film, however, imitation might only be linked to the behavior they saw on screen, and to imagining the possibilities of replicating, at some point in their own lives, the film's domestic scene. In no way is this a purer, more admirable form of imitation; it is, however, a form that typically has not been remarked upon.

Just as the inmates saw their own lives in the movie while also seeing the lives they would like to lead, so too did these viewers experience *It's a Wonderful Life* as both escapist and instructive. One inmate wrote that the film "was something wonderful," explaining that, "for as long as the pic[ture] was on I forgot I was in San Quentin." At the same time, the inmate said he learned a lesson, and it was one of those that so many of the men linked to the rehabilitative function of the film. "The picture had this effect on me," he said, that "as long as a man has friends he isn't lost and that it cost so little to do a good turn than to do other-wise."[108] As Duffy had hoped when he instituted screenings at San Quentin, this film, for at least a couple of hours, let the men forget about being in prison. But also as Duffy had hoped when he gave the men their written assignment, *It's a Wonderful Life* seemed to provide lessons for life outside of jail.

Thus we come to the significant similarities as well as differences in the audiences examined here. For the American soldiers, German prisoners of war, and San Quentin inmates, military and prison officials hoped that Capra's films might have educational effects on the men. In the case of the soldiers the effects were to be immediate as they came to understand the reasons for the war and the necessity of their own involvement in it. For the German and San Quentin prisoners, the results would be prospective, after their release. Even with the *Why We Fight* films, however, military social scientists wanted to use their audience to test the postwar educational possibilities of films in general and documentaries in particular. In each case, then, and despite the differences between the goals of psychologists and sociologists on the one hand and a prison warden on the other, we see in practice the era's belief in the possible therapeutic nature of the movies.

For these experts and overseers, motion pictures had the ability to work positive and measurable changes in the people watching them; in particular films were capable of assimilating audiences to preferred but unfamiliar cultures, from military collective to democratic citizenship to law-abiding domesticity.

Chapter Six

Politics and Pedagogy near the End of a Career:

From Feature Films to Television Production

In May 1948 Susan Clark of Yakima, Washington, wrote an appreciative letter to Capra, in which she told the director "yesterday, as you
know, was Mother's Day and for my special treat we went to see *State
of the Union*. Thank you, Mr. Capra, for every moment of that story portrayed and 'lived' on that screen as only Americans could portray and 'live'
that particular phase of our life."[1] For Clark, Capra's latest film celebrated
both the national and the familial, capturing and combining the country's
values and those of Mother's Day. In other words, *State of the Union* was a
Capra film very much like the movies he had made before. Despite Clark's
endorsement, and the sense of its continuity with the rest of Capra's filmography, the movie marks the beginning of that period of the director's
career that has most typically been seen in terms of decline. *State of the
Union*, which was the director's second production for Liberty Films (and
distributed by MGM), now seems more like one of the lesser films from
the Spencer Tracy–Katharine Hepburn cycle than it does a Capra movie.
Capra himself, in his autobiography, lamented somewhat melodramatically
that *State of the Union* was to be his "last independent production," and
that afterward he "hocked [his] gifts in his finest hour" by signing a long-
term contract with Paramount, "where he slowly drank the hemlock of
champions." Joseph McBride, in his biography of Capra, writes that with
State of the Union the director suddenly "developed an inability to think in
visual terms," and that this malaise indicated the onset of a case of "creative catatonia." In the most extended scholarly analysis of Capra's work,
Ray Carney calls *State of the Union* "a disappointing and confused film,"
and he dispenses with the four feature films Capra made after *State* in a
brief and sketchy final chapter.[2] Most film scholars give even shorter shrift
to the science films that Capra made for television between 1956 and 1958.

This scholarly disapproval is from a remove of forty or fifty years, but at the time of *State of the Union*, and his features from the early 1950s (*Riding High* [1950] and *Here Comes the Groom* [1951]), Capra's audiences understood the director as a celebrity of international significance. They also noticed, and were only too glad to write Capra about, major problems with his films. Before and during World War II, the perceived quality of Capra's movies validated his reputation as an engaged filmmaker. After the war, that reputation came to be reinforced by what some viewers saw as the political and religious significance of Capra's films, and by their status as objects worthy of significant intellectual inquiry, perfectly suited for analysis in the college classroom. Nevertheless, Capra's position as one of the great men of American cinema also served to heighten his fans' disappointment over their sense of the inadequacies of his new films.

I plan here to look at the period of Capra's "decline" and to complicate received notions of the end of his career. As Capra moved from the film studio to a different kind of corporation, AT&T, for which he made his science films, his career may certainly have changed for the worse. But it may also have found its most logical extension, as the director whose films figured so prominently in a variety of educational projects now made films for an audience of students. The fan mail that Capra received about *State of the Union*, which tells the story of a failed run for the Republican presidential nomination by an idealistic politician, echoes that for *Meet John Doe* by coming from an audience of politically engaged film viewers. The mail also, finally, demonstrates the appropriateness of Capra's place in the academy as something of a master teacher. With the broadcast of his science films, Capra's mail further asserts the director's pedagogical skill. The audiences for those films were also carefully tracked by AT&T, with the results of various polls and questionnaires placing Capra in a role central to the dissemination of scientific knowledge, just as, fifteen years before, he had spread the word about World War II to millions of young men in the armed forces.

"The First Film I Wanted to See Was a Capra Film"

For some of his fans, the story of Capra's life seemed far more important than the stories of his new films. Probably to publicize the opening of *Riding High* in 1950, Capra appeared on a series of radio shows. Mrs. Earl L. Summers, after she heard one of them, wrote to Capra to extol the biography of the successful immigrant and to explain the connection she felt to Capra's origins. "I was quite thrilled . . . to hear you say you were from Sicily," she wrote, and then continued, "I am very proud of my heritage," adding that "both my Mother and Dad were born in Palermo." She closed by telling Capra that "you just thrilled me with your story . . . & especially coming from my people's native land."[3] Another Italian American felt a similar closeness to Capra's background, and so wrote the director to voice his own concerns about Hollywood's representational practices. After praising *Riding High*, Peter T. Campon complained that "I deeply regret to see that a new picture called *The Black Hand* is about to be thrust upon the public, for I feel that it will give a wrong impression of our people." He then linked his disappointment to the standard criticism of Jews in Hollywood, asking Capra, "How would Mr. Schenck [MGM executive Nicholas Schenck] feel should a picture be produced detrimental to his Racial group?" Campon answered his own question, insisting that Schenck "would be the first to holler to the high heavens."[4]

As he typically did with his fan mail, Capra took this letter quite seriously and responded by stating that "No, Mr. Schenck wouldn't like it if his race was belittled, as witness the row over the character of Fagin in the *Oliver Twist* picture made in England." Capra then reasoned that "the only way to overcome these racial sensitivities is by understanding and education and not by suppression."[5] Here Capra took on the role of pedagogue, not so much in relation to his current film but in the broad terms of a postwar enlightened liberalism marked by communal harmony and racial understanding. In each case, though, with Mrs. Summers and Peter Campon, Capra had taken on a significance based on his celebrity as a director yet exceeding any of the implications of a film as slight as *Riding High*, a horse-race fantasy that was a remake of Capra's own *Broadway Bill* from 1934. The fans of *Meet John Doe* saw Capra as the leader of a political movement that would grow from the movie. A decade later, at least some of his fans used Capra's new film as a pretext for telling him of his status as an exemplary immigrant, as an inspiration to others with similar family histories, and to make an appeal to this shared background in order to get Capra to do something about perceived slights to Italians in the standard Hollywood studio product.

Thus to at least some audiences in the United States, apparently those with a familial link to Capra's heritage, the director was viewed as signifying the possibilities of the melting pot and the potential for increased understanding among national, racial, and ethnic groups. Of course, as well as standing for a kind of postwar international humanism, Capra also had a significant international audience. Those viewers, or at least those who wrote fan mail, had for many years been unfailingly supportive. With his postwar films, however, that audience became a somewhat more vexed one, pointing out the apparent volatility in these viewers' understanding of Capra's films and his career.

Echoing requests for copies of John Doe's radio speeches, one viewer in Canada asked Capra if there were any way he could "get ahold of a [*State of the Union*] script (or, failing this, Mr. Tracy's 'honest' political speeches)."[6] We can get a sense here of a film culture extending well beyond the theater, in which a movie becomes a literary artifact, worthy of being read as well as seen, and in which those declarative moments so typical of Capra's films—Doe on the radio, Mr. Smith in the senate chamber, Mr. Deeds in court—might serve as continuing inspiration. To go along with this belief in the political uplift of Capra's films, there was also a significant international fan base that viewed Capra as a major star. After seeing *Here Comes the Groom*, one fan in Brazil wrote to Capra, asking him "a great favor: your photograph, to put it in the first place of the producers page on my album." He explained that he had a scrapbook of some 680 photographs, with "artists, producers, directors, etc."[7] He also took the opportunity to ask Capra for pictures of some of the performers in the film. Capra sent a script to the viewer from Canada and an autographed photo to the fan in Brazil, thereby acknowledging at least to some extent his singular importance to an international audience as a director of political films and also his participation in a Hollywood star system that extended its reach to most of the countries in the world.

Yet another fan familiar with Capra from an international context wrote to express his deep disappointment with one of the director's recent films. Similar to so many of Capra's American viewers who saw his films as allegories of Americanism, this one equated the importance of coming to the United States with the significance of the director's movies. As a result, having "first arrived from France to the states," the viewer wrote, "the first film I wanted to see was a Capra film."[8] He went on to speak for all of the French, and to assert the same kind of importance for Capra's films for that national audience that was claimed by so many American viewers: "Nobody in my country has forgotten *Mr. Smith* or *Why We Fight*."[9] Thus aware of Capra's filmography, he could only write to tell the director that, after seeing *Here Comes the Groom*, he "was terribly disappointed." He admonished Capra by saying that the "candy-sweet stuff" of the film "is not true Capra," and that "you are worth more than the 'Cool Cool of the Evening' [the song in the film], the tap-dance sequence or that awful part . . . where Anna Maria [Alberghetti] sings and where everybody is crying without exactly knowing why."[10]

These letters indicate an extraordinary relationship between viewer and director, one in which the viewer expected continued work of inspirational and political importance far beyond the range of most films. Then, when the director delivered a standard Hollywood film, that viewer felt emboldened to express disappointment directly. The French fan went on to tell Capra that "I am really sorry to write such hard things but as I said, I like you too much not to tell you what I think," and he urged Capra to "do a trip to Europe," and then "come back and give us another Masterpiece."[11] According to this criticism, then, Capra's Americanism needed to be refreshed by a new, global consciousness, one that could come from seeing postwar Europe. Here Capra, whom scholarship typically views as having been uniquely in touch with the American viewer, instead had lost contact with his international audience, to which he owed yet another great film.

The letter from the French viewer seems like a reasoned, intelligent one, without the dramatic family histories related by some of the fans who wrote Capra or, worse, the antisemitism. It serves to further indicate the vast audience with high expectations of Capra's films, and it provides a hint of at least some of the pressure Capra must have felt to reproduce the success of his earlier movies. The correspondence that so clearly addressed Capra's international celebrity also echoed the range of opinions about the filmmaker as well as *State of the Union* and some of the later films, and came from viewers with no stated links to other countries or cultures and who were concerned primarily with the potential of American cinema.

To those fans who professed to being sick of the typical studio product, Capra stood out as an anti-Hollywood hero, just as he had with *Mr. Smith Goes to Washington* and *Meet John Doe*. From Iowa, Joseph Hull wrote to Capra in May 1948, and as if to underscore Capra's connection to the political Hull also sent a copy of the letter to Iowa senator Bourke Hickenlooper in Washington, D.C. Hull then showed his common cause with Capra, saying that while "your business is making moving pictures and my business is manufacturing fur coats . . . the government of this nation is both of our businesses." Thus in praising Capra's film Hull addressed the director as a man of singular talent and also as an equal, stating "I enjoyed [*State of the Union*] more than any picture I can remember." Hull had "been a regular patron of the movies" but gave up on them after seeing Bing Crosby and

Bob Hope's latest "road" picture. That movie convinced him that "filmfare was at a low level for my money and my time was better spent with books, radio and hobbies." For Hull, this "fan letter, which is the first to my recollection," was designed to tell Capra, one of the two or three most famous and successful directors of the era, that rather than representing an industry he stood apart from it.[12] Even after the war, and bringing to mind some of the fan response to *Meet John Doe*, Capra made serious-minded films for people who did not like movies and who had even stopped going to them, and who rejected the escapist frivolousness of films like the "road" movies made by Hope and Crosby.

The Road to Rio (1947), of course, might seem too easy a target. But viewers who shared Hull's opinion also rejected the high-quality Hollywood superproduction, a kind of film not dissimilar, in budget and star power, from many of Capra's movies. From Maplewood, New Jersey, Addie Witherspoon Caroulli asked Capra, after seeing *State of the Union*, "Why can't we have more such movies?" Just the week before she had seen David O. Selznick's *Duel in the Sun*, thinking that she "was in for a grand show." "Instead," she continued, "I saw the most disgusting of characters portrayed by stars who have become almost legend for ability in this country," and she added that the film was "a perfect example of what a waste of money Hollywood can perform, to say nothing of the bad influence it could have on the young people of today." We tend today to think of Selznick as a man who specialized in respectable middle-brow culture. Here, though, his films signaled the worst of Hollywood: lavishly overexpensive and detrimental to the audience. Thus a Capra film stood between the meaningless comedy of Hope and Crosby and the bloat of Selznick, an example of the uplift of which Hollywood was capable, were it not for what Caroulli called "the graft and politics" that plagued the film industry and that only one director seemed willing and able to oppose.[13]

Still another viewer told Capra that she had violated one of her own rules of moviegoing: "I waited in line to see the show—something I vowed I would never do." She continued by saying that her "patience was rewarded," and that she "felt, for one of the few times, I got what I paid for," because *State of the Union* was an "adult" film.[14] These letters to Capra provide evidence that in film studies we must take into account the apparent number of viewers who felt a deep alienation from Hollywood cinema, because of its mindless comedy, its lack of attention to grownup concerns, the money that films cost to make, the money charged to see them, and the time spent waiting in line to watch what in the end were inferior movies.

In this discourse of displeasure Capra becomes a hero of resistance, like a Deeds, Smith, or Doe himself, insisting on making films that stood apart from the usual product and were designed for an audience that had given up on Hollywood. Film studies often concentrates broadly on how the cinema fulfills audience desire. With the letters concerning *State of the Union* and other Capra films, however, we start to get a sense of how for at least some audiences cinema failed time and again in that effort—producing, in general, only disappointment or disgust or fulfilling desires only in very specific cases.

Capra's appreciative viewers enjoyed seeing a film that dealt with political issues during serious times. But they interpreted the film's relationship to the political in different ways, from the international to the national to the local. Exemplifying a late-1940s, United Nations–style global utopianism, Joseph Hull applauded Capra for showing that "today our vote is not alone for our government but indirectly for the government of the world because a 'One World' government is the only salvation for our troubles."[15] Another letter came, in fact, from an organization called the World Republic, which boasted a distinguished advisory board that included doctors, military officers, and religious leaders, as well as the actor Eddie Cantor. The group was "particularly impressed with the concise and logical argument for a world government which Spencer Tracy gave," and felt especially pleased that now, with *State of the Union*, "the idea of world government will reach millions of people through the medium of this motion picture."[16] Coming from a more grass-roots organization, Rachel Holcomb, who lived in Mount Airy, North Carolina, echoed the sentiments of the World Republic. She wrote that her town had "just finished a petition drive for World Government which we took to Washington, D.C." Then she addressed Capra as something of a master teacher on the subject: "We the American people really want World Government," she wrote, further insisting that "we only need to be shown and educated up to it." For her, the cinema had to function as an advertisement for ideological advancement, as she thanked Capra for making a film that served as "the first big publicity step that has been taken toward World Government."[17]

Other viewers expressed concern with universal electoral democracy but overall were more interested in the possibility of Hollywood films helping to send Christianity around the world. The field secretary of the Oklahoma Christian Youth Council made a direct connection between watching *State of the Union* and his own entrance into American democracy by telling Capra that his movie could not have come at a better time, because

"November will be my first election." His main concern, however, was both global and religious, with the United States extending the benefits of its spiritual practices and moral systems to the rest of the world. After telling Capra that he had just come back from the Second World Conference of Christian Youth in Oslo, he insisted that the best way of proselytizing for American religious practices "was seeing them on the screen over there." He closed by imploring "[I] beg of you to work for the exporting of more of a good, moral, and honest kind of movie," just like *State of the Union*.[18]

The Hollywood cinema was seen to have a special responsibility, then, to educate a national audience about the benefits of internationalism, and a global audience about the benefits of the United States. *State of the Union* stood out in this respect, as Capra's films had so often before, but the movie was nothing if not flexible, and it also impressed fans as something of an allegory of nationalism or even small-town localism. One viewer, who asked Capra for his autograph, said without further explanation that the film was "a tribute to all the people of the United States."[19] The same woman who complained about *Duel in the Sun* also used the occasion of seeing *State of the Union* to lodge her complaints about issues of class, family, and religion as they manifested themselves in the site par excellence of postwar modernity, the suburb. "In the community in which I live," she told Capra, "far too many youngsters are shoved off to the movies while mother and daddy spend their time at the club or the links." Then she added that "this, I'm sure, is true of many other suburban communities." The movies, by default, would become the contemporary site of moral educa-tion. "These children can't get any ideals from home," she wrote, so "why not at least give them something to cut their teeth on thru the screen." This necessity seemed even stronger because "most of these children come from homes where church, or any participation there . . . is beneath them, so you can't say 'Leave that to the Sunday Schools.'"[20]

An "ordinary housewife" also wrote to Capra, telling him that his film, standing in stark contrast to the "planned show" of the recent Republica-tion convention, made her think about the potential of American political systems. She wrote that "we attend our local council meetings and try to have some voice in our town's government," but that even there she found "pre-council arrangements," and so wondered what must go on at the fed-eral level. She and her family managed "to have a fairly happy life in this mixed-up world," but she added that "all this anxiety, worry & unrest that surrounds us today is not the heritage we should leave to our sons."[21]

In these letters Capra is made to be an educator and exemplar, teaching citizens about the proper management of government and about the potential for motion pictures. We can also get a sense of the status of his celebrity as he becomes someone people can talk to about the problems in their families and hometowns. His films seemed to promote a sort of direct address among his fans, with the content of the films themselves leading to certain assumptions about Capra as a man who would listen to their political and personal concerns. We would have to examine a great deal more fan mail to determine whether Capra's case was unique or closer to the norm. But we begin to understand nevertheless a film culture that, for some fans at least, and in relation to at least some films and filmmakers, connected very directly to their everyday concerns and activities. These fans wanted an engaged cinema but they also looked to the cinema, perhaps because of their own alienation from political and local leaders, to provide them with people like Capra with whom they themselves could engage on significant issues.

Viewers seemed to feel that they could speak quite personally to Capra, but they also looked to him as someone particularly suited to provide leadership. "You have shown rare courage on a perennial subject," one viewer of *State of the Union* said, and then added that "I say rare courage because you expose the foibles of both parties with candor."[22] As they had with *Meet John Doe*, viewers wanted to see films that dealt seriously with political issues. Indeed, if letters like the one above are indicative, there was a segment of the postwar audience that hoped to see films that formulated broad critiques of American political systems, in this case the practices of Democrats as well as Republicans. Again as they had with *Meet John Doe*, these fans looked to Capra to lead a movement that went beyond cinema, thereby offering an indication of some people's willingness to invest particular members of the entertainment community with significant political authority. To the young man who worked for the Oklahoma Christian Youth Council, Capra had become something of a spiritual hero. But others saw him in a different role. One viewer, writing a fan letter for the first time, spoke of being deeply moved by Capra's film, of having the "strange sensation of being both ashamed and proud of being an American." Then the writer closed by asking Capra, quite directly, "Did you ever think of running for president?"[23]

There were, however, criticisms. Viewers typically told Capra about perceived flaws in his work by first acknowledging his celebrity and his ability and then expressing their disappointment that someone so special could err so gravely. Fans' problems with *Meet John Doe* dealt primarily with the ending of the film and with feeling let down by the ideological shift away from "the little people." With *State of the Union* the criticisms mostly dealt with a particular representational practice, and demonstrated something of the old fashioned in the midst of United Nations–era discussions of world government, with many in the audience objecting to the significant amount of drinking depicted in the film. "There was a time when the name Capra meant a good picture and a sober one." Thus Julia Hendrix chastised the director after seeing his latest film. For her, this "splendid" picture was ruined "because of the drinking bouts." She then reversed the usual trend in Capra's mail, associating the director with everyone else in Hollywood rather than acknowledging his exemplary separateness: "When will you people realize the really patriotic and substantial Americans are not drunken imbeciles either in the home or in public?"[24]

The complaint about drinking came to be framed in the same way by several fans who acknowledged Capra's connection to a film as an assurance of a movie's quality and then expressed subsequent disappointment. "Your name on a theater marquee is a guarantee of a successful, true-to-life movie," one viewer wrote after seeing *State of the Union*, and then she joined "in the applause that [was] being given" to the film. She needed, however, "to reserve my applause in one scene . . . in which Van Johnson pours himself a drink." As a twenty-three year old, she felt close enough to the "teen category" to warn Capra of the "lasting impression" Johnson's drinking might have on a young person.[25]

This fan's letter mirrored at least partially that of another young person writing to Capra, the viewer who worked for the Oklahoma Christian Youth Council and who extolled *State of the Union* for its potential to export American values to the rest of the world. For both viewers, the cinema in general and Capra's films in particular functioned as powerful moral agents capable of influencing vast numbers of people. Their difference came in appraising the value of that influence. More broadly, the fans critical of the film (most of whom singled out the drinking in the movie) and those who supported it viewed *State of the Union* either in regressive terms or as one of the signals of postwar modernity. The film was seen as regressive because of the way it set back the cause of the movies as exemplars of good behavior and marked at least the partial end of public confidence in Capra. At the same time it was also viewed as modern because it showed the possibilities of a United Nations–era global government formed in reaction to the hypernationalist, ideologically fractured ruin of World War II.

The postwar context of *State of the Union* as well as Capra's own history as a director almost certainly encouraged viewers to write about the film as a political object. That same history—Capra as a director of superior films—also allowed viewers to examine the film as an aesthetic object, in the manner of a novel, and as a primer for the budding filmmaker. In this way the film entered the classroom shortly after its release. Of course, Capra's films had been objects of study before. As noted earlier, Robert Gessner screened *It Happened One Night* in a New York University film appreciation class in 1938, and the same film was analyzed by Kannapolis, North Carolina, high school students in 1934. Later, however, Capra's films as educational tools had been used not so much to teach about the cinema as to instruct in ideological development (as in the *Why We Fight* films) and in moral growth (as in *It's a Wonderful Life* at San Quentin). In 1948 Capra's work entered into a developing university curriculum, film production, to be dissected by bright young students seeking to learn from the masters and also to point out their flaws. In the instance of *State of the Union*, one such student provided an interesting critique of the film and, of more value here, some very compelling information about its reception.

In May 1948 for an assignment in a class called "Cinema 280B—Directing II," Leslie Londo wrote "A Criticism of *State of the Union*."[26] The class was taught by Andrew Marton, who had left Hungary to come to the United States as Ernst Lubitsch's editor in the 1920s and then settled in Hollywood for good around 1940. As a director he made such films as the 1964 version of *The Thin Red Line*, and he also worked as a second-unit director on a number of movies, including William Wyler's *Ben Hur* and Nicholas Ray's *55 Days at Peking*. The course itself was almost certainly taught at the University of Southern California, which had established its cinema department in 1929, although Londo, who made it clear in the assignment that he was far from his Michigan home, did not identify the institution. He did, however, send the assignment to Capra for the director's consideration of the student's technical analysis of the film and his overview of audience response, both in a local theater and among his family back home.

Londo began with his "personal reaction," in which he sounds much more like a fan than a student, saying that "I enjoyed the picture so much that I stayed and saw it twice." In this, he appears to be like the other audience members that day, who were the subject of Londo's next three statements of fact. Londo wrote that the "audience reaction" was "very good," because "Capra is skilled in making an audience laugh." He then commented on the size of the crowd when he saw the film, saying that it was "average," and then made a demographic note, by adding that there were "more older people than in the usual audience." The student then dealt with the director's filmography. After the heading "Comparison to other Capra films," Londo wrote that "Frank Capra is one of my favorite directors," and continued by saying that "I think this picture ranks with *Mr. Deeds Goes to Town*, *Lady for a Day*, *It Happened One Night*, and *It's a Wonderful Life*." After the heading "Comparison to other MGM films," he wrote "better than average," and after "Comparison to the general Hollywood product," Londo wrote, again, "better than average." He concluded this first part of the assignment with a note on the direction. "The purpose of a director is to tell a story on film," he wrote, and in this "Capra succeeds." He continued by adding that "maybe he fails to make his big-name stars do their best acting, [and] maybe the cutting and camera angles are bad in spots," but then he concluded, in underlined capital letters, "Capra succeeds in telling his story well."

We get an inkling, at least from fans like Londo, that Capra was indeed experiencing something of a creative decline, on the level of that inability to think in visual terms that McBride described. But Londo's assignment also indicates that for fans who were in some sense students of cinema, Capra had a filmmaking history, and this history was one in which a recent film had to be seen as part of an oeuvre that stood out as superior to the usual Hollywood product, with the apparent highlights of that history being the three films that Londo pointed out: Capra's most recent, before *State of the Union*; one of the political films, *Mr. Deeds*; and also the movie that moved Capra into the pantheon of Hollywood directors. The assignment clearly demonstrates a postwar auteurism that predates Truffaut's "politique des auteurs" as well as American versions from the 1950s and 1960s. This early auteurism should come as no surprise given the emphasis placed on directors in the film studies of the 1930s, with Londo also showing the influence of an earlier era's more scientific approach to cinema (which may have been one of the requirements of Marton's original assignment). Here, the student combined an aesthetic and historical approach to Capra's work with the awareness of a sociologist, as he moved back and forth from subjective judgments of the film to analyses of audience response and demographics.

Londo made the authoritative statements about film technique that one might expect from the film student. He mentioned a scene between Hepburn and Tracy that also appeared in the stage version of *State of the*

Union, and then went on to laud Capra's mastery, the same "technique that changed *It Happened One Night* from just another movie to a popular hit." Capra's intelligent use of close-ups made for a vast improvement over the scene as performed on stage, and Londo continued that "the CLOSE-UP is a valuable tool in telling a story on film," and that "the stage has no such weapon; it just cannot compete." Thus the cinema improves on the theater, with Londo providing us excellent information about how these close-ups played for the audience. "That huge theatre rocked with laughter," he wrote, and added that "the wallop was tremendous."

The audience that day seemed intensely involved in Capra's film, as Londo gives us evocative information about their response. When the presidential candidate's wife found apparent evidence of her husband's infidelity, "the audience gasped," and Capra "had us in the hollow of his hand." In this description of what he called the film's "best sequence," Londo continued by stating that "the elderly chap sitting next to me got a tremendous kick out of it," and wrote that the old man's wife "whispered something about men in general . . . she was mad [and] leaned eagerly forward." The end of the scene, when another character did not understand the evidence, "brought the house down with a roar of laughter."

There is, of course, nothing scientific about this description of audience response. But it does offer wonderful information about how an audience might engage with a film, how individuals might audibly comment on what they saw, or how an entire audience might "roar" their approval. Londo included more specific information, still not necessarily applicable to larger groups of viewers, but interesting nevertheless in light of the possibilities raised for understanding film interpretation through the political inclinations and the general filmgoing practices of individual spectators. Londo devised a simple but intriguing reception project, as he asked members of his family, all of whom lived in the Midwest, to see Capra's film and then send him their responses to it. His immediate family seems almost too much like a cross-section of the postwar American public, as it included Republicans, Democrats, and socialists; businessmen and union members; and ranged from ardent movie fans to those with general contempt for motion pictures.

Before each response from each relative, Londo provided information about political affiliation and the number of movies viewed each week or month. A basic premise of Londo's survey, then, was that *State of the Union* must be interpreted in political terms, and that one's political beliefs may well affect interpretation, as might one's general experience of Hollywood films. Londo's father, for instance, a Republican businessman, saw "about two movies a week." For him, the film indicated regional truths as much as ideological ones, with the politicians in the movie reminding him of "the Republicans from Ohio, Illinois and Wisconsin, that I had just been conferring with." He called all of them "a hungry pack," and said that he would write to them to see the film. He then pointed out that "we Michigan folks can be proud that our Michigan Republicans are not like that," although he indicated that "the damned Michigan Democrats in Detroit fit that movie." For Londo's father, who apparently was active in Republican politics and who seems to have been a fairly avid filmgoer, *State of the Union* reflected something of the rough and tumble of politics, and allowed him to voice, even more than his national partisan preference, his loyalty to his state political party.

Demonstrating the political rifts in his own family, Londo referred to his older brother as a Democrat and as the chairman of the Grievance Committee of his union in Detroit. The brother, far less enamored of the movies than his father, saw only one film a month, but felt that *State of the Union* was the "best picture I saw in a long time." The union leader in the film amused him, as he asked, "Who was that . . . man supposed to be? [United Mine Worker leader] John L. Lewis?" and then added "better write old John L. and tell him to see the movie." He closed his letter more seriously, echoing the standard response to Capra films at least since *It Happened One Night*: "What a picture! We ought to see more of them—damn it, we will, if Hollywood makes some." Londo's brother apparently went to one movie a month because he felt that there were so few films worth seeing, with Capra's movie standing out as the unusual rather than the typical Hollywood film, probably because of how it dealt with contemporary political events. Plausibly, then, for the fan who saw more than one hundred films a year, like Londo's father, a Capra film might seem special but might also blend in with the usual Hollywood product. Indeed, Londo's father seemed primarily amused by the film, which allowed him to identify familiar types from his own political experience. For the viewer who rarely saw a motion picture, like Londo's brother, a Capra film provided a reason to go to the movies, a special event rather than just another aspect of an ongoing habit.

In providing the range of comments from the men in his family, Londo moved left along the political spectrum. The next to weigh in was his uncle, Sam, a teacher and socialist who saw only two movies a year. For him, *State of the Union* demonstrated "that special interests use the two major political parties to further their own corrupt schemes to gain power and enhance financial profits." Thus Sam viewed the film as something of a radical critique of American politics, fully consistent with a socialist analysis. The movie redeemed all movies for this viewer, as it "made him ashamed of some of the things I have said in the past about the motion picture industry," and he added that "the men who made this film should be complimented."

For family members who seem to represent a general cross-section of the American political public, *State of the Union* was indeed a political film but also a malleable one. Capra's film might be a mirror of the antics of real life politicians, a special event that dealt seriously with serious issues, or a radical critique of political corruption. As much as these readings seemed to reflect the ideological positions of the viewers, they may also have been related to the frequency with which they went to the movies. The most serious interpretation seems to have been that of Uncle Sam, who seems to have had utter disdain for Hollywood films and never went to see them. Sam's response may have been a measure of Capra's stature, but it is possible as well that, in analyzing reception, we may have to take into account that many of the people who were least likely to see films were also more prone to treat films as significant cultural texts.

The women in Londo's family were apparently less partisan than the men, and less concerned with the political realities represented by *State of the Union*. At least according to Londo, neither his aunt, Kate, nor his two sisters-in-law had any party affiliations, and they seemed to view the film more in terms of propriety than politics, with special concern for the depiction of women. One sister-in-law, who went to two movies a week, complained, "Why did you tell us to go to that awful movie? A presidential candidate's wife getting drunk! A judge's wife drinking like a female pig! A presidential candidate with a mistress!" Aunt Kate, who also saw two movies a week, went to see *State of the Union* with her sister's husband, Uncle Sam. She wrote that Sam was "crazier than a loon," and that while he thought the movie "was grand," she hated it: "Women drunk all over the place—a nut running for president who takes orders from a blonde vampire. What rot!" Another sister-in-law, a "devoted movie fan" who "sometimes sees as many as four pictures a week," responded like a real film enthusiast, saying "Is Spencer Tracy getting old! Why did they give him the lead instead of Van Johnson? Is that old Adolphe Menjou a spiffy dresser!"

Two of these women echoed typical complaints about the film, usually from female viewers, that Capra had lost all sense of correct behavior by having women drinking so heavily. Their interest in the politics of the film focused less on the representation of the political parties, which was the central focus of the men in Londo's family, than on the fitness of a presidential candidate who would engage in an affair. The most dedicated moviegoer in the family, who went to the movies two hundred times a year, had a different response entirely. Here, too, as with the men in Londo's family, we may have to consider the manner in which one's relationship to film culture generally, and particularly the frequency with which one went to the movies, affected reception. This sister-in-law seemed far removed from a consideration of any larger issues in *State of the Union*. Instead she displayed an interest and expertise that almost certainly came from having seen so many films, and that was fixed far less on theme or story and much more on star appearance. She was able to determine how Spencer Tracy seemed to have aged, that Adolphe Menjou, among male stars, was a superb dresser, and that Van Johnson, in this film a supporting player, would have made a more appealing male lead. Her interest was in performers, especially male performers, with regard to appearance as well as casting practices, and her concerns seemed no less serious than those of the men in Londo's family. For this dedicated viewer the cinema was driven by stars, especially by male stars and how they looked. And in this light Capra films, even with their overdetermined emphasis on the political, were no different from other movies.

We have, then, both political and gendered reception practices in Londo's family, as well as practices that seem related to general interest in movies. There is also evidence that Capra's films in particular, at least from *It Happened One Night* on, appealed to audiences taking the cinema seriously as an object of study. Besides Londo's report, Capra also received a letter from Harvey Brown, a student attending City College in New York. Brown wrote to the director to tell him that "one of my subjects is English Composition," and that "I will have to write a term report on a picture the class picks."[27] The class, in fact, had chosen *State of the Union*, and the assignment called for students "to write on the picture itself, the characters used, the lighting & photography and many more incidentals all summed up in 700 words." Brown then asked Capra to do his work for him, writing that "I would sincerely appreciate it if you can send me some reviews of the picture so as to help me with my term report."

The tone here, of course, is far different from that of Londo, who went to great lengths to write his evaluation of *State of the Union*. The assignment itself, however, hints at how broadly film studies had entered the postwar university curriculum. Film production classes like Londo's maintained a film studies component, and film had also clearly become the province of the English class. In this curriculum, Capra's films apparently held a special place. In the cases of USC and City College, *State of the Union* became the choice of both the individual student and the entire class. Indeed, the range of viewers taking *State of the Union* very seriously was a wide one, and included, among others, citizens concerned about world government, the occasional socialist seeking a critique of political practices, evangelical Christians looking to spread American culture throughout the world, and budding filmmakers and film critics studying movies in the academy. Capra's films were deemed pedagogical by institutions and individuals, and because of this, Capra's career after *State of the Union* and throughout the 1950s might be more complex than scholars have acknowledged. We can certainly view it, with Carney, McBride, and others, in terms of creative decline. But we can also view the latter stage of Capra's career as the logical conclusion to a filmography that had become more and more overtly educational, and increasingly suited to educational settings. In this narrative of Capra's career, the didactic lessons of *Deeds*, *Smith*, *Doe*, *Why We Fight*, *State of the Union*, and other movies perfectly anticipated Capra's collaboration with AT&T on science films for junior high and high school students.

The Television Audience and Science Education in the 1950s

In one of the typical narratives of American education history, the United States mobilized new and improved systems in science instruction after the Soviet Union launched Sputnik in October 1957. As early as 1960, the dividing point marked by Sputnik already had become taken for granted. Frederick Fitzpatrick, writing that year in *Policies for Science Education*, called Sputnik an "awakening," which "although painful, has been attended by . . . a heightened concern about the state of science programs in the schools."[28] In fact, although efforts probably increased after Sputnik, modernizing and improving science education had been of major concern to educators, government officials, and representatives of big business at least since the early 1950s. A number of examples might be used to demonstrate the centrality of science education to pre-Sputnik cold war notions of progress. In 1952, for instance, the National Science Teachers Association established the Future Scientists of America Foundation "to help encourage future scientists," while Stanford University in 1954 published *Science*

Facilities for the Modern High School, a monograph designed to link new and better methods in science education to architectural improvements in school building design.[29]

Of particular interest from the period just before and at the very beginning of the space age, however, because of its reach into millions of households, is the American Telephone and Telegraph Bell System Science Series of one hour, full-color television shows, made in collaboration with Capra, who received credit as writer/producer, and also with the help of the N. W. Ayer & Son advertising agency. Broadcast between 1956 and 1958, the four programs that made up the series—*Our Mr. Sun* (about a variety of solar phenomena), *Hemo the Magnificent* (about the circulation of blood), *The Strange Case of the Cosmic Rays* (dealing with various kinds of radiation), and *The Unchained Goddess* (about the weather)—all combined live-action footage with animation, and together signaled AT&T's vigorous participation in the educational film and television business.[30] But rather than just serving as an indication of the corporation's continuing interest in a variety of telecommunications media, the science series also demonstrated the manner in which science corporations during the cold war interacted with the education and entertainment industries to consolidate their influence in the national economy and on governmental science policy.

As a sign of the importance of the science series to AT&T's various projects in the 1950s the corporation, with the Ayer agency's assistance, carefully tested the first of the programs, *Our Mr. Sun*, before a number of audiences for eighteen months before its first telecast in November 1956 on CBS, and maintained careful records of the responses of many groups of viewers. In gauging response to *Our Mr. Sun*, AT&T paid special attention to four audience groups: students, teachers, housewives, and AT&T employees. The company seemed motivated by pedagogy and publicity, as it tried to determine how the film affected attitudes toward science and science education on the one hand, and AT&T-as-science-corporation on the other.

Examining the reception of *Our Mr. Sun*, as evidenced by the tests, helps us to understand the apparently widely held beliefs in the United States during the postwar period about the various roles people wanted science corporations to play, about their attitudes toward those corporations, and about the proper way to disseminate scientific knowledge. Examining the tests themselves informs us not so much about what audiences wanted but about a kind of corporate desire, that is, what AT&T wanted to know about the people who might use a range of AT&T products, how AT&T wanted to influence them, and which audiences AT&T most wanted to reach, particu-

Presenting scientific information with the drama, excitement and humor of popular entertainment.

The science programs have been in preparation for several years under the guidance of a distinguished scientific advisory group. They are a serious attempt to bring to the public an understanding of the meaning of science and the work of scientists, showing their part in modern life and culture and helping to inspire interest in science among young persons.

"Our Mr. Sun" is a full-hour film in color, deals with solar physics, solar astronomy and the uses of solar energy. Its accuracy and authenticity are assured by a panel of the world's leading scientists in solar studies, including Dr. Farrington Daniels, Dr. Armin Deutsch, Dr. Donald Menzel, Dr. Walter Orr Roberts and Dr. Otto Struve. Produced and directed by the Academy Award-winning director Frank Capra; animated drawings by UPA Pictures, Inc.

An advertisement appearing in *Scientific American* for the television premiere of *Our Mr. Sun* from the Bell System Science Series.

larly in terms of class, location, and gender. In addition, the project of the science series and of the tests themselves reveals many of the period's tensions regarding the control of science, the role of elite science corporations in shaping both educational and scientific policy, and the relationships between those corporations, the state, and the national economy.

As for the science series itself, all of the programs in it stand out as perhaps the decade's most inventive educational films, along with those produced by Walt Disney. *Our Mr. Sun* opens in a television studio, in which professor and TV personality Dr. Frank Baxter, as Dr. Research, and actor Eddie Albert, as the fiction writer, puzzle over the best way to produce a documentary about the sun. When Dr. Research can provide no definitive answer about the sun's creation, the writer, using a "magic" motion picture screen, conjures up two animated characters, Mr. Sun and Father Time.[31] Mr. Sun proceeds to give something of an autobiography, emphasizing the good old days of absolute worship by the ancients and lamenting the rationality and skepticism of the modern age. Dr. Research then takes over the narrative, using his "screen for facts" to show Mr. Sun what scientists have learned about him and to pose questions about the still unanswered mysteries.

The entire program is structured as a series of films-within-the-film, controlled by Mr. Sun on the one hand and Dr. Research and the fiction writer on the other. Reproducing a 1950s-style United Nations discourse of progress and unity, Dr. Research's films stress the work done around the world by an international team of scientists attempting to understand the sun and learn how to harness its energy. In fact, the show proselytizes throughout for the development of solar energy, without which, according to Dr. Research, humankind might eventually be reduced to the primitivism of a new dark age.[32] Ideologically, this equation between the progress of civilization and using the sun as an energy source functions as one of the most interesting aspects of the show to a modern audience. But the film is also an extremely sophisticated one narratively as well as visually. Doubly self-reflexive, Capra's film not only provides information about the sun through a series of movies-within-the-movie, but also spends much of its time discussing issues of representation in terms of how several centuries of telescopic and photographic apparatus have seen the sun. At one point, the fiction writer tells Mr. Sun, "You've been photographed more than all the Hollywood stars put together."

Joseph McBride, Capra's biographer, has described the budgetary conflicts between the filmmaker and AT&T, but none of the programs in the series looks as if it were made on the cheap.[33] The animation in *Our Mr. Sun* was supervised by United Productions of America (UPA), probably the most inventive cartoon studio of the period, which was responsible for the more modernist animation aesthetic apparent in the *Mr. Magoo* series and in such adaptations as *Gerald McBoing Boing* (1951), from Dr. Seuss; *A Unicorn in the Garden* (1953), based on the James Thurber story; and *The Tell-Tale Heart* (1953), from Edgar Allan Poe. With its combination of live-action and animation and its ingenious narrative construction, *Our Mr. Sun* still looks extraordinary today, and even on the black-and-white television sets of the 1950s this color program must have seemed very special at the time of its initial broadcast.

The Educational Context:
TV, the Corporation, and Capra

AT&T's production of the science series and even Capra's participation in it fit well within postwar concerns about education, the relation of the science corporation to the classroom, and the role of film and television as educational media. During the 1950s, particularly in relation to science, major American corporations, both scientific and otherwise, increasingly became educational benefactors. By 1963, a Department of Health, Education, and Welfare guide to parents called *Modern Science and Your Child* could state with confidence that interest in science education had never been higher, and that "government, business, and industry, especially through foundation grants, are supporting numerous science improvement projects."[34] Thus, arguably as a corrective to many of the local experiments in progressive education that occurred throughout the 1930s and 1940s, the 1950s produced a discourse of child development that called for a sort of governmental-industrial complex for the advancement of science education.[35]

Nevertheless, throughout the decade relations between the federal government and the science corporation were not always smooth. For example, AT&T continued to lobby the Federal Communications Commission, with only limited success, to increase the microwave frequencies available to the corporation so as to further its development of long-distance lines for carrying a variety of telecommunications systems, including television signals. In 1956 the Department of Justice concluded a seven-year antitrust suit against AT&T, forcing the corporation to engage only in the telecommunications business and to let other companies make use of its patents.[36]

In part, no doubt, as a public relations response to these and other related problems, science corporations sought to solidify their appeals to the family and to associate themselves with wholesome (and particularly edifying) entertainment, and so moved enthusiastically into television production. In 1954, for instance, as Christopher Anderson has pointed out, a group of "electrical utilities and manufacturers, including . . . General Electric and Westinghouse," guided by "the electric industry's trade organization, the Edison Electric Institute," sponsored *Light's Diamond Jubilee*, a two-hour tribute to Thomas Edison that became the most-watched program in the early history of commercial television.[37]

Assessing the educational promise of television, the popular press paid special attention to this type of programming, and typically pointed out the contradictions between intellectual uplift and commercial concerns. In an article called "Up with Frank Capra," *Newsweek* magazine lauded *Our Mr. Sun* as a show designed "to satisfy both professors and moppets." Less than a month later *Time* magazine singled out for particular commendation "a series of ten half-hour television lessons called *The Elements*," designed by Nobel Prize–winning chemist Glenn T. Seaborg for broadcast on educational television stations. In other words, such barometers of mass taste as *Time* and *Newsweek* clearly viewed television's ideal role as educational and particularly appreciated scientific programming. The magazines also blamed powerful networks and sponsors for neglecting their responsibility to the public. Seaborg's series, for instance, could "build shows on the conception that . . . viewers . . . wanted to be taught and challenged" precisely because the series' producers "were not haunted by the limitations of commercial TV." Indeed, *Time* wrote that before Capra's triumph "only a fool" would have proposed a network program on the issues covered by *Our Mr. Sun*, while *Newsweek* could only marvel at Capra's accomplishment and at the move by CBS to give a slot in prime time to a show about science. "Ordinarily," the magazine lamented, "the hucksters gobble down the prime cuts of television time, while the experimenters, the educators and the innovators have to pick at the spare and bony hours when nobody is looking."[38]

While the commercial networks seemed to neglect their educational mission, teachers and school administrators frequently posited the 1950s as a golden age for the use of educational films and television shows in the classroom. *Educational Screen*, probably the leading magazine on the subject of combining audio-visual media with educational theory and practice, drove the point home in almost every issue. Even the titles of articles in *Educational Screen* proclaimed the faith of many educational experts in new technologies. One such article from October 1956, about a perceived crisis in high school science education, was called, simply, "Film Is the Answer."[39]

AT&T treated the science series just as it would a prototype for a new telephone, and the company staged at least five different tests to assess reception of the initial broadcast and to judge audience attitudes toward the science corporation.[40] On 15 June 1954 in Philadelphia, a test audience of 44 high school science teachers and 142 high school students watched the program (on film rather than on television) and then responded to questionnaires. On 19 June 1955, in Riverside, California, after the regular screening of *Love Me or Leave Me*, a biographical drama about singer Ruth Etting that starred Doris Day, viewers were treated to a sneak preview of *Our*

c. Why film rated "poor"

Teachers who rated the film "poor" said they gave it this rating because of "poor color and sound, lack of central theme" or a "dislike of combining factual material with animation".

Table II

Reason for Rating Film "Poor"

	Teachers 44=100%	Students 142=100%
Total Number		
Film Rated "Poor"		
Number answering "Poor"	5= 11%	4= 3%
Reasons for Rating		
Presentation of film - poor to combine fact and animation, central theme poor	9	1
Educational value - questionable, not too easy to understand	2	1
Content of film - scientific explanations not clear	---	1
Miscellaneous Unfavorable - too long, drawn out, childish	7	1
Miscellaneous Favorable - well done	2	-
Total	20%	4%

B. Parts of Film Liked and Disliked

1. Most Liked Aspect of Film:

When asked to name the one thing liked most in the film, one-third of the students said "the subject matter". One-fifth of the teachers said "the explanations by humor - animation", (21% of the students said this); one-fifth of the teachers said they liked most the "color" (10% of the students named "color"). Almost one-quarter of the students said they liked most the "interesting, simple presentation of science" (11% of the teachers said this).

Table III

Most Liked Aspect of Film

Question: What one thing did you like most above everything else about this film?

Number	Teachers 44=100%	Students 142=100%
Mentions		
"Explanation by humor - animation"	20%	21%
"Color"	20	10
"Form of presentation"	18	-
"Photography"	18	15
"Scientific accuracy combined with religious spirit"	16	1
Human interest - "man's role and benefit from research"	14	2
"Interesting...simple presentation of science"	11	23
Subject matter	-	33
"Everything"	-	4
"Scientific terminology and explanations"	-	1
"Actors and people"	-	1
Length	-	1
No Answer	5	2
Total	122%	114%

Charting the response to the test screening of *Our Mr. Sun*. (Wesleyan Cinema Archives)

Mr. Sun and then were asked to record their opinions. On 11 October 1956, five weeks before the nationwide broadcast, AT&T gathered 52 high school students, 131 housewives, 108 of the corporation's employees, and 12 high school and college teachers to watch the show at the AT&T Long Lines Auditorium in New York. Then, on the day after the 19 November broadcast, AT&T conducted a telephone survey of 3,006 households in Toronto, San Francisco, Philadelphia, and Chicago. Finally, in the week following the broadcast, the phone company mailed questionnaires to AT&T employees in their Pacific and New Jersey companies to determine the workers' reactions to the science show. After the telecast, AT&T also kept careful track of the fan mail that the program generated. Capra himself received copies of all the surveys and deposited them, along with at least a sampling of the *Our Mr. Sun* fan mail, with the rest of his papers at Wesleyan University.[41]

Science, Religion, and Educational Practice

The data from the test audiences for *Our Mr. Sun*, particularly from the fan mail that the program generated, indicate a serious interest during the period in the religious implications of science and science education. The program itself smooths over any perceived differences between the scientific method and religious sensibility. *Our Mr. Sun* begins with a citation from Psalms and ends with an invocation from St. Francis, with members of various test audiences feeling reassured by this expression of religious faith and by how solar phenomena partially came to be explained as God's work.[42] In the audience test at Philadelphia, sixteen of forty-four teachers commented that their "most liked aspect" of *Our Mr. Sun* was the manner in which the program combined "scientific accuracy . . . with religious spirit."[43] None of the *Our Mr. Sun* questionnaires, however, asked specific questions about science and religion, and while many teachers in the Philadelphia audience valued the spiritual aspects of the program, very few members of any other test audience mentioned religion in anything but the most allusive terms.[44] The audience for *Our Mr. Sun* that most valued the program's religious content was the one group of viewers that was the most difficult for AT&T to quantify with any sureness; the people motivated to write fan letters after the program's initial telecast.

Despite the difficulty of determining anything absolute about an audience writing unsolicited letters, AT&T took quite seriously the fan mail it received about *Our Mr. Sun*. From this mail the company determined that, of "a total of 953 letters and postal cards . . . from all over the country," 261, or 27 percent, "praised the religious theme" of the show.[45] These letters, or at least those few included with the other audience documents, point to a desire to have a kind of science education consistent with religious values. They also show the extent to which some people viewed television—the machine rather than any program or series of programs—as the technology that showed the possibility for god and science to combine forces, and that was just waiting for men like Capra to use it properly.

One viewer from North Charleroi, Pennsylvania, separated himself from any educational setting or discourse by letting Capra know that "I don't know how to put this in fancy words, etc. like they usually do." Still, he wanted to tell Capra that he was "a credit to Television itself," and that *Our Mr. Sun* seemed like nothing less than "a message from God, himself." In closing, the viewer told Capra, "You have just demonstrated the most sincere, practical & reverend way of using this god-given medium."[46] For this small-town viewer in 1956, television itself constituted the true miracle of the modern age, the most marked sign of the way that science and religion might work together. But audiences in major urban areas also felt the religious implications of both television and Capra's program. Providing information about the various ways, outside of home viewing, that people watched television in the mid-1950s, a former Capra secretary wrote to her exboss to tell him that she had made special arrangements to see the program in color from "the balcony" at a music shop in Beverly Hills. When a customer walked in to purchase a hi-fi set halfway through the program, the proprietor, also watching from the balcony, called down to say, "You'll have to wait—I'm saying my prayers."[47] Clearly, by 1956 hi-fi technology could be considered determinedly earthbound, attractive to those who were unaware of a truly special media event or of the promise of ultramodern media technology; indeed, that technology, television, at least on occasion, had to be watched reverently and uninterrupted by mere business transactions.

Respecting Science

No doubt AT&T was pleased by the connections that viewers made between the science program and religion. For the most part, however, the corporation hoped that *Our Mr. Sun* would provide students not with an understanding of any eternal mysteries, but with a belief in the absolute centrality of science to their future well-being. Part of AT&T's own faith in science and the scientific method becomes clear in the corporation's belief, apparent in the audience questionnaires, that Capra's program would indeed make for precise, measurable changes in the ways viewers thought about specific topics. The descriptive narrative accompanying the Philadelphia student-teacher test acknowledged the difficulty of the task at hand, but expressed some encouragement about the results. "It is obvious that attitudes can be changed," the description insisted, but it was not so clear how long this might take, or how many "exposures to a new influence" might be necessary. Then, however, in an assertion of an unquestioned belief in the power of media influences to speed up this process and produce specific alterations in audience perception, the test description claimed that *Our Mr. Sun* generated "favorable changes in attitude toward science and, on the other hand, almost no changes in attitude toward any other fields."[48]

This positivist belief that film and television reception could be precisely controlled and then accurately monitored meant, for AT&T, that the corporation could teach students some facts about science and, more important, show them how and what to think about science as a discipline and as a vital provider of the modern conveniences. The Philadelphia test questioned students before the screening and after, and found that prior to seeing *Our Mr. Sun* they had a general appreciation for the solidly white-collar jobs. Responding to the question "Which of these professions do you respect the most?" 28 percent said "science" and 45 percent answered "medicine," with "teaching" and "law" receiving 28 percent and 27 percent, respectively.[49]

After the screening, however, both science and medicine were cited as the most-respected professions by 61 percent of the students (all of whom were able to indicate more than one profession at the top of their lists), while other professions remained about the same.[50] In keeping with the perceived educational imperatives of the period, AT&T certainly hoped to increase scientific knowledge, but a central interest of the corporation, apparent in the test questions, was also that of increasing the regard for the field of science, whether or not this meant increased understanding. Of course, along with this new respect for science might come an interest in science as a career, and whether *Our Mr. Sun* might influence students to become science professionals emerges as one of the main concerns of the Philadelphia test. After inquiring about respect, the questionnaire tried to chart "change in attitudes towards professions" and then in relation to "school subjects." After the screening, many students wanted to "know more about" that which the questionnaire termed the "allied fields" of science, such as teaching and engineering (although the changes here were not so dramatic as the shift in respect for these fields). In addition, most students said that *Our Mr. Sun* made them want to take more science courses in high school (but interest in taking science courses in college tended to stay about the same or decline just a little).[51]

A large number of students also insisted that after seeing the program they would take more courses in French, English, and history.[52] As much as anything else, then, and despite AT&T's confidence that the program increased respect for and curiosity about science and not other fields, *Our Mr. Sun* seems to have been interpreted by students as indicating the value of knowledge and education in general. But for AT&T, the success of *Our Mr. Sun* could be measured to the degree that it made students want to be scientists and to think about other career options related to science. In other words, AT&T hoped that the program would make science seem synonymous with upward mobility and, in keeping with a 1950s corporate/educational imperative, would make students want to be scientific professionals at various levels of expertise, and to see the value of science in all professional endeavors.

Sponsoring Science

Along with increasing the respect for science in general, *Our Mr. Sun* was also supposed to heighten regard for AT&T, the science corporation, in particular. For the corporation, this raised questions of how best to advertise itself on the show and to make the viewing public aware of AT&T's sponsorship without seeming to commercialize an educational project. As a result, AT&T decided to telecast *Our Mr. Sun* with only one commercial, about the corporation's work on the transistor, scheduled to run halfway through the program. But AT&T also hoped that viewers who saw the program in any context would see the ad because they planned to release the program as an educational film with the commercial still there.[53] Clearly, AT&T wanted the audience to know that the corporation had sponsored the show, and they hoped that the program would make viewers think highly of them as a result. The issue AT&T needed to clarify was whether the corporation had achieved this recognition as unobtrusively as possible, with the advertisement and the show itself functioning as publicity for the corporation without seeming too crassly commercial.

The subject of the commercial—the transistor—was no accident. Throughout the 1950s AT&T stressed its work on the transistor as a sign of its commitment to national defense, community involvement, and educational improvement, and implicitly as a sign of the fluid connections between them. As early as 1952, AT&T placed a photo of three transistors on the cover of its annual report (with other covers during the decade typically depicting AT&T employees or customers, or decidedly more photogenic technology such as Princess phones). Inside, the text of the report discussed the transistor's use in the development of military technology and in more effective methods of long-distance dialing. Work on the transistor even signified the corporation's contributions to a diverse national economy and to encouraging a healthy field of telecommunications competitors, with AT&T licensing "38 other companies to make and sell transistors under our patents," a practice in keeping with its policy "of making any of our inventions available for use by others . . . on reasonable terms."[54]

By 1958, AT&T had taken its transistors into the classroom. The corporation advertised the fact that "students and teachers in Washington, D.C. use transistors . . . given [to them] by the telephone company to aid studies in science," and emphasized that Bell Laboratories' "invention of the transistor has created a whole new transistor industry, employing tens of thousands of people in this country and also abroad."[55] Thus the transistor stood out as the product around which AT&T constructed a significant public relations program. In a sense, then, *Our Mr. Sun* functioned as an hour-long means for AT&T to present before the public a few moments explaining its work on the transistor, the technology that served as the basis for so many of the corporation's military projects, domestic telecommunications developments, and discourses of benign involvement in the lives of children and the day-to-day activities of neighborhoods.

All of the test audiences were asked about their feelings toward the commercial, the corporation, and corporate sponsorship. In Philadelphia the questionnaire was used to determine the answer to two central questions: "How well integrated into the film is the transistor commercial?" and "How does the Bell Telephone System rank as a leader in research?"[56] The response pleased AT&T and left the corporation with an understanding of the manner in which programming might be received differently in different settings. After the screening, Bell placed third among teachers and students, trailing General Electric and Du Pont, in a listing of research leaders (after the top four, which included Westinghouse, there was a sharp drop-off to other companies such as RCA and General Motors, with Chrysler Corporation finishing twenty-first and last).[57]

Many of these same viewers, according to the survey results, were not even aware that the commercial constituted a break in the program, so well integrated did the transistor ad seem. "However," the survey cautioned, "there was a definite minority that did feel that the commercial 'did not belong.' " The company concluded that "viewed in the context of commercial programs, the transistor commercial would seem a well integrated one, but in the context of a non-commercial program, it would probably be considered out of place by at least some viewers."[58] Thus the commercial posed a problem that had to do precisely with the reception context. For viewers used to single companies sponsoring programs (which was a typical practice on television during this period), and used to being bombarded by commercials, the ad in *Our Mr. Sun* would seem so subtle as to blend in with the rest of the show. For those, like the Philadelphia audience, seeing the film in an educational setting, the commercial indeed could seem absolutely out of place.

Generally, however, responses to AT&T's sponsorship and the efficacy of the commercial indicate a belief among viewers in the benevolence of science corporations and in the positive benefits of this kind of involvement in television production. On the phone survey, AT&T made no hesitation in getting to what was, for the science corporation, the most important questions. After inquiring whether the person on the phone owned a television set and whether anyone in the household might have seen the program, the questioner asked, quite directly, "Who was the sponsor of *Our Mr. Sun*?" Overall, 41 percent knew the answer while 55 percent (almost all of whom had not seen the show) did not. Moreover, among those respondents who had seen the program, 84 percent felt that it was a "good idea for the Telephone Company to sponsor a television program like *Our Mr. Sun*," while only 2 percent believed it to be a bad idea. Only 7 percent thought that this kind of sponsorship was acceptable "for any big Co.," while most agreed that AT&T's involvement indicated that the phone company was "public minded," "scientific minded," and interested in "high type program[s]."[59]

These findings about viewer attitudes toward AT&T are, of course, partial. At the very least, AT&T's surveys show an urban or suburban middle-class bias. The respondents, for the most part, lived in or around major cities and were either professionals (teachers, phone company employees), students with plans for college, or members of households that had televisions. Among this audience there seems to have been a general agreement that *Our Mr. Sun* accurately indicated the special status of the science corporation as an instrument of education, research, and public welfare. The results demonstrate as well the perception that the educational setting was special, indeed commercially inviolate. *Our Mr. Sun* itself was deemed absolutely appropriate for classroom use. However, any overt assertion of AT&T's sponsorship, or of the company's work in the production of science products in general, might be deemed not so much an inappropriate mix of the corporate and the educational (which few seemed to frown on), but an improper entrance of the rough and tumble of sales and marketing into the realm of pure knowledge.

In addition to the location and class biases of AT&T's inquiries and of the respondent pool, the overwhelming majority of those in the test audiences were, apparently, women. Half of the respondents in the Riverside screening were women. At the New York test screening, AT&T listed 131 of the participants as "housewives," and we can assume that among the rest of the audience members about half of the 52 high school students were female, and at least some of the 12 high school and college teachers and 108 AT&T employees also must have been women.[60] The company did not break down the Philadelphia audience of students and teachers by gender, but once again we can assume that somewhere around half were female. Similarly, while no gender divisions were noted in the test of AT&T employees, some were undoubtedly women, while in the telephone survey, the most imbalanced of all of the tests in which gender was noted, 77 percent of the 2,710 respondents were women.[61] Indeed, after employment and student status, gender was the category that AT&T most typically tried to quantify accurately. Class positions may have been implied but were never specified in any of the tests, and race disappeared entirely as a meaningful category, despite the fact that so many of the tests focused on areas with racially diverse populations (San Francisco, Chicago, and Philadelphia, for instance).

These numbers present a range of interpretive possibilities. The daytime test at the AT&T auditorium may have drawn a disproportionate number of housewives because they would have more flexible time than working men or women to attend the screening. Similarly, AT&T made its telephone test of households on the day following the broadcast of *Our Mr. Sun*, and it makes sense in the 1950s that women, who most likely were also primarily housewives, would answer in greater numbers than men, who would be at work. But it seems just as possible that AT&T, using all of the modern methods of divining information scientifically, might have been aware of the gender demographics of tests given at different times of day, and so was particularly interested in the opinions of women. Certainly, the data generated by the tests largely are data about the relationships of women to the science corporation, science education, and product advertising. It is at least possible that for AT&T women were the central audience for the science corporation to reach and were perceived to have more effect than any other group on shaping overall public opinion about science and in determining household consumption practices.

Our Mr. Sun and the Projects of the Science Corporation

While many women enjoyed *Our Mr. Sun*, they also constituted the toughest audiences for the program. The housewives at the New York screening were particularly hard on it, with only 30 percent of them calling it "entertaining." Indeed, praise for the show was never unanimous among any of the audiences. At the Philadelphia screening, viewers objected to a range of images and ideas, from the shot of a woman's leg (showing the relationship between nylon and the sun) to the vast number of concepts introduced by the show.[62] Moreover, while AT&T's interest in students, teachers, and women seems logical given the period's sense of the connections between the domestic setting and the classroom, the avid interest in tracking the opinions of phone company employees implies that, in some cases, gathering information about science may have played a secondary role to collecting data about workers. The emphasis in all the tests on urban or suburban areas and on middle-class subjects leads one to wonder if the corporation's primary concern was with those viewers who had the best chance of turning into consumers and of using those products that the corporation made.

AT&T's interests in, and most of the responses to, *Our Mr. Sun* demonstrate the belief in a series of logical connections—between the corporation, media technology, and education, for example—and in religion and science emerging as compatible fields rather than two ends of a binary opposition. Even Capra himself signified the linkages made during the period between education and entertainment, and between World War II and the relative peace of the cold war era. Most particularly, in so many of its endeavors from the period, AT&T sought to construct versions of the global and the local that were always connected. The cover of the company's annual report for 1953, for instance, depicts a home telephone on a desk, with a small telephone book on the right and a world globe on the left. In 1957, for the illustration accompanying that section of the report detailing the corporation's progress, AT&T used a photograph of a farmer using a phone in his barn, with which "he can talk with 115 million other" customers, "down the lane and across the world."[63] Within this strategy, *Our Mr. Sun* represented the ultimate connection of the two spaces, with the sun itself brought into the smallest unit of the local, at least to AT&T, the family living room.

All of these areas and issues indicate the increasing number of projects of nationalization, practiced by the government and by corporations, or envisioned by those educators who wanted to develop science curricula for the entire country. More significantly for the science corporations, these efforts would be central to maintaining the position of prominence that the scientific research industry had attained during the war, with this prominence being transformed into power over national science policy and within the national economy.[64] Television would be one of the principal instruments of these nationalizing plans on the part of science corporations, with a program like *Our Mr. Sun*, which could amuse and edify at the same time, playing a central role in these projects. After the first telecast of *Our Mr. Sun*, AT&T explained the reasoning behind the entire science series as that of creating a narrative of never-ending development with the science corporation as the hero of the story: "The purpose of these programs is to show in a dramatic and entertaining way how scientists are working to help mankind toward better and more useful living. We hope they will contribute to a broader understanding of scientific goals, and also stimulate interest in science among young people. The country needs more scientists. The telephone business will always need them, for communication service is based on science and our future success depends largely on scientific progress."[65]

Here, "our future" could be interpreted as indicating both that of the country and the telephone company, a linkage that AT&T no doubt hoped to encourage with *Our Mr. Sun* and the rest of the Bell System Science Series. Indeed, it is the importance of this linkage to a variety of AT&T's efforts during the period that helps explain the care with which the corporation sought to gauge the response to its entrance into television production. For AT&T, television, if used correctly, and the science series, if produced properly, could help to construct a postwar modernity marked by an easy cooperation between corporations and an educated, upwardly mobile, and fully technologized citizenry.

With this science series at the end of his career—after the series' completion Capra made only two more feature length films—the director became a pedagogue once again. He had played that role in the 1930s with the entrance of his films into the film appreciation classroom. He was positioned as a teacher yet again in the 1940s with the *Why We Fight* films and, arguably, with the *It's a Wonderful Life* screening in San Quentin, where inmates were supposed to learn valuable lessons from a movie. Then, of course, *State of the Union* became part of the university curriculum, teaching budding directors about humor, scene construction, and the best ways of addressing an audience. In a biographical overview it is relatively easy to see the AT&T science films as signs of decline, as the sad end to a once astonishingly successful auteurist directorial career. We cannot simply dismiss this notion, because Capra did experience great difficulty in getting films made during the 1950s, and seemed more or less forgotten or at least unappreciated by the film studios. But we might also view the science films as the most fitting finish imaginable to a body of work like Capra's. The didactic pedagogy of *Mr. Smith*'s lessons about democracy, or *Why We Fight*'s arguments for war, or *State of the Union*'s instructions for future directors might well lead logically to *Our Mr. Sun*, with a Hollywood film director finally realizing that television had become the ideal medium for his ideas and for his preferred methods of addressing his viewers.

Conclusion

The Contemporary Capra

When Frank Capra died on September 3, 1991, the domestic and international press offered assessments and interpretations of his career. The *New York Times* put the director's picture on the front page the next day and claimed in a caption that his "movies were suffused with affectionate portrayals of the common man and the strengths and foibles of American democracy."[1] In the longer obituary, the *Times* wrote the standard rags-to-riches immigrant narrative, referring to Capra as "the son of illiterate Sicilian peasants who came to this country by steerage when he was six," and who then became "one of Hollywood's preeminent directors in the 1930's and '40's." The *Times* then stated that Capra stood out as "one of the first whose name appeared on marquees and above the title in film credits." Giving the life story a satisfying arc, the obituary then shifted to decline, informing readers that "by the late 1940's . . . the director's optimism no longer coincided with the mood of Americans and his movies were described by some reviewers as naive, sentimental and sanctimonious."[2]

In Paris, *Libération* also put a photo of Capra on the front page, and then eulogized him in a somewhat similar fashion. "Born of Sicilian immigrants, he would achieve his dream: having his name above the title." *Libération* rather oddly prized *Arsenic and Old Lace* above Capra's other films, and then declared the director "the inventor of American comedy."[3] The *Washington Post* sought out director Edward Zwick, who named his production company Bedford Falls after George Bailey's hometown in *It's a Wonderful Life*, and who was one of the creators of the TV show *thirtysomething*. Pontificating about the Capra aesthetic, Zwick said that "I found his vision of America not unlike that of the Hudson River School of painters—this celestial light of unlimited possibilities." But he also created some distance between himself and Capra, saying that the director's overall vision made it possible to "forgive him things you might otherwise take exception to." The *Post* also quoted one of Capra's friends, who was less condescending than Zwick but who reduced Capra's life to that of one of his characters: "In fact, he was like Clarence," the guardian angel in *It's a Wonderful Life*.[4]

These assessments from 1991 certainly do not seem to match the responses that many audiences had to Capra in the 1930s and 1940s. It is not at all clear that those audiences typically found the director's films full of "optimism," nor that his films after, perhaps, *State of the Union* in 1948 were suddenly considered naive or sentimental, or, in fact, that the mood of Americans would be so easy to characterize in the first place.[5] And while his friend may have thought of him as another Clarence, most of his viewers had far more complicated notions of Capra, ranging from political figure to model Italian American to informed pedagogue.

Of course, Capra himself may have been largely responsible for these contemporary interpretations of his career. He largely resurrected his own reputation with the publication of his autobiography in 1971. He called his life story *The Name above the Title*, which apparently provided the evidence for the assertion that having his name prominently displayed on marquees and in credits was indeed the fulfillment of a great dream. This Capra, celebrated in the director's autobiography and then later feted at a 1982 American Film Institute Lifetime Achievement Award, is the one probably still the most familiar to us, the populist in love with the common man.

This is the reputation earned from a few of his films, most notably the *Deeds*, *Smith*, and *Doe* trilogy in addition to *It's a Wonderful Life*. Indeed those films are also often used now as a sort of political shorthand for underdogs and participatory democracy. In 1993, for example, the *San Francisco Chronicle*, in a story about a House of Representatives floor fight over President Clinton's budget proposal that the president won with the very last vote cast by a wavering congresswoman, wrote that "if politics is theater, as the skeptics say, last night was classic Hitchcock, with a very large dose of Frank Capra." Two years later, after Republicans had gained control of the House of Representatives with the elections of dozens of political novices, the *New York Times* headlined: "73 Mr. Smiths, of G.O.P., Go to Washington."[6]

Yet another contemporary understanding of Capra and his films comes from filmmakers themselves. I have not made a formal survey but it seems to me that from the 1960s to the 1980s, Alfred Hitchcock and John Ford were the filmmakers of choice for gifted young directors to imitate. Lately, though, Capra has taken his place in the group, in terms both of imitation (Francis Ford Coppola's 1988 film *Tucker* comes to mind, as does the Coen brothers' *The Hudsucker Proxy* from 1994) and of remake. This is not absolutely new. After *It Happened One Night*, any number of films invoked scenes from that movie, even up to *Bandits* in 2001, in which Bruce Willis, imitating Clark Gable's "walls of Jericho," hangs a blanket in order to divide the bed he must share with Cate Blanchett. Fairly recently, however, directors seemingly removed from the Capra aesthetic—high-art filmmakers with self-conscious styles, forms, and ideological practices—have chosen to remake and rethink Capra. Here, *Meet John Doe* has become the most significant and, with its emphasis on the connection between media and politics, perhaps the most modern of all Capra films. As long ago as 1957 Elia Kazan remade the film, turning the naive Doe into an incipient fascist in *A Face in the Crowd*. In the last dozen years, Stephen Frears with *Hero* (1992), and Spike Lee with *Bamboozled* (2002), both sought to reinvent *Doe* for new audiences.

Thus contemporary artists constitute an audience for Capra, themselves interpreting his movies just as did the fans who wrote the director letters in the 1930s, 1940s, and 1950s. These artists work in various media and not just film. Along with Coppola, Frears, and Lee, for instance, one would also add David Diao, who reproduced oversized images from *The Bitter Tea of General Yen* on silkscreen and then used the shared title of that work and the movie as the title of his 1995 New York exhibition.[7] In 2002 the San Francisco Mime Troupe, which typically combines a situationist aesthetic with leftist politics, remade Capra's 1939 film with their new play *Mr. Smith Goes to Obscuristan*, which critiqued American adventurism in Afghanistan. Capra's work clearly has entered a modernist and postmodernist aesthetic mainstream—a use of his films, and an understanding of them, that the director probably could not have imagined.

There are also the middle- to low-brow interpretations and reinterpretations of Capra. Most recently, audiences have watched *Mr. Deeds*, the 2002 remake of Capra's film that turns a Depression-era political allegory into a summer movie for teenage boys, and also *Legally Blonde 2: Red, White, and Blonde* (2003), a reworking of *Mr. Smith Goes to Washington* for actress Reese Witherspoon. Capra references appear regularly in television situation comedies, usually in places where a quick allusion to *It's a Wonderful Life* helps to establish a personality, or where the distinction between Bedford Falls and Pottersville corresponds to a dilemma facing a character.[8] Capra's movies have also been made into television shows for new audiences. *Mr. Smith*, for instance, has been reconfigured into network programming at least three times. In the 1962–1963 season, Fess Parker, Disney's Davey Crockett, starred as the senator, then in 1995 Delta Burke played a widow selected to replace her late husband in Congress in *Women of the House*. In 2003 *Mr. Smith* became *Mr. Sterling* on NBC, with the premiere episode virtually duplicating the start of Capra's movie. The television show starts with the death of a senator, after which the governor is awakened with the news. He then recommends a naive nobody for the job, in this case the do-gooder son of a former governor. The party bosses think they can control Sterling, but learn otherwise in each episode. So Capra's stories, in various forms, keep finding new audiences.

Capra has also begun reaching audiences that have perhaps only fully existed in any numbers for the last few years, the audience of owners and collectors. Capra has often inspired a discourse of ownership, some of it coming from his autobiography's "one man, one film" manifesto, in which he asserted primary responsibility for his films. Some of that discourse has also been corporate and deals with questions of who, properly speaking, owns Capra's films. The most notable example is probably that of *It's a Wonderful Life*, which became a ubiquitous holiday film only after it dropped out of copyright, and thus could be shown anywhere by anyone. In my own experience I think of a screening in San Francisco of Capra's newly restored 1928 film *The Matinee Idol*. Before the screening a Sony executive addressed the crowd and said that "Capra made seven films for us in 1928." This was the first I had heard that Capra had worked for Sony. But Columbia, Capra's home studio for so many years, had recently become a division of Sony, so that company could now claim possession of Capra's movies and thus speak proudly of Capra as a onetime employee.

Perhaps the largest audience in this category, though, is the one that browses on eBay. A number of Capra items appear on this Web site, from fairly common videos to rather obscure ephemera. My own collection of eBay purchases includes a 1940 Capra director trading card and a *Lost Horizon* scene card from the same year, both issued by a South African cigarette company as part of much larger sets, with pertinent information on the back in English and Afrikaans; novelizations from 1929 and 1931 of two Capra films, *Flight* and *Dirigible*; a 1935 Big Little Book version (about four by five inches) of *It Happened One Night*, with Clark Gable and Claudette Colbert on the cover; and various 1930s magazines with articles about Capra, including the 1938 issue of *Time* with Capra on the cover. In making these purchases I can own a little something of Capra and, as well, some

Top left: The front of the Max Cigarette Frank Capra trading card,
from about 1940. (Collection of the author) *Top right*: The back of the
Max Cigarette card, in English and Afrikaans, calling Capra "humanity's
champion." (Collection of the author) *Bottom*: The program from the
1997 Capra centennial in Bisacquino, Sicily, where the director was
born. (Provincia Regionale di Palermo Assessorato alla Cultura)

items that his fans possessed at the time of the director's greatest celebrity. Thus Capra has entered a whole new kind of commerce, made up of enthusiasts, historians, and others, and it might well be a form of commerce that Capra, the renowned rare book collector, would have appreciated.

Artifact collecting might constitute a new kind of reception studies, one based on a potential purchaser's valuation of a director or film, on how much one should pay for a Capra souvenir card as opposed to a Hitchcock or a Hawks. While I happily participate in this "audience," my own favorite Capra crowd is still the traditional theatrical one, although not necessarily in the traditional theatrical site. In 1997 I had the chance to take part in the Capra centennial celebration in his hometown of Bisacquino, Sicily, a centennial that took its name from Capra's personal and professional life story: "From Bisacquino to Hollywood."[9] The organizers had arranged screenings of Capra's movies in the small town, but in order to accommodate the crowd they were held outdoors, with the films projected onto the wall of a building. For the silent films, a chain-smoking pianist acted as the accompanist, playing original compositions. It was alternately hot and rainy, and children ran around during most of the screenings.

It is not at all my intention here to romanticize this kind of audience or this kind of travel experience. Seeing the movies in the town square, however, did bring to mind those students who watched *It Happened One Night* at a YMCA in North Carolina; the recruits viewing the *Why We Fight* documentaries in their barracks; the prisoners crying while they watched *It's a Wonderful Life* in San Quentin; and the audiences who saw Capra movies at Radio City Music hall or in neighborhood theaters. From Bisacquino to Hollywood, all of those thousands of pairs of eyes and ears, the audiences that Capra heard from and responded to, did indeed seem like the most important and compelling participants in an ongoing history of the cinema as an institution, and in the continuing career of a director who made his last film in 1961.

Notes

INTRODUCTION: AUDIENCES, FILM STUDIES, AND FRANK CAPRA

1   Frank Capra, *The Name above the Title: An Autobiography* (New York: Macmillan, 1971). Capra refers to "a thousand pairs of eyes and ears" on p. 139 and doing his "thing with film" on p. 297.

2   Janet Staiger, *Interpreting Films: Studies in the Historical Reception of American Cinema* (Princeton: Princeton University Press, 1992); Gregory Waller, *Main Street Amusements: Movies and Commercial Entertainment in a Southern City, 1896-1930* (Washington, D.C.: Smithsonian Institution Press, 1995); Charles Maland, *Chaplin and American Culture: The Evolution of a Star Image* (Princeton: Princeton University Press, 1989); Jackie Stacey, *Star Gazing: Hollywood Cinema and Female Spectatorship* (London: Routledge, 1994); Melvyn Stokes and Richard Maltby, eds., *American Movie Audiences: From the Turn of the Century to the Early Sound Era* (London: British Film Institute, 1999); Melvyn Stokes and Richard Maltby, eds., *Identifying Hollywood's Audiences: Cultural Identity and the Movies* (London: British Film Institute, 1999); Annette Kuhn, *Dreaming of Fred and Ginger: Cinema and Cultural Memory* (New York: New York University Press, 2002).

3   Ben Singer, "Manhattan Nickelodeons: New Data on Audiences and Exhibitors," *Cinema Journal* 34, no. 3 (spring 1995): 5-35; Robert C. Allen, "Manhattan Myopia: or, Oh! Iowa!," *Cinema Journal* 35, no. 3 (spring 1996): 75-103. In the same issue, see Ben Singer, "New York, Just Like I Pictured It . . . ," pp. 104-28, as well as Sumiko Higashi's response to Singer's original essay: "Dialogue: Manhattan's Nickelodeons," pp. 72-74.

4   For the essay on Mass Observation, see Sue Harper and Vincent Porter, "Moved to Tears: Weeping in the Cinema in Postwar Britain," *Screen* 37, no. 2 (summer 1996): 152-73. Emilie Altenloh, "A Sociology of the Cinema: The Audience" (1914), trans. Kathleen Cross, *Screen* 42, no. 3 (autumn 2001): 249-93.

5   Margaret Farrand Thorp, *America at the Movies* (New Haven: Yale University Press, 1939), 1.

6   Gessner sent his syllabus to Capra, who deposited it with his papers at the Cinema Archives at Wesleyan University. The class itself seems to have been an adult educa-

tion course, or perhaps an extension course, and not part of the regular university curriculum, because of the fifteen-dollar fee for all of the sessions or the one-dollar fee for individual sessions.

7   Jane Addams, *The Spirit of Youth and City Streets* (New York: Macmillan, 1909). See, for instance, chapter 4, "The House of Dreams," 75–103. In this chapter, Addams writes of "the absorbed gaze of a child" (75), and also examines the manner in which the impact of the motion picture extends well beyond the space of the theater: "Hundreds of young people attend these five-cent theaters every evening in the week, including Sunday, and what is seen and heard there becomes the sole topic of conversation, forming the ground pattern of their social life" (86).

8   Robert S. Lynd and Helen Merrell Lynd, *Middletown* (New York: Harcourt, Brace and World, 1929).

9   Werrett Wallace Charters, *Motion Pictures and Youth* (New York: Macmillan, 1933); Edgar Dale, *Children's Attendance at Motion Pictures* (New York: Macmillan, 1935); Wendell S. Dysinger and Christian A. Ruckmick, *The Emotional Responses of Children to the Motion Picture Situation* (New York: Macmillan, 1935); Perry W. Holaday and George D. Stoddard, *Getting Ideas from the Movies* (New York: Macmillan, 1933).

10 Leo A. Handel, *Hollywood Looks at Its Audience* (Urbana: University of Illinois Press, 1950).

11 David Riesman and Evelyn T. Riesman, "Movies and Audiences," *American Quarterly* 4, no. 3 (fall 1952): 195–202. For a similar article from a non–American studies perspective, see Mark Abrams, "The British Cinema Audience," *Hollywood Quarterly* 3, no. 2, (winter 1947–48): 155–58.

12 Palter's essay originally appeared in the *Hollywood Quarterly* 3, no. 3 (spring 1948), and was reprinted in *Hollywood Quarterly: Film Culture in Postwar America, 1945–1957*, edited by Eric Smoodin and Ann Martin (Berkeley: University of California Press, 2002), 139–51.

13 Garth Jowett, *Film: The Democratic Art* (Boston: Little, Brown, 1976).

14 Eric Lott, *Love and Theft: Blackface Minstrelsy and the American Working Class* (New York: Oxford University Press, 1993); John Bodnar, *Remaking America: Public Memory, Commemoration, and Patriotism in the Twentieth Century* (Princeton: Princeton University Press, 1992); Mary P. Ryan, *Women in Public: Between Banners and Ballots, 1825–1880* (Baltimore: Johns Hopkins University Press, 1990); Jane Gaines, *Contested Culture: The Image, the Voice, and the Law* (Durham: Duke University Press, 1991).

15 Edward Buscombe, "Notes on Columbia Pictures Corporation, 1926–1941." This essay originally appeared in *Screen* 16, no. 3 (autumn 1975): 65–82. The citation here is taken from a volume that has anthologized Buscombe's essay: Janet Staiger, ed., *The Studio System* (New Brunswick: Rutgers University Press, 1995), 24.

16 Ien Ang, *Watching Dallas: Soap Opera and the Melodramatic Imagination* (London: Methuen, 1985), 11; Stacey, *Star Gazing*, 71 (Stacey, on the same page, is my source for the statement by Ang).

17 Frank H. Ricketson Jr., *The Management of Motion Picture Theatres* (New York: McGraw-Hill, 1938).

18 Ibid., 122.

19 In his autobiography, for example, Capra wrote that after his divorce from his first wife and the failure of his 1927 film *For the Love of Mike*, he wondered whether "he should go back to Caltech and try for a Ph.D." (*The Name above the Title*, 77).

20 Eva Basquill to Capra, 1 December 1935, Capra Collection, Wesleyan Cinema Archives (all subsequent fan letters are from this collection).

21 K. Dowsett [or Dorsett], to Capra, 26 January 1935.

22 Katherine Rainey to Capra, 1 September 1937.

23 A. A. Narayan to Capra, 19 August 1937.

24 Joseph McBride provides an excellent review of Capra's work for Project Vista in his biography *Frank Capra: The Catastrophe of Success* (New York: Simon and Schuster, 1992), 588–95.

25 I received Capra's FBI file through a Freedom of Information Act request. The apparent reference to Buchman (like most FOIA files, Capra's is heavily redacted) comes in a document labeled "Security Information—Confidential," dated 29 January 1952, 5; It also appears in a document labeled "Office Memorandum to Mr. Nichols," dated 1 July 1953, 6–7. Capra's FBI files are numbered 100-384984, 7-2403, and 123-12626.

26 The accusations all come in "Office Memorandum to Mr. Nichols."

27 Capra defends himself throughout "Office Memorandum to Mr. Nichols." For patterns of charitable giving, see 6; on his dealings with the Soviet Union, see 8–9.

28 Capra, *The Name above the Title*, 305.

I THE NATIONAL AND THE LOCAL:
BALLYHOO AND THE U.S. FILM AUDIENCE

1 "Highlights about *Flight*, The All-Talking Roadshow Sensation," in "Exhibitor's Campaign Book," n.p., Library of Congress.

2 Capra's filmography from the period includes *The Strong Man* (1926); *Long Pants* (1927); *For the Love of Mike* (1927); *That Certain Thing* (1928); *So This Is Love* (1928); *The Matinee Idol* (1928); *The Way of the Strong* (1928); *Say It with Sables* (1928); *Submarine* (1928); *The Power of the Press* (1928); *The Younger Generation* (1929); *The Donovan Affair* (1929); *Flight* (1929); *Ladies of Leisure* (1930); *Rain or Shine* (1930); *Dirigible* (1931); *The Miracle Woman* (1931); *Platinum Blonde* (1931); *Forbidden* (1932); *American Madness* (1932); *The Bitter Tea of General Yen* (1933); and *Lady for a Day* (1933). While this was a steady workload for a major director, it was by no means unusual, or even extraordinary. During the same period, for instance, William Wellman directed at least thirty-three feature films, while John Ford made at least twenty-one.

3 Tino Balio, *Grand Design: Hollywood as a Modern Business Enterprise, 1930-1939* (Berkeley: University of California Press, 1995), 28–29. Balio notes that by 1934, after "independent producers and exhibitors" convinced the National Recovery Administration to legalize double bills, "nearly every theater in competitive situations—the markets that generated the bulk of the domestic box-office gross—had fallen into line" and were showing two films (29).

4   Janet Staiger, "Announcing Wares, Winning Patrons, Voicing Ideals: Thinking about the History and Theory of Film Advertising," *Cinema Journal* 29, no. 3, (spring 1990): 3–31. Douglas Gomery also has commented on the movement toward national advertising strategies. See his *The Hollywood Studio System* (New York: St. Martin's Press, 1986), 19.

5   Roland Marchand, *Advertising the American Dream: Making Way for Modernity, 1920–1940* (Berkeley: University of California Press, 1985). Marchand first lists the significant magazines from the period in the frontmatter on xvi. For the work of advertisers during World War I, see 5–6. For initial discussions of AT&T and Proctor and Gamble, and also the National Casket Company, see 5.

6   Ibid., xvi.

7   Stuart Ewen and Elizabeth Ewen, *Channels of Desire: Mass Images and the Shaping of American Consciousness* (Minneapolis: University of Minnesota Press, 1992); Jackson Lears, *Fables of Abundance: A Cultural History of Advertising in America* (New York: Basic Books, 1994); Stephen Fox, *The Mirror Makers: A History of American Advertising and Its Creators* (Urbana: University of Illinois Press, 1997).

8   Lizabeth Cohen, "The Class Experience of Mass Consumption: Workers as Consumers in Interwar America," in *The Power of Culture*, ed. Richard Wightman Fox and T. J. Jackson Lears (Chicago: University of Chicago Press, 1993); Kathy M. Newman: *Radio Active: Advertising and Consumer Activism, 1935–1947* (Berkeley: University of California Press, 2004).

9   Richard deCordova, *Picture Personalities: The Emergence of the Star System in America* (Urbana: University of Illinois Press, 1990); Kathryn Fuller, *At the Picture Show: Small-Town Audiences and the Creation of Movie Fan Culture* (Washington, D.C.: Smithsonian Institution Press, 1996); Gaylyn Studlar, *This Mad Masquerade: Stardom and Masculinity in the Jazz Age* (New York: Columbia University Press, 1996); Shelley Stamp, *Movie-Struck Girls: Women and Motion Picture Culture after the Nickelodeon* (Princeton: Princeton University Press, 2000).

10   Richard Wightman Fox, "Intimacy on Trial: Cultural Meanings of the Beecher-Tilton Affair," in *The Power of Culture: Critical Essays in American History*, ed. Richard Wightman Fox and T. J. Jackson Lears (Chicago: University of Chicago Press, 1993), 123.

11   "Production of *Flight* a Romantic Undertaking: Capra Directed Film Wholly by Wireless Communication," "Exhibitor's Campaign Book," n.p.

12   "Government Cooperated on Columbia Air Film: Marine Corps Eager to Assist in Film of *Flight* Calibre," "Exhibitor's Campaign Book," n.p.

13   Ibid.

14   "*Flight* Is a Great Woman's Picture," "Exhibitor's Campaign Book," n.p.

15   Jowett, *Film*, 264.

16   The attendance numbers are given in Jowett, *Film*, 260.

17   Irwin R. Franklyn, *Flight* (New York: Grosset and Dunlap, 1929).

18   The quotation and the suggestion for bookstore windows come from "Window Displays that Bring Extra Dollars," "Exhibitor's Campaign Book," n.p.

19   "Here Is a Way to Build Extra Matinee Business," "Exhibitor's Campaign Book," n.p.

20 Richard deCordova, "Ethnography and Exhibition: The Child Audience, The Hays Office, and Saturday Matinees," *Camera Obscura* 23 (May 1990): 91–107.

21 The other significant story about Capra that appeared in the "Exhibitor's Campaign Book" was "Capra Ace Director: Has Won Universal Acclaim for Several Films." This appears on the same page (although no page number is provided) as "Director Capra Expert at Every Phase of Talkie." See also, in the same campaign book, "Director Self-Supporting since Early Childhood."

22 "Fashion Forecast in *Ladies of Leisure*," "Exhibitor's Campaign Book," n.p.

23 Charles Eckert, "The Carole Lombard in Macy's Window," in *Fabrications: Costume and the Female Body*, ed. Jane Gaines and Charlotte Herzog (New York: Routledge, 1990), 100–21.

24 Kathy Peiss, *Cheap Amusements: Working Women and Leisure in Turn-of-the-Century New York* (Philadelphia: Temple University Press, 1986).

25 Nan Enstad, *Ladies of Labor, Girls of Adventure* (New York: Columbia University Press, 1999), 17.

26 Siegfried Kracauer, "Die kleinen Ladenmädchen gehen ins Kino," in *Das Ornament der Masse* (Frankfurt am Main: Suhrkamp, 1963).

27 Laura Mulvey, "Visual Pleasure and Narrative Cinema," *Screen* 16, no. 3 (autumn 1975): 6–18.

28 Stacey, *Star Gazing*, 146.

29 "Stunts That Fill Seats," *Ladies of Leisure* "Exhibitor's Campaign Book," n.p.

30 "Exploit and Prosper with Columbia," *Ladies of Leisure* "Exhibitor's Campaign Book," n.p.

31 Miriam Hansen, *Babel and Babylon: Spectatorship in American Silent Film* (Cambridge: Harvard University Press, 1991), 2. For an extension of Hansen's argument beyond the cinema, see Anne Friedberg, *Window Shopping: Cinema and the Postmodern* (Berkeley: University of California Press, 1993).

32 Ben Singer, *Melodrama and Modernity: Early Sensational Cinema and Its Contexts* (New York: Columbia University Press, 2001); see chapter 3, "Sensationalism and the World of Urban Modernity," 59–99. For the discussion of Simmel, overstimulation, and hyperstimulation, see 61, 63, and 65.

33 Peiss, *Cheap Amusements*; see chapter 5, "The Coney Island Experience," 115–38.

34 Our understanding of the woman in public has changed significantly in the last twenty years. Thanks to Mary Ryan and other historians, we know that women were visible in public long before the beginning of the twentieth century, although the "female flaneur" that has become so central to contemporary cultural studies may well be a relatively recent development. For a debunking of the traditional "public/private" divide that has pre-twentieth-century American women in the home rather than out in public, see Ryan, *Women in Public*. See also *No More Separate Spheres! A Next Wave American Studies Reader*, ed. Cathy Davidson and Jessamyn Hatcher (Durham: Duke University Press, 2002).

35 For an example of the insistence on the link between modernity and the urban, see Leo Charney and Vanessa Schwartz, eds., *Cinema and the Invention of Modern Life* (Berkeley: University of California Press, 1995). In their introduction the editors write: "Modernity cannot be conceived outside the context of the city, which pro-

vided an arena for the circulation of bodies and goods, the exchange of glances, and the exercise of consumerism. Modern life seemed urban by definition, yet the social and economic transformations wrought by modernity recast the image of the city in the wake of the eruption of industrial capitalism in the second half of the nineteenth century" (3).

36 See, for example, Fuller, *At the Picture Show*.

37 *Motion Picture Herald*, 21 November 1931, 66.

38 *Motion Picture Herald*, 3 January 1931, 38.

39 All of these campaigns are discussed in the *Motion Picture Herald*: 26 September 1931, 61; 14 November 1931, 68; 6 February 1932, 76; 16 July 1932, 76; 28 November 1931, 66.

40 See, for instance, Raymond Bellour, "Segmenting/Analyzing," in *Narrative, Apparatus, Ideology: A Film Theory Reader*, ed. Philip Rosen (New York: Columbia University Press, 1986), 66–92. In the same volume, see also Bellour, "The Obvious and the Code," 93–101.

41 Newman, *Radio Active*.

42 Ricketson, *The Management of Motion Picture Theaters*, 219.

43 "Columbia Starts *Dirigible* Ballyhoo over Radio Feb. 8," *Motion Picture Herald*, 31 January 1931, 34.

44 In the promotional material designed, apparently, for exhibitors, Columbia stressed the realism of *Dirigible*: "An authentic and thrilling drama . . . Every phase of the experiences encountered on such a venture together with details of life aboard an up-to-date blimp are shown with faithful realism." Columbia Pictures publicity flyer, "The Superior Twenty, 1930–1931 Season," (Library of Congress, *Dirigible* copyright records, document 2007). Print ads for the film also stressed its realism, in part through the expertise of those involved in the production. Frank Wead, who wrote the story (although not the screenplay) figured prominently here, typically as "Frank Wilber Wead, U.S.N." This was, of course, the same Frank "Spig" Wead who later wrote screenplays for John Ford. See, as an example, the advertisement for *Dirigible* in *Motion Picture Herald*, 3 January 1931, 26–27.

45 *Motion Picture Herald*, 31 January 1931, 34.

46 Advertising for the film stressed his experience as a director of military films, citing the successes of *Submarine* (1928) and *Flight* (1929). See, for example, *Motion Picture Herald*, 3 January 1931, and 28 February 1931, 28–29.

47 *Motion Picture Herald*, 31 January 1931.

48 *Motion Picture Herald*, 26 December 1931, 58.

49 Ibid.

50 Ibid.

51 Ibid.

52 "Broadway Gets a Taste of Real Oldtime Ballyhoo—and Likes It," *Motion Picture Herald*, 9 September 1933, 11.

53 Ibid.

54 *Motion Picture Herald*, 11 November 1933, 63. Robson's generous response may well indicate that Columbia was closely involved in this campaign, as it seems likely that

the studio would have facilitated communication between the theater manager and the film star.

55 *Motion Picture Herald*, 11 November 1933, 63.

56 Ibid.

57 The phrase in quotes comes from architect S. Charles Lee, who designed theaters from the 1920s through the 1950s. See Maggie Valentine, *The Show Starts on the Sidewalk: An Architectural History of the Movie Theater* (New Haven: Yale University Press, 1994).

2 REGULATING NATIONAL MARKETS: CHINESE CENSORSHIP AND *THE BITTER TEA OF GENERAL YEN*

1 Frederick L. Herron to Willys R. Peck, 31 May 1933, State Department file 893.4061 (Motion Pictures), document 76, National Archives, Washington, D.C. (hereafter cited as DSF).

2 Ruth Vasey discusses Herron's appointment in *The World According to Hollywood, 1918-1939* (Madison: University of Wisconsin Press, 1997), 38.

3 For a case study of local censorship in the United States during the 1930s, by both government and independent interests, see Greg M. Smith, "Blocking *Blockade*: Partisan Protest, Popular Debate, and Encapsulated Texts," *Cinema Journal* 36, no. 1 (fall 1996): 18-38. Some form of federal censorship extended at least into the 1940s. For a study of how the Office of War Information influenced film production, see Rick Worland, "OWI Meets the Monsters: Hollywood Horror Films and War Propaganda, 1942 to 1945," *Cinema Journal* 37, no. 1 (fall 1997): 47-65.

4 Maltby discusses the studios' responses to censorship debates in Balio's *Grand Design*, 37-72. Other useful histories of Hollywood movie censorship include: Gregory D. Black, *Hollywood Censored: Morality Codes, Catholics, and the Movies* (Cambridge: Cambridge University Press, 1994); Jowett, *Film*; and Francis G. Couvares, ed., *Movie Censorship and American Culture* (Washington, D.C.: Smithsonian Institution Press, 1996).

5 Vasey, *The World According to Hollywood*; Kristin Thompson, *Exporting Entertainment: America in the World Film Market, 1907-1934* (London: British Film Institute, 1985); Ian Jarvie, *Hollywood's Overseas Campaign: The North Atlantic Movie Trade, 1920-1950* (Cambridge: Cambridge University Press, 1992); Thomas J. Saunders, *Hollywood in Berlin: American Cinema and Weimar Germany* (Berkeley: University of California Press, 1994).

6 McBride, *Frank Capra*, 281.

7 The film made $80,000 in its first eight days at Radio City, an extraordinary amount of money for the period. The next-highest grossing film in New York, for instance, during the same period (in this case only seven days) was *A Farewell to Arms*, which earned $52,500. Much of the earnings of Capra's film, however, might be attributable to the opening of Radio City and to the relatively high ticket prices ranging from $.35 $1.65, while patrons of the Paramount, where *Farewell* played,

paid only $.35 to $.99. That same week, in Chicago and Los Angeles, Capra's film earned, respectively, 30 percent and 8 percent less than the films playing the previous week (see *Motion Picture Herald*, 28 January 1933, 32, 34). At Radio City Music Hall, the week after *Bitter Tea* played there, *The King's Vacation* in seven days earned $88,000 (*Motion Picture Herald*, 4 February 1933, 42).

8 For a review of the historical events that form the context for the film, see David Palumbo-Liu, "The *Bitter Tea* of Frank Capra," *positions* 3, no. 3 (winter 1995): 759–89.

9 One theater manager complained that the film contained too much "war, Chinese and horrible things our patrons have had too much of," indicating that at least some audiences in the United States may have been tired not only of films about China, but of events taking place in China (*Motion Picture Herald*, 1 July 1933, 49). For the analysis of small-town movie tastes, see *Motion Picture Herald*, 20 May 1933, 45, and 24 June 1933, 45. Stanwyck is quoted in McBride, *Frank Capra*, 281. I have found no evidence to support her claim, but it seems plausible that some of the groups—of women, teachers, parents, etc.—that judged the suitability of films for young audiences would have objected to the interracial romance in *Bitter Tea*. For the theater manager's report on small towns and the Depression, see *Motion Picture Herald*, 1 July 1933, 49.

10 Palumbo-Liu, "The *Bitter Tea* of Frank Capra," 766, 767. For a superb analysis of the film as a captivity narrative, see Gina Marchetti, *Romance and the "Yellow Peril"* (Berkeley: University of California Press, 1993), 49–57.

11 There is, to my knowledge, no extended scholarship on the film's problems with British censors. For brief discussions, see McBride, *Frank Capra*, 282; and Vasey, *The World According to Hollywood*, 150. In his autobiography, Capra claimed that the film indeed had been "banned in Great Britain and in the British Commonwealth countries, due to the shocking implications of a love affair between a yellow man and a white woman" (Capra, *The Name above the Title*, 141–42). Existing Hays Office files, housed at the Academy of Motion Pictures Margaret Herrick Library, indicate very smooth sailing with the Hays Office. On 11 July 1932, Jason Joy, in charge of the office's Studio Relations Committee, wrote to Columbia Pictures studio head Harry Cohn, stating: "We have read with very much pleasure Script #3, *The Bitter Tea of General Yen* and believe that it is satisfactory from the standpoint of the [Production] Code and that it is free of any reasonable censorship worries." On 4 November 1932, James Wingate, who had succeeded Joy, also wrote to Cohn: "Recently we had the pleasure of reviewing the Columbia picture, *The Bitter Tea of General Yen*. We found it to be an excellent picture, free from elements to which official censorship could take serious objection . . . We had no suggestions whatever to make to the studio as regards any necessity for prerelease cuts." Columbia did, however, have to make some cuts in the film for showings in New York, Pennsylvania, Ohio, and Massachusetts (for the latter, sequences only needed to be cut for Sunday showings of the film, but it is doubtful that theaters showed one print six days of the week and another print on Sundays).

12 By the end of the nineteenth and the beginning of the twentieth centuries, the United States had moved from the position primarily of buyer of Chinese goods—

silk and tea, for instance—to selling American goods in China. For more on this topic, see Mira Wilkins, "The Impacts of American Multinational Enterprise on American-Chinese Economic Relations, 1786–1949," in *America's China Trade in Historical Perspective: The Chinese and American Performance*, ed. Ernest R. May and John K. Fairbank (Cambridge: Harvard University Press, 1986), 259–88. As just one example of American business involvement, in 1921 Henry Ford became interested in China, and in 1928 "decided to open a sales and service branch in Shanghai to cover China, French Indochina and the Philippines" (Wilkins, "The Impacts of American Multinational Enterprise," 275–76). As Wilkins points out, however, there were a variety of American investors in China during the period: "Not all U.S. investors in Chinese industry were part of multinational enterprises. There were also individual American businessmen resident in China" (279).

13 C. F. Remer, *Foreign Investments in China* (New York: Macmillan, 1933); Carl Crow, *400 Million Customers: The Experiences—Some Happy, Some Sad of an American in China* (New York: Harper and Brothers, 1937). For an additional view of American business interests in China from this period, see *China through the American Window*, compiled by Julean Arnold, commercial attaché in China for the United States Department of Commerce (Shanghai: American Chamber of Commerce, 1932). According to Arnold: "I believe I echo the sentiments of our American business public in China in expressing the ardent hope that as modern means of communications bring these two great Pacific countries into closer and more intimate contact and as the ever expanding interchange of commodities accentuate their interdependence, the urge to intelligent mutual understanding may lead to the development of enduring foundations of good will and friendship" (14).

14 Crow, *400 Million Customers*, 12, 33.

15 Bruno Lasker, ed., *Problems of the Pacific 1931: Proceedings of the Fourth Conference of the Institute of Pacific Relations, Hangchow and Shanghai, China, October 21 to November 2* (Chicago: University of Chicago Press, 1932), 467.

16 "The Motion Picture Industry in China," completed 4 October 1932, supervised by Richard P. Butrick, DSF, doc. 69.

17 Ibid., 21.

18 Ibid., 52.

19 Ibid., 20–23.

20 Ibid., 22.

21 Ibid., 72.

22 Ibid., 28–29.

23 For a discussion of the national cinemas that were popular in Shanghai, see ibid., 47. For information on Hollywood practices of subtitling and dubbing, see Vasey, *The World According to Hollywood*, 63–99.

24 Frederic Wakeman Jr., *Policing Shanghai 1927–1937* (Berkeley: University of California Press, 1996), 10–11.

25 "The Motion Picture Industry in China," 25.

26 For information on the "party-republic" and on "national construction," see Wakeman, *Policing Shanghai*, xv.

27 Wakeman, *Policing Shanghai*, 8. Throughout this section on Shanghai, I am in-

debted to Wakeman's exemplary study. Other very useful studies of China during this period include Albert Feuerwerker, *The Chinese Economy, 1912–1949* (Ann Arbor: University of Michigan Press, 1968); Edwin E. Moise, *Modern China: A History* (London: Longman, 1986); and May and Fairbank, eds., *America's China Trade in Historical Perspective*.

28 Wakeman, in *Policing Shanghai*, discusses the crackdown on "vice" in chapter 7, 97–115. See 238–39 for a discussion of the efforts to police the film industry.

29 Wakeman, *Policing Shanghai*, 11.

30 See "The Motion Picture Industry in China," 2–4, for an examination of the formation of and rules governing the Censorship Committee, as well as a definition of the "Three People's Principles."

31 See "The Motion Picture Industry in China," 4, for a reference to the banned films and the reason why most films were banned. See p. 5 for Butrick's estimate on the percentage of films that needed to be reedited.

32 Wakeman, *Policing Shanghai*, 58.

33 Peck related this conversation in a memo to the Secretary of State, 15 April 1932, DSF, doc. 59.

34 Ibid.

35 See memo from the Department of State, Division of Far Eastern Affairs, 24 June 1932, DSF, doc. 61.

36 For a discussion of other forms of film censorship in China, see "The Motion Picture Industry in China," 9; see p. 14 for a discussion of the Shanghai American Women's Club.

37 Peck discusses the objections of the Chinese students in Germany in a memo to the Secretary of State, 9 August 1932, no. D-318, DSF, doc. 64.

38 Peck mentions the complaint from Chinese students in Germany in a memo to Nelson Trusler Johnson, American Minister, Peiping, 21 June 1932, Despatch no. 1592, DSF, doc. 61. An anonymous memo from the Department of State, Division of Far Eastern Affairs, 10 August 1932, DSF, doc. 61, mentions the complaint from Chinese students in the United States.

39 DSF, doc. 61.

40 Peck to Secretary of State Henry L. Stimson, 9 August 1932, DSF, doc. 64.

41 Ibid.

42 Memorandum of Conversation, Johs. Albeck, Representative for the Far East of the Columbia Pictures Distributing Company, Inc., on "Objection of the Chinese National Board of Film Censors to the Film *Bitter Tea of General Yen*," 23 May 1933, DSF, doc. 74.

43 For the complaints from Batavia, Sumatra, and Java see J. H. Seidelman, Foreign Manager, to Mr. Kiang, Chinese Consulate, Los Angeles, 6 October 1933, DSF, doc. 101. The objections from Cuba are described by Willys R. Peck in a memo to Nelson Trusler Johnson, American Minster in Peiping, 12 October 1933, doc. 89. For Chicago objections, see Peck to Johnson, 20 June 1933, doc. 80.

44 Herron to Peck, 31 May 1933, DSF, doc. 76.

45 Maltby, in Balio, *Grand Design*, 49.

46 Vasey, *The World According to Hollywood*, 84.

47 Ibid., 80.

48 Memorandum of Conversation, Johs. Albeck and Willys Peck, 23 May 1933, DSF, doc. 74.

49 Albeck and Peck discussed the $60,000 investment in ibid. Albeck mentioned the proposed branch office in Shanghai in a memo to Peck, 24 November 1933, DSF, doc. 97. For the agreement to make the cuts, and the apology to the Chinese government, see Albeck to Peck, 25 May 1933, and Albeck to An Shih Ju, Chairman of the National Board of Censors, Nanking, 25 May 1933 (both in DSF, doc. 76).

50 Albeck to An Shih Ju, 25 May 1933, DSF, doc. 76.

51 For the dialogue to which the Chinese censors objected, see Despatch to the American Legation, no. L-36 Diplomatic, from Nanking, China (no date or document number given).

52 Peck to Johnson, 31 May 1933, DSF, doc. 74.

53 See, for instance, Herron to Peck, 31 May 1933, DSF, doc. 76. See also Peck to Johnson, 7 June 1933, DSF, doc. 76.

54 Seidelman to Kiang, Los Angeles, 6 October 1933, DSF, doc. 101; Peck to Johnson, 12 October 1933, DSF, doc. 89.

55 Douglas Gomery has written that during the 1930s studios typically made about four hundred prints of a film, although it is not clear if Gomery is speaking here only of domestic prints or of global prints as well (see Gomery, *The Hollywood Studio System*, 18).

56 Albeck to Puma Films Ltd., Shanghai, 11 December 1933, DSF, doc. 101.

57 Charles Roberts to Albeck, 10 October 1933, DSF, doc. 101.

58 Peck to Dr. Louis N. Tchou, Director of Department of International Affairs, Waichiaopu, Nanking, 3 October 1933, DSF, doc. 88. For the report on the Dutch East Indies, Singapore, Manila, and Calcutta, as well as Batavia, see Peck to Johnson, 6 October 1933, DSF, doc. 88.

59 Despatch to the American Legation, no. L-34 Diplomatic, from Nanking China. Subject: *The Bitter Tea of General Yen*, 6 October 1933, DSF, doc. 88.

60 Memorandum of Conversation, Albeck and Peck, 23 May 1933, DSF, doc. 74.

61 Albeck to An Shih Ju, 25 May 1933, DSF doc. 76.

62 Peck to Johnson, 12 October 1933, DSF doc. 89.

63 Memorandum of Conversation, Albeck and Peck, 23 May 1933, DSF doc. 74.

64 Peck acknowledges not having seen the film in his memo to Johnson recording his meeting with Chaucer H. Wu of the Chinese Foreign Office, 12 October 1933, DSF doc. 101 (in fact, at this time, Wu also had not seen the film).

65 "The Motion Picture Industry in China," 10.

66 Memorandum of Conversation, Albeck and Peck, 23 May 1933, DSF doc. 74.

67 It is precisely this "structuring absence" of the romance that has been of primary interest to contemporary scholars. For the best analysis of the relationship between Megan and General Yen, see Marchetti, *Romance and the Yellow Peril*, 46–57.

68 Peck to Johnson, 12 October 1933, DSF doc. 89.

69 Albeck to An Shih Ju, 25 May 1933, DSF doc. 76.

70 Peck to Albeck, 1 December 1933, DSF doc. 97.

71 William Phillips to Johnson, 3 August 1933, DSF doc. 74.

72 Ibid.

73 Ibid.

74 Peck to Johnson, 12 October 1933, DSF doc. 89.

75 Peck to Johnson, 12 October 1933, DSF doc. 89.

76 Peck expressed his admiration for the prologue solution in his memo to John-son, ibid. For Albeck's act of forwarding the idea to Columbia, cautioning about the time that implementation might take and also stressing Columbia's pledge for future productions, see Albeck to Peck, 12 December 1933, DSF doc. 101.

77 The last document in the file is dated 1 February 1934.

78 Some of the documents relating to *Oil for the Lamps of China* and *The General Died at Dawn* have been published in *Foreign Relations of the United States: Diplomatic Papers; Vol. 4, The Far East* (Washington, D.C.: GPO, 1936).

79 In 1927, the last year for which I have figures, China accounted for only 0.8 percent of Hollywood's foreign income. Japan accounted for 3.1 percent, and Cuba for 1.25 percent. Great Britain, where *Bitter Tea* also experienced severe censorship prob-lems, accounted for 30.5 percent of foreign income, by far the largest percentage of any foreign territory (see Vasey, *The World According to Hollywood*, 84).

3 FILM EDUCATION AND QUALITY ENTERTAINMENT FOR CHILDREN AND ADOLESCENTS

1 Nelle J. Brown to Fred J. Powell, 8 May 1934, Capra Collection, Wesleyan Cinema Archives (all subsequent fan letters are from this collection).

2 Fred J. Powell to Frank Capra, 11 May 1934.

3 Lea Jacobs, "Reformers and Spectators: The Film Education Movement in the Thirties," *Camera Obscura* 22 (January 1990): 29–49.

4 Jacobs discusses the Teaching Film Custodians films in "Reformers and Specta-tors," primarily 35–44.

5 DeCordova, "Ethnography and Exhibition," 91–197. See p. 97 for a description of the matinee in Rochester, New York, where audience members sang "America the Beautiful"; deCordova, "The Mickey in Macy's Window: Childhood, Consumer-ism, and Disney Animation," in *Disney Discourse: Producing the Magic Kingdom*, ed. Eric Smoodin (New York: Routledge, 1994), 203–13 (deCordova discusses club activities, including the yell, the creed, and the patriotic song, on p. 207).

6 For a discussion of issues concerning the development of the cinema and other in-stitutional and political practices, see, for example, Ella Shohat, "Gender and Cul-ture of Empire: Toward a Feminist Ethnography of the Cinema," *Quarterly Review of Film and Video* 13, nos. 1–3, (1993): 45–84; Fatimah Tobing Rony, "Those Who Squat and Those Who Sit: The Iconography of Race in the 1895 Films of Félix-Louis Regnault," *Camera Obscura* 28 (January 1992): 263–89; and Lisa Cartwright, *Screening the Body: Tracing Medicine's Visual Culture* (Minneapolis: University of Minnesota Press, 1995), in particular chapter 5, "Decomposing the Body: X-Rays and the Cinema," 107–42.

7   Selwyn K. Troen discusses these shifts in American education in "The Discovery of the Adolescent by American Educational Reformers, 1900–1920: An Economic Perspective," in *Schooling and Society: Studies in the History of Education*, ed. Lawrence Stone (Baltimore: Johns Hopkins University Press, 1976), 239–51.

8   Joel H. Spring, "Mass Culture and School Sports," *History of Education Quarterly* 14, no. 4, (winter 1974): 491.

9   Ibid., 495.

10 This is not to imply that there was no interest in movies and adolescents before this time. For discussions of various censorship efforts aimed at protecting children and teenagers, see, for instance, Jacobs, "Reformers and Spectators"; Jowett, *Film*; and Stamp, *Movie-Struck Girls*, in particular chapter 2, "Is Any Girl Safe? Motion Pictures, Women's Leisure, and the White Slavery Scare," 41–101.

11 Apropos of the perceived significance of movies in family relations, William Lewin, in *Photoplay Appreciation in American High Schools* (New York: D. Appleton-Century Company, 1934), 13, noted, for example, that "it would appear that the most common habit of high-school students in relation to selecting a photoplay is *discussing it with a member of the family*" (emphasis in original).

12 Ibid., 16.

13 The NEA report is cited in Jowett, *Film*, 274.

14 Edgar Dale, *How to Appreciate Motion Pictures: A Manual of Motion-Picture Criticism Prepared for High-School Students* (New York: Macmillan, 1933); Sarah McLean Mullen, "How to Judge Motion Pictures: A Pamphlet for High School Students," published by *Scholastic*, the American High School Weekly, New York, 1935; Richard Lewis and Helen Rand, *Film and School: A Handbook in Moving-Picture Evaluation*, a publication of the National Council of Teachers of English (New York: D. Appleton-Century Company, 1937); Barrett C. Kiesling, *Talking Pictures: How They Are Made, How to Appreciate Them* (New York: Johnson Publishing Company, 1937).

15 Lewin, *Photoplay Appreciation*, 47.

16 Ibid., 102.

17 Rand and Lewis, *Film and School*. The authors discuss these issues in their book's first chapter, "Moving Pictures: A Social and Educational Force," 1–14. War as a subject is dealt with on pp. 11–14 and class on pp. 3–5. The question about race (which, as a subject, gets less attention than class and much less than war) can be found on p. 11. Rand and Lewis also take an identifiably progressive position toward crime and criminals, saying that movies should show that, "in most cases," criminals are made by "environment," and that criminals "are not naturally bad, but people—and often exceptionally bright people—who have grown up in bad surroundings" (10).

18 The question about imperialism appears in *Film Survey*, March 1937, 3 (published bimonthly for Associated Film Audiences).

19 Lewin, in *Photoplay Appreciation*, 21, referred to the film studies curriculum as part of "a new deal for the child," thereby further emphasizing the connection between educational reform and 1930s-style liberal politics.

20 Arthur Zilversmit, *Changing Schools: Progressive Education Theory and Practice, 1930-1960* (Chicago: University of Chicago Press, 1993), page 1. The first chapter of Zilversmit's book, "Progressive Education: A Definition," 1–18, offers an outstanding synopsis of the goals of this mode of education.

21 Ibid., 5.

22 Zilversmit discusses the furniture of the progressive schoolroom in *Changing Schools*, 21.

23 Ibid., 7.

24 C. A. Bowers's *The Progressive Educator and the Depression: The Radical Years* (New York: Random House, 1969) remains one of the best discussions of the political factions within the progressive education movement. The debate among progressives tended to center on whether teachers should act as avatars of a new social order—that is, take sides on social issues and work to indoctrinate students—or reject "direct teacher involvement in partisan politics" (18).

25 Arthur Zilversmit, "The Failure of Progressive Education, 1920–1940," in *Schooling and Society: Studies in the History of Education*, ed. Lawrence Stone (Baltimore: Johns Hopkins University Press, 1976), 252–63.

26 In 1930, for example, Capra's *Flight* was Columbia's top-grossing film (*Motion Picture Herald*, 3 January 1930, 10). In 1931, in ads for *Dirigible*, Capra received third billing, in lettering as big as the two male stars, Jack Holt and Ralph Graves, and larger than that of the female lead, Fay Wray, who got fourth billing. The ad copy refers to two other Capra films that also starred Holt and Graves, and refers as well to Capra himself, in addition to Graves and Holt, as "the inimitable trio that made *Flight* and *Submarine*" (*Motion Picture Herald*, 28 February 1931, 28).

27 Dale, *How to Appreciate Motion Pictures*, 179, 182–83.

28 Dale mentions no women directors in his textbook. He does, however, quote Frances Marion, "the well-known screen writer," about proper plot construction (91).

29 Lewin, *Photoplay Appreciation*, 44.

30 Ibid., 16.

31 Ibid., 26.

32 Lewin explains the test in chapter 4 of *Photoplay Appreciation*, 23–29, and provides further explanation and copies of the score sheets on pp. 89–93. Some of the films evaluated by students and teachers (in addition to *Cavalcade* and the films discussed later in this chapter) included *Silver Dollar*, *King's Vacation*, *State Fair*, *Robber's Roost*, *I Am a Fugitive from a Chain Gang*, *The Conquerors*, *You Said a Mouthful*, *Tess of the Storm Country*, *A Successful Calamity*, *Prosperity*, *Topaze*, *Rasputin*, *A Farewell to Arms*, *Twenty Thousand Years in Sing Sing*, *Smilin' Through*, and *All Quiet on the Western Front*.

33 Lewin, *Photoplay Appreciation*, 28. Other films that generated wide swings in teacher evaluations were, among others, *You Said a Mouthful* (220/-35) and *A Successful Calamity* (210/-10),

34 Ibid. The scores from these classes can all be found on p. 26; Mrs. Mullen's score, though not given, is discussed on p. 27.

35 Ibid., 27–28. Neither of these films was uniformly popular among teachers. Miss Mary V. Harris in Montana gave *Forty-Second Street* a score of "less than zero,"

for example, while Mrs. Mary A. Abbott in New York gave *The Sign of the Cross* a score of 25.

36 I have found no information about any connection between the Hollywood studios and the Photographic History Service of Hollywood, but film companies from this period would not have tolerated any unlicensed use of stills from their films. In addition, the studios clearly were interested in film education, perhaps because of its public relations value during a time when the motion picture industry received a great deal of criticism and generated a great deal of concern about the apparent effects of movies on children (the Payne Fund studies stand out as the most famous of the era's examinations of the effects of film on young viewers). As Lea Jacobs points out in "Reformers and Spectators," 36, the MPPDA, the film industry trade association, provided backing for Teaching Film Custodians beginning in 1935, which provided schools with edited excerpts of Hollywood films to facilitate class discussion around a number of issues.

37 For a description of the study units, see *Educational Screen*, September 1934, 197.

38 *Educational Screen*, November 1934, 241.

39 "Bending the Bough," *Nation*, 26 September 1934, 342.

40 For a discussion of the Hays Office and *Sign of the Cross*, see Black, *Hollywood Censored*, 65–70.

41 A brief cycle of films during this period dealt with Westerners in a primitive, exotic "East": in addition to *Madame Butterfly* and *The Bitter Tea of General Yen*, for instance, see also Josef von Sternberg's *Shanghai Express* (1932). Capra himself earlier had directed a film (*Flight*, 1929) about the necessity of the U.S. presence in Nicaragua, another country going through a civil war.

42 Lorraine Noble, ed., *Four Star Scripts* (New York: Doubleday, Doran and Co., 1936).

43 In a cover letter to Capra that Gessner included with his syllabus, he wrote: "You might . . . be interested in knowing that the film holds up remarkably well, after almost four years, which is a pretty good test. If anything, the story interest is a little too thin, or at least, not as meaty as *Mr. Deeds Goes to Town*. But you're one of the few directors who can *tell* a story, and that's the paramount function" (Gessner to Capra, 13 January 1938). Even before Gessner's class, however, *It Happened One Night* was being discussed as a great film. In 1935 the *Nation* saw fit to review the film a second time, after having at first given it a positive but hardly laudatory review. Originally, William Troy wrote that "to claim any significance for the picture, apart from its successful use of what may turn out to be a very good method for the screen, would of course be a mistake." The second time around, Troy changed his opinion, with the title of the review itself signifying the shift: "On a Classic" (see *The Nation*, "Picaresque," 14 March 1934, 314; and "On a Classic," 10 April 1935, 426).

44 Some of the other films on the syllabus include *The Four Horsemen of the Apocalypse* ("The Early American Spectacle"), *The Love of Jeanne Ney* ("The Psychological Film"), *The Last Command* and *Plane Crazy* ("The End of the Silent Era"), *The Last Laugh* ("The Moving Camera in Germany"), and *Fury* ("The American Film of Protest").

45 For detailed information on Cabarrus County, see *The People of North Carolina* (Raleigh: North Carolina State Planning Board, 1938). Population information can be found in plate 2; occupational information in plate 11.

46 Between 1890 and 1930, the white population had grown by at least 195 percent; the "Negro" population by no more than 48 percent.

47 An invaluable source of information about education in North Carolina during the period is the *Biennial Report of the Superintendent of Public Instruction of North Carolina for the Scholastic Years 1933-34 and 1935-36*, part 3, statistical report, publication no. 207, issued by the State Superintendent of Public Instruction, Raleigh, North Carolina. For information on the number of students, see p. 6; for teachers, see p. 56–57.

48 *The People of North Carolina*, 74.

49 Ibid., 68–69.

50 "Study of Local School Units in North Carolina: 1937," publication no, 199, issued by the State Superintendent of Public Instruction, Raleigh, North Carolina, 177.

51 Ibid.

52 Gordon W. Lovejoy, coordinator, *Paths to Maturity: Findings of the North Carolina Youth Survey 1938-1940*, (Chapel Hill: University of North Carolina, 1940); see p. 145 for the discussion of how students spent their leisure time, and p. 156 for the chart on movie attendance. As for white high school boys, who went to movies in greater numbers than any other group in the same age category, 34.7 percent saw one movie a week, 21.5 percent two a week, 6.6 percent three a week, 1.3 percent four a week, and 1.8 percent more than four a week. "Negro" high school girls saw the fewest movies: 21.6 percent one a week, 16.9 percent two a week, 4.9 percent three a week, 0.7 percent four a week, and 0.5 percent more than four a week.

53 Ibid., xi. The complete description of this "average" teenager is interesting: "The most frequent North Carolina youth is white; comes from farm life and agricultural occupations; is from a family of over five people; has resided all his life where he now resides; is from a home with an annual income of less than $1,000; has failed at least one grade in school; left school before sixteen years of age for financial reasons; wishes to enter a profession; will be an unskilled or semi-skilled laborer; has had no special vocational training; his or her teacher said that he or she should have been provided with training for a trade; is a member of a church; has had a full-time job at the time this Study was made; earned on this first full-time job less than $17 a week; worked on that job between 40 and 55 hours a week; found his position through a personal application or the assistance of friends; belongs to no organization except a church club; has no hobby; is apparently in fair health, and a little above the national average in weight as compared to height."

54 Lewin, *Photoplay Appreciation*, 4.

55 The best sources for information about the history of the American high school probably remain Edward A. King's *The Shaping of the American High School: Volume One, 1880-1920* (Madison: University of Wisconsin Press, 1969) and *Volume Two, 1920-1941* (Madison: University of Wisconsin Press, 1972). The information cited here comes from "The General Subjects in the Twenties," vol. 2, 77–79.

56 Beatrice Cartner to Powell, 7 May 1934.

57 Jean Overcass to Powell, undated.

58 Lenore Campbell to Powell, 7 May 1934.

59 Edith Whitley to Powell, 7 May 1934.

60 Lenore Campbell to Powell, 7 May 1934; Ruth Sides to Powell, 8 May 1934; Nelle J. Brown to Powell, 8 May 1934.

61 Mullen, "How to Judge Motion Pictures," 48.

62 Ibid.

63 Mary Bele Anderson to Powell, 8 May 1934.

64 Le Roy [last name illegible] to Powell, 8 May 1934.

65 Capra to Powell, 23 May 1934.

66 By far the most important work on the Payne Fund studies is Garth S. Jowett, Ian C. Jarvie, and Kathryn H. Fuller, *Children and the Movies: Media Influence and the Payne Fund Controversy* (Cambridge: Cambridge University Press, 1996). The authors point out the seriousness of the studies, their indebtedness to the "modern" social sciences, and also their often nuanced investigations into the "problem" of movies. As the authors point out, the Payne Fund studies themselves were published in eight volumes by Macmillan between 1933 and 1935. Henry J. Forman, who did not take part in the studies, published a single-volume summary of the results under the title *Our Movie-Made Children* (New York: Macmillan, 1933). "This best-seller became *the* representation of the PFS [Payne Fund studies] in the public mind and gave the false impression that the researchers had lent themselves to a moralizing crusade" (Jowett, Jarvie, and Fuller, *Children and the Movies*, 7).

67 The Production Code is reproduced in Jowett, *Film*, 468–72. The discussion of maturity and immaturity can be found on p. 472 ("reasons 3A and 3C").

68 For discussions of the structure of the various women's reform movements during this period, see Rosalind Rosenberg, *Divided Lives: American Women in the Twentieth Century* (New York: Hill and Wang, 1992), chapter 4; and Linda Gordon, "Putting Children First: Women, Maternalism, and Welfare in the Early Twentieth Century," in *U.S. History as Women's History: New Feminist Essays*, ed. Linda Kerber, Alice Kessler-Harris, and Kathryn Kish Sklar (Chapel Hill: University of North Carolina Press, 1995), 63–86.

69 Black, *Hollywood Censored*, 13.

70 For excellent discussions of the formation and activities of the National Board of Review, see Black, *Hollywood Censored*; Jowett, *Film* (Jowett discusses the relationship between the board and the film industry on p. 127); and Robert Sklar, *Movie-Made America: A Cultural History of American Movies* (New York: Vintage, 1975).

71 Henry Forman, "To the Movies—But Not to Sleep!" *McCalls*, September 1932, 12–13; "Movie Madness," *McCalls*, October 1932, 14–15; "Molded by Movies," *McCalls*, November 1932, 17.

72 The newspaper told readers that "this bulletin, published monthly, is available free to community leaders upon application to the Motion Picture Producers & Distributors of America, Inc." (*The Motion Picture and the Family*, 15 April 1936, 4).

73 Keisling, *Talking Pictures*, 20.

74 Ibid., 20. The other films on the list were *Trader Horn* (an "educational" film about

Africa); *Sequoia* (a nature film based on the novel *Malibu*); *A Tale of Two Cities*; *Les Miserables*; *Little Women*; *Anthony Adverse*; *Last of the Mohicans*; *The House of Rothschild*; *Maytime* (another MacDonald-Eddy light opera); *Captains Courageous*; *Grand Hotel*; *Little Lord Fauntleroy*; and *Lloyds of London*.

75 Terry Ramsaye, "Sex Lure Looms Again," *Motion Picture Herald*, 24 April 1937, 14. Ramsaye's editorial served as a lead-in to articles about movies, sexuality, and censorship, including David F. Barrett, "Sex Not Returning to Studios, Hays Tells St. Louis MPTO"; "B[alaban] & K[atz] Oriental Signs Girl in Nudity Trial" (no author listed); and James P. Cunningham, "Issue Not for Code Administration but Hays, Breen Holds."

76 Ramsaye, "Sex Lure Looms Again," 14–15, 27–28. The reference to *Mr. Deeds* appears on p. 14. Ramsaye also was the author of *A Million and One Nights: A History of the Motion Picture through 1925* (New York: Simon and Schuster, 1926).

77 William R. Weaver, "The Case for and against Longer Feature Pictures," *Motion Picture Herald*, 11 April 1936, 18, 28–20, 33. The article itself is quite long by *Herald* standards, perhaps indicating the perceived significance of the issues of double bills and running times.

78 Ibid. The Goldwyn and Bernhard quotes are from p. 18.

79 Ibid.

80 Ibid., 28. Some of the other reasons given in favor of longer films were "higher admission prices," "longer runs," and "extended drawing radius." Arguments against included "admission sales resistance," "deflected habitual patronage," "inadequate responsiveness," and "public indifference."

81 "Family Movie Guide," *Parents*, July 1936, 34, 47.

82 Agnes Benedict, "What's Ahead in the Movies?" *Parents*, September 1936, 30–31, 52, 54, 56.

83 Ibid., 52.

84 Ibid., 52, 54.

85 Benedict mentions *Show Boat* on p. 52, placing it with a group of musicals including *The King Steps Out* and *Naughty Marietta*, as well as those movies featuring Lily Pons and Paul Robeson.

86 Sarah McLean Mullen, "Films for the Pupil and Teacher," *The Motion Picture and the Family*, 15 April 1936, 4, 8.

87 For a discussion of *Show Boat*, see Mullen, "Films for the Pupil and Teacher," *The Motion Picture and the Family*, 15 May 1936, 6; for *Romeo and Juliet*, see 15 October 1936, 5–6.

88 Howard M. Le Sourd, "Lessons Learned from the Movies," *The Motion Picture and the Family*, 15 May 1936, 5–6. The poem Le Sourd cites is by Gerald Raftery and appeared in the *New York Times*. It begins, "Out of the theater he strides / Back to the city street— / But in his kindled heart he rides / A broncho, and the beat / Of prancing hoofs keeps step with him; / The words he mutters low / Are cowboy language, drawled and grim, / That elders do not know."

89 Ibid., 6.

90 "Inquiring Photographer Contest Used on *Deeds*," *Motion Picture Herald*, 11 July 1936, 128.

91 "Over 300 Boys and Girls Choose Their 10 Best Films of 1936," press release from the National Board of Review Collection, Box 172, New York Public Library.

92 Ibid. Although they did not like child stars, the voters did like *The Devil Is a Sissy*, a film "which contemplates the problems of juvenile delinquency in pretty vigorous terms." Thus, members of the Young Reviewers and 4-Star clubs appreciated it when the moves dealt seriously with the problems of children rather than simply reducing all children to "cute kids."

93 Ibid., 2.

94 Ibid.

95 For a discussion of the shift from educational hygiene to child development, see Edna W. Bailey, Anita D. Laton, and Elizabeth L. Bishop, *Studying Children in School* (New York: McGraw-Hill, 1939), 3.

96 Ibid., 31, 35, 37.

97 Agnes E. Benedict and Adele Franklin, *Your Best Friends are Your Children: A Guide to Enjoying Parenthood* (New York: Appleton-Century-Crofts, 1951).

98 "Over 300 Boys and Girls Choose Their 10 Best Films of 1936," 2.

99 "Over 350 Boys and Girls Choose Their 10 Best Films of 1937," National Board of Review Collection, Box 172, New York Public Library. The ten-best list as voted on by film reviewers and trade journal editors closely matched the selections of the Young Reviewers and 4-Star clubs. As announced in *Film Daily*, the choices were *The Good Earth*, *Captains Courageous*, *Lost Horizon*, *A Star is Born* (which placed seventh among young voters); *Romeo and Juliet* (which had been considered a 1936 "ten-best" film in the National Board of Review voting); *Stage Door* (eighth among young viewers); *Dead End*, *Winterset* (not mentioned by the National Board voters); and *The Awful Truth* (also not mentioned). In the only significant differences from the choices of the adults, the young voters chose *The Plainsman* and *Stella Dallas* as the last two films on their list.

100 Joseph Mersand, "Facts and Fiction about the Educational Values of the Cinema," *Educational Screen*, December 1938, 319.

101 Ibid., 320. *The Good Earth* also performed quite well among students, with 25 out of 31 viewers giving it four stars. For *The Prisoner of Zenda*, 19 out of 23 students awarded it four stars. Of films seen by a substantial number of students, *Annapolis Salute* fared the worst: of the 25 students who saw the film, 13 gave it two stars and 8 gave it only one.

102 "What the Picture Did For Me," *Motion Picture Herald*, 20 November 1937, 101; 4 November 1937, 65; 11 December 1937, 69; 18 December 1937, 59. To be sure, some small towns enjoyed the picture. From Marion, Indiana, for instance, the exhibitor wrote, "A lavish production that pleased all patrons" (23 October 1937, 77). Moreover, the manager at the Rialto in Paynesville, Minnesota, who felt that the film was "a little above the heads" of most of his customers, thought that his most aged moviegoers fully appreciated the film: "The older people thought it wonderful, but they like a picture that makes them think, and this one will" (18 December 1937, 59).

103 "Hays Warns against Propaganda in Films," *Motion Picture Herald*, 4 April 1936, 52.

104 "New Research Exhibits Lend Added Interest to Film Study," *The Motion Picture and the Family*, 15 October 1936, 1.

105 Ibid., 5.

106 "Classics of This and an Earlier Day are Featured in the Cleveland Library Bookmarks of the Month," *The Motion Picture and the Family*, 15 October 1936, 7. In addition to the "Bookmarks of the Month" program, the Cleveland Public Library also began printing *Books and Films*, "a mimeographed publication, devoted to suggestions for library-film cooperation" (see "Makes Its Bow in Printed Form," *The Motion Picture and the Family*, 15 October 1936, 7).

107 Rand and Lewis, *Film and School*, 22–25.

108 The relationship between movies and radio flourished in particular after 1935, "when AT&T removed the double transmission rates, which required networks to pay for the transmission of a broadcast both to and from New York." After this change, "NBC and CBS built new studios in Los Angeles," and began producing significant amounts of programming with movie stars. And, of course, the film industry, centered in Los Angeles, could also now make use of local radio talent (Balio, *Grand Design*, 171). Orson Welles adapted the Capra films for his 1938–1940 *Campbell Playhouse* radio program: *Lost Horizon*, with Sigrid Gurie, aired on 3 December 1939; and *Mr. Deeds Goes to Town*, starring Gertrude Lawrence and Welles, on 11 February 1940. No date is available for *It Happened One Night*, which starred Miriam Hopkins and William Powell.

109 For information about Youthbuilders, see Sabra Holbrook, *Children Object* (New York: Viking, 1943). Holbrook discusses the Nazi children in chapter 1, "Converts from the *Gleichschaltung*," and the incipient Communists in chapter 3, "Communists and Innocents."

110 "Lyons, over WNYC, Asks End of WNYC," *New York Times*, 3 April 1939, 3; "City Council Wins Power for Inquiry: Upheld by Court of Appeals in WNYC Row with Mayor—Relief Study to Go On," *New York Times*, 5 April 1939, 1.

111 For that day's programming information, see "Today on the Radio," *New York Times*, 6 December 1939, 36.

112 Michele Hilmes, in *Radio Voices: American Broadcasting, 1922–1952* (Minneapolis: University of Minnesota Press, 1997), 151–82, in chapter 6, "Under Cover of Daytime," discusses the daytime audience and the radio industry's determination to construct that audience as a female one.

113 "Children as Movie Critics," *Your Child Series*, broadcast for Youthbuilders, station WNYC, 6 December 1939, 1. This is labeled "first copy—revised," as opposed to the "announcer's continuity." The former is far longer than the latter, although it is not clear precisely which text was aired. Both transcripts are in the National Board of Review Collection, Box 172, New York Public Library.

114 Ibid., "Announcer's Continuity," 3.

115 Ibid., 2.

116 Ibid., 3–4.

117 Ibid., "First Copy—Revised," 3.

118 Ibid., 3.

119 Ibid., 5.

120 Richard M. Ugland, "'Education for Victory': The High School Victory Corps and Curricular Adaptation during World War II," *History of Education Quarterly* (winter 1979): 435.

121 Ibid., 436.

122 Ibid. The quote is from p. 438; the number of schools adopting the program is on p. 439.

4 THIS BUSINESS OF AMERICA: MR. SMITH, JOHN DOE, AND THE POLITICIZED VIEWER

1 For Reagan's speech, see the *Washington Post*, 14 October 1987, A6. The reference to *Mr. Smith* was eventually dropped from the final version of the president's defense of the Bork nomination; for Ross Perot, see the *New York Times*, 6 March 1994, E7, citing the *Wall Street Journal*; about Richard Riordan, see the *Washington Post*, 7 June 1993, A5.

2 The report on Riordan's fortune comes from the *Los Angeles Times*, 7 June 1993, A6.

3 See, for example, Paul Richard, "Norman Rockwell, American Master (Seriously!)," *Washington Post*, 6 June 1993, G1, 8–9. For a more self-conscious and methodologically sophisticated conflation of Capra and Rockwell, see Robert B. Westbrook, "Fighting for the American Family: Private Interests and Political Obligation in World War II," in *The Power of Culture: Critical Essays in American History*, ed. Richard Wightman Fox and T. J. Jackson Lears (Chicago: University of Chicago Press, 1993), 194–221.

4 For a discussion of the "Star-Spangled Banner" debate, see W. C. Ruediger, "Saluting the Flag," *School and Society*, 25 February 1939, 249. Mrs. Roosevelt disapproved of playing the anthem at movie theaters.

5 Kathryn Fuller, "'What the Picture Did for Me': Small Town Exhibitors in the Great Depression" (unpublished paper), 1.

6 The Academy of Motion Picture Arts and Sciences Library in Los Angeles has an extensive collection of *Photoplay Studies*. The study guide to *Mr. Smith Goes to Washington* can be found there and also at the Pacific Film Archive in Berkeley, California, in the *Mr. Smith* clippings file.

7 Department of State documents about *Mr. Smith Goes to Washington* are stored in the National Archives in Washington, D.C., in a file labeled "Adult Education, 1940–44."

8 *Motion Picture Herald*, 4 November 1939, 57; and 25 November 1939, 51.

9 Bodnar, *Remaking America*.

10 Ibid., 83.

11 Warren I. Susman, *Culture as History: The Transformation of American Society in the Twentieth Century* (New York: Pantheon Books, 1984), see particularly chapter 9, "The Culture of the Thirties," 150–83, and chapter 10, "Culture and Commitment," 184–210.

12 For a discussion and analysis of the 150th anniversary celebrations, see Michael Kammen, *A Machine that Would Go of Itself: The Constitution in American Culture* (New York: Vintage Books, 1987), 282–312.

13 For photographs of World's Fair statuary, see *Newsweek*, 25 March 1940, 18–19; for a discussion of *Land of Liberty*, see Allen W. Palmer, "Cecil B. DeMille Writes America's History for the 1939 World's Fair," *Film History* 5, no. 1 (March 1993): 36–48.

14 See, for instance, "Jefferson Memorial Woes: Strike Is Latest in the Series of Rows Harassing Project," *Newsweek*, 28 August 1939, 22.

15 "Ballad of All Americans," *Newsweek*, 25 March 1940, 40.

16 "Four Faces in Granite: Borglum's Black Hills Colossus Is Nearing Completion," *Newsweek*, 10 July 1939, 23.

17 "What the Picture Did for Me," *Motion Picture Herald*, 25 November 1939, 51.

18 Exhibitors' advertising strategies for *Mr. Smith* were almost certainly influenced by the press kit that Columbia produced for Capra's film. I have not, however, been able to locate such a kit in either the Library of Congress or the Academy of Motion Picture Arts and Sciences Library.

19 *Motion Picture Herald*, 4 November 1939, 65; 11 May 1940, 68; and 3 February 1940, 74.

20 About the universal appeal of the film, see "Will Click with the Masses 100 Per Cent" *Motion Picture Herald*, 18 November 1939, 63; "Pleased 100%," 2 December 1939, 64: "This Picture Drew above Average and Is the Kind that Builds Good Will amongst Theatregoers," 30 December 1939, 57. For the comment from the Canadian exhibitor, see *Motion Picture Herald*, 25 November 1939, 51. For an indication of the perceived divisions in the audience, see *Motion Picture Herald*, 2 December 1939, 64, along with the theater manager's comment about *Ice Follies of 1939*: "Too Much Dialogue for Small Town."

21 *Motion Picture Herald*, 23 December 1939, 51; and 16 December 1939, 59.

22 *Motion Picture Herald*, 4 December 1939, 57.

23 For a discussion of the Payne Fund studies and the relationship between the movies and the Legion of Decency, see Jowett, *Film*, 220–59.

24 *Motion Picture Herald*, 25 November 1939, 51; and 4 November 1939, 57.

25 The Production Code Administration file on *Mr. Smith*, stored at the Academy of Motion Picture Arts and Sciences's Margaret Herrick Library in Los Angeles, includes memos about the feelings of journalists toward the film. See Frank Knox to Will Hays, 14 November 1939; and Joseph Breen to Will Hays, 6 December 1939. For coverage of the screening for the Senate, see "*Mr. Smith* Riles Washington," *Time*, 30 October 1939, 49.

26 *Motion Picture Herald*, 25 November 1939, 51; and 7 October 1939, 38.

27 "Ideas Swapped by 3,000 at the 'Country Store' Forum on Education for Democracy," *Newsweek*, 28 August 1939, 25; "Challenge," *Time*, 9 October 1939, 46. The journal under consideration was the October 1939 issue of the *Survey Graphic*. See also "Compulsory Schooling up to 16 Urged at White House Parley," *Newsweek*, 29 January 1940, 36; "For Better Citizens," *Time*, 6 November 1939, 61.

28 "Art Via the Air Waves: Both CBS and NBC Starting New Cultural Programs,"

Newsweek, 6 November 1939, 30; "War of Words: Town Meeting Opens Fifth Explosive Season," *Newsweek*, 9 October 1939, 39; "All-American Program: Deems Taylor and a Symphony to Wave Musical Flag," *Newsweek*, 29 January 1940, 44.

29 All of the articles mentioned appeared in *School and Society*: Floyd S. Gove, "Educational Planning in a Democracy," 25 June 1938, 829–30; William F. Russell, "Education for Democracy," 31 December 1938, 862–64; J. Cayce Morrison, "The Unique Function of Education in American Democracy," 30 July 1938, 132–37; and William H. Kilpatrick, "Propaganda, Democracy, and Education," 1 April 1939, 405–9. President Roosevelt's address, given on 30 June 1938, was reprinted in *School and Society*, 9 July 1938, 29–31.

30 *Photoplay Studies: A Magazine Devoted to Photoplay Appreciation* 5, no. 21 (1939): 3.

31 Ibid., 3.

32 Ibid., 7, 10, 12. It is quite possible that some aspects of the film itself encouraged the rather narrow, fact-based, civics-lesson approach of the study guide. I am thinking here of the scene in which Saunders teaches Smith all about the process through which a Senate bill is written, introduced, and passed.

33 Ibid., 5.

34 Lauren Berlant, "The Theory of Infantile Citizenship," *Public Culture* 5, no. 3 (spring 1993): 397.

35 Ibid., 407.

36 For an analysis of the relations during this period between the federal government and the motion picture industry in terms of furthering foreign policy, see my *Animating Culture: Hollywood Cartoons from The Sound Era* (New Brunswick: Rutgers University Press, 1993), chapter 5.

37 Thomas Burke to Mr. Long, Mr. Briggs, Mr. Bonsal, and Mr. Duggan, 21 March 1940, Department of State file "Adult Education, 1940–44," National Archives (all subsequent memos are from this collection).

38 Ibid.

39 J. Holbrook Chapman to Secretary of State Cordell Hull, 29 July 1940.

40 For the memo questioning Burke's judgment, see Mr. Bonsal to Mr. Briggs and Mr. Daniels, 19 March 1940.

41 Thomas Burke to Mr. Long, Mr. Briggs, Mr. Bonsal, and Mr. Duggan, 21 March 1940.

42 Laurance Duggan to Mr. Long, Mr. Burke, and Mr. Thomson, 21 March 1940.

43 For the complaints about *Mr. Smith*, see Burke to Long et al., and Bangkok Legation to Secretary of State Cordell Hull, 2 January 1941.

44 Bonsal to Mr. Daniels and Mr. Briggs, 19 March 1940.

45 Thomas Burke to Mr. Thomson, 11 February 1941.

46 "*Mr. Smith* Riles Washington," 49.

47 James B. Stewart to Secretary of State Cordell Hull, 30 January 1941.

48 Paul Virilio, *War and Cinema: The Logistics of Perception*, trans. Patrick Camiller (London: Verso, 1989).

49 Mrs. E. Coate to Capra, 26 June 1941, Capra Collection, Wesleyan Cinema Archives (all subsequent fan letters are from this collection).

50 David Morley, *The Nationwide Audience* (London: British Film Institute, 1980).

51 Janet Staiger, *Interpreting Films*; Steven J. Ross, *Working-Class Hollywood: Silent Film and the Shaping of Class in America* (Princeton: Princeton University Press, 1998).

52 Barbara Foley, *Radical Representations: Politics and Form in U.S. Proletarian Fiction, 1929-1941* (Durham: Duke University Press, 1992).

53 Alva Johnston, "Capra Shoots as He Pleases," *Saturday Evening Post*, 14 May 1938, 72.

54 Ibid.

55 Geoffrey T. Hellman, "Profiles: Thinker in Hollywood," *New Yorker*, 24 February 1940, 23-24.

56 For a discussion of Pope Pius and Catholic activism in general, see Michael Kazin, *The Populist Persuasion: An American History* (New York: Basic, 1995), 116-18.

57 I have read all of the *Meet John Doe* fan mail. Those letters that I have not transcribed nevertheless correspond closely, in terms of concerns, interests, and criticisms, to those that I have looked at most closely and that make up the letter sample used in this chapter. When I refer to the number of letters on a given topic, I mean the number that can be taken from the sample of letters that I have transcribed and studied the most carefully.

58 Both citations come from Capra, *The Name above the Title*, 136.

59 Ibid., 303, 297.

60 In his autobiography, Capra discusses the difficulty of finding the right ending for *Doe*. He claims that he shot five versions and then finally settled on the one we know today, in which the John Doe club members convince Doe not to jump (*The Name above the Title*, 302-5). In his biography of Capra, Joseph McBride provides a much more complete story of the film's ending. Capra apparently only shot two endings, with other versions being edited from this footage. The ending in which Norton becomes a sympathetic character was shown to the press and to some early audiences and was almost universally criticized. Capra quickly replaced that ending, and then a few weeks later added the footage that showed the members of the John Doe clubs as the real heroes of the film (see *The Catastrophe of Success*, 431-36).

61 David Stephens to Capra, 13 June 1941.

62 Linda Schoen to Capra, undated.

63 Joyce Eden to Capra, 24 June 1941.

64 "Textbooks Brought to Book," *Time*, 3 March 1941, 39-40.

65 "Youth Hear Defense Plea," *Los Angeles Times*, 7 March 1941, A12.

66 William B. Phillips to Capra, 14 March 1941.

67 Ibid.

68 Letters to Capra from, respectively, Mrs. T. M. Cantwell, 11 February 1941; Ezilda Marie Suton, 29 March 1941; Mary Hagedorn, 9 April 1941; Horace E. Levin, 17 March 1941.

69 "Hedda Hopper's Hollywood," *Los Angeles Times*, 2 March 1941, C3; Edwin Schallert, "*Meet John Doe* Hailed as Capra Victory," *Los Angeles Times*, 13 March 1941, A16; David Platt, "*Meet John Doe* Lets Film Audiences Down," *Daily Worker*, 15 March 1941, 7; *Hollywood News* 7, no. 13 (27 January 1941); "Gary Cooper,

Barbara Stanwyck Star in Capra Production *Meet John Doe*," Warner Bros. press book (no date).

70 For promotional tie-in information, see, for example, "*John Doe* Gets 4-City Opening," *Motion Picture Herald*, 29 March 1941, 66.

71 Read Kendall, "Stars, Fans Brave Rain to Attend Gay Film Event," *Los Angeles Times*, 13 March 1941, A16.

72 Letters to Capra from, respectively, Howard V. C. Davis, 26 February 1941; Maurine Robison, 9 March 1941; and Miss Grace Rasche, 19 August 1941.

73 E. C. Olson to Capra, 13 June 1941.

74 Ingeborg Tillisch to Capra, 23 March 1941.

75 M. Gluck to Capra, 13 March 1941.

76 Letters to Capra from, respectively, Louis A. Meli, 14 May 1941; Mary Hagedorn, 9 April 1941; and Mr. and Mrs. David Greenburg, 19 May 1941.

77 Charles H. Martin to Capra, 13 May 1941.

78 George B. Nordman to Capra, undated.

79 Capra to Charles H. Martin, 16 May 1941.

80 Nick Browne, "System of Production/System of Representation: Industry Context and Ideological Form in Capra's *Meet John Doe*," in "*Meet John Doe*," ed. Charles Wolfe (New Brunswick: Rutgers University Press, 1989), 284–85.

81 M. Gluck to Capra, 13 March 1941; Keith Gordon to Capra, undated.

82 All citations are from *Time* magazine: "Of Thee I Sing," 24 February 1941, 55; "Folk Songs in the White House," 3 March 1941, 57; "MBS Soapbox," 24 March 1941, 61; "Democracy on Pedestals," 24 February 1941, 66.

83 All citations are from the *Los Angeles Times*: "Threatened Demonstration at Kaltenborn Talk Fizzles," 5 March 1941, B1; "Eva [*sic*] Curie Arrives in City," 7 March 1941, B1-2; "Philip F. LaFollette Will Speak Monday," 7 March 1941, B1.

84 "Get Your Tickets Today for Foster Mass Meeting," *Daily Worker*, 14 March 1941, 4.

85 See, for example, Alida Ducker to Capra, 27 February 1941.

86 See, for example, Bill McNutt to Capra, 4 August 1941.

87 For a discussion of the discourses of the New Deal, including both government policy and the work of the Lynds, see Gary Gerstle, "The Protean Character of American Liberalism," *American Historical Review* 99, no. 4 (1994): 1043–73.

88 Capra, *The Name above the Title*, 305.

5 COERCIVE VIEWINGS: SOLDIERS AND
PRISONERS WATCH MOVIES

1 Admittedly, my claim here is difficult to prove. Many filmmakers had their films screened in prisons and other similar locations. Given the available evidence, however, it is difficult to think of other filmmakers who might rival Capra in terms of viewers who were, in some manner or other, forced to watch their movies.

2 The letter, dated Christmas 1939, came from an inmate who apparently once had met Capra when the director was "busy cutting *Mr. Deeds Goes to Town*," and had also once done some work at the film studios. The letter writer, in addition

to praising the film, asked Capra for help in reestablishing his contacts in the film industry. The letter can be found in the *Mr. Deeds Goes to Town* files, among the Capra papers at the Wesleyan Cinema Archives.

3   Michel Foucault, *Discipline and Punish: The Birth of the Prison*, trans. Alan Sheridan (New York: Vintage, 1995). Foucault writes about the architecture of observation on pp. 170–76. For his discussion of the elements of the examination, see p. 184.

4   Ibid. For the description of the 1757 public execution, see pp. 3–6. See p. 9 for his discussion of the shift in the spectacle of punishment.

5   George Raynor Thompson, Dixie R. Harris, Pauline M. Oakes, and Dulany Terrett, *United States Army in World War II: The Technical Services: The Signal Corps: The Test (December 1941 to July 1943)* (Washington, D.C.: Office of the Chief of Military History, Department of the Army, 1957), 415–16.

6   There are several excellent sources for a history of Capra's involvement with the military. See, for instance, McBride, *The Catastrophe of Success*, chapter 16; and Charles Maland, *Frank Capra* (New York: Twayne Publishers, 1995), chapter 5. See also Capra's autobiography, *The Name above the Title*, chapters 16–18.

7   Dorothy Jones, "The Hollywood War Film: 1942–1944," *Hollywood Quarterly*, 1, no. 1, (October 1945): 1–19. Jones discusses "Films Telling Why We Fought" on pp. 3–4.

8   Allan Bérubé, *Coming Out under Fire: The History of Gay Men and Women in World War Two* (New York: Free Press, 1990), 1–7.

9   Iris Barry, "Why Wait for Posterity?" *Hollywood Quarterly* (January 1946): 131. Along with the *Why We Fight* films, another Capra film, *It Happened One Night*, was also included in Barry's list of films worthy of inclusion in the museum's collection.

10 Robert Rahtz, "Movies for Classrooms," *Hollywood Quarterly* 2, no. 3 (April 1947): 323.

11 Robert G. Lord, Lt. Col., Signal Corps, 7 October 1943. National Archives Record Group 111, Box 169, Decimal #062.2.

12 Ibid.

13 Westbrook, "Fighting for the American Family," 195–221.

14 Capra's memo is included in a memorandum for the Directorate of Administration, 22 August 1942, written by Colonel K. B. Lawton of the Signal Corps. National Archives Record Group 111, Box 170.

15 The military reports on the reception of these films can be found in the *Why We Fight* file at the Wesleyan Cinema Archives; see, for example, pp. 1085–112.

16 Ibid., 1100–101 and 1111–112.

17 See Dale, *How to Appreciate Motion Pictures*, 212, for a discussion of the value of scientists' findings regarding the effects of motion pictures on women and children.

18 Ellen Herman, *The Romance of American Psychology: Political Culture in the Age of Experts* (Berkeley: University of California Press, 1996), 5–6.

19 See ibid., chapter 2, for a discussion of the World War II era mobilization of psychological and psychiatric experts.

20 Ibid., 55.

21 Ibid.

22 The rationale for the tests, and the tests' results, eventually were published by
    Carl I. Hovland, Arthur A. Lumsdaine, and Fred D. Sheffield in *Experiments on
    Mass Communication*, vol. 3 (Princeton: Princeton University Press, 1949). The cita-
    tions concerning goals come from p. 13; and concerning techniques, from p. 3.

23 Ibid., 13.

24 Ibid., 15.

25 For a discussion of the effects of *The Battle of Britain*, see Hovland, Lumsdaine,
    and Sheffield, *Experiments on Mass Communication*, chapter 2, "The Orientation
    Film, *The Battle of Britain*," 21–50.

26 Ibid., 38.

27 Ibid., 44.

28 Ibid., 60.

29 Ibid., 45.

30 Citations here come from Hovland, Lumsdaine, and Sheffield, *Experiments on Mass
    Communication*, chapter 3, "General Implications Derived from the Orientation
    Film Experiments," 51.

31 Ibid., 65.

32 Ibid., 68.

33 Ibid., 72.

34 The figure comes from Ron Robin, *The Barbed-Wire College: Reeducating German
    POWs in the United States During World War II* (Princeton: Princeton University
    Press, 1995), 3, 6. Robin's work is an invaluable one, and I have used it through-
    out the first part of this chapter to establish the history of the reeducation program
    in the camps. There is at least a limited bibliography concerning the POW camps.
    For the best review of life in the camps, see Arnold Krammer, *Nazi Prisoners of
    War in America* (Briarcliff Manor, N.Y.: Stein and Day, 1979); see also Judith M.
    Gansberg, *Stalag USA: The Remarkable Story of German POWs in America* (New
    York: Thomas Y. Crowell Company, 1977) (in chapter 4, "The Factory," Gans-
    berg provides an excellent discussion of camp culture, including films). For an ac-
    count of the camps by a former German prisoner, see Reinold Pabel, *Enemies Are
    Human* (Philadelphia: John C. Winston Company, 1955). See also Günter Bischof
    and Stephen E. Ambrose, eds., *Eisenhower and the German POWs: Facts against
    Falsehood* (Baton Rouge: Louisiana State University Press, 1992); and Nicholas Pro-
    nay and Keith Wilson, eds., *The Political Re-Education of Germany and Her Allies
    after World War II* (London: Croom Helm, 1985). There is relatively little work on
    the Japanese and Italian POWs, see, however, Arnold Krammer, "Japanese Prisoners
    of War in America," *Pacific Historical Review* 52, no. 1 (February 1983): 67–91; and
    Louis E. Keefer, *Italian Prisoners of War in America, 1942–1946: Captives or Allies?*
    (New York: Praeger, 1992). It is unclear, both from these sources and from govern-
    ment records, just what the role of film was in the camps for Japanese and Italian
    prisoners.

35 Robin, *The Barbed-Wire College*, 19–24.

36 Ibid., 10.

37   For a discussion of the manner in which prisoners were separated, see Robin, *The Barbed-Wire College*, 41. For the course curriculum, see p. 10; for the introduction of film, see pp. 8–9.

38   See "Films for the Prisoner of War Motion Picture Circuit," National Archives Record Group 389, Box 1605.

39   Jaye E. Gordon, "Operation Celluloid," *Hollywood Quarterly* 2, no. 4 (July 1947): 417.

40   The prison populations seemed to vary in relation to a state's need for POW labor, available space, and weather. More POWs were imprisoned in Texas than any other state, and it was here that camps might number as many as four thousand. As a point of comparison, during the course of the war Minnesota held only six thousand prisoners in twenty-one camps across the state. Several Web sites offer invaluable information about the camps, including the number of men imprisoned in them. See, for example, http://www.tsha.utexas.edu/handbook/online/articles /print/GG/qug1.html; http://www.mnlegion.org/paper/html/minnesota_pows .html; http://ktwu.wuacc.edu/journeys/articles/concord.html; and http://home .arcor.de/kriegsgefangene/usa/index.html.

41   Gordon, "Operation Celluloid," 418.

42   Gordon discusses Dalton Trumbo and *Captains Courageous* in "Operation Celluloid," 419.

43   "*Lost Horizon*, a Columbia Feature, starring Ronald Colman, directed by Frank Capra," 1. Document C-404, National Archives Record Group 389, Box 1605.

44   "Talk No. 4: Showing of *Why We Fight* Series No. 2 with German Commentary," 1, in "Report covering 9 November 1944–1 August 1945," held in the National Archives.

45   Ibid., 1.

46   Ibid., 2.

47   Ibid., 3–4.

48   Gordon, "Operation Celluloid," 417.

49   Pabel, the former prisoner, suggested that the men in his camp did not respond in the manner that Gordon hoped they would:

> One day we were marched to the camp movie to watch a Buchenwald picture. We were warned in advance not to utter a word either during the showing of the film or on the return to camp. The documentary movie was intended to convey an impression of that horror camp and its unfortunate inmates. A narrator commented on the beastly deeds committed in this camp by representatives of the Hitler regime.
>
> I imagine the idea was that we prisoners should be shown what we had done and thus be prevailed on to repent. The experiment was a complete failure. On our way home and in the barracks, whenever that movie was mentioned, the men either declared it a fake or said, "Why the hell did they show that to *us*; we didn't do it" (*Enemies are Human*, 160).

50   Robin, *Barbed-Wire College*, 60. Robin provides his own discussion of Wintergerst's document on pp. 60–61.

51 Oskar Wintergerst, "*Why We Fight* Series and Re-Education of the German Prisoners of War." The document can be found in the National Archives Record Group 389, Box 1616.

52 Hovland, Lumsdaine, and Sheffield, *Experiments on Mass Communication*, 38. The experiment determined that, of the men who had not seen *The Battle of Britain*, 27 percent believed that Germany planned to invade the United States; among those who had seen the film, 36 percent so believed.

53 Wintergerst "*Why We Fight* Series and Re-Education," 1–2, 4.

54 Clinton T. Duffy, *San Quentin: The Story of a Prison* (London: Peter Davies, 1951), 1.

55 Ibid., 11–12.

56 Ibid., 162. Duffy discusses films in San Quentin on pp. 162–67.

57 Ibid., 163.

58 H. A. Gray, "Prison Education and the Sound Film," *School and Society*, 8 August 1942, 114.

59 Ibid., 114.

60 For a description of the Aristophanes reading group, see "Nor Iron Bars," *Newsweek*, 28 February 1949, 78. The newspaper of San Quentin, the *San Quentin News*, ran a report on Great Books programs in the issue of 23 May 1947, 7, titled "Great Books play Prominent Part in Adult Education." The newspaper criticized the typical program for its European bias and its reliance on the usual canon of books: "There is nothing at all from India, China, Japan, Persia, Arabia, Portugal, South America, or Iceland," the newspaper reported, "though each of those countries has produced very great books."

61 See "Ignorance Is Not Bliss," *Colliers*, 10 June 1950, 86, for a description of graduation ceremonies at Statesville Prison in Joliet, Illinois.

62 Gray, "Prison Education and the Sound Film," 114. In discussing prisoners' cultural and recreational tastes before prison, Thomas Blakeley wrote that "these are often limited to the pool hall, the saloon, the house of prostitution, gambling dens, etc" (Blakeley, "An Evaluation of the Administration of the Educational Program at San Quentin," Ph.D. dissertation completed in the Department of Education at the University of California, 1949, 24).

63 Roy Franklyn, "Theatre in Prison," *Theatre Arts* (July 1946): 418. Franklyn himself seems to have been an inmate at Danbury, a prison for first offenders, where he prepared an adaptation of *Pagliacci*.

64 Gray, "Prison Education and the Sound Film," 115.

65 John Law, L. W. Davis, and Gerald Curtin wrote in 1939 that "motion pictures are shown in practically every institution in the country. They provide the emotional relaxation that is nowhere more salutary than in institutional life" ("Physical Education and Recreation," in *Correctional Education Today* ed. Walter M. Wallack, Glenn M. Kendall, Austin H. MacCormick, and Edward R. Cass (American Prison Association, 1939), 231.

66 "What the Picture Did for Me," *Motion Picture Herald*, 6 November 1937, 83; 22 January 1938, 59; 25 November 1939, 51; 16 December 1939, 59; and 18 December 1943, 52.

67 "San Quentin: Behind Its Bars 4,600 Men Live, Work and Sometimes Reform,"

with photographs by Charles E. Steinheimer, *Life*, 27 October 1947, 116–25. The article mentions California's penal system on p. 116; Duffy's friendliness on p. 118; and prison letter writing on p. 122.

68 Even these correspondence courses were seen as a significant improvement in prison education when they were instituted at San Quentin and the Wisconsin State Prison at Waupun. See Wallack, Kendall, MacCormick, and Cass, eds., *Correctional Education Today*, 25.

69 For information regarding Duffy's education program at San Quentin, see Blakeley, "An Evaluation of the Administration." For the formation of the program, see p. 4. Blakeley provides the numbers of students and graduates on pp. 4 and 7, and he discusses class subjects on p. 8. "The San Quentin News," in *Scholastic Notes*, of 29 August 1947, 7, reported that "a total of 1,757 inmates were enrolled in the school classes of the Educational Department" at the prison. The newspaper went on to state that "of these, 1,206 were enrolled in academic subjects, 368 in vocational studies, and 183 in commercial activities." In addition, 433 inmates were taking correspondence classes, 173 were in University Division courses, and 260 in Department of Corrections courses.

70 John Tagg, "Power and Photography," *Screen Education* 36 (Autumn 1980): 17–55.

71 "Convicts See a Movie of Their Own Escape," *Life*, 2 August 1948, 72–74.

72 Ibid., 72–73.

73 For information about the New Year's show, see *San Quentin News*, 3 January 1947, 1–3. The prisoner who thanked the warden for the show did not identify himself.

74 For Booth's talk, see *San Quentin News*, 3 January 1947, 1, 5. The orchestra is discussed in "S.Q.'s 'Toscanini' Parlays Two-Finger Brahms, 'Margie,' and 'Taps' into Band," *San Quentin News*, 25 April 1947, 7.

75 The book reviews appeared in "A Capsule of Atomic Havoc, Told with Utter Simplicity," *San Quentin News*. Ann Blyth appeared in the issue of 3 January 1947, 5; Barton in the issue of 31 January 1947, 5.

76 "Film Schedule," 3 January 1947, 7.

77 See the film schedules for 3 January, 17 January, and 31 January 1947 (all on p. 7).

78 *San Quentin News*, 3 January 1947, 1.

79 Ibid., 50.

80 Fred McDermott to Duffy (all letters to Duffy are in the Capra Collection, Wesleyan Cinema Archives).

81 The quotes here are from letters to Duffy from, respectively, William Denton, A. Rayle, Albert H. Minter, and unidentified.

82 Letters to Duffy from, respectively, Chris Whys; "A Motion Picture Fan"; John B. Ries; Jorgenson (no first name); and Gordon Bishop.

83 "San Quentin," *Life*, 122.

84 Letters to Duffy from, respectively, Eggleston (no first name); unsigned; H. Hall; Lee Alvis; and Jesse P. Bibbs.

85 Harper and Porter, "Moved to Tears," 152–73.

86 Eggleston to Duffy; Frank Carswell to Duffy.

87 Stacey discusses these forms of identification in chapter 5 of *Star Gazing*. For transcendence, and for the response of the woman who sees herself on screen, see p. 145.

88   Paul J. Fisher to Duffy; unsigned to Duffy.

89   Letters to Duffy from, respectively, "A4873"; J. B. Thomas; unsigned; and L. H. Cummings.

90   Charles Morrill to Duffy. *San Quentin News* discusses the prison's AA meetings in "A.A. Meeting Hears Records," 25 April, 1947, 7. This article reports as well that Warden Duffy himself spoke on an "A.A. radio program" originating in Detroit, "as the representative of the San Quentin Chapter of A.A."

91   Cummings to Duffy.

92   Thomas to Duffy.

93   Unsigned letter to Duffy.

94   Unsigned to Duffy.

95   Alvis to Duffy.

96   Durant (no first name) to Duffy.

97   Richard Hanlen to Duffy; unsigned to Duffy.

98   "Piper" to Duffy.

99   Fred McDermott to Duffy.

100 Joseph M. Thierry to Duffy; Irwin Unger to Duffy.

101 The first two responses to Duffy are unsigned; followed by, respectively, Freddy Martin Padilla and Jens P. Miller.

102 Letters to Duffy from, respectively, Harold E. Dennis; Jesse P. Bibbs; and Fred C. Tieman.

103 The first two comments to Duffy were unsigned; the third is from Glen R. High.

104 The first critical response to Duffy was unsigned; the second is from Fitzgerald.

105 Response is unsigned.

106 Response is unsigned.

107 Stacey, *Star Gazing*, in particular chapter 5.

108 Fred Telles to Duffy.

6 POLITICS AND PEDAGOGY NEAR THE END OF A CAREER: FROM FEATURE FILMS TO TELEVISION PRODUCTION

1   The letter is from 10 May 1948, Capra Collection, Wesleyan Cinema Archives (all subsequent letters about *State of the Union* are from this collection).

2   Capra, *The Name above the Title*, 398–99; McBride, *The Catastrophe of Success*, 538–39; Ray Carney, *American Visions: The Films of Frank Capra* (Middletown, Conn.: Wesleyan University Press, 1996), 451.

3   Mrs. Earl L. Summers to Capra, 15 April 1950.

4   Peter T. Campon to Capra, 16 April 1950.

5   Capra to Campon, 28 April 1950.

6   Harold Chetkow, Vancouver, British Columbia, to Capra, 27 May 1948.

7   Alberto O. Andreotti, Campinas, Brazil, to Capra, undated.

8   Henry Singer, Elmhurst-Queens, New York, to Capra, 2 October 1951.

9   Ibid. In his autobiography, Capra wrote that "one theater in a French village in the Vosges Mountains played *Mr. Smith* continuously during the last thirty days be-

fore the ban," instituted by the Nazis, on all American films in 1942. He also cited from the 4 November 1942 *Hollywood Reporter*, which wrote that *Smith* had been "chosen by French theaters as the final English-language film to be shown before the recent Nazi-ordered countrywide ban on American and British films went into effect," and added that the film "was roundly cheered" (*The Name above the Title*, 292–93).

10 Singer to Capra, 2 October 1951.

11 Ibid.

12 Joseph Hull, Marshalltown, Iowa, to Capra, 10 May 1948.

13 Addie Witherspoon Caroulli, Maplewood, New Jersey, to Capra, undated.

14 Miss R. E. Stallings, Murfreesboro, Tennessee, to Capra, 17 June 1948.

15 Hull to Capra, 10 May 1948.

16 The World Republic letter was written on 24 July 1948, by chairman of the Board of Directors William F. Byron.

17 Rachel L. Holcomb to Capra, 26 May 1948.

18 Charles Johnson, Tulsa, Oklahoma, to Capra, undated.

19 J. Sewell to Capra, 5 June 1948.

20 Addie Witherspoon to Capra, undated.

21 Mrs. Joseph L. DePatta, San Anselmo, California, to Capra, 25 June 1948.

22 John V. Crane, Duquesne, Pennsylvania, to Capra, undated.

23 The question about the presidency comes from an undated, unsigned letter.

24 Julia Hendrix, Lexington, South Carolina, to Capra, 15 May 1948.

25 Mrs. George Kimmons, Birmingham, Alabama, to Capra, 8 May 1948.

26 All citations from Londo are taken from the assignment he sent to Capra, which Capra deposited with his papers at the Wesleyan Cinema Archives, and which is dated Thursday, May 20, 1948.

27 Harvey Brown to Capra, 27 July 1948.

28 Frederick L. Fitzpatrick, "Science Manpower and Science Education," in *Policies for Science Education*, ed. Frederick L. Fitzpatrick (New York: Bureau of Publications, Teachers College, Columbia University, 1960), 1.

29 For a brief description of the Future Scientists of America Foundation, see *Science: the Junior High School: A Report of the 1958 West Coast Summer Conference* (Washington, D.C.: Department of the National Education Association, 1959), frontispiece. Paul DeH. Hurd, *Science Facilities for the Modern High School* (Stanford: Stanford University Press, 1954). For an interesting analysis of the general popularity of science and the increased emphasis on science education after World War II, see John C. Burnham, *How Superstition Won and Science Lost: Popularizing Science and Health in the United States* (New Brunswick: Rutgers University Press, 1987). Burnham charts public interest in science, roughly, by decade, and for the first half of the twentieth century he has located the greatest interest in the 1920s and the 1950s (171). In addition, he notes that "beginning in the 1950's, important figures in American science, almost all of them college and especially graduate school teachers, introduced major changes into American science teaching on the elementary and secondary level" (186).

30 At around the same time as the collaboration with Capra, AT&T also contracted

with Warner Bros. to produce four one-hour science specials. One of the shows, *The Alphabet Conspiracy*, featured a segment with Buster Keaton, although according to series producer Jack Warner Jr., AT&T officials insisted that the Keaton footage be eliminated before the telecast, "because nobody remembered Buster Keaton anymore" (Jack Warner Jr., "Story of a Lost Film," *The Keaton Chronicle* 1, no. 3 [autumn 1993]: 1).

31   The voice of Father Time was supplied by Lionel Barrymore, who played the evil Mr. Potter in Capra's 1946 film *It's a Wonderful Life*, and here gave one of the last performances before his death in 1954.

32   By the time of the production of *Our Mr. Sun*, AT&T had developed an apparently serious interest in solar energy. In its annual report in 1954, the corporation emphasized that it had "invented a device to convert sunlight directly into electricity" (3).

33   McBride, *The Catastrophe of Success*, 616. McBride reports that each of the films in the series "wound up costing about $400,000, about three times as much as originally estimated." Quoting animator Shamus Culhane, who worked on the series, McBride also writes that "every time [N.W. Ayer & Son's] Don Jones asked AT&T for more money, 'he might just as well have asked for a pound of bone marrow'" (616).

34   William J. Gruver and Albert Piltz, *Modern Science and Your Child* (Washington, D.C.: U.S. Department of Health, Education, and Welfare, 1963), 7.

35   For a discussion of local implementation of progressive educational systems during the 1930s and 1940s, see Zilversmit, *Changing Schools*.

36   For information about AT&T's relationship with the FCC, see AT&T's annual reports from 1957 (7), 1958 (8), and 1959 (7). The antitrust action is discussed by Maurice Tannenbaum in "The Historical Evolution of U.S. Telecommunications," *Technology in Society* 15 (1993): 270.

37   In two of the instances of this linkage between the media and the government, television showed an atomic weapons test for the first time in 1952, while in September 1954 President Eisenhower himself appeared as the television emcee at the Pennsylvania groundbreaking of the country's first commercial atomic energy plant. See Christopher Anderson, *Hollywood TV: The Studio System in the Fifties* (Austin: University of Texas Press, 1994); for the description of the sponsorship of *Light's Diamond Jubilee*, see pp. 84–85. Anderson describes the first televised bomb test on pp. 93–94, and Eisenhower and the energy plant groundbreaking on pp. 97–99.

38   "Up with Frank Capra," *Newsweek*, 3 December 1956, 92, 94; "Elementary," *Time*, 31 December 1956, 36–37; "Light Subject," *Time*, 3 December 1956, 43–44.

39   Henry Chauncey, "Film Is the Answer," *Educational Screen*, October 1956, 340–41. For another discussion of the quality of science films in the 1950s, see Robert B. Churchill, "Science Comes to Life," *Educational Screen*, May 1956, 176–177, 199.

40   During this period, AT&T discussed its own testing and marketing techniques as extensions of a commitment to the neighborhood and to the needs of ordinary people. In 1956, for instance, the corporation stressed in its *Annual Report* that "we ask the public at regular intervals what they think about the service and about the Bell System." Then, normalizing the presence of the science corporation in the everyday lives of AT&T customers, the report continued by stating that "telephone users who

are acquainted with telephone employees, and see them and talk with them, usually have a better understanding of what we are trying to do, and a higher regard for our efforts" (22). In other annual reports during the 1950s AT&T stressed seeking out the opinions of customers about new communications technologies and emphasized the numerous market tests of new products and the open houses where managers and employees would meet with customers to talk about products and other matters (see *Annual Report*, 1957, 9; 1958, 14, 19).

41 See the following reports in the Frank Capra Collection, Wesleyan Cinema Archives: "Final Report: Audience Research: Students-Teacher Evaluation of *Our Mr. Sun*"; "Results of preview of *Our Mr. Sun* by Frank Capra Productions in Riverside, California"; "What Do Viewers Think of *Our Mr. Sun* as Telecast in Black-and-White: A Study of Students, Housewives and AT&T Long Lines Employees Who Saw the Program, Closed Circuit Telecast"; "Telephone Survey of *Our Mr. Sun* Viewers"; and "Study of Employee Reactions to *Our Mr. Sun*."

42 *Our Mr. Sun* opens with "The heavens declare the glory of god," from Psalms, and ends with "Be praised my lord in what you have created; above all else be praised in our brother Master Sun," from St. Francis. After this quote Beethoven's "Ode to Joy" plays over the end credits. Also during the program, Father Time reminds viewers to "ask, inquire, seek the truth. It's right that you should know, or the good Lord wouldn't have given you that driving curiosity." He concludes by telling us to "measure the outside with mathematics, but measure the inside with prayer. Prayer is research, too."

43 Final Report: Audience Research: "Students-Teacher Evaluation of *Our Mr. Sun*, Full Tabulation," 2. There was, however, some criticism of the religious content of the film. Two teachers in the Philadelphia test complained about the program's "incompatible philosophy of science and religion." In another part of the questionnaire, two teachers once again (and almost certainly the same two as before), along with three students, mentioned the "emphasis on prayer [and] religion" as those items "not belonging in [the] film," while five teachers and two students called the "religious references" their "least liked aspect" of *Our Mr. Sun* (3–4).

44 A few members of the Riverside audience called the film "inspirational," while some of the telephone respondents felt that science could only be truly important if used ethically. See "Written-in Comments" in "Results of Preview of *Our Mr. Sun* by Frank Capra Productions in Riverside, California." See also tabulation of answers for question 5 in the "Telephone Survey of *Our Mr. Sun* Viewers," in which 5 percent of viewers and 2 percent of nonviewers felt that science was either "very important or quite important" only "if used ethically" (2).

45 The numbers about fan mail appear in an undated, unsigned memo in the *Our Mr. Sun* file at the Wesleyan Cinema Archives. The memo details important statistics about the program's initial telecast, for instance, the fact that *Our Mr. Sun* aired opposite programs starring Robert Montgomery and Lawrence Welk, and held its own against them in terms of "Trendex" ratings. The average sets in the use/rating share for *Our Mr. Sun* was 12.8/27, compared to 11.8/24.8 for Montgomery and 14.2/29.7 for Welk.

46 Peter Machurak to Capra, 19 November 1956.

47   Ciel Arshack to Capra, 20 November 1956.

48   Final Report: Audience Research: "Students-Teacher Evaluation," 4–5.

49   Ibid., "Full Tabulation," 10.

50   Ibid.

51   Ibid., 12–13.

52   Ibid., 13.

53   For evidence of AT&T's interest in showing the film in schools with the commercial in place, see "Final Report: Audience Research: Students-Teacher Evaluation: Implications of Findings," 7: "There might be some question about whether the commercial should be left in the film for school showings."

54   AT&T, *Annual Report*, 1952, 20.

55   AT&T, *Annual Report*, 1958, 16.

56   Final Report: Audience Research: "Students-Teacher Evaluation of *Our Mr. Sun*," 6.

57   Ibid., "Full Tabulation," 16.

58   Ibid., "Summary and Interpretation of Findings," 6.

59   "Telephone Survey of *Our Mr. Sun* Viewers," 1, 3.

60   At the Riverside screening, 165 women and 164 men responded to the questionnaires; another 67 respondents neglected to indicate either their age or gender. See "Results of Preview of *Our Mr. Sun* by Frank Capra Productions in Riverside, California." For the reference to housewives at the New York Screening, see "What Do Viewers Think of *Our Mr. Sun*."

61   While 3,006 households were contacted, only about 90 percent of them (2,710) had television sets. To determine sentiment about the program and about AT&T, only those people who lived in homes with sets were surveyed.

62   "Final Report: Audience Research: Students-Teacher Evaluation, Full Tabulation," 3.

63   AT&T, *Annual Report*, 1957, 4.

64   For an excellent analysis of the development of U.S. science policy during and after World War II and the relationship between the science corporation and the federal government, see Daniel Lee Kleinman, *Politics on the Endless Frontier: Postwar Research Policy in the United States* (Durham: Duke University Press, 1995).

65   AT&T, *Annual Report*, 1956, 40.

CONCLUSION: THE CONTEMPORARY CAPRA

1   *New York Times*, 4 September 1991, A1.

2   Peter B. Flint, "Frank Capra, Whose Films Helped America Keep Faith in Itself, Is Dead at 94," *New York Times*, 4 September 1991, B10.

3   "Frank Capra éteint les projecteurs," *Libération*, 4 September 1991, 44. The obituary called Capra "l'inventeur de la comédie américaine," which refers to American comedy from around 1930 to 1960.

4   Tom Shales, "Director Frank Capra Made the Movies that Warmed Everyday People," *Washington Post*, 4 September 1991, B1, B9 (both citations appear on B9). Expressions of superiority to Capra and his films were common after the director's

death. The ABC television show *Nightline* devoted a special program to Capra on 3 September 1991, just after he died. When host Ted Koppel asked film critic Gene Siskel for a critical appraisal, Siskel said, "Well, I think in terms of film technique, I don't think that Mr. Capra was the most exciting filmmaker" (to be fair, Siskel did go on to praise Capra's storytelling talents). Koppel asked filmmaker (and partner of Edward Zwick) Marshall Herskovitz to explain having once called *It's a Wonderful Life* "the best film ever made." Herskovitz responded, "Well, I missed *Citizen Kane*."

5   At least as early as 1941, critics would chastise Capra using the very terms that the *Times* obituary claimed only appeared with the director's postwar films. In 1941, for instance, Anthony Bower wrote of Capra's latest movie that "for muddled thinking and mawkish sentiment *Meet John Doe* undoubtedly deserves a special academy award . . . a gilt crocodile in tears" ("Recent Films," *Nation*, 29 March 1941, 39).

6   Michael Wines, "First-Term Lawmaker Brought Clinton Plan Back from Brink," *San Francisco Chronicle*, 6 August 1993, A9. Robin Tucker, "73 Mr. Smiths, of G.O.P., Go to Washington," *New York Times*, 8 January 1995, A1, A10.

7   For an examination of Diao's *Bitter Tea of General Yen* (and also for a photograph of the silkscreen), see Mira Schor, *Wet: On Painting, Feminism, and Art Culture* (Durham: Duke University Press, 1996), 41–45.

8   For references, either brief or extended, to Capra's films in sitcoms, see, among others: *Married with Children*, Fox, 18 December 1994; *Friends*, NBC, 4 April 1995; *Mad about You*, NBC, 18 May 1995; and *Ellen*, ABC, 13 September 1995.

9   The centennial took place from 30 July to 5 August 1997.

Bibliography

MANUSCRIPT COLLECTIONS

Federal Bureau of Investigation, Frank Capra File numbers 7-2403, 100-384984, and 123-12626.
Library of Congress, Washington, D.C., Motion picture copyright records.
Margaret Herrick Library, Academy of Motion Pictures Arts and Sciences, Los Angeles, California.
    Frank Capra Clippings File.
    Production Code Administration Files.
National Archives, Washington, D.C.
    Department of State, file 893.4041 Motion Pictures (documents relating to film censorship in China).
    Department of State, "Adult Education, 1940–44," (documents relating to international release of *Mr. Smith Goes to Washington*).
    Record Groups 111 and 389 (documents relating to armed forces motion picture production, distribution, and reception during World War II).
New York Public Library, National Board of Review records.
Wesleyan Cinema Archives, Middletown, Connecticut, Frank Capra Collection.

BOOKS AND ARTICLES

"A.A. Meeting Hears Records." *San Quentin News*, 25 April 1947, 7.
Abrams, Mark. "The British Cinema Audience." *Hollywood Quarterly* 3, no. 2 (winter 1947–48): 155–58.
"A Capsule of Atomic Havoc, Told with Utter Simplicity." *San Quentin News*, 14 February 1947, 6.
Addams, Jane. *The Spirit of Youth and City Streets*. New York: Macmillan, 1909.
"All-American Program: Deems Taylor and a Symphony to Wave Musical Flag." *Newsweek*, 29 January 1940, 44.
Allen, Robert C. "Manhattan Myopia; or, Oh! Iowa!" *Cinema Journal* 35, no. 3 (spring 1996): 75–103.

Altenloh, Emilie. "A Sociology of the Cinema: The Audience," (1914) trans. Kathleen Cross. *Screen* 42, no. 3 (autumn 2001): 249–93.

Anderson, Christopher. *Hollywood TV: The Studio System in the Fifties.* Austin: University of Texas Press, 1994.

Ang, Ien. *Watching Dallas: Soap Opera and the Melodramatic Imagination.* London: Methuen, 1985.

Arnold, Julean, comp. *China through the American Window.* Shanghai: American Chamber of Commerce, 1932.

"Art via the Air Waves: Both CBS and NBC Starting New Cultural Programs." *Newsweek,* 6 November 1939, 30.

Bailey, Edna W., Anita D. Laton, and Elizabeth L. Bishop. *Studying Children in School.* New York: McGraw-Hill, 1939.

Balio, Tino. *Grand Design: Hollywood as a Modern Business Enterprise, 1930–1939.* Berkeley: University of California Press, 1995.

"Ballad of All Americans." *Newsweek,* 25 March 1940, 40.

Barry, Iris. "Why Wait for Posterity?" *Hollywood Quarterly* 1, no. 2 (January 1946): 131–37.

Bellour, Raymond. "Segmenting/Analyzing." In *Narrative, Apparatus, Ideology: A Film Theory Reader,* ed. Philip Rosen. New York: Columbia University Press, 1986.

"Bending the Bough." *Nation,* 26 September 1934, 342.

Benedict, Agnes. "What's Ahead in the Movies?" *Parents,* September 1936, 30–31, 52, 54, 56.

Benedict, Agnes, and Adele Franklin. *Your Best Friends are Your Children: A Guide to Enjoying Parenthood.* New York: Appleton-Century-Crofts, 1951.

Berlant, Lauren. "The Theory of Infantile Citizenship." *Public Culture* 5, no. 3 (spring 1993): 395–410.

Berubè, Allan. *Coming Out under Fire: The History of Gay Men and Women in World War Two.* New York: Free Press, 1990.

Biennial Report of the Superintendent of Public Instruction of North Carolina for the Scholastic Years 1933–34 and 1935–36, part 3, statistical report. Publication no. 207, issued by the State Superintendent of Public Instruction, Raleigh, North Carolina.

Bischof, Günter, and Stephen E. Ambrose, eds. *Eisenhower and the German POWs: Facts against Falsehood.* Baton Rouge: Louisiana State University Press, 1992.

Black, Gregory D. *Hollywood Censored: Morality Codes, Catholics, and the Movies.* Cambridge: Cambridge University Press, 1994.

Blakeley, Thomas. "An Evaluation of the Administration of the Educational Program at San Quentin." Ph.D. diss., University of California, Los Angeles, 1949.

Bodnar, John. *Remaking America: Public Memory, Commemoration, and Patriotism in the Twentieth Century.* Princeton: Princeton University Press, 1992.

Bower, Anthony. "Recent Films." *Nation,* 29 March 1941, 39.

Bowers, C. A. *The Progressive Educator and the Depression: The Radical Years.* New York: Random House, 1969.

"Broadway Gets a Taste of Real Oldtime Ballyhoo—and Likes It." *Motion Picture Herald,* 9 September 1933, 11.

Browne, Nick. "System of Production/System of Representation: Industry Context and Ideological Form in Capra's *Meet John Doe*." In *Meet John Doe*, ed. Charles Wolfe. New Brunswick: Rutgers University Press, 1989.

Burnham, John C. *How Superstition Won and Science Lost: Popularizing Science and Health in the United States*. New Brunswick: Rutgers University Press, 1987.

Buscombe, Edward. "Notes on Columbia Pictures Corporation 1926–1941." *Screen* 16, no. 3 (autumn 1975: 65–82).

Capra, Frank. *The Name above the Title: An Autobiography*. New York: Macmillan, 1971.

Carney, Ray. *American Visions: The Films of Frank Capra*. Middletown, Conn.: Wesleyan University Press, 1996.

Cartwright, Lisa. *Screening the Body: Tracing Medicine's Visual Culture*. Minneapolis: University of Minnesota Press, 1995.

"Challenge." *Time*, 9 October 1939, 46.

Charney, Leo, and Vanessa Schwartz, eds. *Cinema and the Invention of Modern Life*. Berkeley: University of California Press, 1995.

Charters, Werrett Wallace. *Motion Pictures and Youth*. New York: Macmillan, 1933.

Chauncey, Henry. "Film Is the Answer." *Educational Screen*, October 1956, 340–41.

Churchill, Robert B. "Science Comes to Life." *Educational Screen*, May 1956, 176–177, 199.

"City Council Wins Power for Inquiry: Upheld by Court of Appeals in WNYC Row with Mayor—Relief Study to Go On." *New York Times*, 5 April 1939, 1.

"Classics of This and an Earlier Day are Featured in the Cleveland Library Bookmarks of the Month." *The Motion Picture and the Family*, 15 October 1936, 7.

Cohen, Lizabeth. "The Class Experience of Mass Consumption: Workers as Consumers in Interwar America." In *The Power of Culture*, ed. Richard Wightman Fox and T. J. Jackson Lears. Chicago: University of Chicago Press, 1993.

"Columbia Starts *Dirigible* Ballyhoo over Radio Feb. 8." *Motion Picture Herald*, 31 January 1931, 34.

"Compulsory Schooling up to 16 Urged at White House Parley." *Newsweek*, 29 January 1940, 36.

"Convicts See a Movie of Their Own Escape." *Life*, 2 August 1948, 72–74.

Couvares, Francis G., ed. *Movie Censorship and American Culture*. Washington, D.C.: Smithsonian Institution Press, 1996.

Crow, Carl. *400 Million Customers: The Experiences—Some Happy, Some Sad of an American in China*. New York: Harper and Brothers, 1937.

Dale, Edgar. *Children's Attendance at Motion Pictures*. New York: Macmillan, 1935.

———. *How to Appreciate Motion Pictures: A Manual of Motion-Picture Criticism Prepared for High-School Students*. New York: Macmillan, 1933.

Davidson, Cathy N., and Jessamyn Hatcher. *No More Separate Spheres! A Next Wave American Studies Reader*. Durham: Duke University Press, 2002.

DeCordova, Richard. "Ethnography and Exhibition: The Child Audiences, the Hays Office, and Saturday Matinees." *Camera Obscura* 23 (May 1990): 91–107.

———. "The Mickey in Macy's Window: Childhood, Consumerism, and Disney Animation." In *Disney Discourse: Producing the Magic Kingdom*. New York: Routledge, 1994.

————. *Picture Personalities: The Emergence of the Star System in America*. Urbana: University of Illinois Press, 1990.

"Democracy on Pedestals." *Time*, 24 February 1941, 66.

Duffy, Clinton T. *San Quentin: The Story of a Prison*. London: Peter Davies, 1951.

Dysinger, Wendell S., and Christian A. Ruckmick. *The Emotional Responses of Children to the Motion Picture Situation*. New York: Macmillan, 1935.

Eckert, Charles. "The Carole Lombard in Macy's Window." In *Fabrications: Costume and the Female Body*, ed. Jane Gaines and Charlotte Herzog. New York: Routledge, 1990.

"Elementary." *Time*, 31 December 1956, 36–37.

Enstad, Nan. *Ladies of Labor, Girls of Adventure*. New York: Columbia University Press, 1999.

"Eva Curie Arrives in City." *Los Angeles Times*, 7 March 1941, B1–2.

Ewen, Elizabeth, and Stuart Ewen. *Channels of Desire: Mass Images and the Shaping of American Consciousness*. Minneapolis: University of Minnesota Press, 1992.

Feuerwerker, Albert. *The Chinese Economy, 1912–1949*. Ann Arbor: University of Michigan Press, 1968.

Fitzpatrick, Frederick L., ed. *Policies for Science Education*. New York: Bureau of Publications, Columbia University, 1960.

Flint, Peter B. "Frank Capra, Whose Films Helped America Keep Faith in Itself, Is Dead at 94." *New York Times*, 4 September 1991, B10.

Foley, Barbara. *Radical Representations: Politics and Form in U.S. Proletarian Fiction, 1929–1941*. Durham: Duke University Press, 1992.

"Folk Songs in the White House." *Time*, 3 March 1941, 57.

"For Better Citizens." *Time*, 6 November 1939, 61.

Foreign Relations of the United States: Diplomatic Papers; Vol. 4, the Far East. Washington, D.C.: GPO, 1936.

Forman, Henry J. "Movie Madness." *McCalls*, October 1932, 14–15.

————. "Molded by Movies." *McCalls*, November 1932, 17.

————. *Our Movie-Made Children*. New York: Macmillan, 1933.

————. "To the Movies—But Not to Sleep!" *McCalls*, September 1932, 12–13.

Foucault, Michel. *Discipline and Punish: The Birth of the Prison*, trans. Alan Sheridan. New York: Vintage, 1995.

"Four Faces in Granite: Borglum's Black Hills Colossus Is Nearing Completion." *Newsweek*, 10 July 1939, 23.

Fox, Richard Wightman. "Intimacy on Trial: Cultural Meanings of the Beecher-Tilton Affair." In *The Power of Culture: Critical Essays in American History*, ed. Richard Wightman Fox and T. J. Jackson Lears, eds. Chicago: University of Chicago Press, 1993.

Fox, Stephen. *The Mirror Makers: A History of American Advertising and Its Creators*. Urbana: University of Illinois Press, 1997.

"Frank Capra éteint les projecteurs." *Libération*, 4 September 1991, 44.

Franklyn, Irwin R. *Flight*. New York: Grosset and Dunlap, 1929.

Franklyn, Roy. "Theatre in Prison." *Theatre Arts*, July 1946, 418.

Friedberg, Anne. *Window Shopping: Cinema and the Postmodern*. Berkeley: University of California Press, 1993.

Fuller, Kathryn. *At the Picture Show: Small-Town Audiences and the Creation of Movie Fan Culture*. Washington, D.C.: Smithsonian Institution Press, 1996.

———. "'What the Picture Did for Me': Small Town Exhibitors in the Great Depression." Unpublished paper.

Gaines, Jane. *Contested Culture: The Image, the Voice, and the Law*. Durham: Duke University Press, 1991.

Gansberg, Judith M. *Stalag USA: The Remarkable Story of German POWs in America*. New York: Thomas Y. Crowell Company, 1977.

Gerstle, Gary. "The Protean Character of American Liberalism." *American Historical Review* 99, no. 4 (October 1994): 1043–73.

"Get Your Tickets Today for Foster Mass Meeting." *Daily Worker*, 14 March 1941, 4.

Gordon, Linda. "Putting Children First: Women, Maternalism, and Welfare in the Early Twentieth Century." In *U.S. History as Women's History: New Feminist Essays*, ed. Linda Kerber, Alice Kessler-Harris, and Kathryn Kish Sklar. Chapel Hill: University of North Carolina Press, 1995.

Gomery, Douglas. *The Hollywood Studio System*. New York: St. Martin's Press, 1986.

Gordon, Jaye E. "Operation Celluloid." *Hollywood Quarterly* 2, no. 4 (July 1947): 416–19.

Gove, Floyd S. "Educational Planning in a Democracy." *School and Society*, 25 June 1938, 829–30.

Gray, H. A. "Prison Education and the Sound Film." *School and Society*, 8 August 1942, 114–16.

"Great Books Play Prominent Part in Adult Education." *San Quentin News*, 23 May 1947, 7.

Gruver, William, and Albert Piltz. *Modern Science and Your Child*. Washington, D.C.: U.S. Department of Health, Education, and Welfare, 1963.

Handel, Leo A. *Hollywood Looks at Its Audience*. Urbana: The University of Illinois Press, 1950.

Hansen, Miriam. *Babel and Babylon: Spectatorship in American Silent Film*. Cambridge: Harvard University Press, 1991.

Harper, Sue, and Vincent Porter. "Moved to Tears: Weeping in the Cinema in Postwar Britain." *Screen* 37, no. 2 (summer 1996): 152–73.

"Hays Warns against Propaganda in Films." *Motion Picture Herald*, 4 April 1936, 52.

Hellman, Geoffrey T. "Profiles: Thinker in Hollywood." *New Yorker*, 24 February 1940, 23–28.

Herman, Ellen. *The Romance of American Psychology: Political Culture in the Age of Experts*. Berkeley: University of California Press, 1996.

Higashi, Sumiko. "Dialogue: Manhattan's Nickelodeons." *Cinema Journal* 35, no. 3 (spring 1996): 72–74.

Hilmes, Michele. *Radio Voices: American Broadcasting, 1922–1952*. Minneapolis: University of Minnesota Press, 1997.

Holaday, Perry W., and George D. Stoddard. *Getting Ideas from the Movies*. New York: Macmillan, 1933.

Holbrook, Sabra. *Children Object*. New York: Viking, 1943.

Hopper, Hedda. "Hedda Hopper's Hollywood." *Los Angeles Times*, 2 March 1941, C3.

Hovland, Carl I., Arthur A. Lumsdaine, and Fred D. Sheffield. *Experiments on Mass Communication*, vol. 3. Princeton: Princeton University Press, 1949.

Hurd, Paul DeH. *Science Facilities for the Modern High School*. Stanford: Stanford University Press, 1954.

"Ideas Swapped by 3,000 at the 'Country Store' Forum on Education for Democracy." *Newsweek*, 28 August 1939, 25.

"Ignorance Is Not Bliss." *Colliers*, 10 June 1950, 86.

"Inquiring Photographer Contest Used on *Deeds*." *Motion Picture Herald*, 11 July 1936, 128.

Jacobs, Lea. "Reformers and Spectators: The Film Education Movement in the Thirties." *Camera Obscura* 22 (January 1990): 29–49.

Jarvie, Ian. *Hollywood's Overseas Campaign: The North Atlantic Movie Trade, 1920–1950*. Cambridge: Cambridge University Press, 1992.

"Jefferson Memorial Woes: Strike Is Latest in the Series of Rows Harassing Project." *Newsweek*, 28 August 1939, 22.

"*John Doe* Gets 4-City Opening." *Motion Picture Herald*, 29 March 1941, 66.

Johnston, Alva. "Capra Shoots as He Pleases." *Saturday Evening Post*, 14 May 1938, 8–9, 67, 69, 71–72.

Jones, Dorothy. "The Hollywood War Film: 1942–1944." *Hollywood Quarterly* 1, no. 1 (October 1945): 1–19.

Jowett, Garth. *Film: The Democratic Art*. Boston: Little, Brown, 1976.

Jowett, Garth, Ian C. Jarvie, and Kathryn H. Fuller. *Children and the Movies: Media Influence and the Payne Fund Controversy*. Cambridge: Cambridge University Press, 1996.

Kammen, Michael. *A Machine That Would Go of Itself: The Constitution in American Culture*. New York: Vintage, 1987.

Kazin, Michael. *The Populist Persuasion: An American History*. New York: Basic Books, 1995.

Keefer, Louis E. *Italian Prisoners of War in America, 1942–1946: Captives or Allies?* New York: Praeger, 1992.

Kendall, Read. "Stars, Fans Brave Rain to Attend Gay Film Event." *Los Angeles Times*, 13 March 1941, A16.

Kiesling, Barrett C. *Talking Pictures: How They Are Made, How to Appreciate Them*. New York: Johnson Publishing Company, 1937.

Kilpatrick, William H. "Propaganda, Democracy, and Education." *School and Society*, 1 April 1939, 405–9.

King, Edward A. *The Shaping of the American High School*, Madison: University of Wisconsin Press, 1969, 1972.

Kleinman, Daniel Lee. *Politics on the Endless Frontier: Postwar Research Policy in the United States*. Durham: Duke University Press, 1995.

Kracauer, Siegfried. *Das Ornament der Masse*. Frankfurt am Main: Suhrkamp, 1963.

Krammer, Arnold. "Japanese Prisoners of War in America." *Pacific Historical Review* 52, no. 1 (February 1983): 67–91.

———. *Nazi Prisoners of War in America*. Briarcliff Manor, N.Y.: Stein and Day, 1979.

Kuhn, Annette. *Dreaming of Fred and Ginger: Cinema and Cultural Memory*. New York: New York University Press, 2002.

Lasker, Bruno, ed. *Problems of the Pacific 1931: Proceedings of the Fourth Conference of the Institute of Pacific Relations, Hangchow and Shanghai, China*. Chicago: University of Chicago Press, 1932.

Law, John, L. W. Davis, and Gerald Curtain. "Physical Education and Recreation." In *Correctional Education Today*, ed. Walter M. Wallack, Glenn M. Kendall, Austin H. MacCormick, and Edward R. Cass. American Prison Association, 1939.

Lears, Jackson. *Fables of Abundance: A Cultural History of Advertising in America*. New York: Basic Books, 1994.

Le Sourd, Howard M. "Lessons Learned from the Movies." *The Motion Picture and the Family*, 15 May 1936, 5–6.

Lewin, William. *Photoplay Appreciation in American High Schools*. New York: D. Appleton-Century Company, 1934.

Lewis, Richard, and Helen Rand. *Film and School: A Handbook in Moving-Picture Evaluation*. New York: D. Appleton-Century Company, 1937.

"Light Subject." *Time*, 3 December 1956, 43–44.

Lott, Eric. *Love and Theft: Blackface Minstrelsy and the American Working Class*. New York: Oxford University Press, 1993.

Lovejoy, Gordon W., ed. *Paths to Maturity: Findings of the North Carolina Youth Survey 1938–1940*. Chapel Hill: University of North Carolina, 1940.

Lynd, Robert S., and Helen Merrell Lynd. *Middletown*. New York: Harcourt, Brace, and World, 1929.

Lyons, over WNYC, Asks End of WNYC." *New York Times*, 3 April 1939, 3.

"Makes Its Bow in Printed Form." *The Motion Picture and the Family*, 15 October 1936, 7.

Maland, Charles. *Chaplin and American Culture: The Evolution of a Star Image*. Princeton: Princeton University Press, 1989.

———. *Frank Capra*. New York: Twayne Publishers, 1995.

Marchand, Roland. *Advertising the American Dream: Making Way for Modernity, 1920–1940*. Berkeley: University of California Press, 1985.

Marchetti, Gina. *Romance and the Yellow Peril: Race, Sex, and Discursive Strategies in Hollywood Fiction*. Berkeley: University of California Press, 1993.

May, Ernest R., and John K. Fairbank, eds. *America's China Trade in Historical Perspective: The Chinese and American Performance*. Cambridge: Harvard University Press, 1986.

"MBS Soapbox." *Time*, 24 March 1941, 54.

McBride, Joseph. *Frank Capra: The Catastrophe of Success*. New York: Simon and Schuster, 1992.

Mersand, Joseph. "Facts and Fiction about the Educational Values of the Cinema." *Educational Screen*, December 1938, 319–20.

Moise, Edwin E. *Modern China: A History*. London: Longman, 1986.

Morley, David. *The Nationwide Audience*. London: British Film Institute, 1980.

Morrison, J. Cayce. "The Unique Function of Education in American Democracy." *School and Society*, 30 July 1938, 132–37.

"*Mr. Smith* Riles Washington." *Time*, 30 October 1939, 49.

Mullen, Sarah McLean. "Films for the Pupil and Teacher." *The Motion Picture and the Family*, 15 April 1936, 4, 8.

———. "How to Judge Motion Pictures: A Pamphlet for High School Students." Scholastic, New York, 1935.

Mulvey, Laura. "Visual Pleasure and Narrative Cinema." *Screen* 16, no. 3 (autumn 1975): 6-18.

Newman, Kathy M. *Radio Active: Advertising and Consumer Activism, 1935-1947*. Berkeley: University of California Press, 2004.

"New Research Exhibits Lend Added Interest to Film Study." *The Motion Picture and the Family*, 15 October 1936, 1.

Noble, Lorraine, ed. *Four Star Scripts*. New York: Doubleday, Doran and Co., 1936.

"Nor Iron Bars." *Newsweek*, 28 February 1949, 78.

"Of Thee I Sing." *Time*, 24 February 1941, 55.

Pabel, Reinold. *Enemies Are Human*. Philadelphia: John C. Winston Company, 1955.

Palmer, Allen W. "Cecil B. DeMille Writes America's History for the 1939 World's Fair." *Film History* 5, no. 1 (March 1993): 36-48.

Palter, Ruth. "Radio's Attraction for Housewives." In *Hollywood Quarterly: Film Culture in Postwar America, 1945-1957*, ed. Eric Smoodin and Ann Martin. Berkeley: University of California Press, 2002.

Palumbo-Liu, David. "The Bitter Tea of Frank Capra." *positions* 3, no. 3 (winter 1995): 759-89.

Peiss, Kathy. *Cheap Amusements: Working Woman and Leisure in Turn-of-the-Century New York*. Philadelphia: Temple University Press, 1986.

The People of North Carolina. Raleigh: North Carolina State Planning Board, 1938.

"Philip F. LaFollette Will Speak Monday." *Los Angeles Times*, 7 March 1941, B1.

Platt, David. "*Meet John Doe* Lets Film Audiences Down." *Daily Worker*, 15 March 1941, 7.

Pronay, Nicholas, and Keith Wilson, eds. *The Political Re-Education of Germany and Her Allies after World War II*. London: Croom Helm, 1985.

Rahtz, Robert. "Movies for Classrooms." *Hollywood Quarterly* (April 1947): 323-25.

Ramsaye, Terry. "Sex Lure Looms Again." *Motion Picture Herald*, 24 April 1937, 14-15, 27-28.

Remer, C. F. *Foreign Investments in China*. New York: Macmillan, 1933.

Richard, Paul. "Norman Rockwell, American Master (Seriously!)." *Washington Post*, 6 June 1993, G1, 8-9.

Ricketson, Frank H. Jr., *The Management of Motion Picture Theatres*. New York: McGraw-Hill, 1938.

Riesman, David, and Evelyn T. Riesman. "Movies and Audiences." *American Quarterly* 4, no. 3 (fall 1952): 195-202.

Robin, Ron. *The Barbed-Wire College: Reeducating German POWs in the United States during World War II*. Princeton: Princeton University Press, 1995.

Rony, Fatimah Tobing. "Those Who Squat and Those Who Sit: The Iconography of Race in the 1895 Films of Félix-Louis Regnault." *Camera Obscura* 28 (January 1992): 263-89.

Roosevelt, Franklin Delano. "Address of the President of the United States." *School and Society*, 9 July 1938, 29–31.

Rosenberg, Rosalind. *Divided Lives: American Women in the Twentieth Century*. New York: Hill and Wang, 1992.

Ross, Steven J. *Working-Class Hollywood: Silent Film and the Shaping of Class in America*. Princeton: Princeton University Press, 1998.

Ruediger, W. C. "Saluting the Flag." *School and Society*, 25 February 1939, 249.

Russell, William F. "Education for Democracy." *School and Society*, 31 December 1938, 862–64.

Ryan, Mary P. *Women in Public: Between Banners and Ballots, 1825–1880*. Baltimore: Johns Hopkins University Press, 1990.

"San Quentin: Behind Its Bars 4,600 Men Live, Work, and Sometimes Reform." *Life*, 27 October 1947, 116–25.

Saunders, Thomas J. *Hollywood in Berlin: American Cinema and Weimar Germany*. Berkeley: University of California Press, 1994.

Schallert, Edwin. "*Meet John Doe* Hailed as Capra Victory." *Los Angeles Times*, 13 March 1941, A16.

Schor, Mira. *Wet: On Painting, Feminism, and Art Culture*. Durham: Duke University Press, 1996.

Science: The Junior High School: A Report of the 1958 West Coast Summer Conference. Washington, D.C.: Department of the National Education Association, 1959.

Shales, Tom. "Director Frank Capra Made the Movies That Warmed Everyday People." *Washington Post*, 4 September 1991, B1, 9.

Shohat, Ella. "Gender and Culture of Empire: Toward a Feminist Ethnography of the Cinema." *Quarterly Review of Film and Video* 13, nos. 1–3 (1993): 45–84.

Singer, Ben. "Manhattan Nickelodeons: New Data on Audiences and Exhibitors." *Cinema Journal* 34, no. 3 (spring 1995: 5–35).

———. *Melodrama and Modernity: Early Sensational Cinema and Its Contexts*. New York: Columbia University Press, 2001.

———. "New York, Just Like I Pictured It. . . ." *Cinema Journal* 35, no. 3 (spring 1996): 104–28.

Sklar, Robert. *Movie-Made America: A Cultural History of American Movies*. New York: Vintage, 1995.

Smith, Greg M. "Blocking *Blockade*: Partisan Protest, Popular Debate, and Encapsulated Texts." *Cinema Journal* 36, no. 1 (fall 1996): 18–38.

Smoodin, Eric. *Animating Culture: Hollywood Cartoons from the Sound Era*. New Brunswick: Rutgers University Press, 1993.

Smoodin, Eric, and Ann Martin. *Hollywood Quarterly: Film Culture in Postwar America, 1945–1957*. Berkeley: University of California Press, 2002.

Spring, Joel H. "Mass Culture and School Sports." *History of Education Quarterly* 14, no. 4 (winter 1974): 483–99.

"S.Q.'s 'Toscanini' Parlays Two-Finger Brahms, 'Margie,' and 'Taps' into Band." *San Quentin News*, 25 April 1947, 7.

Stacey, Jackie. *Star Gazing: Hollywood Cinema and Female Spectatorship*. London: Routledge, 1994.

Staiger, Janet. "Announcing Wares, Winning Patrons, Voicing Ideals: Thinking About the History and Theory of Film Advertising." *Cinema Journal* 29, no. 3 (spring 1990): 3–31.

———. *Interpreting Films: Studies in the Historical Reception of American Cinema.* Princeton: Princeton University Press, 1992.

———. *Perverse Spectators: The Practices of Film Reception.* New York: New York University Press, 2000.

———, ed. *The Studio System.* New Brunswick: Rutgers University Press, 1995.

Stamp, Shelley. *Movie-Struck Girls: Women and Motion Picture Culture after the Nickelodeon.* Princeton: Princeton University Press, 2000.

Stokes, Melvyn, and Richard Maltby, eds. *American Movie Audiences: From the Turn of the Century to the Early Sound Era.* London: British Film Institute, 1999.

———. *Identifying Hollywood's Audiences: Cultural Identity and the Movies.* London: British Film Institute, 1999.

Studlar, Gaylyn. *This Mad Masquerade: Stardom and Masculinity in the Jazz Age.* New York: Columbia University Press, 1996.

"Study of Local School Units in North Carolina: 1937." Publication no. 199, issued by the State Superintendent of Public Instruction, Raleigh, North Carolina.

Susman, Warren I. *Culture as History: The Transformation of American Society in the Twentieth Century.* New York: Pantheon Books, 1984.

Tannenbaum, Maurice. "The Historical Evolution of U.S. Telecommunications." *Technology in Society* 15 (1993): 263–72.

Tagg, John. "Power and Photography." *Screen Education* 36 (autumn 1980): 17–55.

"Textbooks Brought to Book." *Time*, 3 March 1941, 39–40.

Thompson, Kristin. *Exporting Entertainment: America in the World Film Market, 1907–1934.* London: British Film Institute, 1985.

Thompson, George Raynor, Dixie R. Harris, Pauline M. Oakes, and Dulany Terrett. *United States Army in World War II: The Technical Services: The Signal Corps: The Test (December 1941 to July 1943).* Washington, D.C.: Office of the Chief of Military History, Department of the Army, 1957.

Thorp, Margaret Farrand. *America at the Movies.* New Haven: Yale University Press, 1939.

"Threatened Demonstration at Kaltenborn Talk Fizzles." *Los Angeles Times*, 5 March 1941, B1.

"Today on the Radio." *New York Times*, 6 December 1939, 36.

Troen, Selwyn K. "The Discovery of the Adolescent by American Educational Reformers, 1900–1920: An Economic Perspective." In *Schooling and Society: Studies in the History of Education*, ed. Lawrence Stone. Baltimore: Johns Hopkins University Press, 1976.

Troy, William. "Picaresque." *Nation*, 14 March 1934, 314.

———. "On a Classic." *Nation*, 10 April 1935, 426.

Tucker, Robin. "73 Mr. Smiths, of G.O.P., Go to Washington." *New York Times*, 8 January 1995, A1, 10.

Ugland, Richard M. " 'Education for Victory': The High School Victory Corps and Curricular Adaptation During World War II." *History of Education Quarterly* (Winter 1979): 435–51

"Up with Frank Capra." *Newsweek*, 3 December 1956, 92, 94.

Valentine, Maggie. *The Show Starts on the Sidewalk: An Architectural History of the Movie Theater*. New Haven: Yale University Press, 1994.

Vasey, Ruth. *The World According to Hollywood, 1918–1939*. Madison: University of Wisconsin Press, 1997.

Virilio, Paul. *War and Cinema: The Logistics of Perception*, trans. Patrick Camiller. London: Verso, 1989.

Wakeman, Frederic Jr. *Policing Shanghai 1927–1937*. Berkeley: University of California Press, 1996.

Wallack, Walter M., Glenn M. Kendall, Austin H. MacCormick, and Edward R. Cass, eds. *Correctional Education Today*. American Prison Association, 1939.

Waller, Gregory. *Main Street Amusements: Movies and Commercial Entertainment in a Southern City, 1896–1930*. Washington, D.C.: Smithsonian Institution Press, 1995.

Warner, Jack Jr. "Story of a Lost Film." *The Keaton Chronicle* 1, no. 4 (autumn 1993): 1.

"War of Words: Town Meeting Opens Fifth Explosive Season." *Newsweek*, 9 October 1939, 39.

Weaver, William R. "The Case for and against Longer Feature Pictures." *Motion Picture Herald*, 11 April 1936, 18, 28–30, 33.

Westbrook, Robert B. "Fighting for the American Family: Private Interests and Political Obligations in World War II." *The Power of Culture: Critical Essays in American History*, ed. Richard Wightman Fox and T. J. Jackson Lears. Chicago: University of Chicago Press, 1993.

Wilkins, Mira. "The Impacts of American Multinational Enterprise on American-Chinese Economic Relations, 1786–1949." In *America's China Trade in Historical Perspective: The Chinese and American Performance*, ed. Ernest R. May and John K. Fairbank. Cambridge: Harvard University Press, 1986.

Wines, Michael. "First-Term Lawmaker Brought Clinton Plan Back from Brink." *San Francisco Chronicle*, 6 August 1993, A9.

Worland, Rick. "OWI Meets the Monsters: Hollywood Horror Films and War Propaganda, 1942–1945." *Cinema Journal* 37, no. 1 (fall 1997): 47–65.

"Youth Hear Defense Plea." *Los Angeles Times*, 7 March 1941, A12.

Zilversmit, Arthur. *Changing Schools: Progressive Education Theory and Practice, 1930–1960*. Chicago: University of Chicago Press, 1993.

———. "The Failure of Progressive Education, 1920–1940." In *Schooling and Society: Studies in the History of Education*, ed. Lawrence Stone. Baltimore: Johns Hopkins University Press, 1976.

Index

Audience (*continued*)
Payne Fund Studies; Production Code
Administration

Back Street, 33
Back to Bataan, 176
Back Where I Come From, 156
Bailey, Edna, 107-108
Balio, Tino, 25
Bamboozled, 238
Barry, Iris, 165-166; on film education,
163-164
Barrymore, Lionel, 199
Barton, Joan, 189
Baxter, Frank, 221
Beh Chuan Peng, 60-61
Benedict, Agnes, 103-104; on family re-
lations, 108; in praise of Hollywood,
101-102
Ben Hur, 213
Berlant, Lauren, 133
Berubé, Allan, 163
The Big Game, 109
Birds, 185
Bishop, Elizabeth, 107-108
The Bitter Tea of General Yen, 15, 31, 50,
51, 87, 89, 238; in Cuba, 65-66, 75;
and film education, 77, 162; Chinese
censorship of, 61, 64-67, 69-71, 74;
Hays Office and, 250 n.11; interna-
tional censorship of, 54; interracial
romance in, 53, 68-69, 84-85, 92;
in Japan, 67, 71, 75; lobbying efforts
against, 66; prologue for, 71-73; as
quality film, 52; religion, 86; in small
towns, 53. *See also* Department of State
Black, Gregory D., 96
Black Fury, 101
The Black Hand, 205
Blanchett, Cate, 238
Blyth, Ann, 188
Bodnar, John, 10; on public memory,
123-124
Booth, Maud Ballington, 188
Bork, Robert, 119

Borzage, Frank, 82
Boudoir Diplomat, 58
Boystown, 115
Brenon, Herbert, 82
Bringing Up Father, 189
Broadway Bill, 205; and double bills, 100;
and escapism, 158
Broken Lullaby, 82
Browne, Nick, 155
Brute Force, 182
Buchman, Sidney, 20
Burke, Delta, 239
Burke, Thomas, 134
Buscombe, Edward, 10-11
Butrick, Richard P., 55-56, 58

The Cabinet of Dr. Caligari, 87
Canon City, 187
Cantor, Eddie, 56
Capra, Frank: against Hollywood, 98-
99, 207-208; and American values,
120, 127; and auteur criticism, 74,
133, 165-166, 214; celebrity, 16, 18,
21, 23, 24, 32, 50, 81, 127, 142, 204-
206, 211; centennial celebration, 241;
and Communism, 19-22, 142-143;
contemporary influence of, 237-239;
and double bills, 99-100; as educator,
17, 43-44, 77, 81-84, 86, 91-94, 116-
118, 210-211, 213, 219, 234-235; fans'
criticism of, 155-158, 206-207, 217-
218; as filmmaker, 14-15, 24, 54, 203,
218, 237; international audiences, 18-
19, 206-207; and Italian heritage, 205;
and the military, 23, 28-29, 118, 157-
158, 162-163, 165-166; obituaries for,
237-238; as political filmmaker, 102,
140-142, 153, 209-210; and prison
inmates, 160-162, 189-201; as quality
filmmaker, 28-29, 32-33, 97, 108, 149;
and religion, 151, 210; responses to
fans, 94, 153-155, 159, 205; and science,
224; souvenirs of, 239-241; views on
audience, 1, 22; and young audiences,
89-94, 116

Captains Courageous, 109–110; and German POWs, 176
Carlyle, Thomas, 90
Carney, Ray, 203, 219
"The Carole Lombard in Macy's Window," 34
Carson, Jack, 189
Catholic Legion of Decency, 129
Cavalcade, 84
Censorship, 50, 100; attitudes of Hollywood studios, 52, 60; Chinese system of, 57–60; historiography of, 52; international, 51, 53, 64, 66; and literature, 111–112; young audiences, 109. See also *The Bitter Tea of General Yen*
Centennial Summer, 189
Chaplin, Charles, 1, 3, 55; and film education, 82; as model for Capra, 153; and U.S. Government, 122
The Charge of the Light Brigade, 105, 108–109
Chevalier, Maurice, 56
Chiang Kai-shek, 55, 57
Child and adolescent audiences, 77–78
Children's Attendance at Motion Pictures, 8
Churchill, Winston, 21
Cinema Journal, 3
The Citadel, 115; and prison screenings, 186
City Lights, 56, 82
Clair, René, 82, 91
Cleopatra, 85–86
Clinton, Bill, 237
Clouds, 185
Coen brothers, 238
Cohen, Lizabeth, 27
Cohn, Harry, 63
Colbert, Claudette, 18, 92, 239
Colman, Ronald, 56
Come and Get It, 113
Compton, Juliette, 34
Conrad, Joseph, 90
Cooper, Gary, 97, 145–147
Coppola, Francis Ford, 238

Coughlin, Father, 141, 143
Counts, George, 80
Columbia Pictures, 1, 23–24, 28, 29–37, 39–44, 46–48, 50, 54, 56, 60, 62, 64–65, 67, 69, 70–72, 75, 81, 177, 239
Crain, Jeanne, 189
Crawford, Joan, 57
Crosby, Bing, 207
Crow, Carl, 55
Cukor, George, 98, 100, 105
Cummings, Bob, 186
Curie, Eve, 156
Curtiz, Michael, 105

Daily Worker: on *Meet John Doe*, 150
Dale, Edgar, 79, 81–84, 97, 102, 169
David Copperfield, 98
Davis, Natalie Zemon, 10
Day, Doris, 224
Dead End, 109–110
DeCordova, Richard, 27
DeMille, Cecil B., 1; and double bills, 100; and film education, 77, 82, 85–86; and New York World's Fair, 125
Department of State, 13, 29; concerns with censorship, 51, 59–60, 67, 69, 134; on global film markets, 70–71, 122, 133–134
The Devil Is a Sissy, 105, 108
Dewey, John, 80–81, 117
Diao, David, 238
Dickens, Charles, 90, 98, 101
Dieterle, William, 105
Dirigible, 15, 23, 32, 47, 48–49; education, 42–43, 82; local publicity for, 38–41; and military, 42; national publicity for, 42; novelization, 239
Dishonored, 82
Disney, Walt, 1, 239; and film education, 77; and films in prison, 189; mass appeal of, 127; and quality films, 101–102; and science films, 221; and young audiences, 116
Dodsworth, 109, 113
Double Bills, 25, 79, 99–100

Doyle, Arthur Conan, 90
Dracula, 58
Dream of Spring, 176
Dr. Jekyl and Mr. Hyde, 58
Duel in the Sun, 208, 210
Duffy, Clinton T., 193, 198–199; as father figure, 196–197; and prisoner rehabilitation, 182–183, 186–188, 194, 201; and film screenings for prisoners, 183, 186

EBay, 239
Eckert, Charles, 34
Eddy, Nelson, 98
Edison, Thomas, 164, 223
Education: for democracy, 130–131; in science, 219–220, 223–224; High School Victory Corps, 117–118; in prison, 183–187; progressive, 80–81, 223; and religion, 226–227; textbook controversy in, 146–147. *See also* Film Education Movement; Progressive Education; Radio
Educational Screen, 12, 85–86, 110
Eisenstein, Sergei, 82
Eliot, George, 90
Emergency Committee in Psychology, 170
The Emotional Response of Children to the Motion Picture Situation, 8
Enstad, Nan, 34
Etting, Ruth, 224
Ewen, Elizabeth, 26
Ewen, Stuart, 26

A Face in the Crowd, 238
Fang and Claw, 101
A Farewell to Arms, 82
Federal Bureau of Investigation, 13, 19–22
55 Days at Peking, 213
Film: The Democratic Art, 9
Film and School, 79; on *Lost Horizon*, 114; progressive politics, 80, 255 n.17
Film Education Movement, 43, 77–78, 173; changes in, 116–118; and gender, 81–82, 84, 114; and high school curriculum, 79; and importance of

director, 81–84; and literature, 114; opposition to, 131; and progressivism, 89–92, 164. *See also* Education
Film Studies: analysis of fan mail, 143–144, 158; for confined audiences, 160–162, 165; for German POWs, 177–178; and the historical audience, 139–140; history of, 3–9, 17, 164–165; and the impact of films, 144; in high schools, 79–96, 121–122; and masculinity, 160, 162, 182; and the museum, 163–164; for postwar period, 164; in prisons, 185; and scientific research, 168–170, 173–174, 181–182, 201–202; at the university, 213–214, 218–219. *See also* Film Education Movement
Fitzpatrick, Frederick, 219
Flight, 15, 23, 28, 45, 48–50; and fashion industry, 34–35; and female fans, 29–35; and military, 28, 42; and modernism, 37; and publishing industry, 30–31, 34–35, 44, 239
Flinn, Errol, 176
Foley, Barbara, 140
Folsom State Prison, 160, 185
Ford, John, 105, 237
Foreign Investments in China, 55
Forman, Henry, 94, 96
Forty-Second Street, 85
Foucault, Michel, 161
400 Million Customers, 55
Four Star Scripts, 87
Fox, Richard Wightman, 27
Fox, Stephen, 26
Franklin, Sidney, 98, 100
Franklyn, Irwin R., 31
Frears, Stephen, 238
The Free Company, 156
Freund, Karl, 86
Fuller, Kathryn, 27, 38, 94, 121
Fury, 101

Gable, Clarke, 18–19, 92, 238–239
Gaines, Jane, 10
Garbo, Greta, 57

Wu, Chaucer, 67–68, 71–72
Wyler, William, 102, 213

You Can't Take It With You, 15, 144; and
  democracy, 117; and film education, 77;
  and young audiences, 95, 115, 116

You Were Never Lovelier, 176
Your Best Friends are Your Children, 108
Your Child, 96

Zilversmit, Arthur, 81
Zwick, Edward, 236–237

Eric Smoodin is a professor of American studies
at the University of California, Davis.

Library of Congress Cataloging-in-Publication Data
Smoodin, Eric Loren.
Regarding Frank Capra : audience, celebrity, and
American film studies, 1930–1960 / Eric Smoodin.
p. cm.   Includes bibliographical references and index.
ISBN 0-8223-3384-8 (cloth : alk. paper)
ISBN 0-8223-3394-5 (pbk. : alk. paper)
1. Capra, Frank—Criticism and interpretation. I. Title.
PN1998.3.C36S66 2005   791.4302'33'092—dc22   2004011859